D1128933

# North American Indian Anthropology

WITHDRAWN

# North American Indian Anthropology

*Essays on Society and Culture*

EDITED BY

RAYMOND J. DEMALLIE

AND

ALFONSO ORTIZ

UNIVERSITY OF OKLAHOMA PRESS : NORMAN AND LONDON

BY RAYMOND J. DeMALLIE

(edited with Elaine A. Jahner) *Lakota Belief and Ritual,* by James R. Walker (Lincoln, Nebr., 1980)

(edited) *Lakota Society,* by James R. Walker (Lincoln, Nebr., 1982)

(edited) *The Sixth Grandfather: Black Elk's Teachings Given to John G. Neihardt* (Lincoln, Nebr., 1984)

(edited with Douglas R. Parks) *Sioux Indian Religion: Tradition and Innovation* (Norman, 1987)

(with Royal B. Hassrick) *Vestiges of a Proud Nation: The Ogden B. Read Northern Plains Indian Collection* (Burlington, Vt., 1987)


BY ALFONSO ORTIZ

*The Tewa World: Space, Time, Being, and Beocming in a Pueblo Society* (Chicago, 1969)

(edited) *New Perspectives on the Pueblos* (Albuquerque, 1972)

(edited) *Southwest,* vols. 9 and 10, *Handbook of North American Indians* (Washington, D.C., 1979, 1983)

(edited with Richard Erdoes) *American Indian Myths and Legends* (New York, 1985)

*The Pueblo* (New York, 1994)

**Library of Congress Cataloging-in-Publication Data**

North American Indian anthropology: essays on society and culture / edited by Raymond J. DeMallie and Alfonso Ortiz.
   Includes bibliographical references and index.
   ISBN 0-8061-2614-0 (alk. paper)
   1. Indians of North America. 2. Ethnology—United States. 3. Eggan, Fred, 1906-91. I. DeMallie, Raymond J., 1946- . II. Ortiz, Alfonso, 1939- .
E77.2.N65   1994                           94-20618
306'.08997073—dc20                       CIP

The paper in this book meets the guidelines for permanence and durability of the Committee on Production Guidelines for Book Longevity of the Council on Library Resources, Inc. ∞

Copyright © 1994 by the University of Oklahoma Press, Norman, Publishing Division of the University. All rights reserved. Manufactured in the U.S.A.

2 3 4 5 6 7 8 9 10

E
77
.2
.N65
1994

To the memory of
FRED EGGAN,
scholar, teacher, friend

# Contents

Part II. Culture History

# List of Illustrations

## Plates and Figures

# Maps

# List of Tables

INTRODUCTION

# Fred Eggan and American Indian Anthropology

Fred Eggan, about 1983. Arroyo Seco, Santa Fe, N.Mex.
*photograph © Seth Roffman*

INTRODUCTION

# Fred Eggan and American Indian Anthropology

RAYMOND J. DEMALLIE

Fred Eggan (1906-1991), long-time Professor of Anthropology at the University of Chicago, was the preeminent scholar of North American Indian social anthropology. Trained in both American ethnology and British social anthropology, Eggan developed a distinctive approach to the American Indian that combined social and cultural anthropology, situated in historical context. The many students with whom he worked over more than forty years continue to perpetuate Eggan's vision of anthropology. The essays in this volume were written by students of Eggan in his honor and include studies of kinship systems, social organization, and a wide variety of cultural topics; methodologically, most of them are comparative and ethnohistorical. They all reflect aspects of Eggan's own interests and together they represent a broad spectrum of approaches to American Indian anthropology.

The development of anthropology in the United States and Canada has been intimately related to the study of Native American peoples. The parameters of anthropology were largely drawn during the second half of the nineteenth century by the pioneering work of Lewis Henry Morgan (1871, 1877), who defined the distinctiveness of American Indian peoples in terms of cultural patterns—kinship, social organization, politics, religion—interpreted as steps in a developmental sequence by which humankind rose from savagery to civilization. Building on this foundation, J. W. Powell and the members of the Smithsonian's Bureau of American Ethnology recorded a massive quantity of descriptive information on native groups throughout the continent. Using the "comparative method," they were content to situate tribal groups along a scale from simple to complex that was understood to characterize social evolution, and they assumed that the data needed no further analysis. Comparison focused on like institutions—government, sign language, burial customs, picture writing—within geographically dispersed cultural groups organized in perceived scales of complexity that paralleled (and thereby were considered to validate) the broader

3

evolutionary scheme. Within the cultural experiences of Native Americans lay reflections of the common human past, and their significance was not intrinsic to specific cultural groups but was measured collectively as part of the holistic story of the development of culture considered as humankind's distinctive achievement.

Reacting against that comparative method and its evolutionary assumptions, Franz Boas introduced his distinctive historical approach to ethnology, beginning with an emphasis on understanding the integrity of each cultural entity, and later situating cultures historically through detailed comparisons of cultural traits among geographically proximate groups to reconstruct patterns of diffusion. Boas defined cultural units linguistically, following the accepted practice of nineteenth-century anthropology, but he emphasized the understanding of cultures as integral wholes and the description of languages in terms of their individual uniqueness rather than in relation to the grammars of classical languages (see Stocking 1974). During the first decades of the twentieth century, Boas's students developed academic anthropology in the United States, following his methods but proceeding far less cautiously than their teacher. Clark Wissler (1917) and Alfred L. Kroeber (1939), in particular, broadened the scope of comparison to reconstruct patterns of historical relationship throughout the continent. Their "age-area" hypothesis, which assumed that the more widely spread a cultural trait, the older it must be, ultimately proved oversimplistic; yet the "culture areas" they defined have had lasting heuristic value for organizing research in Native America. More significant for the ethnographic record are the detailed bodies of descriptive data on the various tribal groups that they preserved, very much in the tradition of the Bureau of American Ethnology. Cumulatively, the efforts of American anthropologists from the mid-nineteenth to the mid-twentieth centuries make American Indian cultures among the most richly documented in the world.

The Boasians shared with their predecessors who adhered to social evolutionism the basic goal of mapping the diversity of New World peoples, recording something about every group before they all disappeared. Although the Boasians, in contrast to their predecessors, no longer perceived this as "evolution," the "loss" of culture was apparent to them; documentation of "traditional" cultures was for them as much of a race against time as it had been for the evolutionists. Effort could not be wasted, therefore, and each anthropologist found one or perhaps a number of related tribes on which to focus; thus individual anthropologists were considered to have a degree of proprietary interest in the tribes that they studied, and they did not welcome intrusions by other anthropologists, particularly those affiliated with rival universities or museums. The implicit argument was that only by parsing out human resources in such a manner could the task of cultural mapping have a chance of succeeding.

A new perspective was introduced into American Indian anthropology when A. R. Radcliffe-Brown, a Cambridge-trained anthropologist, came to teach at the University of Chicago in 1931. During the previous decade he had developed programs in social anthropology at the University of Cape Town and the University of Sydney; he remained at Chicago until 1937, when he returned to England to accept a chair of social anthropology at Oxford University. At the University of Chicago Radcliffe-Brown introduced his version of British social anthropology, a radical departure from the Boasian approach that, if initially unsettling, ultimately proved revitalizing to American anthropology. He envisioned a "natural science of society" that focused very precisely on social structure as fundamental to understanding tribal life. Group boundaries were defined by patterns of social interaction, rather than language, and culture was relegated to a derivative position. Thus Radcliffe-Brown was interested in classifying Native American peoples from the point of view of social structure, centering on the kinship system and other social institutions. He considered the kinship system to be fundamental to understanding Native American peoples; as Eggan later phrased it, kinship provided an "index" to social structure (1950:11). Defining the range of types of social systems in North America laid a basis for broad generalizations as well as new dimensions to historical reconstructions (see Radcliffe-Brown 1954: chap. 3). Radcliffe-Brown took his inspiration from Morgan, but narrowed the subject to a precise focus that he believed could provide more in-depth understanding of Native American peoples than Boas's historical ethnological approach. Perhaps because the research task was so specifically defined, he encouraged work on the problem of social structure throughout North America, ignoring the long-standing interests of American anthropologists in various tribes, and he freely declared that his students were providing the first adequate accounts of American Indian kinship and social systems.

Most of the Boasians perceived Radcliffe-Brown's methods as threatening to the relativistic approach they had so carefully nurtured against the earlier social evolutionists. Anthropologists at the University of Chicago, however, perceived Radcliffe-Brown as an ally, rather than a threat. He had been invited there by Fay-Cooper Cole, himself a student of Boas. Radcliffe-Brown's influence at Chicago was greatest with the students, and with none more than Fred Eggan, a graduate student who assumed the job of serving as his research assistant.

From the very start of his career, Eggan displayed a remarkable pragmatic ability to balance diverse, even opposing points of view and, stripping away the personalities involved, bring their fundamental ideas into harmony. He developed a deep interest in Illinois archeology, and with training from Cole, Edward Sapir, Leslie Spier, and Paul Radin, he proposed a dissertation on "The Ethnological Interpretation of Archeological Cultures," bringing the diverse methods of American historical anthropology together to develop a fuller picture of the American Indian past in the eastern United States. Though he published a sketch of this work in 1952—still as insightful a summary as has yet been accomplished—the larger project was put aside in the fall of 1931 when Radcliffe-Brown came to Chicago and Eggan, with Cole's encouragement, spent six months working as Radcliffe-Brown's research assistant (Kelley 1978:30; Eggan 1974:8).

It was apparent at that time, Eggan later wrote, that theory was needed both to record and analyze ethnographic data, and that "American anthropologists were looking for new and more satisfying paradigms" (Eggan 1974:9). He told his students (for example, on the first day on his kinship seminar at the University of Chicago in 1968) that when he started his career, he had been concerned above all with data. "'Ethnographer' was a term of highest praise," he commented; the first duty of an anthropologist, an essential part of his training, was to contribute to the body of ethnographic data. Yet the analyses of Boasian anthropology, reconstructing historical patterns of borrowing and diffusion, "provided little understanding of the cultures." In the "functional" approach of Radcliffe-Brown, exemplified in *The Social Organization of Australian Tribes,* Eggan found "a new and productive way of thinking about culture and society" (Eggan 1974:8).

Paralleling his Australian study, Radcliffe-Brown's project while at the University of Chicago was to be "The Social Organization of North American Tribes." In 1925, only six years earlier, Leslie Spier had published a survey article that outlined eight types of kinship systems in North America based on differences in the classification of cross cousins. Spier characterized his study as descriptive, and included maps to show the geographical distribution in North America of societies classified on the basis of kinship type. Spier (1921) had applied the same method to a distributional study of elements of the Sun Dance, and from it he had drawn historical conclusions concerning patterns of diffusion. But the method failed to make sense out of the geographical distribution of societies classified on the basis of kinship type. Here was a tailor-made problem to test the value of a new approach. Radcliffe-Brown began his project by referring his assistant, Eggan, back to Morgan's classic 1871 compendium as the starting place from which to compile information on American Indian kinship systems and social structures. Radcliffe-Brown left Chicago for Oxford in 1937, leaving the study unfinished, but the project he had initiated became a major focus for Eggan's lifework.

From Radcliffe-Brown, Eggan adopted a concept of kinship system as comprising "*both* the terminology and the patterns of social behavior between relatives," as well as the idea "that the kinship system was an integral part of the total social structure" (Eggan 1966:15). This provided him with a powerful methodological tool for recording and analyzing data about the American Indian that could be used for systematic comparison to go far beyond Morgan's explanation of similarities among social groups to understand the differences among them as well. Building both on Radcliffe-Brown's work and on Boasian anthropology, Eggan proposed that a kinship system could be understood as comprising both social and cultural components, that is, a system of social *relations* between individuals and a system of social *usages*—conventional behavioral patterns characterizing the relationship between pairs of individuals. Understood as a dynamic social and cultural system, kinship terms could not be relegated—as Kroeber (1909) and other American anthropologists had argued—to strictly linguistic phenomena (Eggan 1950:4, 10).

For Eggan, the first practical test of Radcliffe-Brown's approach came in the summer of 1932 when he participated in the Santa Fe Laboratory of Anthropology Field School directed by Leslie White among the Hopis. With a focused research problem, he was able in three months to record the data needed to document the Hopi social system, which was based on matrilineal clans, matrilocal families, and a Crow-type kinship system that reflected kin relations across generations. At the same time his focus helped Eggan to fit his project into the larger field school goals so that, for example, his work was complementary to that of Mischa Titiev, who was also gathering data for a dissertation on the Hopis. For Eggan, it was the beginning of a life-long commitment to the Hopi people.

In order to put the Hopis in comparative perspective, Eggan summarized the data on kinship and social organization for the other Western Pueblos—Hano, Zuni, Acoma, and Laguna—using published sources. Searching to explain divergences among these groups from a common Western Pueblo pattern, Eggan interpreted the differences as reflecting differing ecological and historical circumstances. In contrast to the Western Pueblos, he found that among the Eastern Pueblos a different type of social organization—bilateral, with weak development of clans—underlay the apparent homogeneity of Pueblo culture, with the Keresan Pueblos forming a bridge between east and west. Although he completed his dissertation in 1933, a combination of other projects and the interruption of the Second World War delayed its revision and publication until 1950. Even then the approach was fresh, and the succinct summary of the principles of social anthropology, set in the broader context of American cultural anthropology and used to introduce the study of the Western Pueblo data, is as clear and convincing a presentation of Radcliffe-Brown's approach as any in the literature.

With this background of understanding the workings of the Crow-type system of the Hopis, Eggan turned to interpreting the data on kinship terminologies of the tribes of the Southeast that he had first summarized for Radcliffe-Brown. He had found in Morgan's kinship tables an intriguing series of variations on the Crow type in which, among the Choctaws, for example, the characteristic line of father's sisters marking the father's *matri*lineage had shifted to become a line of fathers, marking the father's sister's son's *patri*lineage. He suspected that this must represent a change in the kinship system. Visiting the Choctaws in Mississippi in the summer of 1933, Eggan found that the aberrant system reported by Morgan was still in use. Then, the discovery of a historical documentary account confirmed Eggan's hypothesis that earlier in the nineteenth century, before Morgan's time, the Choctaw system had been of the normal Crow type. This was a major breakthrough, for it clearly documented change in the kinship system over time. As Eggan expressed it, the Southeastern data showed that patterns of kinship terminology are "remarkably sensitive indicators of social and cultural change" (Eggan 1966:38). Under pressure to adapt to Euro-American society, Southeastern kinship systems had shifted from matrilineal to either patrilineal or generational. Correlating the variations on the Crow system with relative degree of acculturation of the tribes as documented in the historical studies of Grant Foreman (1934) and Angie Debo (1934), Eggan found support for his general hypothesis that the kinship systems of the less-acculturated tribes were most like the Crow type, while those of the more-acculturated tribes were the least Crow-like.

Two major theoretical conclusions came from this study: first, that changes in the kinship system resulted from changes in behavioral patterns, and second, that the approaches of British social anthropology and American ethnology could be combined profitably. Furthermore, both could be enriched by the study of documentary sources—the ethnohistorical method, an approach that was fostered by Cole at the University of Chicago. Publishing the Choctaw study in the *American Anthropologist* enabled Eggan to demonstrate the validity and utility to American ethnology of Radcliffe-Brown's as yet controversial approach (Eggan

1937a). The work of Alexander Spoehr, Eggan's first student, beginning in 1938, tested the hypothesis of change in Southeastern kinship systems, confirming it independently with a comparison of the Seminoles of Florida and Oklahoma, and recorded among the Creeks the whole sequence of change in kinship pattern from Crow to generational (Spoehr 1947).

After leaving the Choctaws in summer 1933, Eggan continued field study for two more months with the Cheyennes and Arapahos of Oklahoma. The Plains was then the best known North American culture area, but there had been little systematic study of Plains kinship systems. In this regard the Cheyennes were particularly significant because the pioneer work of George Bird Grinnell (1923) had suggested former matrilineal descent, an hypothesis later strengthened by the archeological work of William Duncan Strong (1940), who traced the tribe to an earlier existence as earth lodge village-dwellers in the Prairie Plains. The Cheyennes of 1933, however, were bilateral and generational in their kinship system, a change that Eggan interpreted by invoking Radcliffe-Brown's principle of the "solidarity and unity of the sibling group," reflecting the cooperation among brothers, cousins, and male friends necessary to ensure the success of cooperative buffalo hunting on the High Plains. Rather than look to patterns of diffusion, following the Boasian method, Eggan invoked ecological factors to explain why tribes that came into the Plains with a variety of backgrounds developed similar kinship systems and social structures (1937b:92-93).

Studying kinship among the tribes of the Northeast and Great Lakes region, Eggan focused on the role of cross-cousin marriage in structuring small bands, a pattern that Strong (1929) reported in practice among the Naskapis of Labrador. Drawing on W. H. R. Rivers's (1914) suggestion of the importance of cross-cousin marriage in the area, which he based on kin term equivalences taken from Morgan, Eggan hypothesized a series of historical changes, as groups became larger and more economically secure, which led to the abandonment of cross-cousin marriage in favor of lineage organization (1966:175). Earlier, in his first published paper, Eggan (1934a) had hypothesized on the basis of kin terminology that the ancient Mayas had practiced cross-cousin marriage, a theoretical issue that interested him throughout his life.

For Eggan, acceptance of Radcliffe-Brown's social anthropology did not imply rejection of Boasian ethnology. Rather, he sought to synthesize the two, positing *society* and *culture* as independent variables: "A society is a group of individuals who have adjusted their interests sufficiently to co-operate in satisfying their various needs. Culture is the set of conventional attitudes and behavior patterns by which the mutual adaptation and co-operation is carried out" (1950:4). In his studies, Eggan sought to analyze the relationship between society and culture to explain change over time. He called this approach the "method of controlled comparison," a means by which groups are compared holding as many contextual variables constant as possible—geographical, cultural, linguistic, and historical relationship—thereby allowing for generalizations that may be helpful in understanding social and cultural change. He analyzed the patterned differences as well as the similarities in social and cultural systems to reconstruct the forces of change through time. Rather than the "universal laws" envisioned by Radcliffe-Brown, Eggan sought more limited generalizations, which, borrowing from the sociologist Robert K. Merton (1949:5), he characterized as "the middle range of theory" (Eggan 1954:748). In this manner Eggan preserved the older comparative method, controlled it to prevent its misuse for fortuitous comparisons, and forged it to relate the interests of both social anthropology and ethnology. Although this synthesis began to take shape in the 1930s, and is evident in the introductory methodological section of *Social Organization of the Western Pueblos* (1950), it is most eloquently articulated in his 1953 presidential paper presented to the American Anthropological Association, "Social Anthropology and the Method of Controlled Comparison" (Eggan 1954).

In his concern for studying change over time and tracing the accultura-tive effects of Euro-American society on American Indian social systems, Eggan broke from the ahistorical approach of British social anthropology as well as from the American ethnological approach of historical recon-struction by continuing his studies up to the present day. Eggan never relegated American Indians to the past. His fieldwork had introduced him to a variety of American Indian situations and heightened his awareness of contemporary problems. Responding to a Bureau of Indian Affairs circular, Eggan (1934b) wrote to Commissioner John Collier: "From my experience it seems necessary for the Government to have more than one policy . . . It is obvious that the same procedure will not fit the Hopi, the Mississippi Choctaw, and the Cheyenne, for example." Eggan suggested that in the Southwest, tribal cultures should be allowed to develop as they wished, encouraging literacy to foster native language literatures. In Mississippi, on the other hand, the Choctaws needed government help to rescue them from economic straights. The Cheyennes and Arapahos, he believed, would benefit from communal lands and from the official encouragement of their Sun Dance, "which is the most important integrating factor at present."

Thirty years later Eggan devoted the last of his Morgan Lectures at the University of Rochester to the topic of "Lewis Henry Morgan and the

Future of the American Indian," applauding the 1961 American Indian Chicago Conference—organized by his long-term colleague and fellow social anthropologist, Sol Tax—where representatives from ninety tribes forged "A Declaration of Indian Purpose." "In the last analysis," Eggan concluded, "it is the Indians themselves who will solve their problems" (1966:168).

Throughout his career Eggan worked with contemporary Indian peoples—in a study of food and nutrition in the Southwest in 1941-42, and later with land claims cases at Zuni and the land dispute between the Hopis and Navajos. Out of the latter came his 1967 essay "From History to Myth: A Hopi Example," which argues for the cross-referencing of oral and documentary accounts for historical reconstruction and to develop understanding of American Indian conceptions of the past. It also led him to plan what he liked to call "a biography of the Hopi tribe," drawing on the work of Julian Steward to reconstruct Hopi origins in the ancestral forms of social organization characterizing Great Basin Shoshoneans (Eggan 1980).

Many of the hypotheses found in Fred Eggan's social anthropological studies have received further attention from his students and others who have refined, tested, and reinterpreted his conclusions. He had an uncanny ability to formulate problems, synthesize relevant data, and generalize insightfully. In part this reflects his life-long commitment to controlled comparison, to "the middle range of theory," and his dictum that "generalizations do not have to be universal in order to be useful" (1950:8). He also felt the responsibility periodically to summarize progress as a way of organizing future research. Eggan's contribution on Cheyenne and Arapaho kinship and social organization to the 1937 Festschrift for Radcliffe-Brown, *Social Anthropology of North American Tribes,* includes a classification and summary of Plains kinship systems, with broader comparisons to tribes living in the East. To the expanded edition of 1955 he added a masterful summary of progress in American Indian social anthropology, both methodological and substantive, during the previous two decades. Here he again argued for the complementarity of the generalizing British social-structural approach and the historical American cultural approach, expressing his conviction that if the common ground between them could be enlarged, "anthropology as a whole will advance" (1955:491). The 1964 Morgan Lectures once again reviewed the progress of American Indian social anthropology, this time in relation to Morgan's pioneering studies. These summaries have been important for orienting and inspiring successive generations of students.

From 1935 to 1974 Eggan taught his own distinctive synthesis of social anthropology and ethnology at the University of Chicago, continuing to devote much of his own attention as well as that of many of his students to the American Indian. In addition, following the lead of Fay-Cooper Cole, Eggan also carried on field work with the Tinguians in the Philippines, and directed the Philippines Study Center at Chicago from 1953 until the mid-1960s. After the Second World War, overseas research burgeoned, and studies of the American Indian waned. Many anthropologists assumed that there was little left to study among North American Indians, and they traveled instead to distant places where peoples were presumed to have been less influenced by contact with the modern world. Only in recent years, as we have labeled the world "postmodern" and come to a realization of its very real interconnectedness, have American Indian studies in anthropology begun to be again in the forefront of theoretical work in general anthropology.

More than any other single anthropologist of his generation, Eggan directed the course of American Indian anthropology in the years after the Second World War. He never abandoned the research goal suggested by Radcliffe-Brown of surveying the types of native North American societies and developing generalizations about their change over time. Through his teaching and writings he inspired a small but steady stream of journeyman anthropologists who studied kinship, social organization, and cultural change among native groups throughout North America. Many of them used the method of controlled comparison as a foundation for their studies. Although Eggan remained committed to Radcliffe-Brown's social anthropology, he was always receptive to developments in the field and was open to the possibilities that each successive innovation in anthropological approach had to offer. With Eggan's encouragement, his students continually explored new methods and theories in the service of a common goal. The cumulative record of their theses and dissertations, and their subsequent publications, have enormously enriched anthropological understanding of the American Indian. Many of those students have continued to specialize in American Indian studies throughout their careers, and in their turn have inspired successive generations to continue the work.

The essays in this volume were all written by students of Fred Eggan, and were prepared in his honor. Together they comprise an inventory of progress in the field not unlike the 1937 *Social Anthropology of North American Tribes*. Like the earlier volume, these essays make descriptive contributions to American Indian anthropology, but they are more disparate in their theoretical and methodological orientations, reflecting the diversity of anthropological approaches that have developed since the Second World War. French structuralism, Marxism, ethnohistorical methods, interpretive anthropology, symbolic analyses, and the recent emphasis on reflexivity and humanistic approaches have all had their productive influence on American Indian anthropology, and all are represented to different degrees in various of these essays. As a group they reflect Eggan's concern for historicity and the documentation of change and stability over time. Some of the essays use Eggan's technique of comparing social structures and cultural patterns and assessing the differential rates of change between them. Many of them make explicit use of the method of controlled comparison.

Part I, "Kinship and Social Organization," comprises seven chapters that directly address questions of social organization and cultural patterning of social life in a variety of Native American groups. In Chapter 1, "Biology and Social Relationship in the Kin Terminology of an Inuit Community," Joseph Maxwell examines the meaning of kin terms and the patterning of kin terminology using data from his field studies of the Inuit of Repulse Bay (located on the northwest side of Hudson Bay, in the Northwest Territories of Canada). Combining both genealogical and cultural (symbolic) approaches to the meaning of kin terms, and examining the extent to which kin terminology reflects social structure, Maxwell interprets Inuit kinship systems as adaptations to uncertain food resources, mobility, and sharing. He concludes that Inuit define kinship both in terms of biological connection and behavioral-emotional relationship and that this pattern is best explained in terms of its adaptive value.

In Chapter 2, "Historical Changes in the Chipewyan Kinship System," the late James G. E. Smith uses the method of controlled comparison to examine data collected from the nineteenth century to the present to reveal changes in Chipewyan kinship and social organization. Sorting out the many inconsistencies in the data, he identifies three categories of kin terminologies and argues against attempting to reconstruct from those variants any single ancestral pattern. At the same time, he concludes on the basis of ecological factors that contrary to the pattern of patrilateral cross-cousin marriage hypothesized for the Chipewyans by Eggan (1955:543), their kinship system was both bilateral and generational. A modern tendency toward patrilineality may reflect influence from European-derived Canadian culture.

In Chapter 3, "Kinship, Social Class, and Religion of Northwest Peoples," June M. Collins uses the method of controlled comparison to examine three geographically separate Salish-speaking peoples in Washington State and British Columbia. Focusing on the kinship and social systems, the presence or absence of social class and other forms of social rank, and religious beliefs and practices, she examines each group to assess the functional consistency of the three variables and on that basis draws historical conclusions. The egalitarian Interior Salish, who moved inland from the coast, reveal the closest approximation to her reconstruction of the ancestral Salish pattern. The Coast Salish, who remained behind, acquired concepts of rank and privilege from the Kwakiutls and Nootkas, and at the time of European contact their kinship and religious systems were still in the process of changing to reflect new social realities. The third group, the Bella Coolas, had been separated longest from the other Salish, and, reflecting Kwakiutl influence, had more fully integrated social class into both their kinship and religious systems.

In Chapter 4, "Central Algonkian Moieties," the late Charles Callender addresses the problem of the nature of dual organization and uses the method of controlled comparison to examine the historical evidence in regard to the Central Algonkian tribes. The Menominis and Miamis were reported to have had classical moieties based on clans, and by extension this might also apply to the Illinois. The Sauk, Fox, Potawatomi, and Kickapoo tribes had nonunilineal dual divisions whose primary function was to structure competition and joking. Fox dual divisions have been interpreted as representing an expansion of warrior societies to replace earlier clan-based moieties, later reflected in ceremonial reciprocity; Callender hypothesizes that the same was true of the Sauks and Kickapoos. The Shawnees lacked dual divisions altogether. Callender notes that even though on the basis of the rest of their culture it would be logical to assume that the Central Algonkian tribes practiced dual organization, none of them carried it through consistently, either in structure or function. While it might be considered as diagnostic of decay, this inconsistency has persisted at least from the early nineteenth century, leaving the means by which those cultures achieved symbolic integration as a problem not yet solved.

In Chapter 5, "Kinship and Biology in Sioux Culture," Raymond J. DeMallie takes a symbolic approach to examine kinship and social organization from Sioux cultural perspectives. Based on the study of nineteenth- and twentieth-century sources he discusses kinship as a central focus of Sioux culture. Kinship is symbolized by the sacred pipe, a religious gift that creates and maintains relationships between humans and the spirit world and regulates relationships among humans. Through the analysis of the symbols of kinship DeMallie concludes that active relationship rather than biological connectedness was its defining feature. By means of a semantic analysis he identifies the implicit principles of the Sioux kinship classification. This leads to a rejection of W. H. R. Rivers's old hypothesis, discussed by Eggan (1966:98-103), that the distinctive Sioux cross-cousin terms derived from the earlier practice of cross-cousin marriage, and supports Alexander Lesser's hypothesis that those terms reflect the systematic practice of the sororate and levirate. The chapter suggests the possibility of developing classifications of kin terminologies based on cultural symbols to complement those based on structural features.

In Chapter 6, "Northern Cheyenne Kinship Reconsidered," Anne S. Straus compares the data on Cheyenne kinship recorded by Eggan in 1933 with information on contemporary Cheyenne kinship. Her analysis confirms that the system as recorded among the Southern Cheyennes fifty years earlier was basically identical to that of the Northern Cheyennes, and that only minor changes have occurred since, reflecting influence from the patterning of English kin terms and the increasing importance of the nuclear family in reservation society. Contrary to Eggan's hypothesis (1955:537), Straus finds no evidence to support an earlier practice of matrilineality by the Cheyennes, and concludes that the system was historically bilateral, just as it is today. Significantly, she is led to this conclusion by examining Cheyenne concepts of male and female, arguing that the cultural ideology they embody has been incorrectly interpreted as representing social patterns of unilineality. She also discusses the use of variant kin terms as tactical strategies and considers the relevance of the life cycle to understanding the relationship between brothers and the pattern of generational terminology that characterizes Plains kinship systems.

In Chapter 7, "The Social Organizations of the Southeast," Greg Urban uses the method of controlled comparison to reevaluate the question of the diversity of social types in the Southeast. On the basis of John R. Swanton's earlier studies, Eggan (1966:18-19) had assumed a single, homogeneous type of social organization throughout the entire culture area, characterized by matrilineality and Crow-type kinship terms. However, analysis of the literature reveals nine distinct patterns of kin classification, closely correlated with linguistic subdivisions and with terminology reflecting Crow, Omaha, and bilateral (Dakota) patterns. Internal complexity of types of social organization offers the challenge to correlate these variants with settlement patterns and political types and to relate them to the archeological record in order to reconstruct a fuller picture of the development of tribal groups in the Southeast.

Part II, "Culture History," comprises nine chapters that investigate a broad range of problems in the analysis of American Indian social and cultural systems. In Chapter 8, "Fur Trade as Centrifuge: Familial Dispersal and Offspring Identity in Two Company Contexts," Jennifer S. H. Brown compares the social and cultural characteristics of the fur traders who comprised the Hudson's Bay Company and North West Company on the western frontier of British America in the period before 1821. Ethno-historical study of the documentary record reveals that the members of the two companies were of different social backgrounds and interacted with American Indians in different ways; understanding those differences dispels the ethnohistorical myth of a unitary mode of interaction between Indians and fur traders. This chapter focuses on the intermarriage of traders and Indian women. The Hudson's Bay Company refused to recognize those relationships as legitimate marriages and made no provisions for the offspring when traders ultimately retired to the east; their Indian wives and mixed-blood children were expected to return to tribal society. The North West Company, in contrast, not only recognized such marriages, but their fur traders sent their mixed-blood sons east to be educated, where many assimilated into the larger society, while their wives and daughters formed the nucleus of the developing Métis population arising on the frontier. In consequence, the mixed-blood offspring of the fur traders from the two companies evolved radically different social identities with significant implications for subsequent developments in the Canadian Northwest.

In Chapter 9, "The Civilization Strategy: Gros Ventres, Northern and Southern Arapahos Compared," Loretta Fowler contrasts the different historical experiences of three closely related Algonkian peoples. Beginning in the eighteenth century as members of a larger Arapaho-speaking population, with very similar social structures and cultural perspectives, the three groups developed different strategies to cope with advancing American settlement and with life on reservations. They all adopted what Fowler calls a "civilization strategy" during early reservation years. In Montana, the Gros Ventres focused on gaining independence from restraints of government officials and politically dominating the Assiniboines with whom they shared the Fort Belknap Reservation. They abandoned traditional religion in favor of Christianity and developed secular ceremonies to promote prestige and social integration. In Wyoming, the Northern Arapahoes shared the Wind River Reservation with the Shoshones; their strategy aimed at maximizing material benefits for tribal members and countering repressive measures against tribal religion. In Oklahoma, the Southern Arapahos, confronted with the loss of their reservation, relied on their chiefs to protect the interests of tribal members. Increasingly the chiefs were viewed as ineffective, which undermined both their political and religious authority. Introduction of the Native American Church offered a new means to achieve religious and political leadership. Fowler suggests that controlled comparison of the strategies used by tribes in adapting to federal policies can help explain the nature and extent of variation among contemporary American Indian political structures.

In Chapter 10, "The Roots of Factionalism among the Lower Brule Sioux," Ernest L. Schusky takes an ethnohistorical approach to examine the development of factions. Eggan argued that societies should be looked at in terms of the problems of adaptation (1955:494) and he hypothesized that societies with bilateral kinship systems had an easier time adapting to change than unilineal ones (1966:127). The Lower Brule Sioux provide a good test case and support the hypothesis. Living during the nineteenth century in fluid bilateral bands, factional disputes were settled by fission, and disgruntled individuals could leave to join other bands. Once settled on the reservation, however, factionalism developed around the issue of cooperation with government policies, and has continued in the present century around mixed-blood versus full-blood identity as well as specific issues. However, rather than being entirely negative in their effect, these two factions work together; mixed-bloods are seen as intermediators with white society, while full-bloods give credibility to the group as Indian. Lower Brule society remains fluid and has successfully adapted to the reservation context.

In Chapter 11, "'Reading Back' to Find Community: Lumbee Ethno-history," Karen I. Blu addresses a methodological issue in ethnohistorical study. Using historical documents relating to the Lumbee Indians of Robeson County, North Carolina, she shows how "reading back" from the contemporary Lumbee social and cultural landscape provides insights for identifying continuities in the historical record that, because of the fragmentary nature of the documents, would be otherwise meaningless and therefore overlooked. Blu also raises general questions concerning the nature of community in relation to local and national identities and to processes of change and persistence.

In Chapter 12, "The Dynamics of Pueblo Cultural Survival," Alfonso Ortiz utilizes cultural analysis to demonstrate that Pueblo Indian peoples, despite linguistic differences and the lack of any single cultural feature that can be said to be common to them all, have shared a cultural similarity from early prehistoric times that sets them apart from other American Indians. Differences among the Pueblos can be ascribed to historical processes, but they all share the fact that they have never moved from their homelands, giving a strong sense of place that is important to their enduring identity. The coming of Europeans to their country has been only the latest in a long series of changes to which the Pueblos have adapted, resulting repeatedly in cultural revitalizations that have been the means of their survival.

In Chapter 13, "Hopi Shamanism: A Reappraisal," Jerrold E. Levy examines shamanism among the Hopis, using the method of controlled comparison to show that, while sharing in a general Puebloan shamanistic tradition, the Hopi form differs in the absence of several widespread characteristics: bear shamanism (and associated trance state), spirit helpers, the concept of soul loss, the idea that an individual's state of mind is an important element in disease, and the prominence of shaman societies. Tentatively, he suggests that Hopi shamanism developed separately from that of the Eastern Pueblos, and that the Hopis rejected Keresan influences accepted both by the Tanoan Pueblos and the Zunis.

In Chapter 14, "Patterns of Leadership in Western Pueblo Society," Triloki Nath Pandey examines the recent history and present structure of economic and political institutions in Hopi and Zuni pueblos. He compares the political and religious structure of the two pueblos as examples of theocracies, examines changes documented through time, and discusses patterns of leadership. Differences between the two pueblos lead to understanding of the greater adaptive success of Zuni in dealing with the federal bureaucracy.

In Chapter 15, "Indian Law and Puebloan Tribal Law," Bruce B. MacLachlan builds on Eggan's study of the Pueblos (1950) to describe Santa Clara as representative of the Eastern Pueblo type, focusing in particular on the significance of legal institutions in social change and persistence. Factions of long standing at Santa Clara, characterized either as conservative or progressive, and each bifurcated along moiety lines, came together in 1934 in a single coalition to adopt a tribal government based on the Indian Reorganization Act. Ultimate authority remained vested in religious leadership, but secular officials were granted discretionary authority in a sphere responsive to, but not directed by, religious leaders. When the council enacted a law granting tribal membership only to the children of Santa Clara men, it codified a cultural principle of patrifiliation that exists in the absence of a unilineal clan system. In ensuing years, Santa Clara women tried unsuccessfully to enroll their children by alien men, and in 1971 a suit was brought claiming that the tribal law violated the 1968 Indian Civil Rights Act. The Supreme Court, however, disavowed jurisdiction over controversies arising from the Indian Civil Rights Act, thereby upholding the priority of tribal law. Acceptance of the elected form of tribal government as a social institution and the codification of tribal law may therefore serve as a force for cultural persistence as well as for change.

In Chapter 16, "Cultural Motifs in Navajo Weaving," Gary Witherspoon reexamines a familiar area of anthropological study from historical, cultural, and linguistic perspectives to determine its roots and explore its meaning as expressing the essence of being Navajo. The symmetry of Navajo weaving is interpreted as symbolic of *hózhǫ́*, the concept of holistic essence that permeates Navajo culture. Basic weaving designs are cultural motifs built upon the emblems of the principal Navajo deities, and from this perspective Navajo weaving may be interpreted as an abstract art built upon cultural motif. The emblems used in weaving replicate those of other domains of Navajo culture, specifically, certain ritual equipment, the hair buns of both men and women, and the petroglyphs found throughout Navajo country. Witherspoon argues that to Navajos, weaving is a source of national pride and identity, expressing the vitality, strength, and integration of Navajo society. The remarkable historical persistence of design elements similarly asserts their power as semiotic expressions of cultural meanings central to Navajo identity through time.

In Chapter 17, "On the Application of the Phylogenetic Model to the Maya," Evon Z. Vogt employs the method of controlled comparison to understand the development of Mayan groups in Highland Chiapas. The phylogenetic model limits itself to the consideration of groups sharing physical type, systemic patterns, and phylogenetically related languages, thereby providing maximum control for the comparison. The proposed analysis requires data from all the subfields of anthropology to follow eight steps in defining the Maya from reconstructed proto-language and proto-culture to the linguistic and ethnographic variation found today. This chapter focuses on the identification of systemic patterns—those of great antiquity among the Maya that might have evolved at the proto-time level or shortly thereafter. These include patterns of subsistence, settlement, social structure, religious specialists, ancestral gods, and the religious equivalence of mountains and pyramids. Recent advances in scholarship on the Maya will allow for further development of the model, which can lead to fuller understanding of the divergence of groups from ancestral culture and the specific social and cultural processes that have led to the variations observed among the Maya today.

This collection of essays was first proposed by DeMallie and Ortiz in 1980; they attempted to contact all of Fred Eggan's students whose professional studies centered on American Indians. The authors of these chapters represent a cross-section of Eggan's students who received their doctorates between 1948 and 1978. Many others, whose work is equally important and representative of Eggan's influence, are not represented here, both because of practical considerations of time and space, and the decision to give coherence to the volume by limiting it to the native peoples of North America.

By the time all the essays were submitted, two of the contributors were deceased. Charles Callender died in 1985; he had been the first to complete his essay for this volume. James G. E. Smith died in 1989, only weeks after submitting his completed essay. We mourn their passing and take hope in the fact that the inclusion of their contributions here keeps their work alive as a contribution to the ongoing intellectual enterprise of which we are all part.

Fred Eggan himself died in 1991, when these essays were in the final stages of preparation. This volume is dedicated to his memory, in testimony to his enduring influence as scholar, mentor, and friend. We know that his many students and colleagues join us in honoring Fred Eggan's memory and acknowledging the invaluable role he played in furthering the study of native North America and in developing the discipline of anthropology at large.

Financial assistance in the preparation of this volume was generously provided by the Peabody Museum, Harvard University; the President's Council on Social Science and by the Office of Research and the University Graduate School, Indiana University; and the Department of Anthropology, University of New Mexico. Seth Roffman, Santa Fe, New Mexico, kindly provided the photograph of Fred Eggan that precedes this introduction. Maps were drawn by Janis Kearney and Sherri Hilgeman, Glenn A. Black Laboratory of Anthropology, Indiana University. The text was prepared for publication by Christina Burke, Rita Crouch, Alex Eulenberg, Erik Gooding, Wallace Hooper, Jason Baird Jackson, and Paula Wagoner, all of the American Indian Studies Research Institute, Indiana University.

## References

Debo, Angie
    1934    The Rise and Fall of the Choctaw Republic. Norman: University of Oklahoma
            Press.
Eggan, Fred
    1934a   The Maya Kinship System and Cross-Cousin Marriage. American Anthropol-
            ogist 36:188-202.
    1934b   Letter to John Collier, Commissioner of Indian Affairs, January 11. Records
            Relating to the Wheeler-Howard Act, file 4894-1934-666 (part 10-A).
            Records of the Bureau of Indian Affairs, Record Group 75, National Archives
            and Records Service, Washington, D.C.
    1937a   Historical Changes in the Choctaw Kinship System. American Anthropologist
            39:34-52.

1937b    The Cheyenne and Arapaho Kinship System. *In* Social Anthropology of North American Tribes, edited by Fred Eggan, 33-95. Chicago: University of Chicago Press.

1950     Social Organization of the Western Pueblos. Chicago: University of Chicago Press.

1952     The Ethnological Cultures and Their Archeological Backgrounds. *In* Archeology of the Eastern United States, edited by James B. Griffin, 34-45. Chicago: University of Chicago Press.

1954     Social Anthropology and the Method of Controlled Comparison. American Anthropologist 56:743-63.

1955     Social Anthropology: Methods and Results. *In* Social Anthropology of North American Tribes, edited by Fred Eggan, 485-551. Enlarged ed. Chicago: University of Chicago Press.

1966     The American Indian: Perspectives for the Study of Social Change. Chicago: Aldine Publishing.

1974     Among the Anthropologists. *In* Annual Review of Anthropology, vol. 3, edited by Bernard J. Siegel, 1-20. Palo Alto, Calif.: Annual Reviews.

1980     Shoshone Kinship Structures and Their Significance for Anthropological Theory. Journal of the Steward Anthropological Society 11:165-93. Urbana, Ill.

Eggan, Fred, ed.
1937     Social Anthropology of North American Tribes. Chicago: University of Chicago Press.

Foreman, Grant
1934     The Five Civilized Tribes. Norman: University of Oklahoma Press.

Grinnell, George Bird
1923     The Cheyenne Indians: Their History and Ways of Life. 2 vols. New Haven: Yale University Press.

Kelley, Lawrence C.
1978     Fred Eggan Interview, University of Chicago. May 31 and June 2, 1978. Typescript. Fred Eggan Papers, Special Collections, Regenstein Library, University of Chicago.

Kroeber, Alfred L.
1909     The Classificatory System of Relationship. Journal of the Royal Anthropological Institute 39:77-84

1939     Cultural and Natural Areas of Native North America. University of California Publications in American Archaeology and Ethnology, no. 38. Berkeley and Los Angeles: University of California Press.

Merton, Robert K.
1949     Social Theory and Social Structure. Glencoe: The Free Press.

Morgan, Lewis Henry
1871     Systems of Consanguinity and Affinity of the Human Family. Smithsonian Contributions to Knowledge, vol. 17. Washington, D.C.

1877     Ancient Society, or, Researches in the Lines of Human Progress from Savagery through Barbarism to Civilization. New York: Henry Holt.

Radcliffe-Brown, A. R.
1952     Structure and Function in Primitive Society: Essays and Addresses. Glenco: Free Press.

Rivers, W. H. R.
  1914    Kinship and Social Organization. New ed., London School of Economics Monographs on Social Anthropology, no. 34. New York: Humanities Press, 1968.
Spier, Leslie
  1921    The Sun Dance of the Plains Indians: Its Development and Diffusion. Anthropological Papers of the American Museum of Natural History, vol. 16, no. 7. New York.
  1925    The Distribution of Kinship Systems in North America. University of Washington Publications in Anthropology, vol. 1, no. 2. Seattle.
Spoehr, Alexander
  1947    Changing Kinship Systems. Field Museum of Natural History, Anthropological Series, vol. 33, no. 4. Chicago.
Stocking, George W., Jr., ed.
  1974    The Shaping of American Anthropology, 1883-1911: A Franz Boas Reader. New York: Basic Books.
Strong, William Duncan
  1929    Cross-Cousin Marriage and the Culture of the Northeast Algonkian. American Anthropologist 31:277-88.
  1940    From History to Prehistory in the Northern Great Plains. In Essays in Historical Anthropology of North America. Smithsonian Miscellaneous Collections 100, 353-94. Washington, D.C.
Wissler, Clark
  1917    The American Indian: An Introduction to the Anthropology of the New World. New York: Douglas C. McMurtrie.

# PART I

# Kinship and Social Organization

# 1

# Biology and Social Relationship in the Kin Terminology of an Inuit Community

## JOSEPH MAXWELL

The study of kin terminology[1] has been dominated recently by a controversy between two schools. One, which I will refer to as genealogical, has had as its major representative Harold W. Scheffler (1972a, 1972b, 1972c, 1976, 1978, 1982, 1984; Scheffler and Lounsbury 1971). The other, which I will call cultural, has been most vigorously advanced by David M. Schneider (1964, 1968, 1969a, 1969b, 1972, 1976, 1980, 1984). Proponents of these two schools have tended to take opposing positions on both of the major questions in the study of kin terminology: the meaning of kin terms, and the causes of particular patterns of kin terminology.

On the first issue, the meaning of kin terms, the genealogical approach tends to see biological (actually, ethnobiological) relatedness as basic and primary, with other meanings being secondary and derived from the primary biological meanings of the terms by genealogical or metaphoric extension. The arguments for this position have been both definitional (if biology were not the primary meaning, we would not call them *kin* terminologies) and empirical (evidence from numerous societies demonstrates the primacy of biological meanings). The cultural approach holds that biological meanings are only one of several possibilities, and that the relationship between these different meanings must be determined empirically for each culture. Schneider (1969a) claims that genealogical analyses have systematically overlooked or excluded evidence that would challenge the primacy of biological meanings.

On the second issue, the causes of particular patterns of kin terminology, the genealogical position tends to be that the semantic structure of a kin terminology is a reflection of the social structure. Floyd G. Lounsbury (1965), for example, held that the semantic rules that generate a pattern of terminology are reflections of particular social rules, such as those governing descent, residence, and inheritance. The cultural position denies that social determinism, and holds that the structure of a kin terminology

25

is a reflection of more basic cultural principles that manifest themselves in a variety of cultural domains.

However, there is a third tradition in the study of kin terminology, best exemplified by the work of Fred Eggan (1937, 1955, 1966) and some of his students (Bellah 1952; Callender 1962; Cottrell 1965; cf. Maxwell 1978). This approach has devoted considerable attention to changes in kin terminology, rather than focusing exclusively on synchronic analyses of kinship, and has attempted to relate differences in terminology to ecological factors, employing a method that Eggan (1954) termed controlled comparison: the comparative study of societies that are historically or geographically related. In so doing, it has emphasized the adaptive value of systems of kin classification, an issue that the other approaches have generally ignored or settled by theoretical fiat.

The analytic approach I have adopted here draws to a significant extent on all three of these traditions. I apply it to the kin terminology used by the Inuit inhabitants of Repulse Bay, N.W.T., Canada. The data presented here were collected during a year of fieldwork in Repulse Bay; most of the information was obtained through interviews in Inuktitut (the term these Inuit prefer for their own language), without the use of an interpreter.

My purpose and methods in presenting an account of this kin terminology are somewhat different from those of Scheffler or Schneider. I do not attempt to provide a formal semantic analysis of this kin terminology, in the sense of an abstract model that replicates the distribution of kin terms over kin types (Scheffler and Lounsbury 1971:49–50). My goals and methods are much closer to those described by Schneider (1980): to provide a "cultural account" of the terminological system. However, I do not accept Schneider's view that cultural analysis consists of "abstracting" symbols and meanings from behavior, and therefore I disagree with his position that behavioral data can provide nothing more than examples, and in no way can lend factual support to an interpretation. Schneider has in fact labeled the sort of argument that I present here "cheating" (Schneider 1980:124). In contrast to Schneider, I take culture to be mental rather than behavioral (Maxwell 1986). While culture itself cannot be observed (or even "abstracted" from behavior), it is inferred in order to make behavior intelligible (Goodenough 1971). This perspective implies that cultural analysis requires evidence from behavior (including verbal behavior) for its validation (Maxwell 1992).

In my view, a cultural account must not only meet criteria of simplicity, adequacy, and logical coherence (Scheffler 1978:385), but must also address potential "validity threats" to the analysis (Cook and Campbell 1979; Maxwell 1992)—that is, alternate explanations that could more plausibly account for the data. I have therefore tried to take account of such plausible alternatives to my analysis; in particular, based on Scheffler's (1976) critique of Schneider's interpretation of American kinship (1968), I have constructed an alternative analysis to the one I propose here and have presented the evidence that leads me to reject this alternative interpretation.

## The Basic Model of Kin Terminology

Before describing the kin terminology used in Repulse Bay, I must address a few definitional matters. First, when I use the phrase *kin term,* I am referring to a culturally defined category: those terms that are valid responses to the questions *qanuq ilagiviuk* 'How do you have him or her as a relative?' or *sugiviuk* 'What do you have him or her as?' At first, I was told that these two questions are synonymous, but later I found that there is a significant difference between them. Basically, *sugiviuk* is a request for the term actually used to address a person. If no term is used, the reply is *suginngittara,* literally, 'I don't have him as what', though if the person is a relative that fact would normally be mentioned. On the other hand, *qanuq ilagiviuk* is a request for the actual relationship, regardless of terminological usage. While some informants were quite explicit on this point, it is not a rigid or universally employed distinction, and in practice either question may receive as an answer either the term used or the actual relationship. *Sugiviuk* is used much more commonly than *qanuq ilagiviuk*, and is the standard way of asking about kin relationships.

Second, I use the term *natal* to refer to a relative or a relationship that a person acquires by virtue of being born into a particular nuclear family (Guemple 1966). Thus, natal relationships are distinguished both from putative biological relationships (such as that with a "natural" father) and from those relationships that are acquired following birth, such as those resulting from adoption.

The basic terminological structure used in Repulse Bay (figs. 1–5) is similar to that described by David Damas (1963), Nelson Graburn (1964), and Lee Guemple (1966) for other Canadian Inuit groups. The structure is "basic" in that it contains the terms that are most fundamental to the semantic structure of the kin terminology. Most other kin terms either are formed by modification of the basic terms, or are isolates and form no systematic structure with the other terms. A more detailed analysis of these basic terms is provided in Maxwell (1986).

Genealogical charts such as these are often taken to refer to biological (or putative biological) and procreative relationships. However, this is not the intent of these figures, nor do I believe it to be an accurate interpretation

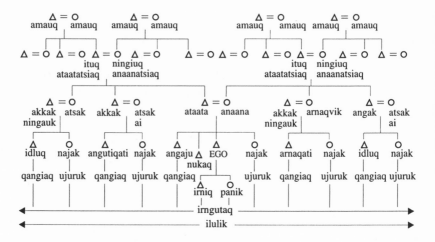

**Figure 1.** Inuit consanguineal kin terms: male ego.

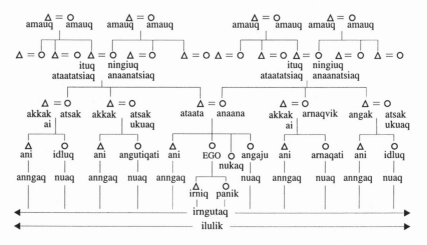

**Figure 2.** Inuit consanguineal kin terms: female ego.

of genealogical diagrams generally, as these are used to present kin terminologies. The figures represent only the logical structure of the linguistic constructions used to define terms and specify relationships, in which certain terms function as logical primitives. These logical primitives are used to define other terms, but are themselves undefined (Leaf 1971).

In these diagrams, the Inuktitut terms used as logical primitives, and their English glosses, are *ataata* 'father', *anaana* 'mother', *irniq* 'son', *panik* 'daughter', *angaju* 'older same-sex sibling', *nukaq* 'younger same-sex sibling' *ani* 'brother, female speaking', *najak* 'sister, male speaking',

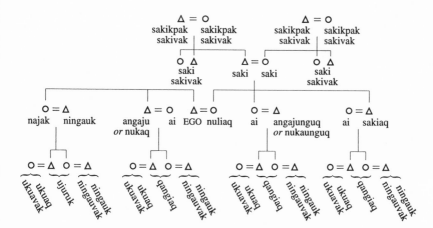

**Figure 3.** Inuit affinal kin terms: male ego.

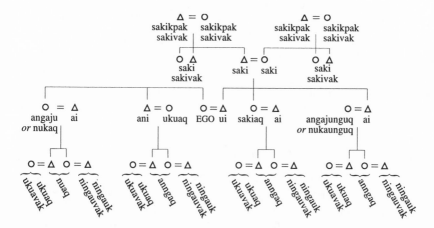

**Figure 4.** Inuit affinal kin terms: female ego.

*ui* 'husband', and *nuliaq* 'wife'. A vertical line upward represents a link to a person's *ataata* and *anaana;* downward, to his or her *irniq* or *panik*. A horizontal line represents a link to a person's *angaju, nukaq, ani,* or *najak,* depending on the sex and relative age of the two persons. An equals sign represents a link to a person's *ui* or *nuliaq.*

Neither the diagram, nor my use of English glosses as convenient labels for Inuktitut terms, should be taken to indicate that these terms refer to enthnobiological relationship (contra Scheffler and Lounsbury 1971:50), or to any other particular content. At this point I am concerned only with the structure of the terminology; I will later address the question of what

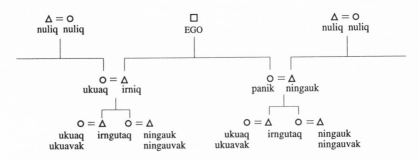

**Figure 5.** Inuit affinal kin terms (continued): male or female ego.

meaning can be assigned to these terms apart from that implied in this structure.

For some kinship positions, there is significant variation in the terms used. The most important source of such variation is the fact that the people of Repulse Bay are divided, and see themselves as divided, into two groups, one with social and kinship ties northeastward to Igloolik, the other with ties northwestward to Pelly Bay. There are significant differences in the kin terminologies used by the two groups, and those differences are indicated on the diagram by alternate terms. There is also a certain amount of idiosyncratic variation in terminological models; that variation is not indicated on the diagram, but is addressed in my discussion of semantic diversity.

## Modifications of the Basic Model

There are several ways in which the basic terminology is modified or extended by means of particular social practices. These practices fall into two classes. First, there are those that can be (and often have been) seen as creating extensions of the basic meanings of kin terms: remarriage, adoption, betrothal, polygamy, and spouse exchange. The relationships created by these practices are primarily incorporated into the terminology through modifying postbases that indicate the specific nature of the relationship, as with English *step* or *in-law*. Second, there are the practices surrounding naming and name sharing; terminologically these practices involve both a set of statuses, separate from the genealogical network, and a set of rules by means of which name-sharing relationships affect the genealogical ascription of kin terms. The name-sharing practices have a profound effect on the use of kin terms in Inuit communities (cf. Guemple 1965), but are not relevant to the main issues of this paper, and will not be discussed further. A more extended treatment of these practices is given in Maxwell (1986).

*Remarriage*

Relationships involving a subsequent marriage are "marked" with respect to those based on an initial marriage. Two postbases are employed for this marking. The first, *-taaq*, is the same postbase used generally with the meaning 'gets' or 'takes' (e.g., *umiaktaaqpuq* 'he gets a boat'). This construction is the usual way of referring to marriage (e.g., *nuliaqtaaqpuq* 'he takes a wife'). The *-taaq* postbase can be used to modify any basic kin term where the relative in question, or a linking relative, is a subsequent spouse; for example, one's father's brother's second wife is one's *atsaktaaq* and not one's "real" *atsaq* (*atsadlataaq*).

If the relationship is the result of the remarriage of one's own father or mother, or reciprocally, of one's marriage to someone having children by a former marriage, a second postbase, *-ksaq*, is used. This postbase is used generally to mean 'potential' or 'material for' (e.g., *igluksaq* 'material for [building] a house'). Used with kin terms, it has roughly the same meaning as English *step-*, but can be used to modify any basic kin term (fig. 6). The terms *angutiksaq* and *arnaksaq*, derived from *angut* 'man; male' and *arnaq* 'woman; female', are synonymous with *ataataksaq* and *anaanaksaq*, but are commonly used only by the Pelly Bay group, while the latter terms are used by both groups.

The *-ksaq* and *-taaq* postbases are often ignored in actual usage; normally a relative by remarriage will be addressed and referred to by the basic term without the postbase, while the postbase will be used to explain the relationship or specify the relative more precisely. Particularly for *-ksaq*, this pattern is due to its connotation that the relationship is less than fully 'real' (*-dlataaq*) or 'genuine'. Nonuse of the *-ksaq* postbase was often

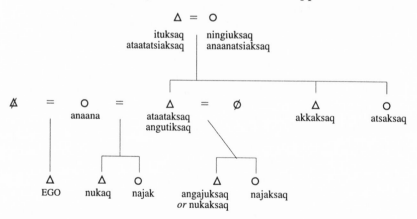

**Figure 6.** Inuit kin terms resulting from one parent's remarriage.

explained to me as a result of closeness and absence of uncomfortableness (*ilira–*) in the relationship, and the postbase is often dropped as the social relationship becomes stronger. Members of the Igloolik group, especially, feel that the *–ksaq* terms are uncomfortable (*iłuanngittut*), and dislike using them.

*Adoption*

Kin relationships arising from adoption in infancy are, at least in principle, quite distinct from those resulting from remarriage. There are distinct terms for an adopted child and for an adopting parent (*tiguaq* and *tiguaqsi*, respectively) that are kin terms in the strict sense; that is, they are valid answers to the question *qanuq ilagiviuk* 'How are you related to him or her?'

The *tiguaq*–based terms are derived from the root *tigu–* 'to take or grasp'. The postbase *–aq*, in other contexts, means 'that which is or does'. The meaning of the postbase *–si* is unclear, but it may be a contracted form of *–siji* 'one who _____', since *tiguaqsiji* 'one who adopts' is used for an adoptive parent in other areas. The verbal form for adoption is *tiguaqpuq* 'he/she adopts'.

For all other adoptive relationships, one uses (at least ideally) the same terms as for natal relatives. Most of my informants insisted that the *–ksaq* postbase was not correct for adoptive relatives, but only for step-relatives. That was contradicted by other informants, and was not entirely consistent even with the former informants' own genealogies. However, it constitutes both a widely held ideal rule and a general tendency in terminological usage. In no case did I find *–ksaq* terms used for adoptive parent or child when the adoption took place in infancy, although a few informants accepted those terms as correct in principle. One informant, who had denied that *–ksaq* terms were correct for adoptive parents' siblings, backtracked when I pointed out just such a usage in her own genealogy, and said that they could correctly be used in such cases to make the relationship clearer to someone, and that she had heard them used in stories. In talking of such usages, she used the phrases *nalunaikkutaq* and *nalunanngijjutik*, which have roughly the sense of 'that which is used to reduce ignorance'. Since there exist both an accepted use of the *–ksaq* terms for adoptive relatives and a feeling that such a usage is not really ideal, it is not surprising that different people develop varying ideas about the absolute "correctness" of this usage.

There is considerable optionality in the terms used between adoptive parents and children. Everyone agreed that either natal (basic) or *tiguaq*–based terms were acceptable, and my genealogies show that both are frequent. In the fairly common case of an unmarried woman's child being adopted by her parents, the latter may use *tiguaq, irniq/panik* ('son/ daughter'), or *irngutaq* ('grandchild'). The *tiguaq*–based terms, like the –*ksaq* terms, may be dropped as the child grows older, but they need not be, and are often maintained throughout the life of the relationship. They do not seem to have the same negative connotations as the –*ksaq* terms, and in general the adoptive relationship is seen as more "genuine" than that resulting from remarriage; some reasons for this perception are discussed below in considering ideas about the parent-child bond.

In the case of children who are orphaned after infancy and adopted by another couple, the *tiguaq*–based terms do not seem to be used; in the cases of this sort in my genealogies, –*ksaq* terms were employed. The "orphan" relationship is notoriously problematic in Eskimo society; such children are often mistreated, and the relationship tends to be unstable and easily broken. Some of the reasons for this situation are discussed later; the salient point here is the use of –*ksaq* rather than *tiguaq*–based terms (despite the verbal use of *tiguaq*– in describing the relationship) in a situation that rarely conforms to the ideal closeness of the parent-child bond.

## Betrothal

The –*ksaq* postbase is also used to mark relationships based on or deriving from betrothal. The terms for betrothed husband and wife are *uiksaq* and *nuliaksaq*, respectively; in this case, the use of –*ksaq* is strictly consistent with its more general meaning of 'potential' or 'material for'. There are also cases in my genealogies of the use of –*ksaq* for more distant relationships that involve a betrothal link (e.g., *ukuaksaq* for son's betrothed wife), and many informants considered such persons to be relatives. However, opinions differed on the proper terminology. Some informants claimed that the use of –*ksaq* terms for these relatives was completely correct, and a valid answer to *qanuq ilagiviuk*, even if the person was called by a different term; others said that while the –*ksaq* postbase could be used to make the relationship clearer to someone, the person correctly should be called by the normal affinal term (e.g., *ukuaq*) without the postbase. Despite this disagreement, all informants said that the relationship would not be "real" (–*dlataaq*) until the marriage occurred.

## Polygamy

Although polygamy is no longer practiced in Repulse Bay, the kin terms used in a polygamous relationship are known to many people (fig. 7). None of the terms can be considered basic in the sense defined above; all are either derived from terms with a more general, nonkinship meaning, or are formed from basic terms by the addition of a postbase. The term for co-

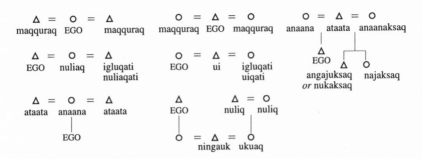

**Figure 7.** Inuit kin terms resulting from polygamy.

husband or co-wife, *igluqati*, means literally 'house-companion'. Co-husband and co-wife are also called *nuliaqati* and *uiqati*, respectively, from the terms for wife and husband plus the postbase *–qati* 'companion'. According to some informants, the term *aipaq* can be used between same-sex partners in a polygamous relationship, but this term is generally used for exchange relationships, as discussed below.

The term used by a man or woman for one of two spouses in a polygamous marriage, *maqquraq*, is derived from *maqquq* 'two'. I was told that this was the normal term used in polygamous marriage, rather than *ui* or *nuliaq*, and was a valid answer to *qanuq ilagiviuk*. (The postbase *–taaq*, discussed above, is used only for sequential marriage, not for polygamy.)

The terms used for and by the children in a polygamous marriage were different for polygyny and polyandry. In the case of a man with two wives, each woman used natal terms for her own children, and natal terms plus *–ksaq* for those of the other woman; her children used *anaanaksaq* for the other woman, and sibling terms plus *–ksaq* for her children. For a woman with two husbands, all the participants in the relationship used natal terms; I was told that all these relationships were *–dlataaq* 'real', and that the children thus had two "real" fathers.

For affinal relatives of the members of a polygamous marriage, the normal affinal terms were extended to include all participants. For example, one's daughter's husband's other wife is one's *ukuaq*, the same term as for son's wife. For more distant consanguineal relatives, the terminology merges with the natal or remarriage terminology.

*Spouse Exchange*

Like polygamy, spouse exchange (*kipuqtuk* 'they two exchange places or pass one another') in the traditional manner is no longer practiced in Repulse Bay, but relationships deriving from former exchanges are still operative (fig. 8). With the doubtful exception of *aipaq*, none of the terms

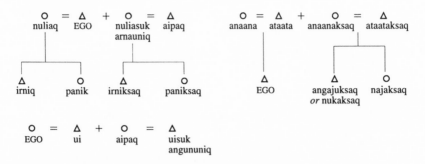

**Figure 8.** Inuit kin terms resulting from spouse-exchange.

can be considered basic; they are all formed from either basic kin terms or other roots by the addition of some postbase. The terms for 'exchange-husband' and 'exchange-wife' are formed from the terms for 'husband' and 'wife' by the addition of the postbase *–suk*. These terms are generally used for any man or woman with whom one has intercourse outside marriage; younger people use them in the sense of 'boyfriend' or 'girlfriend'. An alternate set of terms for these relationships, *angununiq* and *arnauniq*, is derived from the terms for 'man' (*angut*) and 'woman' (*arnaq*).

The term for exchange-partner (i.e., the person of the same sex as ego in the relationship; ego's exchange-spouse's spouse) is *aipaq*. In addition to exchange-partner and (as mentioned above) co-spouse in a polygamous marriage, it is also used between sequential spouses of the same person, after divorce and remarriage. Though it has a more general meaning elsewhere, it is used only in a kinship sense in Repulse Bay.

The terms used for and between children born to the exchanging couples follow a pattern similar to that for polygamy. Children of the other couple born after the exchange takes place are called by natal terms plus *–ksaq*, and the children of one couple use natal terms plus *–ksaq* for the other couple and for the latter's children. The child's natal parents (i.e., his mother and mother's husband) are his "real" (*–dlataaq*) parents, while his mother's exchange-husband is not his *ataatadlataaq*, but his *ataataksaq*.

I was told that in Igloolik there is a separate postbase, *–ksaarjuk*, which is used instead of *–ksaq* to refer specifically to relationships deriving from spouse exchange, distinguishing them from relationships resulting from remarriage and polygamy. This postbase seems to consist of *–ksaq* plus the diminutive *–arjuk*, which like other diminutives has the connotation of 'nice' or 'good' in many contexts. There is also another term for exchange-partner, *aipaarjuk*, which consists of *aipaq* plus *–arjuk*. The *–arjuk* postbase seems to function to counteract the negative connotations of the *–ksaq* postbase, which are particularly strong for the Igloolik group.

My informants were unsure whether or not the consanguineal relatives of one couple became related to the other couple through the exchange. The two couples themselves were relatives (*ilait*) only while the exchange was actually in effect and ceased to be related after the exchanging ended. However, the children born from the exchange continued to be related both to the other couple and to the latter's children.

## The Concept of *ila* 'Relative'

The central term in the Inuit conceptualization of kinship is *ila*. It has a range of meanings which are not confined to kinship, and an understanding of the significance and implications of the term in the area of kinship requires an analysis of both the kinship and nonkinship meanings it possesses.

In its most general sense, *ila* means 'part'. It is most commonly used, not for a part of a homogeneous mass or for one of a number of objects that simply happen to be together, but for something that has a separable identity yet is a necessary or functioning part of a larger whole, such as a part of a motor or harpoon. In referring to persons, *ila* has the general meaning of 'partner' or 'companion'. It is used for someone who accompanies one on a trip; one of the two verbs regularly used for that activity, *ilauvuq*, means literally 'he is an *ila*'. It is also used for any coparticipant in some activity, in particular for persons on the same side in games involving two teams. In talking about these uses of the term, informants emphasized not simply the physical proximity of the individuals classed as *ilagiit*, but the cooperation and assistance involved, often in the context of one person being more capable (*ajunnginniqsaq*) than another, and aiding the latter.

The use of *ila* to designate genealogical relatives shares much of the meaning of the more general uses of the term. In this context *ila* is often opposed to *adlaq* 'stranger, nonrelative'. In discussing these terms informants emphasized the importance of helping (*ikajuq–*), love (*nagli–*), being "mindful" and concerned (*isumaqatsiaq–*), and not being afraid or uneasy (*ilira–*) as distinguishing *ilait* from *adlait*. However, the definition of *ila* also involves the concept of genealogical connection. Informants would discuss in abstract genealogical terms which kinsmen were one's *ilait* and which were not, and while there was no universal agreement on a definite boundary for one's *ilagiit* (those who are *ila* to one another) in genealogical terms (for example, one informant said that one's *nuliq* was not one's *ila*, a statement rejected by all other informants questioned on this point), there was a rough consensus that some persons denoted by kin terms were definitely included and some were definitely not, and that one of the relevant criteria for this was some sort of genealogical connection.

It seems easy, at first, to interpret this information in terms of a purely genealogical definition of *ila*, to treat the social and attitudinal components as connotations of the term rather than as part of its designative meaning, and to consider the broader uses of *ila* outside the field of kinship to be metaphorical extensions of the concept that are likewise not involved in its basic meaning. This is the way in which several kin terminologies have been handled by Scheffler; nongenealogical meanings of kin terms are seen as secondary and metaphorical (e.g., "God the Father"), and the semantic core of kinship is considered to be the concept of biological relationship.

This interpretation encounters difficulties when applied to Inuit kinship. Social relatedness, as opposed to biological connection, is incorporated in the Inuit conceptualization of kinship in two important ways. First, the Inuit concept of "genealogy," as an ascriptive basis for kin relationship, itself involves social factors, so that it is impossible to analyze "genealogical" reckoning purely in terms of ethnobiological or procreative relationships. Second, the concept of *ila* involves attitudinal and behavioral criteria as well as genealogical ones. Informants spoke of love, aid, and lack of fear not simply as things that *ilait* normally or ideally felt and did for one another, but as characteristics that to a significant extent were incorporated in the definition of the term, and that determined whether or not someone was "really" one's *ila*.

### "Real" Relatives: *–dlataaq* and *–mmarik*

The claim that certain meanings of a term are more fundamental than others depends to an important extent on the meaning of the postbases that I have glossed as 'real' or 'really': *–dlataaq* and *–mmarik*. As far as I could discover, the two are synonymous, and to some extent are regional variants, *–dlataaq* being used more to the northeast of Repulse Bay, and *–mmarik* to the south and northwest. While *–mmarik* is the more common in general, *–dlataaq* is used more frequently with kin terms. Both are used with both verbs and nouns, and like the English terms *real* and *really,* can mean both 'truly' and 'very'. Thus, *surammariktuq* 'it's really broken' can mean both 'it's truly broken' (if someone doubts the fact) or 'it's very broken'; *inummarik* 'a real Inuk' can mean both a true Inuk (biologically), or a person who is very Inuit either in physical features or in maintaining a traditional way of life.

When used with kin terms, *–dlataaq* and *–mmarik* have several standard meanings. They are most commonly used in opposition to *–ksaq*, to indicate that the relationship is natal rather than being adoptive or a step-relationship; that is the usual reply I received when I asked directly about the meaning of terms containing *–dlataaq* and *–mmarik*. Also in opposition to *–ksaq*, they can indicate that, for an affine, the couple in question is actually married rather than only betrothed; for example, *ningaudlataaq* '"real" son-in-law', as opposed to *ningauksaq* 'daughter's betrothed husband'. Third, they can be used in contrast to *–taaq*, to distinguish relationships based on a first marriage from those involving remarriage; for example, one's father's brother's second wife is one's *atsaktaaq* and not one's *atsadlataaq*. Fourth, they may distinguish genealogical relationships from those involving name-based skewing, or from what I call idiosyncratic kin relationships (*tuqłirarniq*) based on criteria other than genealogy. Fifth, they can be used to separate close from distant genealogical relatives who are classed together under one kin term; for example, one informant said that her husband's parents' siblings were her *sakiit*, but not her *sakidlataat*, restricting the latter term to husband's parents. Sixth, they can refer to biological rather than social relationships; *ataatadlataaq* is often used in this sense, with roughly the same meaning as *real father* in English. Finally, they can have the opposite sense from the previous use: they may distinguish natal or social relationships from merely biological ones. For example, Jerome Rousseau (1970) cites the case of a man who, after discussing his adoptive mother and comparing her favorably with his biological mother, said, "It is she, rather, who is my true mother."

This last usage is uncommon in pure form (I have no unequivocal examples of it), but it is involved in a number of standard uses of these postbases. The child of an unmarried woman without a regular *uisuk* (lover), whose biological paternity is thus uncertain, is said to have no "real" father (*ataatadlataaq*); only if one knew unequivocally who the father was (*nalunanngippat*), I was told, would the child be said to have an *ataatadlataaq*. In cases of spouse exchange, it is the child's mother's husband, rather than her exchange-husband, who is the child's *ataatadlataaq;* the latter is the child's *ataataksaq*. In a polyandrous marriage, when both men have a socially recognized relationship to the child's mother, the child has both men as its *ataatadlataaq*. (Most older people, in telling of cases in which a person had an Inuit social father and a white biological father, said simply that the person had two fathers, and would not spontaneously use *–dlataaq* for the biological father, although they generally accepted my use of the postbase in that sense.) What accounts for the denotations of *ataatadlataaq* in these situations is not presumed biological connection, but the presence of an established social relationship between a man and the child or its mother.

Which of these different meanings of *–dlataaq* and *–mmarik* is understood by the hearer depends on the context, and the terms are therefore "shifters" (Silverstein 1976), indexing features of the speech situation as well as communicating situation-independent referential meanings. This point has also been made by Kelley (1982:74) with respect to the English term "real"; he states that "real" does not in itself designate a particular sufficiency condition for the use of a kin term, but simply denotes the sufficiency condition that is considered to be critical to a given conversation. He argues that the statistical predominance of references to biological ties in American English is a result of Americans' belief that the social order derives from the natural order rather than vice versa. This belief is not present to the same extent in Inuit culture.

If *–dlataaq* terms in fact derive part of their meaning from their context of use, different persons would be expected to interpret them differently when the terms are used without any defining context. For example, I asked a number of people if one's cousin of the opposite sex (*ani* or *najak*, the same term as for brother or sister) was one's *anidlataaq* or *najadlataaq*. Most of them replied that the cousin would be *–dlataaq*, as long as they were natal relatives, not adopted or step-relatives, although if asked about the relationship they would explain that they had different parents. (I have heard *najammarik* used for a female cousin in speaking to a child.) A minority of informants, using the criterion of genealogical distance rather than natal relationship, denied that opposite-sex cousins were *–dlataaq*, saying that only *nangminiik* (one's own siblings) were *–dlataaq*. The interpretation of the term depends not on some absolute, context-free meaning of the postbase, but on what the hearer thinks is being asked about.

When used with *ila* rather than with kin terms, the meaning of these postbases is somewhat different. The terms *iladlataaq* and *ilammarik* are not usually employed to designate "real" relatives, as opposed to some other, less genuine sort of relatives, but to mean 'really a relative', in response to doubt. Whenever I asked directly about these terms, I was told that anyone who is one's *ila* is one's *iladlataaq*—that includes adoptive, step, and affinal relatives as well as consanguines. In explaining kinship matters to me, however, informants would often use *ila* in a number of different senses and ranges of inclusiveness, and in such cases they used *–dlataaq* and *–mmarik* to distinguish the narrower and more central meanings from the peripheral and more general ones. Two criteria are involved in these "focal" meanings marked by *–dlataaq* and *–mmarik*: genealogical closeness and social closeness.

Genealogical closeness is reckoned in much the same way as in English-speaking cultures, and depends on both the number and the type of links connecting the speaker with the relative in question. One's closest relatives are one's parents, siblings, and children—those relationships that are labeled by the logically primitive kin terms. (My informants were at a loss to decide whether one's husband or wife was one's *ila;* answers varied, and no one seemed especially confident of his or her conclusion.) There is a term, *ilammarigiit* 'those who are real relatives to one another', that is used for one's closest kin; whenever I was given a genealogical definition of the term, it was limited to the children and grandchildren of one couple. Genealogically more distant relatives (considered in terms of the number of genealogical steps between the speaker and the relative)—such as parents' siblings, cousins, and siblings' children—are not generally considered part of a person's *ilammarigiit*. Affines are likewise excluded from the *ilammarigiit* as genealogically defined, as are persons related through name sharing. However, adoptive and (at least in principle) step-parents, -siblings, and -children are part of one's *ilammarigiit*. In this pattern of inclusion and exclusion, the term is similar to, and was often translated by English-speaking informants as, 'family'.

Informants also used *iladlataaq* and *ilammarik* (usually the latter) to refer to social rather than genealogical closeness. The term *ilammarigiit* was defined by one informant as *ikajuqpaktut* 'they who frequently help (one another)'. That informant explained that if your relatives treated you well and loved you, they would be *ilammariit*, while if they didn't they would be *adlait*. When I asked about the relative importance of genealogical connection and proper action, he said that one's attitude and behavior were most important, that in principle anyone in the world could be one's *ilammarik* if he acted and thought in the right way toward one.

Thus, there are two ways in which these postbases are used with *ila* and with kin terms: genealogical and social. This dichotomy supports the earlier analysis of the term *ila* itself, which suggested that the term has two semantic dimensions—genealogical connection and social relatedness—and constitutes evidence against the suggestion that biological relationship is the primary meaning of the term and the social meanings of the term are secondary and metaphorical. My conclusion here is similar to Schneider's in his analysis of American kinship (1968)—that there are two defining criteria for being a relative, shared substance ("blood") and code for conduct ("diffuse, enduring solidarity").

Social relationship is incorporated at two levels in Repulse Bay Inuit kinship. It is a factor in the reckoning of genealogy itself, since genealogical connection is not simply a matter of shared biological substance, but incorporates social factors as well. Social relationship also operates as a separate consideration from genealogy in the assessment of kinship relations.

## The Parent-Child Bond

Part of the explanation for this importance of social relatedness, and for the particular forms that it takes, can be found in Inuit ideas about the nature and development of the parent-child bond. A child's mind (*isuma*) is regarded as unformed at birth, and develops gradually during the first few years of its life, as a result of the care and attention the child is given by its parents. The bond between parent and child is seen primarily as a result of this love and nurture, rather than of a biological connection between the two. Therefore, the connection between a child adopted as an infant and its adoptive parents is seen as being much stronger than any intrinsic tie to its natural parents, even though a social relationship may exist with the latter.

A number of features of the structure and use of kin terms can be seen as consequences of this view of the parent-child bond. First, it explains why adoptive relationships are considered both "real" and genealogical (i.e., these relatives are considered *iladlataat* in abstraction, regardless of the actual social relationship), and why the genealogical meaning of *ataatadlataaq* depends on social factors as well as putative biological paternity (because the genealogical link between parent and child involves social as well as biological factors). It also accounts for the strong feeling of most of my informants that *–ksaq* terms are not appropriate for adoptive relationships, but only for step-relationships. When the child is adopted as an infant, the social bond between it and its adoptive parents is in theory as strong as if the latter were the child's natal parents. That being so, natal terms can be used between adoptive parent and child, and should be used between adoptive siblings, rather than the *–ksaq* terms, which imply that the relationship is not fully "genuine." However, *–ksaq* terms, like those containing the postbases *–dlataaq* and *–mmarik*, can be used to express a variety of distinctions, so that in explaining a relationship a *–ksaq* term may be used to indicate that the relationship is adoptive rather than natal.

Conversely, this conceptualization of the parent-child bond explains why the *–ksaq* terms are frequently used by and for orphans (*iliijait*) and other children adopted later in life, as well as for step-children. In such cases there has been no bond formed between the child and its adoptive or step-parents and the relationship usually lacks the closeness and affection that exist when the child is born into the family or adopted at birth. At present, the same situation can arise when a young child becomes ill and is sent out of the settlement for extended medical care during the period when the parent-child bond is supposed to develop. Such children are often not successfully reintegrated into the family on their return, and their status and treatment can approach that of step-children or orphans.

## Validity of the Analysis

My analysis of Repulse Bay kin terminology[2] asserts that there are two components to the meaning of specific kin terms and of the term *ila* 'relative'. These two components can be labeled "procreative connection" and "nurture/support." Either of these two components is a sufficient condition for a person to be denoted by the term *ila*, although ideally both components are present. Either component can also constitute a sufficient condition for the denotation of a person by a particular kin term, although procreative connection is the usual basis for the assignment of kin terms.

The validity of this analysis hinges on how well it explains the data I have collected on the use and explanation of kin terms by Repulse Bay Inuit. In particular, the analysis must provide a better account of those data than alternative explanations. The most plausible alternative to my analysis would seem to be a "genealogical" account along the lines of Scheffler (1976).

Such an account would take procreative connection to be the defining feature of *ila* and of the basic kin terms. "Real" relatives are those with whom one has a connection through a procreative relationship. Relatives through remarriage or name sharing, betrothed kin, and more distant members of particular kin categories are "relatives" in a secondary and derived sense, resulting from genealogically based extensions of the terms; this is evident from the various postbases that mark many of these relatives as not being "real" kin. Adoptive relatives, on the other hand, are "relatives" only through metaphoric extension of the kin terms to persons who substitute for particular "real" relatives, fulfilling the social obligations of the kin role. In this instance, the social obligations of love, nurture, and support—which are nondistinctive features (connotations) of the term *ila* and of particular kin terms—function as sufficient conditions for their use. The application of particular kin terms to persons with whom one lacks a genealogical relationship is also based on this sort of metaphorical extension.

I accept Scheffler's argument that modification of the basic terminology by means of postbases (as for relatives through remarriage and betrothed kin), and the use of kin terms for more distant genealogical relatives and for relatives connected through name sharing, involve a genealogical extension of the primary meanings of these terms. However, I question whether that is a valid analysis of the meaning of the basic kin terms, of *ila*, and of the terms for adoptive relatives, *tiguaq* and *tiguaqsi*. The key question is the relative plausibility of an interpretation based on two components of the meaning of those terms, versus an account that treats one of these components as nondistinctive and connotative, rather than part of the designative meaning of the terms.

I have rejected the view that this assessment can be based entirely on formal criteria of adequacy and parsimony in predicting a limited set of denotata of the terms (e.g., Katz 1972), even though I feel that my analysis is in fact more adequate than the alternative in its explanation of the use of these terms. Consequently, I will provide a number of different kinds of evidence for an interpretation that employs two components of the meaning of kin terms: on the one hand, procreative connection, and on the other hand, nurture and support.

The first type of evidence is based on the use of the terms, particularly in connection with the postbases *-ksaq*, *-dlataaq*, and *-mmarik*. Adoptive relatives tend not to be marked by the *-ksaq* postbase, and my genealogies contain no instances of the use of *-ksaq* terms for adoptive parent or adopted child when the adoption took place in infancy. This situation is in sharp contrast to adoptions taking place when the child is older, which invariably involved the use of *-ksaq* rather than *tiguaq–* terms. While the *-dlataaq* and *-ksaq* postbases can be used to distinguish procreative relationships from adoptive ones, *-dlataaq* can also be used (although this is less common) to denote adoptive relatives in contrast to procreative kin for whom the component of nurture and support is absent. The term *ataatadlataaq* is also used for one's natal father in an exchange relationship, rather than for one's presumed genitor, the exchange-father, who is denoted by *ataataksaq*.

The second type of evidence consists of the explanations that Repulse Bay Inuit give for the meaning and appropriate use of the term *ila*. The features of love, help, and concern were explained to me not simply as connotations or role obligations of *ila*, but a part of the meaning of the term, along with genealogical connection, and as criteria for separating *ilammariit* from relatives in general.

The third sort of supporting evidence derives from the conceptualization of the parent-child bond, which emphasizes the role of love and nurture rather than procreative connection, although the latter is also involved. This conceptualization provides a basis for the incorporation of two components not only in the meaning of kin terms, but in Inuit views of social relationship generally. It seems to me not only plausible, but highly likely, that Inuit would, in gaining an understanding of kin terms, incorporate these non-procreational concepts into the meanings of the terms. However, I do not claim that all Inuit, even in a single community, share the same cognitive model of the meaning of kin terms. It is conceivable that some people in Repulse Bay have a "Schefflerian" understanding of kinship, and others a "Schneiderian" one.

A fourth argument can also be used to support the two-component analysis, based primarily on the approach to kinship of Eggan, rather than the "genealogical" or "cultural" schools. This argument is that a semantic model that incorporates attitudinal and behavioral criteria for being a relative is of considerable adaptive value in Inuit societies. Inuit place great value on creating and extending kinship ties, and the flexibility and "negotiability" of Inuit kinship have been noted by many researchers (e.g., Guemple 1972). The ecological reasons for that flexibility are connected with the uncertainty of subsistence resources, the frequent need to change residence, and the importance of cooperation and sharing food. The incorporation of nurture and support into the meaning of *ila* and of kin terms in general can be seen as providing cultural support for that flexibility, allowing relationships established through means other than genealogical connection to be treated as "real" kinship. This analysis draws on Eggan's explanation for the extension of sibling terms to cousins in many Plains tribes in response to the increased uncertainty in hunting and warfare resulting from moving onto the plains and the consequent need for greater flexibility in kinship structure (Eggan 1955, 1966; Maxwell 1978).

## Conclusions

The meaning of Repulse Bay kin terms is not centered on the concept of procreative connection, nor are other meanings of the term secondary to, or extensions of, the putative biological link between individuals resulting from the "universal facts" of sexual intercourse and birth. Scheffler, the main proponent of the genealogical position, has in fact disavowed this extreme position (1976:87–88), although he argues that opponents of this view have failed to make a convincing case. My disagreement with this position is both methodological and empirical. As argued above, the genealogical method as normally employed rests on the use of certain terms as logical primitives, and by itself it says nothing about the meaning of those terms. Their meaning must be empirically investigated, rather than assumed from parallels with the investigator's kin terminology; as Scheffler (1976:88) acknowledges, relatively few studies of kin terminologies have systematically undertaken that task.

My analysis suggests that biological connection is only one component of the meaning of Repulse Bay kin terms, the other being similar to what Schneider has called "diffuse, enduring solidarity." The existence of these two components of the meaning of kin terms, biological relationship and behavioral-emotional relationship, has been asserted for the kinship systems of numerous other societies, including groups in the Pacific

(Silverman 1971; Carroll 1970; Pynkiewich 1974; Glasse 1969; Labby 1976; Shore 1976; Clay 1977; Feinberg 1981), South Asia (Inden and Nicholas 1977), and Native America (Witherspoon 1975; DeMallie, this volume). It seems to me that it may be a common feature of kinship semantics.

A valid account of the meaning of Repulse Bay kin terms requires the insights of all three approaches discussed here: Scheffler's "genealogical" analysis, Schneider's "cultural" analysis, and Eggan's emphasis on adaptation. A theory of kin terminology that integrates these perspectives should constitute a significant step toward Eggan's goal of "clarify[ing] the relations between culture, as a set of ideas and symbols, and social structure, as a system of social interaction" (1963:399).

## Notes

1. I prefer the forms *kin term* and *kin terminology* to the more common *kinship terminology* for two reasons. First, they are shorter; second, what is meant are terms designating kin, not all of the terms pertaining to the domain of kinship.

2. I do not claim that *all* Inuit kin terminologies can be analyzed in this way; in fact, evidence presented by Heinrich (1971) and Burch (1975) for Alaska suggests that my analysis may not be valid for the latter area.

## References

Bellah, Robert N.
1952    Apache Kinship Systems. Cambridge: Harvard University Press.
Burch, Ernest S., Jr.
1975    Eskimo Kinsmen: Changing Family Relationships in Northwest Alaska. American Ethnological Society Monograph, no. 59. St. Paul: West Publishing Co.
Callender, Charles
1962    Social Organization of the Central Algonkian Indians. Milwaukee Public Museum Publications in Anthropology, no. 7.
Carroll, Vern
1970    Adoption on Nukuoro. *In* Adoption in Eastern Oceania, edited by Vern Carroll, 121–57. Association for Social Anthropology in Oceania Monograph, no. 1. Honolulu: University of Hawaii Press.
Clay, Brenda
1977    Pinikindu: Maternal Nurture, Paternal Substance. Chicago: University of Chicago Press.
Cook, Thomas D., and Donald T. Campbell
1979    Quasi-experimentation: Design and Analysis Issues for Field Settings. Boston: Houghton Mifflin.

Cottrell, Calvert B.
1965     Changes in Crow Kinship. M.A. Paper, Department of Anthropology, University of Chicago.

Damas, David
1963     Igluligmiut Kinship and Local Groupings: A Structural Approach. National Museums of Canada Bulletin no. 196. Ottawa: Department of Northern Affairs and Natural Resources.

Eggan, Fred
1937     The Cheyenne and Arapaho Kinship System. *In* Social Anthropology of North American Tribes, edited by Fred Eggan, 35–39. Chicago: University of Chicago Press.
1954     Social Anthropology and the Method of Controlled Comparison. American Anthropologist 56:743–63.
1955     Social Anthropology: Methods and Results. *In* Social Anthropology of North American Tribes, enlarged edition, edited by Fred Eggan, 485–551. Chicago: University of Chicago Press.
1963     Cultural Drift and Social Change. Current Anthropology 4:347–55.
1966     The North American Indian: Perspectives for the Study of Social Change. Chicago: Aldine Publishing.

Feinberg, Richard
1981     Anuta: Social Structure of a Polynesian Island. Institute for Polynesian Studies and the Polynesian Cultural Center in cooperation with the Danish National Museum. Provo, Utah: Brigham Young University Press.

Glasse, R. M.
1969     Marriage in South Fore. *In* Pigs, Pearlshells, and Women: Marriage in the New Guinea Highlands, edited by R. M. Glasse and M. J. Meggitt, 16–37. Englewood Cliffs, N. J.: Prentice-Hall.

Goodenough, Ward H.
1971     Culture, Language, and Society. McCaleb Module in Anthropology. Reading, Pa.: Addison-Wesley.

Graburn, Nelson H. H.
1964     Taqagmiut Eskimo Kinship Terminology. Ottawa: Department of Northern Affairs and Natural Resources.

Guemple, Lee
1965     Saunik: Name-Sharing as a Factor Governing Eskimo Kin Terms. Ethnology 4:323–35.
1966     Kinship Reckoning among the Belcher Island Eskimos. Ph.D. diss., University of Chicago.

Guemple, Lee, ed.
1972     Alliance in Eskimo Society. Proceedings of the American Ethnological Society 1971, Supplement. Seattle: University of Washington Press.

Heinrich, Albert W.
1972     Divorce as an Alliance Mechanism among Eskimos. *In* Alliance in Eskimo Society, edited by Lee Guemple, 79–88. Proceedings of the American Ethnological Society 1971, Supplement. Seattle: University of Washington Press.

Inden, Ronald B., and Ralph W. Nicholas
1977     Kinship in Bengali Culture. Chicago: University of Chicago Press.

Katz, Jerrold
1972       Semantic Theory. New York: Harper and Row.
Kelley, William R.
1982       Aspects of the Meaning of American English Kinterms. M.A. Paper,
           Department of Anthropology, University of Chicago.
Labby, David
1976       The Demystification of Yap: Dialectics of Culture on a Micronesian Island.
           Chicago: University of Chicago Press.
Leaf, Murray
1971       The Punjabi Kinship Terminology as a Semantic System. American Anthro-
           pologist 73:545-54.
Lounsbury, Floyd G.
1965       Another View of the Trobriand Kinship Categories. *In* Formal Semantic
           Analysis, edited by E. A. Hammell, 142-85. American Anthropologist 65(5),
           part 2.
Maxwell, Joseph A.
1978       The Evolution of Plains Indian Kin Terminologies: A Non-Reflectionist
           Account. Plains Anthropologist 23:13-29.
1986       The Conceptualization of Kinship in an Inuit Community: A Cultural
           Account. Ph.D., University of Chicago.
1992       Understanding and Validity in Qualitative Research. Harvard Educational
           Review 62:279-300.
Pynkiewich, Michael A.
1974       Coming Home to Bokelab. *In* Conformity and Conflict: Readings in Cultural
           Anthropology, edited by James P. Spradley and David W. McCurdy. 2d ed.
           Boston: Little, Brown, and Company.
Rousseau, Jerome
1970       L'adoption chez les Esquimaux Tununermiut (Pond Inlet, T. du N.-O.) Centre
           d'Études Nordiques, Travaux Divers, no. 28. Québec: Université Laval.
Scheffler, Harold W.
1972a      Baniata Kin Classification: The Case for Extensions. Southwestern Journal
           of Anthropology 28:350-81.
1972b      Kinship Semantics. *In* Annual Review of Anthropology 1, edited by Bernard
           J. Siegel, 309-28. Palo Alto, Calif.: Annual Reviews.
1972c      Systems of Kin Classification: A Structural Typology. *In* Kinship Systems in
           the Morgan Centennial Year, edited by Priscilla Reining, 113-33. Washing-
           ton, D.C.: Anthropological Society of Washington.
1976       The "Meaning" of Kinship in American Culture: Another View. *In* Meaning
           in Anthropology, edited by Keith H. Basso and Henry A. Selby, 57-91.
           Albuquerque: University of New Mexico Press.
1978       Reviews of *The Demystification of Yap,* by David Labby, and *Pinikindu:
           Maternal Nurture, Paternal Substance,* by Brenda Johnson Clay. American
           Ethnologist 5:382-85.
1982       Theory and Method in Social Anthropology: On the Structure of Systems of
           Kin Classification. American Ethnologist 9:167-84.
1984       Kin Classification as Social Structure: The Ambrym Case. American
           Ethnologist 11:791-806.

Scheffler, Harold W., and Floyd G. Lounsbury
    1971    A Study in Structural Semantics: The Siriono Kinship System. Englewood
            Cliffs, N.J.: Prentice-Hall.
Schneider, David M.
    1964    The Nature of Kinship. Man 64:180–81.
    1968    American Kinship: A Cultural Account. Englewood Cliffs, N.J.: Prentice-
            Hall.
    1969a   Componential Analysis: A State-of-the-Art Review. Paper prepared for a
            symposium on Cognitive Studies and Artificial Intelligence Research,
            Chicago, 1969. Wenner-Gren Foundation for Anthropological Research.
    1969b   Kinship, Nationality, and Religion in American Culture: Toward a Definition
            of Kinship. In Forms of Symbolic Action, edited by Robert F. Spencer, 116–
            25. Proceedings of the American Ethnological Society 1969. Seattle.
    1972    What Is Kinship All About? In Kinship in the Morgan Centennial Year, edited
            by Priscilla Reining, 32–63. Washington, D.C.: Anthropological Society of
            Washington.
    1976    Notes Toward a Theory of Culture. In Meaning in Anthropology, edited by
            Keith Basso and Henry Selby, 197–220. Albuquerque: University of New
            Mexico Press.
    1980    American Kinship: A Cultural Account. 2d ed. Englewood Cliffs, N.J.:
            Prentice-Hall.
    1984    A Critique of the Study of Kinship. Ann Arbor: University of Michigan Press.
Shore, Bradd
    1976    Adoption, Alliance, and Political Mobility in Samoa. In Transactions in
            Kinship: Adoption and Fosterage in Samoa, edited by Ivan Brady. Association
            for Social Anthropology in Oceania, Monograph no. 4. Honolulu: University
            of Hawaii Press.
Silverman, Martin G.
    1971    Disconcerting Issue: Meaning and Struggle in a Resettled Pacific Community.
            Chicago: University of Chicago Press.
Silverstein, Michael
    1976    Shifters, Linguistic Categories, and Cultural Description. In Meaning in
            Anthropology, edited by Keith H. Basso and Henry A. Selby, 11–55.
            Albuquerque: University of New Mexico Press.
Witherspoon, Gary
    1975    Navajo Kinship and Marriage. Chicago: University of Chicago Press.

# 2

# Historical Changes in the Chipewyan Kinship System

JAMES G. E. SMITH

The increasing amount of research on North American subarctic cultures by a growing number of students embodying different theoretical and methodological approaches has resulted in substantial questions concerning contact era culture and the subsequent course of change. The accelerating pace is indicated by comparing Richard Slobodin's (1975a, 1975b) evaluation of pre-1970 studies with more recent bibliographies and reviews by Ernest Burch (1979), Shepard Krech (1980), Edward Rogers (1981) and June Helm and Royce Kurtz (1984).

This paper discusses problems of kinship among several divisions of the Chipewyans of subarctic Canada; it includes consideration of environmental adaptation and socioterritorial organization, kindreds, variations in terminology, and marriage. Kinship played an important role in developing and maintaining a social network over a vast area with sparse but seasonally concentrated populations. However, the scope lessened in recent times and internal adaptations were made as a consequence of various acculturative forces. These forces included the fur trade (especially the Hudson's Bay Company), the Church and, finally, the government of Canada, all leading to the contemporary "micro-urban" village (J. G. E. Smith 1978b).

Fred Eggan's (1937a) classic study of change in the Choctaw kinship system pointed out the regularity of changes due to Euroamerican acculturative influences. His study of the western Pueblos (1950) pioneered an approach that synthesized ethnographic research with historical and environmental perspectives. His broad research interests have been particularly insightful in the examination of kinship, marriage, and band organization of the Subarctic and Plains areas (1937b, 1955, 1966).

In his analysis of Northern Algonkian social organization Eggan suggested as a structural type the "bilateral band held together by cross-cousin marriage" (1937b:521). He discussed the possibility of patrilateral cross-cousin marriage among the then little known Chipewyans as a more amorphous form of band integration, but questioned the frequency of the practice (Eggan 1937b:543). About the same time, Julian Steward (1955: 143–50) described subarctic Algonkian and Athapaskan bands as "composite" (i.e., bilateral, but including some individuals without kinship links to the others).

Helm's comparison of kinship among the arctic drainage Athapaskans found that the historically and ethnographically known bands were bilateral and *all* persons were related by primary ties of consanguinity or affinity (Helm 1965; MacNeish 1960). There was no evidence of unilocal residence rules. Helm proposed that bilaterality in this region was a response to the uncertainties of the environment that made the widest network of kinship adaptive. In examining the Hare data, however, she found they had Iroquois cousin terminology but there were no cases of first-cousin marriage, only one of second cross cousins, and the remaining eleven were with terminological cross cousins (Helm 1968b). In another paper, Helm (1980) indicated that population loss attributed to the Northeastern Athapaskans from Old World diseases was exaggerated and was compensated for by the cessation of female infanticide.

In retrospect, Clark Wissler (1915) stressed the similarities of cultural adaptations of the caribou hunters of the north and the buffalo hunters of the Plains. Eggan (1937b) suggested that the generational kinship system of the Cheyennes and Arapahos had parallels among other northern Plains tribes and proposed that this was an aspect of Plains horse-bison adaptation. Eggan (1980:174–75, 179–81) discussed pseudo-cross-cousin marriage among the Shoshones, "in which a step-cross cousin was married rather than a genealogical cross cousin." His analysis of pseudo-patrilateral cross-cousin marriage among the Northern Shoshones indicated it was part of an ecological adaptation involving low density of population but permitting seasonally larger groups, perhaps suggesting parallels to the Plains. Among some Caribou Eaters with equally low population density and with seasonal large regional and local bands, I found some evidence of classificatory or pseudo-patrilateral cross-cousin marriage within a basically generational system (J. G. E. Smith 1978a:81). Here I propose to consider Eggan's hypotheses in the context of the subarctic hunters of the migratory and nomadic caribou.

George Murdock (1955:95) proposed that North American societies were essentially bilateral, and that special considerations led to unilineal organization. In contrast, Elman Service saw the "causes of the modern, fluid, informal, composite band" as the "initial shocks, depopulation, relocation and other disturbances in the early contact period" (1971:77). He held that patrilineal organization preceded bilateral or complex organization, a questionable assumption since the *Man the Hunter* conference (Lee and DeVore 1968). Following Service, however, B. J. Williams (1974:97-102) attributed the assumed loss of patrilocal or patrilineal-patrilocal bands to those factors. In contrast, Charles Bishop and Arthur Ray (1976) presented a similar model of culture change, and Bishop and Shepard Krech (1980) proposed aboriginal "matriorganization" that was also lost as a consequence of hypothesized population loss. However, Service's "D P Hypothesis" (Guemple 1972) has not gained general acceptance among Arctic and Subarctic specialists (e.g., Damas 1969; Helm 1965; Helm et al. 1975; Helm, Rogers, and Smith 1981; Meyer 1985; Rogers and Smith 1973). I. Dyen and D. F. Aberle (1974) asserted that an ancestral Protohistoric Athapaskan matrilineal system gave way to other varieties. Richard Perry (1989) considered Northern Athapaskan matrilineal descent and locality as an anomaly among hunter-gatherers, but erred conceptually by including temporary postmarital matrilocal residence or bride service among his examples. This practice was equally characteristic of the bilateral descent groups of the Northwest Territories (Helm 1965) and Northern Algonkians as far west as Alberta (J. G. E. Smith 1975b:183, 1987:61).

## Chipewyan Ecological Adaptation

The Chipewyans, or "Northern Indians," were first contacted by Europeans about 1700 and thus have a long history recorded in the Hudson's Bay Company Archives (HBCA) and other early fur trade sources. The Caribou Eaters, as they became known, were those who remained in their traditional lands and maintained a commitment as caribou hunters until recent years. Until the final stages of sedentism, caribou were basic to subsistence and to their moral and mythical world (Sharp 1977a, 1977b; J. G. E. Smith 1975a, 1978a).

The relationship of Chipewyans to the caribou is an old one. William Noble (1981:102-6), in an example of the direct historical approach, found evidence that dates the ancestral Chipewyan Taltheilei Shale Tradition from about 500 B.C. to the early historic period. Samuel Hearne (1795) described it as it was between 1769 and 1772; Ernest Burch (1976) described the predator-prey relationship of 1600 to 1800; and Pierre Duchaussois (1935:253) noted the decline of the hunting ranges at the end of the nineteenth century.

The aboriginal Chipewyans occupied the taiga-tundra ecotone from the Seal River northwestward to the Arctic Circle, near the mouth of the Coppermine River (J. G. E. Smith and Burch 1979). The northwestern group was known as the Yellowknife (or Copper or Red Knife) Indians, because of their control and use of copper. In the late eighteenth and nineteenth centuries some Chipewyans moved into the full boreal forest, largely due to the influences of the fur trade (Gillespie 1970, 1975). There subsistence was based on a more diversified fauna and more fur bearers (VanStone 1965; Jarvenpa 1976; D. M. Smith 1982), and more closely resembled that of their former enemies, the Crees. As the southern movement increased, the exploitation of the Barren Lands decreased, until they were completely abandoned by about 1960 (J. G. E. Smith and Burch 1979; J. G. E. Smith 1976b).

The relationship of Chipewyan socioterritorial organization to the Barren-Ground caribou has been considered in detail elsewhere (J. G. E. Smith 1975a, 1976b, 1978a, 1981; Sharp 1977a, 1977b), and will only be summarized here. In this vast area James Isham (1949:177) estimated their population in the 1740s at about 1,000 families, or somewhat more than 4,000 individuals. They were often widely dispersed, but seasonally, large regional bands or even larger groups came together as the herds aggregated (HBCA B.239/a/2, fo. 28d).

The Barren-Ground caribou *(Rangifer tarandus groenlandicus)* is a highly migratory, nomadic and gregarious herd species (Kelsall 1968; Symington 1965; Parker 1972). Three great populations occupied the old Chipewyan regions west of Hudson Bay, the herds migrating into the forest in early winter and returning to the tundra at winter's end. Each population was the subsistence base of several regional bands of the early Chipewyans.

Chipewyan exploitative strategies were based on the seasonal habits of the caribou. The aim was to make efficient major kills during the migrations, minimizing effort and ensuring a large supply of food and raw materials. No other game animals had similar importance, although bear were ritually significant, and moose and musk-oxen (Burch 1977) were a backup resource; however, the flesh of moose and musk-oxen was not considered "substantial food" (Hearne 1795:135, 167). Fish were particularly important during spawning seasons, when they were taken by nets; at other times they were taken by angling.

Within the winter and summer zones the caribou were dispersed in small herds and bands. From November or early December the herds were distributed in the northern transitional zone of the boreal forest, the "land of the little sticks." Major kills were made by regional bands assembled on the migration route. Within the winter foraging ranges, the herds divided into smaller nomadic herds and bands. As they dispersed, so the Chipewyan regional bands dispersed into their constituent local bands or hunting groups. Toward the end of winter the caribou aggregated in anticipation of the summer migration to arrive at their calving areas in June. The dispersed hunting groups again aggregated as regional bands and made major kills during the migration. On reaching the tundra, the caribou scattered in small herds and bands, and the people similarly broke into local bands and hunting groups.

The seasonal movement of the caribou is presented as a model, for many factors affected their distribution: severity of the winter, snow accumulation, temperatures, wind velocity, and avoidance of areas of recent forest fires. There was also probably a population cycle or oscillation of about thirty-five years (Kelsall 1968:205). Herds, for unknown reasons, were also erratic in their movements. Sometimes, too, several herds temporarily aggregated in vast numbers in a limited range, while other areas were almost devoid of animals. The strong element of uncertainty had important consequences for Chipewyan exploitative strategy (J. G. E. Smith 1978a).

The Chipewyan pattern of seasonal aggregation and dispersal formed a system of groups monitoring the concentrations and movements of the herds. Each of the hunting groups was in frequent communication with adjacent groups, and in their entirety they formed a social communications network (J. G. E. Smith 1978a). Thus the changing seasonal distribution of the herds was known to all as information on movements was shared. Most important was the rapidly disseminated information on the apparent migration route, which was of especially critical importance when herds moved in unexpected directions. The overlap of the Kaminuriak and Beverly populations coincided with the overlap of the Barren Lands and Hatchet Lake bands, and widely dispersed kindreds provided a high degree of insurance against the vagaries of herd movements.

The only other major predator on the caribou herds were wolves. Although caribou were not given great attention in the Chipewyan belief system or mythology, wolves were of unusual importance. The wolf was, in effect, identified with the Chipewyans in their relationship to the caribou. The wolf was believed to have human characteristics, living in monogamous families, both parents raising their pups, establishing a residence (den), cooking their food, grouping in packs or bands, and using hunting strategies similar to those of the Chipewyans. Deceased Dene individuals could alternate reincarnation as wolves or humans, and continued reincarnation resulted in men of extraordinary power or $i^nko^nze$. This power was exemplified by the emergence of the Miracle Boy (*denedasikolye* 'man something knows') in the mid 1960s, who healed by the laying on of hands, having received the power from a wolf. Henry S. Sharp (1976, 1978, 1986) has dealt with this issue in some detail, based on his research with the Mission Band.

The ancestral bands that gave rise to the recent three eastern Caribou Eater regional bands (Churchill, Barren Lands, and Hatchet Lake bands) were predators on the Kaminuriak Population. The Beverly Population was hunted by a central division, principally made up of the ancestors of the present Black Lake, Stony Rapids, and Fond du Lac bands, and others. The Yellowknifes extended from Great Slave Lake to the Arctic Circle, based on the herds of the Bathurst Population.[1]

The caribou populations and herds, and the later historical movement of some people into the full forest, resulted in a number of human geographical and possibly dialect divisions. In the eighteenth century, the Hudson's Bay Company (e.g., Hearne 1795) recognized only two divisions, the Northern Indians and the Copper Indians. In the nineteenth century, according to Emile Petitot (1876:26), the recognized divisions were the Caribou Eaters *(Etθen-eldili-dene)* and the Yellowknife *(T'atsanottine)* of the taiga-tundra ecotone; the "Athabaskans" *(Kkpest'ayle kke ottine* 'dwellers in the trembling aspen'), in the full boreal forest between Lake Athabasca and Great Slave Lake; and the Thilanottines *(θilanottine)* who dwelled in the full boreal forest near the headwaters of the Churchill, or English, River. These terms probably represented only a general situation of uncertain boundaries, and probably do not do justice to the mobility of the Chipewyans, the shifting of people from one group to another, and complexities resulting from social realignments and the consequences of the fur trade.[2] Nevertheless, there are hints that there may have been very early cultural distinctions between the Chipewyan populations dependent on the great caribou populations.

The spread of trading posts and the rationalization of the trade after the merging of the Hudson's Bay and Northwest companies in 1821 began to decrease band mobility. Old regional bands or segments became oriented to the area trading fort, to which the mission was later added. Individuals became associated with specific forts and there were pressures against some social traditions. In the 1840s the Roman Catholic Oblates of Mary Immaculate were charged with the conversion of the Indians of the Canadian Northwest. Between 1848 and 1905 conversion was nominally completed, ending polygyny, infanticide, and other "infidel" practices. On his first visit to Fort Chipewyan in 1847, Father Taché baptized 194 "infidèles," all of those polygamists abandoning their "illegitimate" wives. When the mission buildings were completed in 1851, they housed some 150 orphans (Duchaussois 1935:232). Conversion of the Caribou Eaters was not effective until the 1870s and later (Duchaussois 1935:255–78). The introduction of the Canadian "welfare" state began revolutionary rather than evolutionary changes.

## Kindreds

The several forms of the bilateral kindred were of greatest importance until the process of sedentism began to have profound effects. The kindred provided the widespread and large numbers of kin from whom one could expect hospitality and cooperation, and from within which one could maintain or establish new social alignments, in part explaining why the "bands" discussed later had such a high degree of flexibility.

The Caribou Eaters extended over several hundred thousand square miles with a population of perhaps 5,000 and a density of roughly one person per hundred square miles. Although they were organized in regional and local bands, hunting groups, and ephemeral task groups, a network of kinship and marriage tied them together over this great area. For example, between 1769 and 1772 Samuel Hearne (1795), in company with his guide, friend, and trading chief, Captain Matonabbee, explored the region from Prince of Wales's Fort (Fort Churchill) to the mouth of the Coppermine. Only rarely did they encounter a group in which a member of their party did not have kinsmen or "friends." Dialect differences were minor, Hearne comparing them to those of adjacent counties in England.

The significant ego-centered category, as contrasted to groups, was the bilateral kindred, of which the eastern Caribou Eaters recognized two levels, although the Mission Band to the west recognized three (Sharp 1979:19–21). The major kindred was known as *eɫlelotine,* and consisted of all known kin, including affines and even those to whom the precise genealogical connection was unknown. Membership in a kindred provided individuals with associations over a wide area that could be used for information, friendship, and hospitality. It also minimized interpersonal friction and provided the basis for potential social realignments, to relieve the interpersonal tensions described by Joel Savashinsky (1974) and Sharp (1988).

A more restricted nodal or minor kindred could also be referred to as *eɫlelotine,* and then carried the sense of a cooperative group who lived, hunted, and worked together. It could, in fact, indicate a local band or a hunting group, although there were no particular terms to specify those entities.

The second ego-centered class was the *e^nθagabedele,* or "same blood," restricted to lineal kin and immediate collaterals (i.e., ego's own parents, grandparents, siblings, children, and grandchildren). It did not include strictly classificatory kin. The obligations of kinship were strongest within this category. The boundary of the *e^nθagabedele* was relatively clearcut in contrast to the flexible and overlapping nature of the *eɫlelotine.* The large number of individuals in the ego-centered bilateral kindred provided ample opportunity for social realignments and individual manipulation.

## Bands

Band organization throughout the Canadian subarctic has been a frequent subject of theoretical discussion, often for failure to distinguish between small hunting groups or local bands, and larger regional bands or "nations." The flexibility or fluidity of subarctic band membership has also contributed to difficulties of classification. The terms chosen by Helm for the arctic drainage Dene peoples in general (1965) and the Dogribs in particular (1968a) seem appropriate to the Chipewyans and to other Northern Algonkian peoples of the central and eastern subarctic.

The Chipewyans themselves had no terms to describe regional local bands, or hunting groups, their practice being to refer to "the people of _____," typically a lake or other geographical feature. Their word *banen* (Legoff 1889:43) refers only to an indeterminate collective group, often rendered as English 'band'. The bands described below must be considered only in terms of their concepts of kindreds, which provided the basis for the formation of groups larger than the family and hunting group. The kindreds comprised the "pool" from which the socioterritorial groupings were formed and transformed.

A Chipewyan regional band, in Helm's (1965, 1968a) terms, occupied a wide range and was typically known by some geographic feature. For example, the official (Treaty No. 10 of 1907) name Barren Lands Band was a literal translation of the name by which they had been known by their Dene neighbors, *hotelnadidene* 'people of the low land', based on their term for the tundra. Because of the nomadic and erratic nature of the caribou, the range was large, varied and was not exclusive. It was commonly composed of possibly several hundred individuals, related through multiple ties of consanguinity and affinity. Members of a regional band were linked by those ties to members of hunting groups in adjacent regional bands, ensuring access to the herds. This maximal band probably aggregated only at times of the caribou migrations or at other times when large caribou concentrations permitted. In membership, the regional band was the most stable of the types of bands.

Local bands were, conceptually, nodal kindreds. They consisted historically of from two related conjugal pairs or hunting groups to as many as a dozen, and sometimes included more than a hundred people. They typically exploited smaller caribou herds or bands in their wintering ranges and hunted together on the Barren Lands during the summer. Such bands appear in Hearne's narrative of 1769 to 1772, in archival sources of the early 1800s, and to the 1960s (J. G. E. Smith 1976b). Their composition varied considerably over time, often depending on the authority of a successful hunter-chief and dissolving upon his death. Marriages were arranged by parents, sororal polygyny was normative for a successful hunter, and a preferred form was the betrothal of two brothers to two sisters. The practice of bride service, involving temporary matrilocal (uxorilocal) residence, further led to intergroup cooperation—and the potential for social realignment through permanent uxorality. Local bands were usually known by the name of their wintering lake or base camp, such as the *houldaye-tue-dene* 'jackfish lake people'. In the early twentieth century increasing sedentism led the local bands to become the typical all-native log cabin communities (Helm and Damas 1963) of the late Contact-Traditional period (Helm et al. 1975).

The fundamental Chipewyan sociocentric kin unit, the hunting group (Smith 1975a, 1976a, 1976b, 1978a, 1978b; Sharp's 1977a "hunting unit"), was the "primary subsistence unit" (Steward 1968:322). A shallow-depth cognatic descent group, it often operated for much of the year in relative isolation. It was generally based on the unity of brothers and their spouses, and included their sons, wives, and children. The bond of brothers was particularly strong, but brothers-in-law were often found as partners in task groups. A man with an established reputation as a hunter and organizer, or with good hunting "luck," or $i^n ko^n ze$ (cf. D. M. Smith 1973; Sharp 1988), was likely to attract followers (including sons-in-law and others), thus forming a larger group—what is here termed a local band. Demographic problems such as skewing of age and sex, as well as parental wishes, often influenced the choice of relatively permanent postmarital residence.

Age and sex were important in terms of authority, elders dominated younger males, older brothers had authority over younger brothers, and male kin had authority over all females. Marriages were arranged by parents, with a view to the son-in-law's economic contribution as a hunter. Particularly valued was the marriage of two brothers to two sisters (cf. Heinrich and Anderson 1968), which established close ties between the brothers and immediate affines and for the two generations of the extended families or hunting groups involved. The relationship could not be continued due to the resulting incest prohibitions. Temporary postmarital matrilocal residence (or bride service) was mandatory until the birth of a child, but could become permanent. Polygyny, especially sororal, was practiced until the late-nineteenth century, and remarriage in the sororate was occasionally practiced as late as the time of fieldwork. Thus, ego classed stepsiblings as his own siblings and stepchildren as his own.

Among the Barren Lands and Hatchet Lake bands of Caribou Eaters, hunting groups were usually known by geographic terms, but were also known as *etnakwi* 'brothers', which signaled the importance of the sibling bond in Subarctic societies, often the basis for larger local bands. The hunting group had a life cycle, based on the cooperation of brothers. As their sons became hunters, each of the elders was apt to become leader of his own hunting group. But while the sibling bond was emphasized, it was sometimes in conflict with the individual's competing goals of leadership and autonomy, authority and equality (Sharp 1988), sometimes ending in group fission and subsequent social realignments. In terms of Chipewyan concepts, the distinction between "hunting group" and "local band" was possibly a matter of indifference.

The isolation of small hunting groups was typically relieved by frequent visiting, which was an important aspect of the communications network. Indeed, frequent visiting of other local bands in which one had members of his kindred gave some individuals knowledge of a vast territory, and often it was they who became leaders. During the early fur trade period, the visitor with a broad geographic background may have been the trading leader or captain of the "trading Indians."

Marriage during the early historic period, and enduring in many respects until the late-nineteenth or mid-twentieth century, had a number of characteristics shared with other arctic drainage Dene peoples: marriages were arranged by the father of the girl; the groom was chosen because of demonstrated ability as a hunter; sororal polygyny was practiced; the marriage of two brothers to two sisters was highly valued; the groom was commonly much older than the bride, who was betrothed at a very early age; a period of bride service was required, almost necessarily involving temporary matrilocal residence; and female infanticide, by limiting the number of marriageable girls, gave the father great bargaining power in the selection of a groom and thus the establishment of alliances.

During the period of Chipewyan "trading Indians" and "gangs" (ca. 1717–1821), polygyny probably increased as women were needed to carry furs to the great trading center at Fort Churchill and trade goods back to the hinterland, as suggested by Hearne (1795:80). While infanticide apparently was ended by mid-nineteenth century, later male-female ratios indicated that girls were given less care than boys (Records of the Mission St. Pierre de Lac Caribou, Archives of the Oblates of Mary Immaculate).

## Kinship Terminology

Samuel Hearne (1795) discussed many aspects of Chipewyan social life, including the "household" or lodge size, polygyny, sororal polygyny, bride purchase, the practice of men wrestling for young wives, and temporary wife exchange to establish a strong relationship. Using Matonabbee's words, he also indicated the importance of women's work and their low status. Another early explorer, probably John McDonnell of the North West Company (Jenness 1956), described the extended family lodge, polygyny, the practice of men wrestling for young wives, and the low status of women. David Thompson (1916:130) noted the practice of female infanticide in the 1790s, but John Franklin (1828:64) noted that after his second expedition of 1825 through 1827, infanticide was rare among the Chipewyans.

No kinship terminology or description of the behavioral system for the early contact period has yet been found in the archival or published sources of the fur trade; here as elsewhere early explorers and others were apparently uninterested in kinship (Tax 1955:446)—or perhaps bilaterality was familiar and taken for granted.

However, Lewis H. Morgan (1871:281–382), the founder of kinship studies, recorded "Red Knife" (Yellowknife) terminology in 1861. Although he had only two female informants, probably elderly, at the Convent of St. Boniface, Hudson's Bay Company Territory, his terms are important due to their Yellowknife provenience and their early date. Furthermore, in *Ancient Society,* Morgan (1877:179) noted there was no evidence of gentes or clans.

Early linguistic work done by missionaries (Legoff 1889; Penard 1938) among the Thilanottine Chipewyans included some kinship terms. Fang-Kuei Li's (1933) linguistic work at Fort Chipewyan noted a limited number of terms. Other schedules were collected by Edward Curtis (1928) from the Thilanottines, James VanStone (1965) and David M. Smith (1982) from the Athapaskans, and Sharp (1979) and myself from Caribou Eater bands. J. Alden Mason's (1914) visit to the Yellowknives was apparently too late to obtain any useful kinship information.

In table 1, the older kin terms of Lewis Henry Morgan (1871:281–382), and Laurent Legoff (1889:327–31), Edward Curtis (1928:149–51) and J. M. Penard (1938:8–9) are compared. Table 2 includes kinship schedules recorded by anthropologists: June Helm (MacNeish 1960; Helm 1965), James VanStone (1965), David M. Smith (1982), Henry Sharp (1979) and myself (1967-69) for the Barren Lands Band of Caribou Eaters in northern Manitoba.

**Table 1.** Comparative Chipewyan Kinship Terminology (Male Speaking)

| Kin Types | Morgan 1861 | Legoff* 1889 | Curtis 1925 | Penard* 1938 |
|---|---|---|---|---|
| | | CONSANGUINEAL TERMS | | |
| *2d ascending generation*[1] | | | | |
| GF | setseea | setsiye | setseea | setsiye |
| GFB | setseea | setsiye | setseea | setsiye |
| GFZ | setsana | setsounen | setsana | setsounen |
| GM | setsana | setsounen | setsana | setsounen |
| GMB | setseea | setsiye | setseea | setsiye |
| GMZ | setsana | setsounen | setsana | setsounen |
| *1st ascending generation* | | | | |
| F | setha | se'ta | setha | se'ta |
| M | ana | ennen | eha$^n$ | ennen |
| FB | seethene | sede'lshennen | sethe | — |
| FZ | setso | setsoun | setsu$^n$ | setssoun |
| MB | sera | serzhe | sethe | — |
| MZ | sakrea | sankkiye | seha$^n$kiye | sankkiye |
| FFBS | selthene | — | sella | — |
| FFBD | setso | — | setsu$^n$ | — |
| FFZS | — | — | — | — |
| FFZD | setso | — | setsu$^n$ | — |
| MMBS | sera | — | sethe | — |
| MMBD | selthena | — | setsu$^n$ | — |
| MMZS | selthene | — | — | — |
| MMZD | sakrea | — | — | — |
| *Ego's generation* | | | | |
| oB | sunaga | sounaρe | sunaghe | sounnaρe |
| yB | setchileaze | setchele | sechele | setchele |
| oZ | setdezaaze[2] | sare | sehare/sare | sare |
| yZ | sare[2] | seddeze | sedeze | seddezhe |
| FoBS | sunaga | sounnaρe | sella | sella |
| FyBS | setchileaze | setchele | sella | sella |
| FoBD | setdezaaze[2] | sella | sare | sella |
| FyBD | sare[2] | sella | sedeze | sella |

*Continued on next page*

**Table 1** (continued)

| Kin Types | Morgan 1861 | Legoff* 1889 | Curtis 1925 | Penard* 1938 |
|---|---|---|---|---|
| FoZS | sunaga | sella | seghe | sella |
| FyZS | setchileaze | sella | seghe | sella |
| FoZD | setdezeaze[2] | sella | setsu$^n$ | sella |
| FyZD | sare[2] | sella | setsu$^n$ | sella |
| MoZS | sunaga | sella | sella | sella |
| MyZS | setchileaze | sella | sella | sella |
| MoZD | setdezeaze[2] | sare | sehare/sare | sella |
| MyZD | sare[2] | seddeze | sedeze | sella |
| MoBS | sunaga | — | seghe | sella |
| MyBS | setchileaze | — | seghe | sella |
| MoBD | setdezeaaze[2] | setsoun | setsu$^n$ | sella |
| MyBD | sare[2] | setsoun | setsu$^n$ | sella |

*1st descending generation*

| Kin Types | Morgan 1861 | Legoff* 1889 | Curtis 1925 | Penard* 1938 |
|---|---|---|---|---|
| S | seyaze | sinyeze | si$^n$yeze | sinyeze |
| D | seleya | sellinye | seli$^n$e$^n$ | sellinye |
| BS | seyaze | sinyeze | saze/sehaze | saze |
| BD | seleya | sellinye | saze/sehaze | saze |
| ZS | seyaze | saze | saze/sehaze | saze |
| ZD | seleya | saze | saze/sehaze | saze/sellinye |

*2d descending generation*

| Kin Types | Morgan 1861 | Legoff* 1889 | Curtis 1925 | Penard* 1938 |
|---|---|---|---|---|
| GCh | — | setthue | setthuye | — |
| GS | seyazetthare | — | sunaghaze | sounaρaze |
| GD | salezetthare | — | seharaze | saρeρaze |

AFFINAL TERMS

*1st ascending generation*

| Kin Types | Morgan 1861 | Legoff* 1889 | Curtis 1925 | Penard* 1938 |
|---|---|---|---|---|
| WF | setha | serzh'e | sethe | se'erzh |
| WM | setso | setsoun | setsu$^n$ | setssoun |
| HF | setha | serzh'e | sethe | se'erzh |
| HM | setso | setsoun | setsu$^n$ | setssoun |
| FBW | setso | — | setsu$^n$ | — |

*Continued on next page*

**Table 1** (continued)

| Kin Types | Morgan 1861 | Legoff* 1889 | Curtis 1925 | Penard* 1938 |
|---|---|---|---|---|
| MZH | selthena | — | sedelthune | — |
| MBW | setso | — | setsu$^n$ | — |
| FZH | — | — | sethe | — |
| | | | | |
| StepF | setthena | sede'lshennen | sedelthune | se'erzh |
| StepM | sakrea | sankkiye | seha$^n$kiye | sankkiye |
| co-F-in-L (reciprocal) | — | seppe | — | — |
| co-M-in-L) (reciprocal) | saguna | seppe | — | — |

*Ego's generation*

| Kin Types | Morgan 1861 | Legoff* 1889 | Curtis 1925 | Penard* 1938 |
|---|---|---|---|---|
| H | setdenna | sedene | — | — |
| W | setzeana | setsseyanen | — | — |
| WB | saoga | seppe | seghe | sepe |
| WZ | setso | setsoun | setsu$^n$ | setsoun |
| WBW | — | — | — | — |
| WZH | — | — | — | — |
| BW | setso | setsoun | setsu$^n$ | — |
| BWZ | — | — | setsu$^n$ | — |
| BWB | — | — | seghe | — |
| ZH | saoga | — | seghe | — |
| ZHZ | — | — | setsu$^n$ | — |
| WZH | — | — | — | — |
| ZHB | — | — | — | — |
| FBSW | setso | — | setsu$^n$ | — |
| FBDH | saoga | — | seghe | — |
| FZSW | setso | — | setsu$^n$ | — |
| FZDH | saoga | — | — | — |
| MBSW | setso | — | — | — |
| MBDH | saoga | — | — | — |
| MZSW | setso | — | — | — |
| MZDH | saoga | — | seghe | — |

*Continued on next page*

**Table 1** (continued)

| Kin Types | Morgan 1861 | Legoff* 1889 | Curtis 1925 | Penard* 1938 |
|---|---|---|---|---|
| *1st descending generation* | | | | |
| SW/D-in-L | setthuya | saze | sehaze/saze | — |
| DH/S-in-L | setshiya | saze | sehaze/saze | — |
| SWB | — | — | — | — |
| SWZ | — | — | — | — |
| DHB | — | — | — | — |
| BSW | — | — | — | — |
| ZSW | — | — | — | — |
| WZS | — | — | si$^n$yese | — |
| WZD | — | — | seli$^n$e$^n$ | — |

\* The transcriptions from Chipewyan to French follow certain rules: *n* is pronounced as in French, nasalized when it is not an initial sound, hard when it is the initial sound; 'l is now transcribed as ł, sh as θ; apparently rz was Greek delta (δ), while gamma (γ) and rho (ρ) represented gh in some more recent forms, and sounded as the *r* in French *grasseyement* (exaggerated rolling of uvular r); a doubled consonant indicates stress.

[1] Grandparental terms were also applied to great grandparents and to all other old people believed to be related. The suffix *-yune* to any kinship term elevates the individual to a higher age or generation on the basis of relative age.

[2] Comparing sister terms, it appears that Morgan was incorrect in assigning *sare* as yZ and *setdezaaze* for oZ; his informants may have been confused, although it is equally likely that these terms were accidentally transposed.

**Table 2.** Comparative Chipewyan Kinship Terminology (Male Speaking)

| Kin Types | MacNeish 1960 | VanStone 1965 | Sharp 1979 | D. M. Smith 1982 | J. G. E. Smith 1967–69 |
|---|---|---|---|---|---|
| | | | CONSANGUINEAL TERMS | | |

*2d ascending generation*

| Kin Types | MacNeish 1960 | VanStone 1965 | Sharp 1979 | D. M. Smith 1982 | J. G. E. Smith 1967–69 |
|---|---|---|---|---|---|
| GF | setsie | setsiyé | setseia | setsie | setsie |
| GFB | setsie | setsiyé | setseia | setsie | setsie |
| GFZ | setsune | setsounné | setsuna | setsune | setsune |
| GM | setsune | setsounné | setsuna | setsune | setsune |
| GMB | setsie | setsiyé | setseia | setsie | setsie |
| GMZ | setsune | setsounné | setsuna | setsune | setsune |

*1st ascending generation*

| Kin Types | MacNeish 1960 | VanStone 1965 | Sharp 1979 | D. M. Smith 1982 | J. G. E. Smith 1967–69 |
|---|---|---|---|---|---|
| F | seta | se'ta | seta | seta | set'ha |
| M | ene | enne | ena | ene | ene |
| FB | setaze | sede'lthune | se'a | se'e | se'e |
| FZ | setsu$^n$ | sank'iye | sankie | sa$^n$k'ie | setso$^n$ |
| MB | se'e | ser'e | se'a | se'e | se'e |
| MZ | sa$^n$k'ie | sank'iye | sankie | sa$^n$k'ie | sanke |
| StepF | setaze | — | sethuna | seθsene/se'e | selθene |
| StepM | enaze | — | sankie | seθsene/sank'ie | sanke |

*Ego's generation*

| Kin Types | MacNeish 1960 | VanStone 1965 | Sharp 1979 | D. M. Smith 1982 | J. G. E. Smith 1967–69 |
|---|---|---|---|---|---|
| oB | sonaγe | sounnare | sunnara | sonaγe/sela | sunaγe/sela |
| yB | sečele | setchele | secela | setcele/sela | secele/sela |
| oZ | sare | saré | sari | sare/sela | sare/sela |
| yZ | sedeze | seddezé | sedeze | sedeze/sela | sedeze/sela |
| FoBS | sonaγe | sella | sela | sonaγe/sela | sunaγe/sela |
| FyBS | sečele | sella | sela | setcele/sela | secele/sela |
| FoBD | sare | sella | sela | sare/sela | sare/sela |
| FyBD | sedeze | sella | sela | sedeze/sela | sedeze/sela |
| FoZS | — | sella | sela | sonaγe/sela | seγe/sela |
| FyZS | — | sella | sela | setcele/sela | seγe/sela |
| FoZD | setsunaze | sella | sela | sare/sela | setso$^n$/sare |
| FyZD | setsunaze | sella | sela | sedeze/sela | setso$^n$/sedeze |
| MoZS | sonaγe | sella | sela | sonaγe/sela | sunaγe/sela |
| MyZS | sečele | sella | sela | setcele/sela | secele/sela |

*Continued on next page*

# Table 2 (continued)

| Kin Types | MacNeish 1960 | VanStone 1965 | Sharp 1979 | D. M. Smith 1982 | J. G. E. Smith 1967–69 |
|---|---|---|---|---|---|
| MoZD | sare | sella | sela | sare/sela | sare/sela |
| MyZD | sedeze | sella | sela | sedeze/sela | sedeze/sela |
| MoBS | — | sella | sela | sona$\gamma$e/sela | suna$\gamma$e/sela |
| MyBS | — | sella | sela | setcele/sela | secele/sela |
| MoBD | setsunaze | sella | sela | sare/sela | sare/sela |
| MyBD | setsunaze | sella | sela | sedeze/sela | sedeze/sela |

*1st descending generation*

| Kin Types | MacNeish 1960 | VanStone 1965 | Sharp 1979 | D. M. Smith 1982 | J. G. E. Smith 1967–69 |
|---|---|---|---|---|---|
| S | siyeze | sinyeze | seyaze | seyaze | si$^n$yeze |
| D | selie$^n$ | selliyé | selea | sequaze/selie$^n$ze | silie$^n$ |
| BS | siyeze | sinyeze | saze | saze | suna$\gamma$aze |
| BD | silie$^n$ | selliyé | silie$^n$ | saraze | saraze |
| ZS | saze | sinyeze | saze | saze | suna$\gamma$aze |
| ZD | saze | selliyé | saze | saraze | saraze |

*2d descending generation*

| Kin Types | MacNeish 1960 | VanStone 1965 | Sharp 1979 | D. M. Smith 1982 | J. G. E. Smith 1967–69 |
|---|---|---|---|---|---|
| GCh | set$\theta$ue | — | saze | se$\theta$uaze | set$\theta$waze |
| GS | suna$\gamma$aze | sounnaraze | sunaras | suna$\gamma$aze | suna$\gamma$aze |
| GD | saraze | saréaze | saraze | saraze | saraze |

### AFFINAL TERMS

*1st ascending generation*

| Kin Types | MacNeish 1960 | VanStone 1965 | Sharp 1979 | D. M. Smith 1982 | J. G. E. Smith 1967–69 |
|---|---|---|---|---|---|
| WF | se'e | ser'e | — | se'e | se'e |
| WM | setsu$^n$ | setsun | setsu | setso$^n$ | setso$^n$ |
| MZH | — | seré | se'a | se'e | sel$\theta$ene |
| MBW | — | sank'iye | — | — | setso$^n$/sanke |
| FBW | — | sank'iye | sankie | sa$^n$k'ie | setso$^n$/sanke |
| FZH | — | sede'ldhene | se'a | se'e | se'e/sel$\theta$ene |
| WFB | — | — | se'a | se'e | se'e |
| WFZ | — | — | sankie | — | setso$^n$ |
| WMB | — | — | se'a | — | se'e |
| WMZ | — | — | sankie | setso$^n$ | setso$^n$ |

*Continued on next page*

**Table 2** (continued)

| Kin Types | MacNeish 1960 | VanStone 1965 | Sharp 1979 | D. M. Smith 1982 | J. G. E. Smith 1967–69 |
|---|---|---|---|---|---|
| *Ego's generation* | | | | | |
| H | sedene | sedene | senekwi | sedene | senekwi |
| W | setsa$^n$kwie | setsseyane | sesankwi | setsane | setsa$^n$kwi/ setseyane |
| WB | se$\gamma$e | serre | seri | — | se$\gamma$e |
| WZ | setsu$^n$ | setsun | setsu | setso$^n$ | setso$^n$ |
| WBW | — | — | setsu | — | setso$^n$ |
| WZH | — | — | seri | se$\gamma$e | se$\gamma$e |
| BW | setsu$^n$ | setsun | setsu | setso$^n$ | setso$^n$ |
| BWZ | — | — | — | setso$^n$ | setso$^n$ |
| BWB | — | — | — | se$\gamma$e | se$\gamma$e |
| ZH | se$\gamma$e | serre | seri | se$\gamma$e | se$\gamma$e |
| ZHZ | — | — | — | setso$^n$ | setso$^n$ |
| WZH | — | — | seri | se$\gamma$e | se$\gamma$e |
| ZHB | — | — | seri | se$\gamma$e | se$\gamma$e |
| Sweetheart | setsunaze | — | — | setswa$^n$ze | setswa$^n$ze |
| co-F-in-L | se$\gamma$e | — | seri | — | — |
| co-M-in-L | se$\gamma$e | — | seri | — | — |
| Men married to sisters | — | — | — | — | sela |
| *1st descending generation* | | | | | |
| SW | — | saze | saraze | saraze | saraze |
| SWZ | — | — | — | saraze | saraze |
| DH | — | saze | saze | saze | saze |

## Yellowknife

Franklin writing about the Yellowknives, commented that "they frequently marry two sisters, and there is no prohibition to the intermarriage of cousins, but a man is restricted from marrying his niece" (1823:289). As will be seen, Chipewyan terms for 'cousin' vary, and given our knowledge of later systems, Franklin may have provided a useful insight.

Morgan (1871:281–382) described a basically generational system, but with bifurcate collateral terms in the first ascending generation. FZ *(setso)* was distinguished from MZ *(sakrea)*. FB and MB were also terminologically distinct, and the word for MZH *(selthene)* corresponded to stepfather. In ego's generation all consanguineous males were older or younger brothers and all females were older or younger sisters. The classification of all "cousins" as siblings seemingly prohibited any kind of cousin marriage. In the first descending generation, ego's sons and daughters were not differentiated from nephews and nieces (i.e., BZ, BD, ZS, and ZD), as well as other classificatory "sons" and "daughters." Affinal terms indicated the probability of the sororate and levirate. In addition to FZ and FZD as *setso,* Yellowknives also placed in this category WZ, BW, FBSW, MBSW, WM, HM, FBW, MBW (i.e., all women related by marriage). Since relatively few contemporary Chipewyans have a strong interest in genealogy, it is possible that cousins of uncertain genealogical connection may have been potential spouses (cf. Franklin, above). This may easily have happened, since in some systems *cousins* could alternatively include siblings and classificatory siblings, or cousins only, and there seems to be confusion in many cases, including perhaps that of the recorder.

## Thilanottine

Legoff gave a limited description of kinship terms, particularly of the "Montagnais" from the region of Cold Lake, Ile à la Crosse, and Portage la Loche (1889:10, 327-31). Terminology in the first ascending generation is bifurcate collateral. Cousin terminology seems confused, with some cousins classified as siblings; Helm (MacNeish 1960:285-86) pointed out inconsistencies in the cousin terminology that were in disagreement with the asymmetrical marriage system discussed by Curtis. Penard's (1938) much more limited number of terms from adjacent Saskatchewan are identical to Legoff's, but are too few to make a significant contribution.

    The eminent photographer Edward Curtis described the kinship system of the Chipewyans at Cold Lake, Alberta. His kinship material provides a system of terms appropriate to preferential patrilateral cross-cousin marriage. After noting the sororate, levirate, and sororal polygyny, Curtis (or his amanuensis) wrote:

> A favorite marriage was that of a man and his father's sister's daughter *[setso[n]]*. Paternal aunt and mother-in-law therefore become synonymous. By mental processes not comprehensible to us, this female cross-cousin also was designated by the same term as was her mother, that is, maternal aunt (mother-in-law); and since it might be one's brother instead of one's

self that married this female cross-cousin, the same term came to mean also a man's brother's wife. But her sister also was a potential wife of the same man; hence, she, the wife's sister, was designated by the term. Women, as well as men, employ the word in the sense of mother-in-law, although originally its application in this sense must have been restricted to men. [1928:148–51][3]

Helm (MacNeish 1960) obtained kin terms from two Chipewyans who had been hospitalized in Edmonton; they were from LeGoff, Alberta, near Cold Lake, where Curtis and Legoff had worked. Grandparental terms included only two criteria: generation and sex. In the first ascending generation, the terms were bifurcate collateral, with certain exceptions: for both FZ and WM the term *setsuⁿ* is used, related to GM. For FB and MZH, they used a diminutive of F *(setaze < seta)*. In ego's generation, parallel cousins were classed as siblings (differentiated as older or younger) by a woman, but a man used *sela,* a term "pretty near like a brother," for a parallel cousin. However, he called his female cross cousins and sweetheart *setsuⁿaze,* diminutive of *setsuⁿ* for FZ, MBW, and M-in-L and the same stem as GM, *setsune.* The spouse of a *setsuⁿaze,* however, was a *sela,* and there was no term known for a cross cousin.

*Athapaskans*

VanStone's (1965) Snowdrift people were a recent example of the emergence of a trading post band, made up of families who had formerly belonged to various groups between Lake Athabasca and Great Slave Lake. This deme, to use Murdock's (1949:63) term, developed after the Hudson's Bay Company established a store at Snowdrift in 1925. VanStone noted his informants' indifference to discussing kinship terms and the limitations this imposed on his data. However, his terms conform to other schedules and he notes important features for this comparative study. Generation and sex were alone the determinants of grandparental terms. In the first ascending generation, the system appears to be bifurcate collateral, with M and F separated from MZ, FZ, and MB and FB. Apparently old terms were still used to distinguish FB *(sede'ldthene [selθene])* and MB *(ser'e),* but both FZ and MZ were *sank'iye,* and thus distinct from mother-in-law, *setsun.* Lineality was stressed in ego's and first ascending generation, but in the first descending generation S and D terms were also used for nephew and niece. The cousin term *(sela),* does not differentiate by sex, and is of Murdock's (1949:223–28) Eskimo type.

The Chipewyans of Fort Resolution, N.W.T. (D. M. Smith 1982: 20–23) were also a trading post band, but one that developed much earlier from Dene people located principally between Great Slave Lake and Lake Athabasca from the late-eighteenth and into the nineteenth centuries. Although Athapaskans with a historical background similar to Snowdrift Chipewyans, the kinship system was intermediate between the Snowdrift and Mission Chipewyans. In the first ascending generation, terms were bifurcate merging: FZ and MZ were termed *sank'ie,* a term etymologically related to M, while FB and MB were *se'e,* a term undoubtedly related to the word for F *(setha).* The single term *sela* included both ego's true siblings and classificatory siblings ("cousins"), but distinctive terms for oB, yB, oZ, and yZ were alternatively used. In contrast, one's own children were terminologically distinguished lineally from siblings' children. Marriage to genealogically known relatives was prohibited, but in the past sororal polygyny was practiced. David M. Smith does not comment on death and remarriage (i.e., the levirate and sororate).

*Caribou Eaters of the Lake Athabasca Region*

The original Mission Band of northern Saskatchewan (Sharp 1975, 1979) was more similar to the Athapaskans discussed above than to the eastern Caribou Eaters. According to Duchaussois (1935:253), writing in 1922, these Mangeurs de Caribou exploited only the fringe of the Barren Lands by or before the twentieth century, as a result of the fur trade. Members of Sharp's original Mission Band had a system that featured bifurcate merging terms in the parental generation, with FZ and MZ both termed *sankie.* The *sankie* term also included MBW, FBW, WFZ, WMZ, HMZ, and step-mother (i.e., all women of the first ascending generation related by kinship or marriage). Both FB and MB were *se'a,* as well as FZH, MZH, HF, WFB, WMB, HFB, and HMB (i.e., all men of the first ascending generation related by consanguinity or affinity). First-cousin marriage was said to have been permitted, but prohibited after conversion to Christianity. While *setsu* referred to WM, WZ, and BW in both the original and immigrant groups, to the original Mission dialect speakers *setsu* were within the incest prohibitions. Cousin terminology was of the Eskimo type, separating siblings *(sunnara, sechela; sari, sedeze)* from cousins *(sela).* One's own sons and daughters were also differentiated from *saze,* nephews and nieces.

According to Sharp (1975:71–76) this pattern was characteristic of communities near eastern Lake Athabasca (Fond du Lac, Stony Rapids, and Black Lake bands), but not of the more easterly Caribou Eaters and the Thilanottines.

In contrast, the immigrants who joined the Mission Band from Caribou Eater bands of the east (1930s) and other immigrants from the Churchill River region of the south (1920s) had some distinctive features. First-cousin marriage was prohibited, since such persons were categorized as S or D by ego's parents, and thus were siblings. However, Sharp's (1975:74-76) kinship terms of the immigrants from the Brochet area (Barren Lands and Hatchet Lake bands) differ from those collected by Curtis and myself, especially with regard to the distinction between S-D, Ne-Ni, and FZ-FZD.

*Caribou Eaters of the East*

The eastern Caribou Eaters are here represented by the Barren Lands Band and many members of the Hatchet Lake Band after 1958. Since 1859, both bands had traded at the trading post-mission complex at Brochet, at the north end of Reindeer Lake, in Manitoba, but in 1958 a trading post, mission, and school were established at Lake Wollaston, Saskatchewan. Perhaps by coincidence, both provinces imposed trapping regulations and registered traplines, and each band was also administratively in different districts of the Department of Indian Affairs. Thus, because of "administrative convenience" for the government the two bands were separated. Some members of the Hatchet Lake Band transferred their formal membership to the Barren Lands Band, but continued to hunt and trap in their traditional territories in Saskatchewan, resulting in some administrative inconvenience.

Brochet had been at a considerable distance from their hunting and trapping territories, but gradually their center shifted south and about 1967 they briefly settled at Brochet, and then moved back to the north to Jackfish Lake (J. G. E. Smith 1978b).

According to many elders, the kinship terms were changing, and some alternative forms are given in table 2. In the second and third ascending generations all terms are generational, differentiated only by sex. All relatives of significantly greater age were elevated to the next generation, or the suffix -*yune* was added. In ego's parental generation, terms were bifurcate merging, although MZ and FZ were differentiated. The term for FB (*se'e*) was different from MZH and stepfather (*selθene*). The term for MZ (*sankie*) was a derivative of M, but also meant stepmother. FZ (*setsoⁿ*) also meant all women related by marriage in ego's or first ascending generation. It also referred to FZD, and a diminutive (*setswaⁿze*) was the term for sweetheart. Unlike the putative case of Curtis's Cold Lake people, marriage to a true FZD was prohibited, as it was to any person of known genealogical connection. However, marriage to a classificatory FZD (i.e., a patrilateral FZD by marriage) was considered desirable, and extended the bond between families for another generation. Cousin terms were Hawaiian, with sibling terms applied to all cousins except FZD. As ego's

FoBS was usually older, he was commonly referred to as *se 'e*. However, the term *sela* was formerly used for true siblings and for all cousins irrespective of age and sex, as it was in David M. Smith's (1982:22–23) system at Fort Resolution. Lineality was expressed, however, in that ego's S *(si"yeze)* and D *(silie")* were distinguished from siblings' sons *(sunapaze)* and daughters *(saraze),* the same terms used for ego's grandsons and granddaughters.

In recent generations, *sela* has lost any commonly recognized meaning: some use it to refer to FoB children (but not those of father's younger brother), to remote cousins, or even to those who have the same name. *Sitsene* is used as a term for one having the same name, but it also has another important meaning: partner. A new term is *seboye,* derived from English *my boy,* and may refer to kin of unspecific genealogical connection, or to anyone of ego's own age or younger.

At all generational levels, the use of specific terms was also governed by changes due to marriage and remarriage, as death did not necessarily cancel affinal relations, especially given the sororate. In addition, since individuals were commonly related by multiple ties, the usage in specific cases was capable of manipulation.

## Discussion

Leslie Spier (1925:26, cited in MacNeish 1960:279) characterized the Mackenzie Basin kinship type as having Hawaiian cousin terms, with the Yellowknives and Slaveys as his examples. All recorded Chipewyan kinship terms emphasized generation, relative age within the generation, and sex. Known terminologies appear to fall into three major categories based on generation, distinctions in the parental generation, sibling and "cousin" terms, lineality, and in some groups terminology indicative (questionably) of bilateral or patrilateral cousin marriage.[4] In the first ascending generation there was a strong tendency toward bifurcate merging, at least partially. In addition, bride service is still normative, and formerly mandated temporary matrilocal residence. The term *setso",* based on FZ, had variable usage. Among the Eastern Caribou Eaters and the Thilanottines the term included all women related by marriage, a smaller but significant scope among the Yellowknives, but the usage was constricted among other groups (cf. tables 1 and 2). It is unclear whether the different usages actually reflect historically different normative systems, a limited number of informants, relatively new change and confusion, or the limited interests of the researchers.

For the nineteenth century, on kinship criteria, I suggest three groups:[5] (1) The Yellowknives, based on Morgan's small sample, with generational-sex terms for the second ascending generation, bifurcate collateral parental generation terms, Hawaiian cousin terms, generational terms for children, and affinal terms suggesting the sororate. (2) The bands near Lake Athabasca, described by James VanStone (1965) and Henry Sharp (1979), which had generational-sex emphasis in the second ascending generation, "semi-bifurcate collateral/merging" terms in the parental generation, Eskimo cousin terms, and generational terms (VanStone), or terms tending toward lineality (Sharp) in the first descending generation. The sororate was prohibited. (3) The eastern Caribou Eaters, and some Thilanottines, had generational terms for the second ascending generation. In the parental generation, terms were predominantly bifurcate merging, although FZ was distinct *(setsu^n/setso^n)* from MZ, and *setsu^n* or a derivative was used for FZD and sweetheart. Cousin terms tended toward Hawaiian, with pronounced recent confusion over the appropriate terms. For terms in the first descending generation, there is a recent pronounced tendency toward lineality from many consultants. The sororate was part of the marriage system. The people studied by David M. Smith (1982) at Fort Resolution were intermediate, with Hawaiian cousin terms and lineality in the first descending generation. If schedules had been obtained from all Chipewyan bands, possibly further variations would be found.

A modern tendency toward lineality could reflect the Hudson's Bay Company's shift from dealing through trading chiefs to dealing with individuals and accounts, conversion to Christianity and the adoption of family names, and the intervention of the government and the creation of official bands and membership lists. All those factors may give the appearance of patrilocality or patriliny and the false impression of a corporate group.

There are many inconsistencies in the terminologies, probably due to continuing internal readaptations to reduced nomadism and limited interdivisional and perhaps interband contacts, a normally high mortality rate, effects of epidemic and endemic diseases,[6] elimination of polygyny, demographic skewing of age-sex ratios, and local or even individual variations. Sharp (1975:73) also perceived that some terms could be used but with different meanings. It is probable that Eggan's (1963) concept of "cultural drift" was appropriate in both prehistoric and historic periods.

It seems fruitless to argue that any of the kinship classifications discussed above were close to or derived from some single imagined pristine system. Many Proto-Athapaskan speakers may have had matrilineal emphasis in their systems of classification, in the postulated

*Urheimat* in Alaska, many thousands of years ago. However, the ancestral Chipewyans have been in the taiga-tundra ecotone for several thousand years, where bilateral systems were more adaptive to predation on the highly migratory, nomadic, and gregarious barren-ground caribou. It is appealing to recall that this adaptation had similarities to the bison hunters of the Plains, whose kinship systems showed pronounced generational tendencies.

However, given the predation of regional hunting bands on different caribou herds, there were opportunities for variations to have occurred in kinship and related features, both before and after the advent of the fur trade. It can only be maintained that a common ancestral system would have emphasized generation, sex, relative age, bilateral kinship, and social structures of a broad or encompassing nature, manifested in the kindreds noted earlier. Socioterritorial groups were, of necessity, primarily based on changing caribou distribution. Marriage was by parental arrangement, included bride service with temporary postmarital residence, and the sororate was common and united extended families or hunting groups for two or more generations.

There is little real ethnographic evidence of bilateral or asymmetric cross-cousin marriage, although conceivably the vague pattern did once exist. Father A. G. Morice (1906-10:253-54) asserted that patrilateral cross-cousin marriage occurred among the matrilineal Denes (of the Pacific drainage), but only Curtis (1928:150) has argued for this form for any Chipewyans, and those from deep within the full boreal forest. For reasons discussed above any pattern of patrilateral exchange of women would be undependable and impractical, or, in Lévi-Strauss's terms, "cannot realize an overall structure" (1969:xxxii–xxxiii, 451–53).

Eggan (1955:543) considered the possibility of exchange of *husbands or wives* in successive generations, questioned its systematic practice, but observed the possible importance of a son-in-law as the support of his father-in-law, and the subsequent support of the son-in-law by the man's son's son. Sharp (1979:72–74) made a cogent argument that by substituting adoption for marriage in a succeeding generation, the system could be viewed as reciprocal over a three-generation period. This form of reciprocity may have been applicable to an important degree. However, pseudo-patrilateral cross-cousin marriage (male ego to a classificatory FZD, related only through marriage) could continue an alliance for the second and, possibly, a third generation.

The treatment of the aged raises some difficult questions about the dependence of a man on his son-in-law. Those too old to be productive or unable to keep up with the moving group were sometimes abandoned.

Hearne (1795) observed that old people, no longer able to work, were treated with disrespect and one-half of the aged were abandoned to die. In contrast, McDonnell (Jenness 1956:28) does not mention abandonment of the aged among those Chipewyans trading into the North West Company fort on Lake Athabasca. Sons-in-law resided with their parents-in-law only temporarily, although uxorilocal residence could, under some conditions at least, become permanent. Perhaps treatment of the aged depended on the circumstances, but also may have been features of the different major Chipewyan divisions, as was, perhaps, kinship and dialect.

The greater care given to aged people and orphans appears to be a recent development, probably dating to the latter nineteenth century, when missions were able to take on responsibility for their care. As Helm (1980) argued, infanticide probably ended as a means of compensating for severe losses during epidemics, not to mention the distaste of the fur traders. Duchaussois (1935:232) noted that in ending polygyny, the mission at Fort Chipewyan had to house the resulting 150 orphans in 1851. After the Canadian government introduced Old Age Pensions and Family Allowances immediately after World War II, it became more practical and financially rewarding to maintain a superannuated adult in the family, or for elders to adopt young grandchildren. While the amounts paid by the government were relatively small, they were of inordinate importance in bands that lived basically on natural resources.

Adoption as reciprocity must be considered at length elsewhere. Similar patterns occur among the Chipewyans, Bush Crees, Rocky Crees, and Swampy Crees, and there are hints of it among the Dogribs and Slaveys (June Helm, p. c.).

The Crees are of special interest, in view of a different environmental adaptation and a distinct sociocultural history. The Western Woods Crees have bilateral cross-cousin marriage that conceptually involves only two groups in the direct exchange of women. Their economy was based principally on moose, which are individualistic and only mildly nomadic and migratory; this dependence led to distinctive hunting strategies, socioterritorial organization, and a relatively sedentary lifestyle. Among the Crees, bilateral cross-cousin marriage served to establish or maintain close relationships (or alliances) over time between small hunting groups. Occasional marriages with more distant cross cousins were sometimes deliberately arranged with children in often far distant bands to maintain a very large and widespread kindred *(ntotimak)*.

The Dene bands closest to Cold Lake were Beaver, who in modern times, at least, may have had bilateral cross-cousin marriage (Ridington 1969), a form principally found among the Crees, the immediate neighbors and enemies of the southern tier of Chipewyan bands.

The evidence does not indicate a Fall from Unilineal Grace to Bilateral Sin.


## Acknowledgments

The adaptation described is based on fieldwork with the Barren Lands band of Caribou Eaters (1967–68, 1969–70, and the summers of 1973 and 1976), research in the Hudson's Bay Company Archives, other fur trade and missionary sources, and consideration of recent research by anthropologists with the Chipewyans and adjacent groups. I am greatly indebted to June Helm and Henry S. Sharp for their comments on the manuscript.


## Notes

1. Band names have varied through time. The official Barren Lands Band changed its name in 1976 to the Northlands Band; the Churchill Band had also been known as the Duck Lake Band, but in the 1950s was resettled at Churchill, and in the 1970s shifted to Tadoule Lake. The Hatchet Lake Band *(θante-tue dene)* has also been known as the Lake Wollaston or the Lac la Hache Band. All Chipewyans had traded into Churchill from its founding in 1717 until trading forts were established in the hinterland of the Bay, beginning in the late-eighteenth century.

2. The general terms were probably not used by the members of the groups, but applied to them by their neighbors; thus those known as Caribou Eaters thought all Chipewyans hunted caribou and did not use the term themselves, although it was commonly recognized. The Caribou Eaters called themselves Dene, as did all Chipewyans.

3. Marriage of two brothers to two sisters is much more common than Heinrich and Anderson thought. It has also been found among the Western Woods Crees: Rocky Crees of Reindeer Lake (Smith 1975b), Bush Crees (J. G. E. Smith 1987) and the Swampy Crees (Meyer 1985). Although also valued, the marriage of a brother and sister to another sister and brother is not equally desired.

4. Curtis is the only source for putative patrilateral cross-cousin marriage, and there is no corroborating evidence in the historical literature, archives, or fieldwork accounts. Curtis spent only one summer at Cold Lake, during which he also photographed and studied some Woods Crees. Wherever else the terminology is found, actual cousin marriage is prohibited. It is possible that that form of marriage occurred, but it is questionable.

5. Sharp (1975:71–72) suggests a somewhat different tripartite division, but his analysis is based on more limited data.

6. The effects of the 1781 smallpox epidemic on the Chipewyans have been exaggerated. Hearne (1795:115, note) wrote that it had "carried off nine-tenths of them, and particularly those who composed the trade at Churchill Factory." There is ample evidence in other sources to indicate that that figure was very high, but probably applicable to certain bands of "trading Indians." There is little question that other diseases (scarlet fever, mumps, tuberculosis, etc.) affected the Chipewyans in the nineteenth century, but they were also affected by influenza and measles in the twentieth century.

# References

Archives of the Oblates of Mary Immaculate
  Mss.      Provincial Archives of Alberta. Edmonton, Alberta.
Bishop, Charles A., and Shepard Krech III
  1980      Matriorganization: The Basis of Aboriginal Subarctic Social Organization.
            Arctic Anthropology 17(2):34-45.
Bishop, Charles A., and Arthur J. Ray
  1976      Ethnohistorical Research in the Central Subarctic: Some Conceptual and
            Methodological Problems. Western Canadian Journal of Anthropology
            6:116-43.
Burch, Ernest S., Jr.
  1977      Muskox and Man in the Central Canadian Subarctic 1689-1974. Arctic
            30:135-54.
  1976      The Caribou Eater Chipewyan and Their Prey, 1600-1800. Paper presented
            at the Symposium on Ecological Adaptations, 9th Annual Conference of the
            University of Calgary Archaeology Association, Calgary, 4-7 November.
  1979      The Ethnography of Northern North America: A Guide to Recent Research.
            Arctic Anthropology 16(1):62-146.
Curtis, Edward S.
  1928      Chipewyan. The North American Indian. Vol. 18, 3-52, 125-29, 201-5.
Damas, David
  1969      Review of Elman Service's The Hunters. American Anthropologist 71:
            315-16.
Duchaussois, Pierre
  1935      Aux glaces polaires: Indiens et Esquimaux. Paris: Editions Spes.
Dyen, I., and D. F. Aberle
  1974      Lexical Reconstruction: The Case of the Proto-Athapaskan Kinship System.
            Cambridge: Cambridge University Press.
Eggan, Fred
  1937a     Historical Changes in the Choctaw Kinship System. American Anthropologist
            39:34-52.
  1937b     The Cheyenne and Arapaho Kinship System. In Social Anthropology of North
            American Tribes, edited by Fred Eggan, 35-98. Chicago: University of
            Chicago Press.
  1955      Social Anthropology: Methods and Results. In Social Anthropology of North
            American Tribes, edited by Fred Eggan, 485-554. Enlarged ed. Chicago:
            University of Chicago Press.
  1963      Cultural Drift and Social Change. Current Anthropology 4:347-55.
  1966      The American Indian: Perspectives for the Study of Social Change. Chicago:
            Aldine Publishing.
  1980      Shoshone Kinship Structures and Their Significance for Anthropological
            Theory. Journal of the Steward Anthropological Society 11:165-93.
Franklin, John
  1823      Narrative of a Journey to the Shores of the Polar Sea in the Years 1819, 20, 21,
            22. Reprint ed. Edmonton: Hurtig, 1970.
  1828      Narrative of a Second Expedition to the Shores of the Polar Seas in the years
            1825, 1826, and 1827. Reprint ed. Edmonton: Hurtig, 1970.

Gillespie, Beryl
    1970      Yellowknives: Quo Iverunt? *In* Migration and Anthropology, edited by Robert
              F. Spencer, 61-71. Proceedings of the 1970 Annual Spring Meeting of the
              American Ethnological Society. Seattle: University of Washington Press.
    1975      An Ethnohistory of the Yellowknives: A Northern Athapaskan Tribe. *In*
              Contributions to Anthropology, 1975, edited by D. B. Carlisle, 191-245.
              National Museum of Man, Mercury Series, Canadian Ethnology Service Paper
              no. 31. Ottawa.
Guemple, Lee
    1972      Eskimo Band Organization and the "D P Camp" Hypothesis. Arctic
              Anthropology 9(2):80-112.
Hearne, Samuel
    1795      A Journey from Prince of Wales's Fort in Hudson's Bay to the Northern
              Ocean, in the Years 1769, 1770, 1771, and 1772. Edited by R. Glover.
              Toronto: Macmillan, 1958.
Heinrich, Albert C., and Russell Anderson
    1968      Co-Affinal Siblingship as a Structural Feature among Some Northern North
              American Peoples. Ethnology 7:290-95.
Helm, June
    1965      Bilaterality in the Socio-Territorial Organization of the Arctic Drainage Dene.
              Ethnology 4:361-85.
    1968a     The Nature of Dogrib Socio-Territorial Groups. *In* Man the Hunter, edited by
              Richard B. Lee and Irven DeVore, 118-25. Chicago: Aldine Publishing.
    1968b     The Statistics of Kin Marriage. *In* Man the Hunter, edited by Richard B. Lee
              and Irven DeVore, 216-17. Chicago: Aldine Publishing.
    1980      Female Infanticide, European Diseases, and Population Levels among the
              Mackenzie Dene. American Ethnologist 7:259-85.
Helm, June, and David Damas
    1963   .  The Contact-Traditional All-Native Community of the Canadian North: The
              Upper Mackenzie "Bush" Athapaskans and the Igluligmuit. Anthropologica,
              n.s., 5:9-22.
Helm, June, and Royce Kurtz
    1984      Subarctic Athapaskan Bibliography. Iowa City: University of Iowa.
Helm, June, Terry Alliband, Terry Birk, Virginia Lawson, Suzanne Reisner, Craig
Sturtevant, and Stanley Witkowski
    1975      The Contact History of the Subarctic Athapaskans: An Overview. *In*
              Proceedings: Northern Athapaskan Conference, 1971, edited by A. M. Clark,
              vol. 1, 302-49. National Museum of Man, Mercury Series, Canadian
              Ethnology Service Paper no. 27. 2 vols. Ottawa.
Helm, June, Edward S. Rogers, and James G. E. Smith
    1981      Intercultural Relations and Cultural Change in the Shield and Mackenzie
              Borderlands. *In* Handbook of North American Indians, vol. 6, Subarctic,
              edited by June Helm, 146-57. Washington, D.C.: Smithsonian Institution.
Hudson's Bay Company Archives
    1670-1940 York Fort Journal, 1716, HBCA B.239/a/2. Provincial Archives of Manitoba,
              Winnipeg. Microfilm copies in National Archives of Canada, Ottawa, and
              Public Records Office, London.

Isham, James
    1949    Observations on Hudson's Bay, 1743, and Notes on Observations on a Book
            Entitled A Voyage to Hudson's Bay in the Dobbs Galley, 1749. Edited by E.
            E. Rich. Toronto: Published by the Champlain Society for the Hudson's Bay
            Record Society.
Jarvenpa, Robert
    1976    Spatial and Ecological Factors in the Annual Economic Cycle of the English
            River Band of Chipewyan. Arctic Anthropology 13(1):43-69.
Jenness, Diamond
    1956    The Chipewyan Indians: An Account by an Early Explorer. Anthropologica
            3:15-33.
Kelsall, J. P.
    1968    The Migratory Barren-Ground Caribou of Canada. Canadian Wildlife Series
            no. 3. Ottawa: Department of Indian Affairs and Northern Development.
Krech, Shepard, III
    1980    Northern Athapaskan Ethnology: An Annotated Bibliography of Published
            Materials, 1970-1979. Arctic Anthropology 17(2):68-105.
Lee, Richard B., and Irven DeVore, eds.
    1968    Man the Hunter. Chicago: Aldine Publishing.
Legoff, Laurent, O.M.I.
    1889    Grammaire de la langue montaignaise. Montréal: no publisher.
Lévi-Strauss, Claude
    1969    The Elementary Structures of Kinship. Orig. French ed., 1949. Boston:
            Beacon Press.
Li, Fang-Kuei
    1933    A List of Chipewyan Stems. International Journal of American Linguistics
            7:122-51.
MacNeish, June Helm
    1960    Kin Terms of the Arctic Drainage Dene: Hare, Slavey, Chipewyan. American
            Anthropologist 62:279-95.
Mason, J. Alden
    1914    Notes on Northeastern Athabaskan Culture. National Museum of Canada,
            Division of Anthropology, manuscript no. 45. Ottawa.
Meyer, David
    1985    The Red Earth Crees, 1860-1960. National Museum of Man, Mercury Series,
            Canadian Ethnology Service Paper no. 100. Ottawa.
Morgan, Lewis H.
    1871    Systems of Consanguinity and Affinity of the Human Family. Smithsonian
            Contributions to Knowledge, vol. 17. Washington, D.C.
    1877    Ancient Society, or Researches in the Lines of Human Progress from Savagery
            through Barbarism to Civilization. New York: Holt.
Morice, A. G., O.M.I
    1906-10 The Great Déné Race. Anthropos 1:229-77, 438-508, 695-730; 2:1-34, 181-
            96; 4:582-606; 5:113-42, 419-43, 643-53, 969-90. Reprint ed. St. Gabriel-
            Mödling, no date.
Murdock, George P.
    1949    Social Structure. New York: Macmillan.

1955      North American Indian Social Organization. Davidson Journal of Anthro-
          pology 1:85-97.
Noble, William C.
1981      Prehistory of the Great Slave Lake and Great Bear Lake Region. *In* Handbook
          of North American Indians, vol. 6, Subarctic, edited by June Helm, 97-106.
          Washington, D.C.: Smithsonian Institution.
Parker, Gerald R.
1972      Biology of the Kaminuriak Population of Barren-Ground Caribou. Part 1:
          Total Numbers, Mortality, Recruitment, and Seasonal Distribution. Canadian
          Wildlife Service Report Series no. 20. Ottawa.
Penard, J. M., O.M.I.
1938      Grammaire montagnaise. LePas, Manitoba: Eveque.
Perry, Richard J.
1989      Matrilineal Descent in a Hunting Context: The Athapaskan Case. Ethnology
          28:33-52.
Petitot, Emile, O.M.I.
1876      Monographie des Dene-Dindjie. Paris: E. Leroux.
Ridington, Robin
1969      Kin Categories versus Kin Groups: A Two-Section System without Sections.
          Ethnology 8:460-67.
Rogers, Edward S.
1981      History of Ethnological Research in the Subarctic Shield and Mackenzie
          Borderlands. *In* Handbook of North American Indians, vol. 6, Subarctic,
          edited by June Helm, 19-29. Washington, D.C.: Smithsonian Institution.
Rogers, Edward S., and James G. E. Smith
1973      Cultural Ecology of the Canadian Shield Subarctic. Paper presented at the 11th
          International Congress of Anthropological and Ethnological Sciences,
          Chicago.
Savashinsky, Joel
1974      The Trail of the Hare: Life and Stress in an Arctic Community. New York:
          Gordon and Breach.
Service, Elman
1971      Primitive Social Organization. 2d ed., New York: Random House.
Sharp, Henry S.
1975      Introducing the Sororate to a Northern Saskatchewan Chipewyan Village.
          Ethnology 14:71-82.
1976      Man:Wolf:Woman:Dog. Arctic Anthropology 13(1):25-34.
1977a     The Chipewyan Hunting Unit. American Ethnologist 4:377-93.
1977b     The Caribou-Eater Chipewyan: Bilaterality, Strategies of Caribou Hunting
          and the Fur Trade. Arctic Anthropology 14(2):35-40.
1978      Comparative Ethnology of the Wolf and Chipewyan. *In* Wolf and Man
          Evolution in Parallel, edited by R. L. Hall and H. S. Sharp, 55-79. New York:
          Academic Press.
1979      Chipewyan Marriage. National Museum of Man, Mercury Series, Canadian
          Ethnology Service Paper no. 58. Ottawa.
1986      Shared Experience and Magical Death: Chipewyan Explanation of a Prophet's
          Decline. Ethnology 25:257-70.
1988      The Transformation of Bigfoot: Maleness, Power, and Belief among the

Chipewyan. Smithsonian Series in Ethnographic Inquiry. Washington, D.C.
Slobodin, Richard
   1975a    Canadian Subarctic Athapaskans in the Literature to 1965. Canadian Review
            of Sociology and Anthropology 12:278-89.
   1975b    Northern Athapaskan Research: Some Comments. *In* Proceedings: Northern
            Athapaskan Conference, 1971, edited by A. McFadyen Clark, vol. 2, 786-77.
            National Museum of Man, Mercury Series, Canadian Ethnology Service Paper
            no. 27. 2 vols. Ottawa.
Smith, David M.
   1973     I$^{n}$ko$^{n}$ze: Magico-Religious Beliefs of Contact-Traditional Chipewyan Trading
            at Fort Resolution, NWT, Canada. National Museum of Man, Mercury Series,
            Canadian Ethnology Service Paper no. 6. Ottawa.
   1982     Moose-Deer Island People: A History of the Native People of Fort Resolution.
            National Museum of Man, Mercury Series, Canadian Ethnology Service Paper
            no. 81. Ottawa.
Smith, James G. E.
   1975a    The Ecological Basis of Chipewyan Socio-Territorial Organization. *In*
            Proceedings: Northern Athapaskan Conference, 1971, edited by A. M. Clark,
            vol. 2, 389-461. National Museum of Man, Mercury Series, Canadian
            Ethnology Service Paper no. 27. 2 vols. Ottawa.
   1975b    Preliminary Notes on the Rocky Cree of Reindeer Lake. *In* Contributions to
            Anthropology, 1975, edited by David B. Carlisle, 171-89. National Museum
            of Man. Mercury Series, Canadian Ethnology Service Paper no. 31. Ottawa.
   1976a    Local Band Organization of the Caribou Eater Chipewyan. Arctic
            Anthropology 13(1):12-24.
   1976b    Local Band Organization of the Caribou Eater Chipewyan in the Eighteenth
            and Nineteenth Centuries. Western Canadian Journal of Anthropology
            6:72-90.
   1978a    Economic Uncertainty in an "Original Affluent Society": Caribou and Caribou
            Eater Chipewyan Adaptive Strategies. Arctic Anthropology 15(1):68-88.
   1978b    The Emergence of the Micro-urban Village among the Caribou Eater
            Chipewyan. Human Organization 37:38-49.
   1981     Chipewyan. *In* Handbook of North American Indians, vol. 6, Subarctic, edited
            by June Helm, 278-84. Washington, D.C.: Smithsonian Institution.
   1987     The Lubicon Lake Cree. Cultural Survival 11:61-62.
Smith, James G. E., and Ernest S. Burch, Jr.
   1979     Chipewyan and Inuit in the Central Canadian Subarctic, 1613-1977. Arctic
            Anthropology 16(2):76-101.
Spier, Leslie
   1925     The Distribution of Kinship Systems in North America. University of
            Washington Publications in Anthropology no. 1. Seattle.
Steward, Julian
   1955     Theory of Culture Change: The Methodology of Multilinear Evolution.
            Urbana: University of Illinois Press.
   1968     Causal Factors and Processes in the Evolution of Pre-Farming Societies. *In*
            Man the Hunter, edited by Richard B. Lee and Irven DeVore, 321-34.
            Chicago: Aldine Publishing.

Symington, Fraser
    1965      Tuktu: A Question of Survival. Canadian Wildlife Service. Ottawa:
              Department of Indian Affairs and Northern Development.
Tax, Sol
    1955      From Lafitau to Radcliffe-Brown. *In* Social Anthropology of North American
              Tribes, edited by Fred Eggan, 445-81. Enlarged ed. Chicago: University of
              Chicago Press.
VanStone, James W.
    1965      The Changing Culture of the Snowdrift Chipewyan. National Museum of
              Canada Bulletin no. 209, Anthropological Series no. 74. Ottawa.
Williams, B. J.
    1974      A Model of Band Society. American Antiquity 39(4), Memoir no. 29.
Wissler, Clark
    1915      Culture of North American Indians Occupying the Caribou Area. Proceedings,
              National Academy of Sciences, vol. 1, 51-54.

# 3

# Kinship, Social Class, and Religion
# of Northwest Peoples

JUNE M. COLLINS

A social system consists of sets of beliefs or social logics, the structure of the society, and the manifestations of that structure in behavior. The structure of a society consists of groupings according to age and sex, kinship, political organization, status or ranked positions, social class and caste, religion, clubs, and other types of association. All these groupings, of course, are not present in all societies. The social logics by which the members of the society live provide a foundation for social structure. At times in certain societies, and in the present example of the Coast Salish, one set of these logics can be out of phase with another.

Using the method advocated by Radcliffe-Brown (1951) and Eggan (1955), I wish to compare three Salish-speaking peoples—the Central Salish of the American Plateau, the Coast Salish of British Columbia and Washington, and the Bella Coolas of British Columbia—on the basis of kinship and family system; the presence or absence of social class, caste, and of ranked positions; and religious beliefs and practices. In conclusion I will offer suggestions concerning the course of historical development of those aspects among the three groups of Salish speakers.

An assumption set forth by Radcliffe-Brown (Kuper 1977:45ff.) and used here is that each social system shows functional consistency. Further, the degree of consistency varies from society to society. It is very likely, as Radcliffe-Brown said, that "the lowest order, the absence of all conflict, is an order to which . . . a number of simpler societies approximate" (Kuper 1977:48). The Salish societies considered here varied considerably in the degree of inherent or structural conflict. The Central Interior Salish probably had the least conflict, the Coast Salish had the most, and the Bella Coolas were somewhere in between. Any society changes to reduce inherent strains and to approach a higher level of consistency. That process may have been taking place among the Coast Salish at the time of first European contact and had already reached a higher level of internal harmony among the Bella Coolas. Comparing the three groups of Salish-speaking peoples, I conclude that kinship, social classes (or lack thereof), and religious beliefs and practices enjoyed varying degrees of internal harmony among the three spheres. Of the three groups, the Central Interior Salish showed the highest degree of integration of these three aspects, the Coast Salish the poorest fit among the three, and the Bella Coolas an intermediate position.

Part of the evidence for this study comes from my own fieldwork among the Upper Skagit Indians of western Washington and some of their neighbors beginning in 1942 and continuing at intervals to 1980. My methods of field research were primarily interviewing (sometimes structured, sometimes free association) and observation. I also have relied on the literature written by anthropologists who are specialists in Northwest Coast studies and by explorers and other authorities.

## The Interior Salish

Beginning with the Interior Salish, I will concentrate on the Sanpoils and Southern Okanogans, whom Ray (1939:26) regarded as the "most central and isolated" groups on the Plateau. They lived on the main channel of the Columbia River and some of its tributaries in eastern Washington. Like the other Salish considered here, they were food-gathering peoples; they emphasized hunting and root gathering more in their economy and relied less on fishing than the Coast Salish and Bella Coolas. According to Ray, the Sanpoils and Southern Okanogans shared characteristics that made the Plateau distinctive, and presumably they had incorporated relatively few influences from either the Northwest Coast or the Plains. We should expect to find that these Interior Salish people will show some contrasts with the Coast Salish on the one hand, and with the Bella Coolas on the other. The material presented here is derived largely from Ray's (1933) reconstruction of aboriginal Sanpoil and Nespelem society and from Walters's (1938) reconstruction for the Southern Okanogan.

Concerning their kinship system, the consanguineal terms are of the bifurcate collateral type with different terms for mother's brother, father's brother, mother's sister, and father's sister. Further, the terms for all "cousins" and brothers and sisters are divided into four categories: those of the younger male and the younger female relatives, and the older male and the older female relatives. This distinguishing of older consanguineal relatives of one's own generation from younger ones seems to be present in most, if not all, Salish kinship systems.

Kinship, together with sex and age, was probably the most important principle underlying social relations. The Sanpoils and Southern Okanogans had semipermanent winter villages that they left in the summer and fall as wild foods became available. Accordingly, community ties were also influential in their social life. Residence patterns after marriage tended to be patrilocal, although the couple could spend long periods with the wife's family.

Parents usually arranged the first marriage of their children by having the boy's mother approach the mother of the girl. Later the two fathers met, the boy's father promising a bride price. Ray says this sum was not negotiable. The groom's relatives gave the bride price in two successive visits to the bride's family. The bride and her parents did not keep all the food and other articles comprising the bride price but distributed much of it to their relatives. Soon after the second visit, the bride's parents went to see the groom's family, taking with them gifts at least equal in value to the bride price and sometimes greater. This is the basic outline of marriage in all Salish societies: a union arranged by parents or other older relatives of the principals and the two sets of gifts—the bride price and the return of property by the bride's family.

According to both Ray (1933:139) and Mandelbaum (1938:112), individuals known to be blood relatives were not allowed to marry. Speaking of the Sanpoil-Nespelems, Ray says this rule extended as far as three generations removed from ego (1933:139). According to Mandelbaum (1938:112), similar rules existed among the Southern Okanogans. Some second cousins did marry, although such unions were disapproved. This point is emphasized here to provide contrast later with the Bella Coolas.

In addition to monogamous marriages, the Interior Salish permitted plural wives, with a tendency toward sororal polygyny. Ray does not say that wealth was an inducement to polygyny. Nevertheless, his point that shamans, chiefs, and especially good hunters and gamblers had the largest number of wives (1933:142) suggests that earning a good living may have been a consideration in polygyny.

In terms of government, there was some degree of formal political organization; each village had a chief, and sometimes one head chief governed several separate communities. In addition, the chief had a speaker and possibly one or two other officers to carry out his orders. The chief served as judge; otherwise his authority was largely advisory in nature. He did not own or control the use of resources.

There were no social classes or slaves among most of the Plateau Salish:

Peoples of the Plateau have remained impressively unreceptive to the notions of caste which are so strongly emphasized on the Coast. The only tribes in no way influenced are those in direct contact along the boundary of the two areas. The Plateau attitude is not one of passive disregard; on the contrary, the opposite principle, that of equality of man, is given active and emotional support.

The Sanpoil are among the most outspoken in this respect. To them class distinctions are unthinkable, to say nothing to slavery. The latter is looked upon as an unaccountable custom of foreigners. Every adult citizen—man or woman—is a member of the general assembly of his village. When it becomes necessary to select a chief from a new lineage, any man is eligible. The selection is made without regard to any quality suggestive of class. The chief is in no way set apart socially; he is as approachable as any man in the group. Nor does wealth carry any suggestion of advance in status. Indeed, wealth is rare. [Ray 1939:24-25]

Among the Central Plateau Salish, except for the semi-inherited position of chief, there were no inherited privileges or positions. Their religious life reflects this tendency.

The religion of the Interior Salish, like the other Salish, was animistic, believing that the world was populated by a great variety of supernatural beings. Through the guardian spirit quest, any Sanpoil or Southern Okanogan child or adolescent could seek these beings. If the child were successful, he had a dream or vision in which a spirit appeared to him, taught him a song and a dance, and instructed him as to the type of power he was bestowing. The child was expected to repress this memory until adulthood, when he would fall sick with the spirit's return. The adult was then required to sponsor a winter ceremony in which he danced and sang as his spirit had earlier instructed him. Throughout life the guardian spirit assisted him in many different ways, although some spirits bestowed special abilities as in hunting or gambling.

Ray underscores the democratic climate of the religious life: "In the quest for supernatural power equality also plays its role. This activity is open equally to every man and every woman, not to only a privileged few as on parts of the Coast. Very few men fail to achieve at least one guardian spirit" (1939:26). Success or failure in the Plateau spirit quest was not based on inheritance. The decision lay in the hands of the spirit and not of the human beings.

At death, the fetishes that had been used in rituals were interred with the body of the owner. After burial and a feast, the dead person's property, usually scanty, was distributed to the mourners. The father, brothers, and sons—presumably in the case of a dead male—took the most (Ray 1939:

152). Fear of the dead, as among the other Salish, was great. The Central Interior Salish carried out rituals to remove dangerous qualities from property owned by the dead so that living relatives could use the items safely. Ray reports that death removed little property permanently from the living (1933:151). Mandelbaum says that the Southern Okanogans sometimes gave the property of the deceased to nonrelatives (although this was said to be a recent practice) and occasionally razed the dwelling or abandoned the whole village (1938:129). A second ceremony in which gifts were distributed to the living was held about a year after death. Both Mandelbaum (1938:139) and Teit (1930:289) were unsure that this second rite was ancient.

There was no personal ownership of major food-gathering sites among the peoples of the south-central Plateau, and, accordingly, they could not be inherited by individuals. Apparently each village owned the important fishing sites in its own locale. The men of the village constructed the weirs together and shared the fish from them. Visiting relatives were always allowed an equal part of the take. In the case of the Sanpoils, individual men built and owned traps placed on small streams. Similarly, in reference to all the Okanogan, including the Southern peoples, Teit wrote:

> The people of one band did not, as a rule, pick berries or dig roots in the grounds of another band without first obtaining the consent of the chief in charge of the territory, and then only at the proper season. Some grounds were tribal and not under the authority of any particular chief. [1930:277]

In summary, for the Interior Salish, the kinship system, the recognition of residential bonds, and the set of religious beliefs and practices were in harmony. No one, except possibly the chief, had a superior position. The lack of social classes, slavery, and inherited privileges demonstrates the egalitarian nature of these societies.

## The Coast Salish

Moving from the Interior Salish to the Coast Salish of British Columbia and Washington, let us consider first the codes governing kinship and family behavior and the bonds based on coresidence. The period referred to is that of early contact with Europeans, the first part of the nineteenth century.

Like the Interior Salish, the Coast Salish had a food-gathering economy. They relied more on fish, less on game, and much less on vegetable foods than the Interior Salish. They had permanent villages to which they returned each winter, spending the rest of the year in obtaining food at sites where it became available.

Their society, too, was familial, with great emphasis placed on kinship. The codes governing kinship were based on the assumption that all persons known to each individual were either consanguineal or affinal relatives. The kinship system of the Upper Skagits has been described in detail (Collins 1974a:15–28, 1974b:83–110). All Coast Salish systems were not identical in terminology to the Upper Skagit system, but all shared certain principles present also among the Interior Salish. Inherent in these terminological systems were discrimination based on generation, sex, age (whether relatives of the same generation were older or younger than ego), and whether the linking relative was alive or dead. Further, all Salish, both Coast and Interior, have bilateral systems.

While the Central Interior Salish have a bifurcate collateral system, the Coast Salish have a lineal type. For the Upper Skagits and other Puget Salish, this means that they have one term for father, one for mother, a third term for both father's brother and mother's brother, and a fourth for both mother's sister and father's sister.

Among the Straits Salish, such as the Saanich (Barnett 1955:240–41) and Lummis (Suttles 1974:294), there was another variant of this lineal type with distinctive terms for mother and father but the same term used for both "aunts" and "uncles" without regard to sex differences. Again, in all the Salish systems with which I am familiar, there is a pronominal prefix for each kinship term as it is used in reference that designates the sex of the relative. (Although the linguistic evidence is not yet complete—for example, the sound shifts have not been worked out in detail for all the Salish languages—I think the ancestral Salish system may have been bifurcate collateral, which changed to the lineal type among the Coast Salish and the Bella Coolas.)

According to the kinship responsibilities and rights prevailing among the Coast Salish, older relatives of the same generation and those in ascending generations owed protection and assistance to those who were younger or in descending generations. When a parent died, his or her siblings and cousins had increased obligations to the surviving children. In return for this aid from older relatives of ego's generation and from the first ascending generation, ego was expected to obey and to respect them and help them in case of need. Rules governing kin behavior spread as far as relationships could be traced.

In theory, within the society, the obligations and responsibilities toward kin overrode all other structural demands. In practice, kinship rules did not always take precedence, especially in cases where social-class differences were involved.

Among some Coast Salish, particularly those on Vancouver Island and the Straits Salish, the kinship system contained a potential basis for primogeniture. For example, separate terms for the oldest child existed in some societies. Also, the term for younger sibling was used as synonymous for members of junior lines (i.e., the children of siblings younger than the parents). This pattern was reflected to some extent in behavior. Barnett (1955:250–51), speaking about the Coast Salish of British Columbia, says that the oldest son would inherit the name (presumably the most distinguished name belonging to the family). Summing up the emphasis on primogeniture, Barnett states:

> Rank depended, not alone upon birth in a certain family, but also upon the order of birth within it. Within any given family, the possession of valuable items and resources of wealth and of ceremonial prerogatives was the important criterion of status. As a rule, this correlated *pari passu* with order of birth, for in general all rights were inherited. A fifth son in an aristocratic family therefore ranked far below the first, and his first cousin far below him. [1955:247]

Note that the "resources of wealth" included the title to lands such as fishing sites and ownership of such food-getting devices as sturgeon nets.

The oldest son was expected to share lands belonging to the family with other members, but he was in control of those lands and directed their use. Where family masks, dances, and other privileges were concerned, he decided when and under what circumstances they could be used. Inheritance by primogeniture was either entirely absent or rare among the Puget Salish and the Olympic Peninsula Salish south of the Klallams. Families did single out specific children to receive honored hereditary names, but that practice was usually based on an idea of fit between the child and the ancestor. Each child in a family was observed to see which ancestor his or her temperament and talents might best match. The idea that an individual or even a specific family owned certain fishing and hunting grounds or ceremonial displays was not present as far as I know. It was the village and not the family that owned the fishing sites and hunting grounds, although in small villages such ownership might coincide with the large, extended family. Further, it was not customary among these Salish to have any hereditary displays in the form of masks or rites at ceremonies.

In other words, the emphasis on primogeniture noted above seems to diminish among the Washington Coast Salish farther removed from the Strait Salish. For example, among the Upper Skagits who bordered some of the Strait Salish, there was little of this tendency. The only stress on primogeniture among the Upper Skagits was reserved for the oldest relative, usually a man, of one's own generation (among the large group of cousins and siblings). That individual inherited only an advisory position in the sense that younger members of this group were likely to ask his advice and support before planning a potlatch or other joint event. The person had no authority to command younger relatives, and he was not in charge of land use, fishing or hunting practices, or ceremonial regalia. The last were regarded as controlled entirely by the guardian spirit of each person. As far as I know, these ritual items were never inherited. At the time of death, such ceremonial objects were placed in the graveyard with the body of the dead owner and were avoided by the living. Authorities who have written about other Puget and Olympic Salish do not mention special attention to the oldest child in regard to inheritance.

Inheritance practices varied somewhat among the Coast Salish. The net effect was usually that few, if any, items belonging to the deceased, including valuables, passed to the immediate heirs. Fear of the ghost of the dead formed the basis of this tendency. The greatest danger existed for those survivors who were most devoted to and had the closest bonds with the dead person. Among the Upper Skagits and their neighbors, distant relatives or those who felt themselves to be safe came to the house after death and took whatever items they wished. A few days later, through voluntary return, these individuals began to contribute gifts to the household of the deceased.

Allowing those outside the group of close survivors to select items of property should not be confused with the memorial potlatch. This potlatch, which usually included cleaning and reburial of the bones of the dead, could be held at any time in honor of the deceased but had to be given whenever the graveyard was moved.

Barnett describes the Canadian Salish as burning the personal possessions of the dead, although individuals, presumably not the heirs, could select items and pay the heirs for them (1955:218).

The point of this discussion is that in Coast Salish society one would not be likely to accumulate property through inheritance from one's parents or grandparents.

Fear of the association of the ghost with his or her house was handled differently in different parts of the Coast Salish area. Among some of the Coast Salish of Washington, as among the Interior Salish, depending on the decision of the survivors, the house could be permanently or temporarily abandoned. With others, such as the Twanas and the Canadian Salish, apparently that necessity was circumvented by removal of the body through a plank in the wall (so that the ghost could not find the way back) and by ritual purification of the house.

Returning to kinship rules, we should note that the Salish assumed that in-laws should be treated like the comparable blood relatives (mother-in-law like one's own mother, father-in-law like one's own father, etc.). In practice there was often considerable rivalry and jealousy between in-laws.

Coast Salish rules governing marriage of relatives were similar to those of the Interior Salish. Village exogamy was stressed, and, at least among the Upper Skagits, that rule was followed rigidly (Collins 1979:245). Ideally, husband and wife should have no traceable consanguineal relationship (Elmendorf 1974:371). In practice, among some Coast Salish this rule was sometimes amended to permit marriages of individuals known to be related but not nearer than third cousins (Barnett 1955:184).

All societies having social classes try to perpetuate them in part by marriage regulations. The Coast Salish were no exception. First marriages, as in the case of the Interior Salish, were arranged by older relatives, usually the parents, who gave careful attention to the genealogy, social class, and wealth of the prospective spouse. Upper-class parents always attempted to arrange matches between social equals. One preferred form was to seek an upper-class marriage partner in a distant village on another drainage system or saltwater location. This practice had the advantage of increasing the spread of honorable and prestigious alliances for the family and its descendants. Lower-class parents were willing to allow their children to marry upper-class individuals, but they rarely had the opportunity to do so.

The ideal of matching social-class levels in marriage was not always attained. Young people seldom selected their own spouses but occasionally they insisted on marrying below their social class. There are even a few cases among the Upper Skagits and their neighbors of upper-class individuals, despite great opposition from their relatives, marrying slaves. Coast Salish society had no accepted way of handling the critical problems resulting from such unions.

Among Northwest Coast peoples, property exchange at marriage was always a topic for consideration. Among the Coast Salish the family of the groom or the groom himself usually gave property to the bride's father or other close male relative. This gift was regarded as legalizing the union so that children born of it would be legitimate. The bride usually went to live with her husband in his father's home, which was generally in another village. Traditionally, a year after the marriage the parents of the bride paid a visit to their daughter and her husband in which they repaid the bride price and sometimes exceeded it.

While the amounts of the bride price and the return did not affect the legality of the marriage, they did influence the social position of the bride and groom as well as that of their children. The greater the bride price, the higher the prestige of the couple and their descendants. The degree of expense and elaborateness at the time of marriage was highly variable. No ritual other than the giving of the bride price was necessary. At some weddings an additional ceremony was held in which the bride and groom received advice from elders of both their families. Rarely, an upper-class family held a potlatch to celebrate the wedding.

Ruyle (1973:603-11) and others, discussing the Northwest Coast peoples, have raised the question of economic exploitation of the lower class and of slaves by the upper class. The items of such exploitation can be grouped into two categories: access to natural resources (especially food) and exploitation of services under duress.

Concerning the first category, I find that social-class differentiation in access to natural resources was very likely present in only a few villages among the Coast Salish. In at least one Upper Skagit village, the lower-class section was not so advantageously located in regard to the fish runs as was the upper-class part. In the other cases in the literature where the upper-class and lower-class parts of the same village were separated by considerable distances, I am not certain that the latter had the poorer location in regard to fish runs, but it is a possibility. Even if it were so, considering seasonal pursuits throughout the year as well as the different modes of fishing and hunting, I think that the location in itself was probably not a great handicap in obtaining the annual supply of food. In the Upper Skagit village mentioned above, the members of the entire village, upper-class and lower-class, could join in dip-netting in the main channel of the river. In addition, all could fish by dragging the net between two canoes. Both classes hunted in the same locales. Access to roots in the mountains was unrestricted. Only two villages had prairie areas with inherited rights to plots of land containing semicultivated plants. Upper Skagits inherited use of that land through the female line. Due to bilateral descent, with the resulting multiplicity of ancestors, it seems likely that there were few, if any, women with Upper Skagit ancestors who could not use the plots. There probably were some women from neighboring societies, married into Upper Skagit villages, who lacked inherited rights to dig roots in them.

With the exception of the Klahuses, Slaiamans, Sechelts, and some of the Straits peoples, the Coast Salish of Canada seem to follow those of Washington State in regard to open access to the fishing and hunting sites for all members of a village. The first three exceptions had a pattern common to the Kwakiutls, Nootkas, and Bella Coolas, in which the heads of certain extended families owned stretches of land that had fishing sites. Among some of the Straits Salish, the heads of certain families or the entire family owned rights to certain reef-netting locations. In one such arrangement Suttles (1974:222) says that the owner felt obliged to give freely (of fish) to a relative.

The second consideration is the possibility of exploitation of services. There is some evidence that certain lower-class villages had to supply the upper-class people with goods. Jenness (1955:86) gives two examples of such cases among the Coast Salish of the Lower Fraser River in southern British Columbia. One was Coquitlam, which was tributary to the Kwantlem (or New Westminster Indians), and a second (also reported by Duff 1952:27), located near Port Moody, was subordinate to the Squamish of North Vancouver. A third, Nanoose, held the same lower-class position relative to the Nanaimo of Vancouver Island. The people of Sechelt and of Kuiper Island may also have been vassals. Although all these lower-class villages were composed of freemen, the members had to supply firewood, salmon, deer meat, or other required items to the superior community. In addition, the Coquitlams are described by Duff (1952:27) as having to work for the Kwantlems during the fish runs. The lower-class settlement at Dugualla Bay on Whidbey Island had to bring firewood and salmon to the upper-class Swinomish village. Elmendorf (1974:320), speaking of the Suquamish of Puget Sound, also mentions a lower-class branch at Dye Inlet. The literature has few such statements for other Coast Salish villages in Washington and Oregon. It is difficult to tell whether there are gaps in the records or whether such subordinate divisions were not present in the majority of Coast Salish villages.

Apart from requiring food or other goods on a regular basis, the Salish upper class benefitted principally from collecting goods from and mobilizing the services of the lower class for special purposes such as potlatches, namings, weddings, and funerals. Although the upper-class sponsors of those events redistributed the goods and provided the services to their guests (who always included many lower-class individuals), the sponsors were the ones who gained social prestige. In other words, upper-class people used the products and the labor of the lower class to strengthen their position as a class and to raise their rank within their own class.

These practices were carried on throughout the Coast Salish area. The difference between them and the goods and services demanded in the relatively few examples of separate lower-class communities mentioned above is that the gifts and labor were voluntary. Although the upper class presumably was willing to reciprocate by volunteering property and work to affairs of the lower class, these opportunities were rare. Few lower-class individuals held potlatches. Further, they carried out their rites of passage on a small, inexpensive scale.

If the boundaries between the upper and the lower classes were somewhat hazy in some villages, those dividing the freemen from the slaves were clearcut. First, there were few slaves in relation to the total population. A Hudson Bay census conducted in 1838 and 1839 for thirteen Coast Salish "tribes" in the Fort Nisqually District of Puget Sound indicates that slaves made up 4 percent of the population (Taylor 1974:416). That figure rises to 11 percent for the Fraser River Salish in 1839 if the phrase "male and female followers" is taken to mean slaves (Duff 1952:130). Apparently among the Coast Salish the overall ratio of slaves to freemen was not high. Both the census data and the reports of elderly Coast Salish in recent times are in agreement that some villages had no slaves and others had only one or two.

Compared to free persons, slaves were severely disadvantaged. For example, their masters had the right of life and death over them. Barnett (1955:218) says that one or two individuals among the Coast Salish of Canada had heard of a slave being killed when his master died. Duff (1952:83) cites a slave killed at the funeral of an Upper Stalo of the Fraser River. Costello (1967:30) reports that among the Suquamish of Puget Sound, three slaves—husband, wife, and daughter—were threatened with death after their master died. The bodies were to be placed on the grave of their owner. Chief Seattle prevented the killings, saying that the American authorities were opposed to the practice. In general, slaves were regarded as more valuable alive than dead.

Owners assigned their slaves the most menial and unpleasant labor, including cleaning fish, carrying game, and supplying wood and water. Slaves were not taught skills such as woodworking or basketry, but they were allowed to do such work if they already had the training when they were acquired.

Slaves could not marry unless their owner permitted, although apparently they were occasionally allowed to marry if the owner had both male and female slaves. Slaves described for the Upper Skagits and (with one exception) the Lower Skagits did not marry. If the Coast Salish were reluctant to have members of the lower class marry those of the upper, they were even more opposed to the unions of slaves with freemen. Technically, such a union would not constitute a legal marriage. The Coast Salish literature mentions a few exceptions in which a slave married a free person with the sanction of the parents of the free person. In those instances, the latter held a potlatch to obtain social approval of the marriage and of the offspring. Such attempts were not completely successful. The descendants of the union always suffered some social stigma. All parents were not so lenient as those who would give a potlatch for a child who mated with a slave. Barnett (1955:208) speaking of the Squamish, relates an incident in which an upper-class father, whose daughter had sexual relations with a slave, arranged to have both drowned.

Probably the greatest advantage of owning slaves lay in social prestige rather than economic gain. Many Coast Salish from a number of different societies have stated that it was necessary to own a slave in order to be upper-class. It may not have been a universal criterion, but there is no question that possessing a slave helped one to obtain a high position in Coast Salish society.

Turning to the religious life, the Coast Salish had a set of animistic beliefs much like the Interior Salish with further similarities to many western Native American peoples. The Interior Salish believed that there was a host of spiritual beings who gave all good in human life. These beings were sometimes associated with certain animal species and less often with species of trees or plants, with natural phenomena like the sun and moon, and with specific locales such as a lake or a place in the river. In still other cases, the spirits appeared as humanoid figures lacking associations with nature. Health, survival, talents and achievements, and wealth were all attributed to the help of these beings. Individuals sought relation with these spirits during childhood by the quest that included fasting and bathing in isolation, or by quests later in life. Public confirmation of the relationship between the human and the spirit was later displayed in a dance ceremony held at the request of the spirit. At that ceremony, the sponsor needed for assistance the attendance of all people having the same type of spirit as well as other guests. Further, at the end of the ceremony the sponsor gave gifts to all present.

The point for this discussion is that the Coast Salish, like the Interior Salish, believed that these guardian spirits, with one or two exceptions, disregarded social class or rank in accepting a human being. The few exceptions to this rule are discussed below. Since the decision lay in the hands of the spirit, anyone—lower-class or upper-class—could approach a spirit through the quest. There is even some indication in folklore that spirits might be moved by pity to select a person who was lowly or spurned by members of his society.

In comparing the social logics of religious life and of kinship, on the one hand, with those of social class and caste, on the other, the potential for conflict becomes apparent. Neither the codes of kinship nor those of religious life allowed for a social-class and caste system. My interpretation is that the kinship codes and structure as well as religious beliefs were older and had not yet changed to conform with the newer concepts of social class and caste. Kinship was supposed to take precedence over distinctions of social class, rank, and caste.

On the other hand, the fear of contamination from association with the lower class was great. How then should upper-class people behave toward their lower-class kin? The social system provided no generally accepted ways of resolving this problem. Some individuals were noted for giving first priority to their kinship obligations. Others became famous for the rigidity with which they attempted to maintain social-class lines even where their own relatives were concerned. Whatever the individual did in the face of conflicts between the demands of kinship and of social class was not likely to meet with full public approval, as the following examples illustrate.

About the middle of the last century, a Samish man seized a young woman from a neighboring village as a slave, apparently because her father had not repaid him a debt. As was the practice, the slave owner then sold her to a distant village so that she would not likely escape or be rescued. Despite the distance and difficulty of travel, she was able to escape and made her way to an Upper Skagit village where she had relatives. (She did not go to the home of her closest relatives because she feared they would not help her.) In this village she was accepted and treated as a relative, not a slave. One of the upper-class men of the village married her and the two had children. The welcoming villagers, although they had acted in strict accord with the kinship code, violated the rules governing social class and caste. Accordingly, they received severe criticism. To some extent, the couple's descendants remained under a cloud of disapproval for several generations.

In another case, an Upper Skagit man was captured as a slave and taken to a Coast Salish village in what is now British Columbia. An Upper Skagit woman who visited the village with her family made arrangements for his escape, which was effected by trickery. When the Upper Skagit contingent left, they pretended to carry a load of supplies to their canoes. In actuality, the load was the slave concealed in wrappings. The freed slave then returned to his Upper Skagit village, married, and had children. The family that had rescued him, like the Upper Skagit husband in the previous story, had behaved to the letter of the kinship code. Still, they encountered considerable criticism from others. Some said that the freed man, having learned to lie and to steal as a slave, continued to behave in the same way and taught his children, who in turn transmitted the immoral behavior to their descendants. From this point of view, the rescuing family should have left well enough alone and not freed him.

There are stories also of conflicts and difficulties resulting from marriages between upper- and lower-class individuals. According to the strict logics of social class, such marriages should not occur. In practice they occasionally did. In the accounts, the upper-class spouse and his or her relatives suffer repeatedly from the misconduct of the lower-class spouse and in-laws.

At potlatches and at the guardian spirit ceremonies, the sponsors gave gifts to the guests. Here again the conflicts between kinship and social class were apparent. According to the kinship code, an upper-class sponsor with lower-class relatives should not slight them in any way. On the other hand, the cultural logics of the social-class system demanded that the sponsor give first place to the upper-class guests in seating, dining, and in the value of gifts received. Again, individuals probably resolved this problem in different ways on different occasions. They might well be criticized however they handled the situation.

At the time of first European contact, toward the latter part of the eighteenth century and for some years thereafter, a hypothesis formulated by Radcliffe-Brown seems to have been operating: "Whenever marked functional inconsistencies occur, they tend to produce change and that the tendency continues until the inconsistencies are resolved" (1935:531). In Coast Salish societies, religious life came into more harmonious relationship with the social-class system. Those changes seem to have been borrowed from the Coast Salish on Vancouver Island, and from the mainland of British Columbia by those Washington State Salish closest to them. One major area of change lay in the way of getting guardian spirits.

As an example, the Upper Skagits, like most other Salish of Washington State, believed that human association with guardian spirits was the decision of the spirit. How then could they explain lower-class individuals who acquired guardian spirits and became wealthy and successful with their help? The Upper Skagits developed the concept that the guardian spirits often wanted to continue their associations with a particular family. In practice, it meant that a given spirit, when his human associate died, might well want to assist a younger brother, child, or other close consanguineal relative. Because of this feeling, the spirit might then "make it easy" for the relative to become his associate. This view meant that people tended to think it more probable that a certain spirit would remain in one family than go to a nonrelative. However, the logic continued that the choice was entirely within the province of the spirit. Peoples of southern Puget Sound, such as the Puyallups, are not reported as having this idea of the spirit tending to move from one family member to another. This suggests to me that the Upper Skagits had gone one step further than some others in trying to harmonize religious life with the social-class system. Presumably, close family members would belong to the same social class, so willingness of guardian spirits to stay with them would tend to perpetuate the class system.

The partial nature of the integration of religious beliefs with the social-class system is shown by the point that only one type of spirit conveying wealth is reported to consider the social class of the applicant. For example, Haeberlin and Gunther (1930:68) speak of a Samish man whose father was partly of slave descent but whose mother was of high rank. The man encountered a wealth spirit by diving into a whirlpool in the Snoqualmie River. The spirit told him he could give him only half his power because the boy's father was of slave descent. This same type of spirit among the Upper Skagits is described as asking his servant if the applicant is "high-class" before he awards him the entire potential of his power. Elmendorf (1974:33) speaks of similar discrimination by Twana wealth spirits. Even though such a spirit specifically conveyed wealth, most of the other Coast Salish spirits were also regarded as helping people become well-to-do. An important sign of any spirit relationship was the ability to earn a good living and to be able to accumulate enough goods to distribute at the end of the winter dance ceremonial.

Another trend that may have strengthened the social-class system involves the method of acquiring a spirit. Among the Coast Salish of Canada (and also some of the United States), an important way of getting a spirit is by contagion rather than by fasting in isolation—a group of people who share the same type spirit transmit the spirit by "grabbing" and "working on" an individual. This process may happen quickly during a winter dance ceremonial or it may take place over a period of several weeks or months. During the longer period, the group holds the person in secluded quarters. After they seize the person, they raise his body in the air and run around the interior of the ceremonial building with him. They may also blow on him and rub or even bite his body. By these techniques the spirit may be induced into the person. The transmission may take place against the will of the person but with the consent of his or her relatives. The point here is that this technique primarily involves other human agents and is not a matter solely between the individual and his spirit. Such a system makes it possible for the perpetuation of the same spirits within the same social class, for human beings decide who will receive this treatment. (Since the old social-class structure has broken down, selection of "captives" on the basis of social class does not seem likely today.)

Among the Kwakiutls and Nootkas, secret societies formed the principal structure of religious life. Membership in these societies among the Kwakiutls was limited to those who were upper-class or of higher rank. To avoid the controversy as to whether or not the Kwakiutls had social class or only rank, I emphasize that it is the importance of the graded social distinctions, rather than the terminology used, that concerns us here.

One of the secret societies, *xənxanítəl* 'black dance' among some of the Coast Salish, called *klokwalla* among the Quinaults, may have had its origin in the wolf ritual *tło·kwa·na* of the Nootkas (Elmendorf 1948:631; Ernst 1952:99ff.). Drucker, speaking of the Nootkas, emphasizes the social-ranking aspects of the *klokwalla* (which he calls the Shamans' dance): "Basically, the ritual was built around the system of rank; chiefs sponsored the performance on the basis of hereditary right to do so, and similarly owned nearly all the important ritual acts. And these were the same chiefs that held highest rank in the lineages and in the tribes" (1951:388).

In the case of the Kwakiutls, also, specific societies, the *hamatsa*, or Cannibal Dancers, and several of the other orders—grizzly bear and the *hawi:nəl* (a warrior society)—clearly spread to the Comox, their near Salish-speaking neighbors. Barnett (1955:290) points out that the right to join one of these societies was acquired only through inheritance or as part of the groom's marriage gift. Taking part as a member in their ceremonies also required considerable wealth. The sponsor of the initiate, usually a close consanguineal relative or father-in-law, had to pay all the members of the society as well as the assistants, servers, and anyone who had been injured or had property destroyed during the ceremonies.

Moving from the Salish of Vancouver Island to those of the mainland, Barnett states that the Slaiamans (1955:170) and the Klahuses (1955:303) had ritual performances that included masks called *tal*, which had originated among the Kwakiutls. He also says (1955:303) that three other Kwakiutl-derived masked performances, with their foreign names, had just arrived among the Klahuses when they had to give them up and that those performances did not spread farther to the south.

Apart from a few such comments, the literature is not specific as to the exact spread of the Kwakiutl secret societies among the Salish in early historic times. The societies' effect seems to diminish and they disappear completely among Coast Salish distant from the Kwakiutls. For example, the Upper Skagits and their neighbors to the south did not have them.

Duff (1952:110) suggests that the Kwakiutl religious societies had a more pervasive influence than the taking over of the actual societies and ceremonies themselves. For example, he speaks of initiation into a society by "inspiration"—that is, by unsolicited seizure by a spirit held by others present at a winter dance ceremony. He refers here to the Stalos of the Fraser River but adds that Kwakiutl as well as Nootkan influence was present in the initiation ceremony of the Saanich, Cowichans, Naniamos, Squamish, and Musqueams.

In summary, the presence of secret societies and, in general, effects leading to the acquisition of spiritual powers through human agency rather than the supernatural alone appear to have come to the Coast Salish from the Nootkas and the Kwakiutls. These foreign concepts fitted the social-class system well but were antithetical to the dominant and basic idea of the Salish guardian spirit religion. Accordingly, they were imperfectly integrated into the religious system. This lack of harmony explains why many Coast Salish objected to the concepts, saying either that those who claimed to have supernatural power though initiation into a secret society or through contagion or capture were faking and had no such power or that they had only weak power.

## The Bella Coolas

If Coast Salish religion and kinship had only partly come into line with the social-class system, we should expect to find greater harmony among these three aspects among the Bella Coolas. Isolated in their geographical location from other Salish-speakers and closely exposed to Kwakiutl-speaking peoples on two sides, the Bella Coolas could be expected to have the logics underlying their kinship system relatively well integrated with both their social-class system and their religious life. That is exactly what occurred. The Bella Coolas, like other Salish speakers, placed great stress on kinship. They too had a bilateral kinship system, showing some cognates with the Coast Salish. Their inheritance practices stressed the patrilineal side of the family more than those of the Coast Salish did, although the latter tended in this direction, particularly where house and village occupancy was concerned. Perhaps the Bella Coolas stressed the patrilineal side as heavily as they did because they had much more to inherit in the sense of the many social and religious prerogatives. This emphasis on inheritance in general, as well as the specific practice of a man inheriting from his father-in-law, probably shows Kwakiutl influence.

The Bella Coolas provided a careful mapping of social-class and rank distinctions in relation to kinship. This mapping reveals several underlying features, including the first arrival of ancestors in a locale. To be an upper-class person in a Bella Coola village it was necessary to have ancestors who were thought to be among the first residents of the community. Myths telling of the events of arrival were among the valued properties of high-ranking individuals. Primogeniture was also important. The oldest son usually inherited the best of the family's prerogatives, and as a result the descendants of younger sons eventually became lower-class. Further, upper-class status among the Bella Coolas was validated by potlatching. The Bella Coolas, like other Salish, had the pattern number of four and maintained that it was necessary to give four potlatches to confirm upper-class status. Then a man could have a wooden seat built for his use during ceremonies, a tangible symbol of his high rank.

The support of upper-class relatives was essential in order to give a potlatch. McIlwraith (1948, 1:369ff.) describes how a father would take his son aside from time to time and show him sets of material, such as a bunch of twigs and a bundle of nettle fibers, standing for gifts already bestowed on the child at ceremonies. At potlatches, sponsors gave property to certain children because they had upper-class parents and other relatives. The father required his son at an early age to memorize the names of the donors and the value of the gifts. In this way he introduced the boy to the set of obligations and rights he would later have to maintain on his own. Further, it was the father, with his sponsorship at the ceremony in giving an ancestral name to his son, who put the boy's step on the ladder toward adult potlatching.

Upper-class Bella Coola elders, as among the Salish in general, arranged most first marriages. Like the Coast Salish, they took care to match the social class of the bride and groom. Unlike the other Salish speakers, who emphasized village exogamy and disapproved of or forbade marriage among cousins, the Bella Coolas were heavily endogamous within the ancestral family. This large kin unit consisted of individuals related through the father's side of the family to one of the original settlers of the Bella Coola valley. The idea underlying this preferred form of marriage was that the valuable ancestral names and privileges could be kept within the same family unit. It seems likely that the Bella Coolas took this idea from the Kwakiutls, although it was not the only form of marriage permitted to upper-class Kwakiutls (Boas 1966:50). In other words, while the Coast Salish emphasis was on marriage out of the village, the Bella Coolas, who preferred marriage within the ancestral family, often married within the village (McIlwraith 1948, 1:375). The Bella Coolas did not like first cousins to marry. Nevertheless, unlike the Coast Salish and the Interior Salish, they apparently sometimes did allow such marriages and accepted unions of second cousins as well (McIlwraith 1948, 1:375).

In the property exchanges involved in Bella Coola marriages, we see clearly the strong Kwakiutl influences on a basic Salish pattern, which, as we have seen, included bride price and the return to the groom and his family of at least the same amount and sometimes more. Gift exchange between the two sets of in-laws continued afterward at intervals. For the Bella Coolas, the exchange could follow the elaborate format described by McIlwraith (1948, 1:373ff.) for the upper class.

In contrast to the Interior and to many of the Coast Salish, Bella Coola wedding gifts always included names given by both sets of in-laws to the bride and groom as well as ancestral privileges and other property. There was a series of gift-giving events and feasts instead of the two minimal visits described for most of the other Salish. Even the Comox and Pentlatch, who had the most costly and complex exchanges among the Coast Salish, do not seem to have reached the Bella Coola level of property exchange.

Other evidence of Kwakiutl influence appears in the fictive marriages of the Bella Coolas (McIlwraith 1948, 2:422–27). A man without a daughter might ally himself by marriage to a famous chief by supplying a "bride": his finger, leg, hand, or other body part. In one case, the "wife" was a favorite dog (McIlwraith 1948, 2:425). Among the Coast Salish, only a few peoples such as the Comox (Barnett 1955:203) are described as having fictive marriages, also presumably due to Kwakiutl influence.

The point of this discussion is that widespread Salish marriage practices had been altered among the upper-class Bella Coolas to bring kinship into closer cohesion with the structure of social class and rank.

Turning to religion, as we have seen, one of the ideas underlying the guardian spirit complex among the Plateau Salish and the Coast Salish was that of occupational assistance. The help of spiritual beings was credited with enabling all work-related ability, such as carpentry, basketry, fishing, and hunting. Since individuals could seek any one of these spirits by the quest, they did not rely on inheritance.

With their great stress on inheritance of rank and privileges, the Bella Coolas appear to have altered their traditional religious beliefs about occupation accordingly. They had developed a series of named positions (Carpenter, Hunter, Warrior) that were hereditary and were validated by public gift giving (McIlwraith 1948, 1:261ff.). The right to become a Carpenter was contained in an ancestral myth and thus only male descendants of that figure could hold the position. A supernatural being, the Master Carpenter *(Yulatimiut)*, a close associate of the Creator, had been in existence since the beginning of time. The Master Carpenter married a Bella Coola woman; their male descendants were eligible to become Carpenters. The Carpenter, like the Warrior or Hunter, had a dance and song to perform publicly. In his woodworking, the Bella Coola carpenter was able to draw upon the powers of the supernatural Master Carpenter.

The Bella Coolas recognized the possibility that individuals who did not qualify for these inherited positions could build canoes, fight, or hunt successfully. In the case of an able carpenter who lacked the appropriate ancestors, they said that a specific spiritual being, the Model Maker, very likely had appeared to the man and given him the power to make canoes. In Bella Coola society, the man encouraged to specialize as a carpenter was clearly the one with ancestral prerogative. The greater prestige was reserved for the man with the hereditary position rather than for other specialists.

Here the Bella Coolas show that without entirely relinquishing the Salish idea that spiritual beings could at will bestow special powers on any person, they clearly provided a prestigious means of inheriting occupational ability through social position.

Unlike the Coast Salish of Puget Sound and the Interior Salish, the Bella Coolas emphasized secret society rituals in religious life. Following practices of the Kwakiutls, their attention to these rituals was overwhelming. People who joined these societies obtained spiritual help by virtue of their membership. Like the other Salish speakers, they continued to allow individuals with guardian spirits obtained in quests to validate them apart from the secret society performances. These spirit validation ceremonies received minor interest compared to the secret society performances.

For individuals to join their three secret societies, the Bella Coolas required inheritance and payment of fees. One of the secret societies, the *kusiut*, perhaps most closely approximated the old Salish ideal that religious life be open to anyone. Membership in the *kusiut*, like the other two, was obtained through purchase and through validation of ancestral prerogatives. Apparently, the fees were lower for the *kusiut* society than for the other two. In recent history, every Bella Coola inherited one of the prerogatives needed to join. This society may have been more selective for members in the past.

Bella Coola religious life had not completely discarded the idea that religious participation could be available to all. Nevertheless, social-class membership limited participation in Bella Coola rituals to a much greater extent than it did among other Salish speakers. Very likely this pattern was taken from the Kwakiutls, who allowed only upper-class individuals to dance in the performances of their secret societies.

In terms of social class, the Bella Coolas, like the Kwakiutls and Nootkas, did not have separate houses or communities for the lower class, as the Coast Salish often did. Bella Coolas did not seem to fear social harm from association with the lower class. I therefore suspect that Bella Coola class lines were so firmly determined by inheritance that membership involved little uncertainty. If an individual knows that his or her position is primarily fixed by inheritance, he is not so likely to be anxious about association with those at a lower level. It is upper-class people, who fear the encroachment of the socially mobile person or the loss of their own social position, who are likely to avoid interaction with the lower class. The general Bella Coola acceptance of lower-class individuals in the same house and as part of the village indicates that inherited social class and rank was probably more firmly entrenched among them than among the Coast Salish.

In contrast to the Coast Salish, the Bella Coolas had a much larger slave caste, as much as 30 or 40 percent in every village at some time (McIlwraith 1948, 1:158). The position of Bella Coola slaves was similar to those of the Coast Salish. Their masters held the power of life and death over them but apparently seldom killed them. The right to slay a slave was supported by Bella Coola myths concerning the origin of the initiation rites for their religious society, the *kusiut*. The myths in which the ancestor in each case established the right of his descendants to become members of the society include the story of a slave who was killed and buried within the house. While many Bella Coola myths mention slaves, few appear in Coast Salish myths. (Here I use the term *myth* to refer only to the tales recounted of a time when the world was different from its present state—a separate category from the folktales of the recent period.) In other words, Bella Coola mythology, like that of other peoples of the world, was supportive of religious and some social practices. The mythology assumed acceptance of the slave caste, while Coast Salish mythology did not—further evidence for the close interweaving of religion with social-class and caste structure among the Bella Coolas.

## Conclusion

Linguistic evidence at present suggests that Salish languages may have had a place of dispersion at or near the mouth of the Fraser River in what has since become Coast Salish territory. If that were so, the Salish as they spread into the interior may have kept the main characteristics of their ancestral social structure and logics. Among those characteristics is the emphasis on kinship as the principle underlying social relations unmitigated by social class or caste and little affected by inherited rank. Their religious life, with its emphasis on the association with guardian spirits through the quest open to all individuals, fitted such a social structure well.

In terms of the kinship system alone, very likely the Interior Salish form retained a closer approximation to the ancestral Salish. Among the changes in Coast Salish kinship systems from the possible ancestral Salish type are the emphases on primogeniture in the male line among the Strait Salish and the other Salish of Vancouver Island and the British Columbia mainland. Those emphases seem clearly related to the greater importance of social class and inherited rank among the Coast Salish by virtue of their heavier exposure to the Kwakiutls and Nootkas.

In other words, my interpretation is that the Salish group that became the Coast Salish gradually acquired concepts of social class and caste (and, to a lesser extent, inherited privileges) after their relatives who were to become the Interior Salish separated from them. Among the Coast Salish, these newer concepts remained imperfectly integrated with the kinship system and religious belief in guardian spirits. Accordingly, strains and conflicts were present in Coast Salish society. When Europeans first arrived and for some years thereafter, Coast Salish kinship systems and religious beliefs were changing in the direction of greater harmony with social-class and rank distinctions but had by no means achieved complete consistency with them.

The Bella Coolas were presumably separated from the rest of the Salish-speaking peoples for a lengthy period. Compared to the Coast Salish they show a much closer fit between the kinship system and religious beliefs, on the one hand, and the social-class and rank system, on the other. The closer fit is likely due to the Bella Coolas' incorporation of Kwakiutl influences resulting from their location and prolonged association with the latter. That the Bella Coolas had not completely lost their Salish religious heritage is shown by their continuing to permit individuals to acquire guardian spirits through the quest. Even so, through time Bella Coola dance performances validating these spirits had come to form only a minor part of ceremonial life. The major rituals were those of the secret society dancers who inherited their memberships and paid for them.

A major question remains: Why were the Bella Coolas, and to a lesser extent, the Coast Salish, receptive to concepts of social class, inherited rank, and slavery. Did the prestige of the Nootkas and Kwakiutls lead the Coast Salish to emulate them by taking on secret societies and accepting the concept of social classes? The Comox living adjacent to the Kwakiutls occasionally intermarried with them, and Barnett speaks of Comox alliances with the Kwakiutls in warfare (1955:267). Since the Comox had lost territory to the Kwakiutls, they may have fostered these alliances in the hope of reducing Kwakiutl warfare at their expense. This process does not explain why all the Coast Salish had proved willing to take on a system of social classes. It only provides evidence of one avenue by which Kwakiutl concepts and practices could move into Salish society. Very likely similar paths were provided by the association of the Nootkas with the Coast Salish of southern Vancouver Island and the adjacent Washington mainland.

Does part of the explanation lie in a human tendency to bring the supernatural under control? The rigorous demands of the old Salish religion, which emphasized prolonged fasting in isolation, did not guarantee results. Individuals approaching spiritual beings in these traditional ways still could be rebuffed or even harmed. Getting super-natural help depended on the wishes of the spirits, who did not always share their thinking with human beings. In contrast, being able to obtain the help of a spiritual being by joining a secret society was both certain (depending on ancestry and wealth) and relatively easy.

The relationship between the development of the social-class system and religious beliefs and practices is pertinent here. The evidence from both the Coast Salish and the Bella Coolas suggests that the social-class system became well entrenched, while the religious system was changing much more slowly to coincide with it. Shifts in Coast Salish religious life seemed to strengthen the position of the upper class in relation to the lower. It is usual in other parts of the world to find that religious practices, and, in some cases, their logics as well, support the social-class system. The old Salish guardian spirit religion, which did not incorporate social-class differences, was moving in this direction.

Radcliffe-Brown's working hypothesis is applicable here: "Whenever marked functional inconsistencies occur, they tend to produce change and the tendency continues until the inconsistencies are resolved" (1935:351). In the Coast Salish case the inconsistencies were never resolved, although trends toward that end were apparent. Among the Bella Coolas, the inconsistencies had become much fainter, being replaced by a relatively high level of integration between the logics of the society and its social structure.

# References

Barnett, Homer G.
    1955     The Coast Salish of British Columbia. Eugene: University of Oregon Press.
Boas, Franz
    1966     Kwakiutl Ethnography, edited by Helen Codere. Chicago: University of Chicago Press.
Collins, June McCormick
    1974a    The Influence of White Contact on Class Distinctions and Political Authority among the Indians of Northern Puget Sound. In Coast Salish and Western Washington Indians, vol. 2, 89–204. New York: Garland Publishing.
    1974b    Valley of the Spirits: The Upper Skagit Indians of Western Washington. American Ethnological Society Monograph 56. Seattle: University of Washington Press.
    1979     Multilineal Descent: A Coast Salish Strategy. In Currents in Anthropology: Essays in Honor of Sol Tax, edited by Robert Hinshaw, 243–69. The Hague: Mouton.

Costello, J. A.
  1895      The Siwash, Their Life Legends and Tales. Seattle: Calvert Company.
            Reprint. Seattle: Shorey Book Store, 1967.
Drucker, Philip
  1951      The Northern and Central Nootkan Tribes. Smithsonian Institution, Bureau
            of American Ethnology Bulletin 144. Washington, D.C.
Duff, Wilson
  1952      The Upper Stalo Indians of the Fraser Valley, British Columbia. Anthropology
            in British Columbia, Memoirs of the British Columbia Provincial Museum
            no. 1. Victoria.
Eggan, Fred
  1955      Social Anthropology: Methods and Results. *In* Social Anthropology of North
            American Tribes, edited by Fred Eggan, 485-551. Enlarged ed. Chicago:
            University of Chicago Press.
Elmendorf, William W.
  1948      The Cultural Setting of the Twana Secret Society. American Anthropologist
            50:625-33.
  1974      Structure of Twana Culture. *In* Coast Salish and Western Washington Indians,
            vol. 4, 27-576. New York: Garland Publishing.
Ernst, Alice Henson
  1952      The Wolf Ritual of the Northwest Coast. Eugene: University of Oregon Press.
Haeberlin, Hermann, and Erna Gunther
  1930      The Indians of Puget Sound. University of Washington Publications in
            Anthropology no. 4. Seattle: University of Washington Press.
Jenness, Diamond
  1955      The Faith of a Coast Salish Indian. Anthropology in British Columbia, edited
            by Wilson Duff, 3-92. Memoirs of the British Columbia Provincial Museum
            no. 3. Victoria.
Kuper, Adam, ed.
  1977      The Social Anthropology of Radcliffe-Brown. London: Routledge and Kegan
            Paul.
Mandelbaum, May
  1938      The Individual Life Cycle. *In* The Sinkaietk or Southern Okanogan of
            Washington, edited by Leslie Spier, 101-29. General Series in Anthropology
            6. Menasha, Wisc.
McIlwraith, Thomas F.
  1948      The Bella Coola Indians. 2 vols. Toronto: University of Toronto Press.
Radcliffe-Brown, A. R.
  1935      Kinship Terminologies in California. American Anthropologist 37:530-35.
  1951      The Comparative Method in Social Anthropology. Journal of the Royal
            Anthropological Institute 81:15-22.
Ray, Verne F.
  1933      The Sanpoil and Nespelem. University of Washington Publications in
            Anthropology no. 5. Seattle: University of Washington Press.
  1939      Cultural Relations in the Plateau of Northwestern America. Publications of
            the Frederick Webb Hodge Anniversary Publication Fund, vol. 3. Los
            Angeles: Southwest Museum.

Ruyle, Eugene
  1973      Slavery, Surplus and Stratification on the Northwest Coast. Current Anthro-
              pology 14:603-31.
Suttles, Wayne P.
  1974      The Economic Life of the Coast Salish of Haro and Rosario Straits. *In* Coast
              Salish and Western Washington Indians, vol. 1, 41-512. New York: Garland
              Publishing.
Taylor, Herbert C., Jr.
  1974      The Medicine Creek Tribes. *In* Coast Salish and Western Washington Indians,
              vol. 2, 401-73. New York: Garland Publishing.
Teit, James A.
  1930      The Salishan Tribes of the Western Plateau. Smithsonian Institution, Forty-
              Fifth Annual Report of the Bureau of American Ethnology, 23-396.
              Washington, D.C.
Walters, L. V. W.
  1938      Social Structure. *In* The Sinkaietk or Southern Okanogan of Washington,
              edited by Leslie Spier, 71-99. General Series in Anthropology 6. Menasha,
              Wisc.

# 4

# Central Algonkian Moieties

CHARLES CALLENDER

Most Central Algonkian tribes lacked moiety systems, in the classical sense of "half-tribes" based on unilineal descent (Lowie 1948:240). However, among the Iroquois to the east and the Chiwere and Dhegiha Siouans to the west, classical moieties were important social units with multiple functions (Fenton 1978:310-11; Fletcher and La Flesche 1911: 134-41; Radin 1923; cf. Lurie 1978:694-95). Their distribution among the intervening Central Algonkians—Sauks, Fox, Kickapoos, Potawatomis, Shawnees, Menominis, and the various Miami and Illinois tribes—was very limited. These societies fell into three groups, one with classical moieties, another with nonunilineal dual divisions, and a third with neither system.

Moieties based on clans were reported for the Menominis and Miamis, and may be attributed to the Illinois. Like those of neighboring Siouan tribes, these moieties were associated with Earth and Sky. The Menomini forms apparently had important political functions, besides determining seating at tribal councils and structuring opposition in lacrosse games (Hoffman 1896:131-35; Keesing 1939:36-37), but the details of these roles have been obscured by extensive changes in social structure after the fur trade was introduced in the late seventeenth century (Spindler 1978: 712-13). Even less is known about Miami moieties, reported in 1825 by Charles Trowbridge (1938:18), who gives little information beyond noting their existence. They had disappeared by 1860, when the clan system itself was disintegrating (Morgan 1959:80). While no direct evidence confirms moieties among the Illinois, their cultural and linguistic similarities to the Miamis provide grounds for assuming their presence.

The Sauks, Fox, Potawatomis, and Kickapoos have dual divisions that are in no respect descent groups (Callender 1978a:616-17). The first three tribes assign siblings alternately to opposite divisions by their order of birth, producing units that crosscut clans, lineages, and families. The Kickapoos assign some clans to one division or the other, producing an incomplete semblance of Siouan or Iroquoian moieties; but siblings are

108

named into different clans and the clans themselves are no longer unilineal descent groups. The functions of these dual divisions are much more restricted than those of Siouan or Iroquoian moieties. Divorced from political organization, they also lack the complex symbolism of the Omaha forms, which involved Earth-Sky and female-male oppositions as well as the concept of moieties as halves that had to be combined for tribal action and welfare (Fletcher and La Flesche 1911:134-41). The divisions determine seating and other kinds of placement at some public events, including rituals. Their most obvious role is to provide a basis for opposition and rivalry within each tribe by organizing competition in games and contests and by prescribed joking across divisional lines. What might be called integrative functions are much less obvious except for their crosscutting of the patrilineal descent groups that formerly characterized these tribes (cf. Eggan 1950:117).

The Shawnees stood apart from the other Central Algonkians, lacking any kind of moiety system or groups comparable to dual divisions. Opposition and reciprocity were based partly on name group (or clan) affiliation, and partly on gender in forms reminiscent of the Iroquois recognition of male and female principles (cf. Fenton 1978:310-11).

## Fox Moieties

The historical development of Fox social organization has been reconstructed by Ives Goddard (1975), who argues that at the time of contact, in the mid-seventeenth century, each Fox clan had its own village; that these clans were grouped into moieties that later disappeared as such; and that the dual divisions originated in a nineteenth-century expansion of warrior societies to provide moiety functions. The first issue, while relevant to the history of Fox social structure, is not directly involved in the moiety question and will not be dealt with here. The relatively abundant data for this tribe make it a good starting point for approaching the general problem of Central Algonkian dual divisions.

Goddard's argument that a classical moiety system formerly characterized the Fox rests on two points. First, Truman Michelson's accounts of Fox ceremonies in the early part of this century show a consistent grouping of clans for reciprocal ritual services, with the Bear and Wolf clans constituting one group and the Eagle, Fox, and Thunder the other (Fisher in Jones 1939:79). This reciprocity divides the five clans into two groups, although omitting all other clans. His second indication of moieties is Bacqueville de la Potherie's description of the seventeenth-century Fox as consisting of two "*extractions*" (lineages) calling themselves Fox and Red-

Earth (Blair 1911-12, 1:360). *Meškwahki·haki* or Red Earths is the name the Fox currently use for themselves, while *Fox* is the usual outsiders' designation for the tribe.

Although the limitation of reciprocal services to five clans might seem to weaken the argument for the prior existence of a moiety system, it actually strengthens the case. Lists of Fox clans, like those for most Central Algonkian tribes, show marked disagreement outside a central core (cf. Michelson 1925:501). This diversity stems ultimately from the nature of these clans, which among the Sauks, Fox, Kickapoos, and Potawatomis are simultaneously name-owning groups and cults whose corporate property is ritual in nature (Callender 1978a:613-14; Tax 1955). A clan as a cult sponsors ceremonies based on the sacred objects it owns; members of clans with which it is linked in reciprocity help stage these ceremonies and serve at them. Only some clans own such objects and constitute cults. Although clan affiliation was formerly determined by patrilineal descent, it now rests on one's personal name, which among the Fox is still usually taken from one's father's clan. Even in the past, patrilineality seems to have been stronger as concept than practice.

A more immediate factor, operating in conjunction with these innate characteristics, was the incorporation of outsiders through shifts in residence and extensive intermarriage across tribal boundaries. Whatever conditions may have existed before contact, when these four tribes lived in lower Michigan and northern Ohio, mixed settlements and intermarriage were very common by the middle of the seventeenth century after they had moved to Wisconsin. In the years from 1665 to 1667 Claude Jean Allouez described the Sauks and Fox as mingled with the Potawatomis (Thwaites 1896-1901, 51:43). Slightly later Nicolas Perrot (1911-12, 1:270) characterized the Potawatomis as half Sauk, and the Sauks as part Fox. Outsiders coming into a tribe were assigned to clans according to their personal names, either affiliating them with an existing clan or introducing a new one. This process of incorporating members of other tribes continued through the nineteenth century as small Indian groups who had evaded relocation gravitated toward the nearest reservations.

Lists of Fox clans, such as the thirteen units William Jones (1939: 74-75) recorded about 1900, were actually lists of the clans represented among residents of the Fox community, defined by their names. Most of them were very small groups, really clanlets, that did not function as cults and, according to genealogies later collected by Sol Tax, were Sauk, Potawatomi, or Winnebago in origin. Disagreement centered on these clanlets, with informants often denying the existence of one or another (Michelson 1925:501). By 1917 the Fox achieved some surface uniformity by grouping most of them into a Fish clan (Fisher in Jones 1939:75; cf. Tax 1955:269, n. 6; Callender 1962:27 who erroneously calls this a phratry). This so-called clan lacked rituals and its stocks of personal names belonged to constituent lineages without being collectively owned. Arguments about the clanlets it included were as frequent in 1954 as earlier.

By 1954 only five Fox clans were cult groups that owned and performed rituals: Bear, Fox (or War Chief), Wolf, Thunder, and Eagle. These conditions held early in this century; Michelson does not list any other clans as giving ceremonies. The first four are very large groups, comprising most of the tribe. The Eagle clan, smaller than many accreted clanlets, had almost died out by 1932, when it numbered only twelve persons (Tax 1955:265) and its one male was elderly. Yet it has remained ritually active, maintained as a demographically viable unit by giving Eagle names to persons whose fathers belonged to other clans. The ritual activity of the Eagle clan and the obvious Fox concern with its perpetuation significantly differentiate this unit from the clanlets (some of which have died out) and show that in spite of its small size it ranks in importance with the four large clans.

The five clans functioning as cult groups in 1954 were those described by the tribal chief around 1900 as the original Fox clans (Jones 1939:76). His statement is supported by evidence for their existence at the time of contact. In 1672 Allouez named four groups—the Ouagousak, Makoua, Makoucoue, and Mikissioua—which were included in the Jesuit mission to the Fox (Thwaites 1896-1901, 58:40). Goddard (1975) convincingly presents the linguistic evidence to translate these names as Fox, Bear, Wolf, and Eagle, and identifies them as clans. While Allouez said nothing about the Thunder clan, its existence at the time is suggested by other evidence. Pemoussa, a Fox chief at Detroit in 1712, apparently had the Thunder clan name *pe·mosa·ha* (cf. Goddard 1975; Jones 1939:143). Goddard's conclusion seems entirely reasonable that if at the time of European contact only these five clans existed, the reciprocal grouping of Bear and Wolf against Eagle, Fox, and Thunder, would have constituted a moiety system.

Goddard provisionally identifies la Potherie's two *extractions* as Sky and Earth moieties, suggesting that the Sky or Fox moiety included the Fox, Eagle, and Thunder clans while the Earth or Red Earth moiety comprised the Bear and Wolf. On the occasion la Potherie described, Nicolas Perrot visited the Fox tribe in 1683 to persuade them to end hostilities with the Ottawa and Ojibwa and release a captive Ojibwa girl. The chief of the Fox *extraction* holding this position as replacement for his brother, whom the Ojibwa had recently killed, repeatedly rejected Perrot's request to smoke the calumet and come to terms. The Red Earth chief intervened, persuading him to settle the affair. Goddard, following Fisher (Jones 1939:76), identifies the contrasting behavior of the two leaders as those characteristic of war and peace chiefs, respectively. On that basis he suggests that, like the Menomini system, the Sky moiety of the Fox provided the war chief and the Earth moiety the peace chief. He also notes that the Fox peace chief traditionally belonged to the Bear clan and that War Chief is the alternative name for the Fox clan. While that argument is stimulating, I think the evidence is not yet sufficient to identify these *extractions* as moieties, associate them with Earth and Sky, or assume they divided peace and war functions.

While the behavior of the Red Earth chief resembled the moderating actions of a tribal or peace chief, the chief of the Fox *extraction* seems to have been acting from personal grievance over his brother's death rather than exercising the duties of a war chief. The *extraction* he headed might have been simply his clan, rather than a moiety. The two *extractions* may even have been factions rather than descent groups. Records showing that the tribal chief came from the Bear clan have a shallow time depth. One Fox tradition holds that the line of chiefs changed about 1829. We do not know whether this was only a shift from one Bear lineage to another, like one made in 1883, or whether it involved two different clans. The Fox, or War Chief, clan once included a lineage called Peace Chief or Kindly Chief, whose role has never been described, to which *či·koškaka*, whom the United States agent appointed to replace the hereditary Fox chief in 1859, belonged (cf. Jones 1939:138, 141). Whether this lineage affiliation legitimized his abortive assumption of office is uncertain, but the name of his descent group raises the possibility that it once provided the tribal chief.

While I have reservations about Goddard's identification of la Potherie's *extractions* as Earth and Sky moieties, I agree that the seventeenth-century Fox clans were probably grouped into moieties whose traces persist in the present system of ceremonial reciprocity.

## Sauk and Kickapoo Moieties

If clan-based moieties formerly characterized the Fox they should also have existed among the Sauks and Kickapoos, the tribes most closely related to them in language and culture. Investigating this broader aspect of the problem is much more difficult. Comparable data from the contact period are lacking, and information from later times is much scantier.

Lists of Sauk clans show the same discrepancies as their Fox counterparts, stemming from similar causes. A definite resolution of these disagreements like that proposed for the Fox is inhibited by the lack of demographic and genealogical data facilitating the distinction of true clans from clanlets, a much broader shift in this century from patrilineal clans to non-descent-name groups, and much less information about clan rituals. Seven reasonably authentic lists ranging from 1826 to 1955 (Callender 1955; Forsyth 1911-12, 2:190-91; Galland 1869:350; Hewitt 1910; Michelson n.d.a and n.d.b; Skinner 1923-25, 1:13) generally agree upon eleven clans: Bear, Bear Potato, Black Bass, Deer, Eagle, Fox, Ringed Perch, Sea, Sturgeon, Thunder, and Wolf. Although the Sauks, a larger tribe than the Fox, are consistently described as having more clans (cf. Forsyth 1911-12, 2:190-92) that number seems excessive and probably includes accreted clanlets. A statement that only four Sauk clans were really important (Michelson 1927:3) should probably not be taken literally, given the sacred character of the number four, but it points in the same direction.

The Fox system of clan reciprocity, based on accounts of specific ceremonies, is clear. Corresponding information for the Sauks is limited to three very general accounts that often disagree. Isaac Galland (1869:350) describes a division of clans into "chiefs" and "waiters," instituted by the culture hero *wi·sahke·ha*. These groups were defined by services at rituals, which in spite of Galland's labels were reciprocal. Leaving out clans other sources do not confirm, the "chiefs" include the Bear, Ringed Perch, Sturgeon, Sea, Eagle, and Thunder; the "waiters" are the Bear Potato, Deer, Wolf, and Fox. Accounts of ritual reciprocity by Alanson Skinner (1923-25, 1:13-14) and Mark Harrington (1914:162-63) also combine Bear with Ringed Perch, Sturgeon, and perhaps other clans with fish eponyms into one group and Bear, Potato, Deer, and Wolf into another, although otherwise disagreeing. While the evidence is scanty and many details are unrecoverable, there are definite indications of a system of clan reciprocity among the Sauks, best described by Galland, that could, as among the Fox, represent traces of an earlier moiety system.

Establishing the identity of Kickapoo clans and distinguishing them from clanlets is complicated by this tribe's division between sections in Oklahoma and Mexico. Accretions exist, perhaps including all the clans that seem extinct or are reduced to one member (Dillingham 1963:125; Latorre and Latorre 1976:152-53). The four ritually active Mexican Kickapoo clans—Bear, Berry, Buffalo, and Thunder—are also the large clans, to which their smaller counterparts are attached for ceremonies. Rituals among the Oklahoma Kickapoos are also limited to four clans: Berry, Eagle, Raccoon, and Tree.

Two very different kinds of clan groupings are reported for the Kickapoos. One is the assignment of entire clans to the dual divisions. Betty Ann Dillingham (1963:126-27) places Bear, Buffalo, Eagle, and Fox in the *oskasa* division, with the *kiiskooha* division including Berry, Raccoon,

Tree, and Water. The Man and Thunder clans are not assigned; apparently their members may belong to either division. The Divisional clan assignments are even less complete among the Mexican Kickapoo, limited to defining Buffalo as *oskasa* and Berry as *kiiskooha* (Latorre and Latorre 1976:156). While at first sight the Oklahoma Kickapoo groups seem to resemble classical clan-based moieties except for their incompleteness, individuals take their clan and divisional affiliations from relatives selected by their parents to give them names, and parents tend to alternate in choosing namers (Dillingham 1963:120, 126).

Clans are also grouped by reciprocal services in ritual. Ceremonial reciprocity among the Oklahoma Kickapoos combines Berry with Eagle against Raccoon and Tree (Dillingham 1963:148-49) in a pattern different from assignment of those clans to divisions. The Mexican Kickapoos oppose Thunder and Buffalo to Man and Berry (Latorre and Latorre 1976:286-87). Even though details are unclear, the Kickapoo system of ceremonial reciprocity, like Sauk and Fox practice, may be interpreted as the remnants of an older moiety system.

## Potawatomi

The Potawatomis, stemming from a very different cultural background (Callender 1962:83; Clifton 1977; Landes 1970:3-4), were strongly influenced by the Sauks, Fox, and Kickapoos after contact and had clans of the same general type. Skinner (1924-27, 1:18-19) reported an elaborate threefold arrangement of services at clan rituals by the three positions of host, waiter, and speaker but his account is incomplete, often contradictory, and the system he describes is frequently not reciprocal. Unable to find any traces of clan reciprocity in 1935 and 1936, Ruth Landes (1970:288) suggested that Skinner's account was perhaps an artifact of his main informant. This apparent absence of ceremonial reciprocity among Potawatomi clans strengthens the argument for considering it an old pattern among the Sauks, Fox, and Kickapoos, antedating the beginning of their close association with the Potawatomis around 1650.

## Shawnee

The Shawnee name groups described by C. F. and E. W. Voegelin (1935) may also be relevant to the problem of Central Algonkian moieties. In 1933 and 1934 these units, evolved from an older system of patrilineal clans, numbered six, each owning sets of names referring to groups of eponyms.

The Horse name group combined hoofed animals such as deer, buffalo, and elk; Rounded-Foot, carnivores such as fox and wolf; Coon, raccoon and bear; Turtle, all aquatic forms; and Turkey, all birds. Rabbit names designated a gentle and peaceful disposition, rather than specifically referring to any animal.

Shawnee rituals, owned and performed by the political and territorial groups called divisions (Voegelin 1936), did not involve reciprocal services among the name groups, whose interrelations were instead defined by joking and teasing behavior resembling that between dual divisions in other tribes. Rather than each name group opposing all the others in joking, Horse and Rounded-Foot were allied in opposition to a similar alliance of Turtle and Turkey. The very small Coon name group stood alone, without allies, but was particularly opposed to Turkey. This set of alliances and oppositions produced a dichotomy separating land animals from birds and water beings, groupings that the reciprocal systems of the Sauk-Fox-Kickapoo series tended to mingle. While Rabbit was omitted, its names seem to symbolize disposition, without specific eponymous reference, and in any case numbered only one percent of those identified.

The Voegelins deny that these name-group interrelations functioned outside the joking context, but some information they present suggests that their role might once have been broader. Ritual leadership in the Spring Bread Dance, centering on agriculture, was held by members of the Turtle or Turkey groups, while Horse or Rounded-Foot persons exercised this in the Fall Bread Dances, which focused on hunting. One informant described a system of burial reciprocity by name group affiliation, conforming to the joking pattern, and with Coon and Rabbit again holding anomalous positions. This evidence, taken as a whole and including the joking alignments, raises a possibility that the present alliances and oppositions among name groups represent traces of a moiety division, although the argument is much weaker than that for the Sauk-Fox-Kickapoo series.

## The Loss of Moieties

Goddard credits the seventeenth-century Fox with a moiety system whose features included organized opposition as well as ritual reciprocity. He attributes its disappearance to heavy population losses during the eighteenth-century wars with the French and allied Indians, replaced by the large-scale adoption of outsiders belonging to other tribes. These increments introduced new clans lacking the ceremonies of those making up the moiety system, which did not expand to incorporate the accretions and eventually could no longer effectively structure competitive opposition, although ritual reciprocity continued. Moieties thus disappeared as formal units. Rival warrior societies, not based on clan affiliation, later expanded into dual divisions to provide structured opposition.

Some elements of this process undoubtedly occurred. But anthropologists and historians have probably exaggerated the demographic effects of the French wars on Fox population. Even more important, if moieties once characterized the Fox-Sauk-Kickapoo series, and perhaps even the Shawnee, an explanation for their disappearance or transformation must be sought beyond the specific historical experiences of the Fox.

Fisher (Jones 1939:1-7) presents in its most extreme form the traditional view of the consequences of the French wars for the Fox. She describes the Fox as having been repeatedly almost wiped out, each time regenerating themselves by adopting captives and repatriating captive members of their own tribe. Assuming that the outsiders and even the repatriated Fox brought in alien material significantly changing the traditional culture, she warns against assuming that recent Fox culture reflects older Central Algonkian forms. Yet wherever earlier sociocultural forms can be discerned, the Fox have clearly retained them more completely than any other group except perhaps, and only in some respects, the Mexican Kickapoos (Callender, Pope, and Pope 1978:666). The Fox still have the clans that were reported for them at contact, and apparently most closely approximate their earlier grouping into moieties. Fox population certainly diminished during the eighteenth-century wars, but French accounts of those losses were grossly inflated. Little independent evidence corroborates French claims that they ever approached their goal of destroying the Fox, whose eventual offer to surrender was probably impelled by the constant movement needed to evade attack.

In any case, the incorporation of outsiders and the consequent introduction of new clans also characterized the Sauks, whose eighteenth-century history was very different. Similar practices may be assumed for the Kickapoos, culminating in their absorption of the related Mascoutens (Goddard 1978). These processes could have weakened moiety systems in the ways Goddard suggests. Yet it seems probable that if the moieties were not already very weak they could have adjusted to take in new groups, using techniques like the Mexican Kickapoo practice of attaching clanlets to the clans owning ceremonies.

The absence of any evidence that clan-based moieties ever existed among the Potawatomis, as noted above, is reason to assume that they characterized the Sauks, Fox, and Kickapoos before the contact period, when they were living in southeastern Michigan and northern Ohio. This assumption draws some support from the slight indications that such moieties might once have been present among the Shawnees, who share old cultural ties with these tribes (Callender 1978b:622).

In his archeological analysis of the western Lake Erie basin, G. Michael Pratt (1981:135-73) distinguishes a Sandusky tradition, appearing about A.D. 1000 and continuing until the middle of the seventeenth century, which he interprets as representing the spread of Upper Mississippian cultural features derived from a Fort Ancient source to northwest Ohio, later extending into southeastern Michigan. This Sandusky tradition seems to be the archeological representative of the historical Sauks and Fox—and perhaps the Mascoutens—occupying the same areas they held shortly before contact. Fort Ancient culture is probably represented historically by the Shawnees. Marian White's identification of Chautauqua Lake on Nicolas Sanson's map of 1656 (1978:413, 415) suggests that the Kickapoos, whom he placed west of that lake under their Huron name Ontarraronen, may be equated with Whittlesey culture, along the southern shores of Lake Erie, which also showed Fort Ancient affinities.

During the 1640s the Sauks, Fox, Kickapoos, and Mascoutens, under the collective name Assistaronons, came under heavy attack by the Neutrals, who were armed with European weapons (Trigger 1976:624-25). These Neutral campaigns, or the even more devastating attacks the Five Nations Iroquois launched in the next decade, drove those tribes out of their areas and eventually they settled in Wisconsin. Detailed knowledge of their flight and resettlement is lost. A Miami tradition recorded by Charles Trowbridge (1938:69) indicates that the Kickapoos fled down the Wabash. Galinee's report that in 1668 the Senecas placed the Outagames or Fox on the lower Ohio (Kellogg 1917:171), if not a complete misunderstanding, could suggest a similar move by this tribe. Population losses—through epidemics as well as warfare and perhaps the period of unsettled habitation—may have been severe enough to damage the moiety systems irreparably. Conditions in Wisconsin would not have encouraged the revival of these structures. The intertribal settlements common during the early years of contact, combined with the tendency for tribal segments to split off, probably emphasized clans as social units that could be easily equated across tribal boundaries—more easily than moieties. Ritual reciprocity between specific clans that owned ceremonies could have persisted as other features of moieties disappeared, along with their formal recognition as social units.

## Dual Divisions

All the tribes with dual divisions use essentially the same term for one of these units: Sauk and Fox *ki·ško·ha*, Kickapoo *kiiskooha*, and Potawatomi *kišk·o*. The Fox call the opposite division *to·hka·na*, a name apparently borrowed from the *tukala* society of the Iowas (Michelson 1925:548). Its Sauk name, *aškaša*, corresponds to Kickapoo *oskasa* and Potawatomi *wšk·əš*.

The Fox assign the first child born to a couple to the division opposite that of its father, the second child to the father's division, and so on alternately. The Potawatomis usually assign the first born to the *wšk·əš* and the next to the *kišk·o*, but if either parent owns a sacred pack, all the children are placed in the same division as its ancestral owner, while members of a religious society may in that context regard themselves as belonging to the same division but in other contexts retain their original affiliation (Landes 1970:204). Formerly following the Fox rules, the Sauks have shifted to the basic Potawatomi rules. Kickapoo practice, which also seems to rest ultimately on birth order, assigns a child to the division of the person chosen to name it.

Defined as rivals, the divisions formerly organized competition for war honors and still determine sides in games and contests and positions at some public events, besides providing a framework for institutionalized joking. The *ki·ško·ha* division is associated with south and with white or light colors; the *aškaša* (or *to·hka·na*), with north and black or dark colors.

Goddard's hypothesis that the dual divisions were originally warrior societies rests primarily on the earliest descriptions of these groups, by Morrell Marston (1911-12, 2:156-57) in 1820 and Thomas Forsyth (1911-12, 2:192-94) in 1826. Both described the Sauk divisions as rival associations of warriors. Goddard also notes that adopting the name of an Iowa warrior society for one of their divisions suggests that the Fox equated them with such societies, rather than with the Iowa moieties. I agree, but the tendency of some Fox families of Winnebago origin to assign all their offspring to one division could imply their equation of these units with moieties, while the Kickapoo pseudomoieties might have similar implications.

I believe that Marston and Forsyth overlooked other features of the divisions as well as the fact that they included both genders. Agreeing that membership was assigned at birth and that siblings alternated, they describe different rules for the dual divisions that are not confirmed by later studies of the Sauks. This error suggests they may have misunderstood other aspects of the divisions in describing them as associations of warriors.

Moreover, it seems almost impossible that a shift from warrior societies to dual divisions incorporating the entire population occurred among these four tribes between 1826 and 1900.

Nevertheless, Goddard's hypothesis seems tenable if the time period for that shift is pushed back, perhaps to the early contact period. Evidence for warrior societies before 1820 is lacking. Frank Speck (1909:24) noted that although Yuchi descent was matrilineal, membership in the two men's societies was patrilineal, and he suggested that these societies showed some resemblance to the early-nineteenth-century accounts of the Sauk divisions. Given indications of an old Yuchi relationship with the Shawnees (Callender 1978b:623), one could construct a very tenuous working hypothesis, based on almost no evidence, and assume that a system of two men's societies was shared by the Yuchis, Shawnees, Sauks, Fox, and Kickapoos. When massive Iroquoian attacks at the close of the precontact period, followed by extensive tribal movements, crippled clan-based moieties, the Sauks, Fox, and Kickapoos eventually shifted intratribal opposition to the men's societies, opening them to everyone and perhaps revising membership rules to ensure a permanent division of each tribe into two units of approximately equal size that prevented significant numerical imbalance. Through close association with these tribes after contact the Potawatomis borrowed dual divisions.

## Conclusions

While differing with Goddard to some extent about the processes and time periods involved, I substantially agree that the Fox dual divisions represent an expansion of warrior societies to replace an early system of clan-based moieties, still reflected in ceremonial reciprocity. I think this hypothesis can be extended to the Sauks and Kickapoos. I suggest, much more tentatively, that a similar moiety system might have characterized the precontact Shawnees and is now represented only by their alignment of name groups for joking.

Whatever validity these reconstructions may have, they do not seem to explain certain features of these units. Contemporary Central Algonkians have at least two systems of dual organization, using this term in Robert H. Lowie's (1948:240–47) sense of social units rather than the more symbolic-structural approach followed in recent analyses (e.g., Ortiz 1965, 1969).

One system, the dual divisions, has as far back as records go consisted of nondescent groups. Unrelated to marriage regulations, political organization, or settlement pattern, these groups do not perform reciprocal services for each other and express only the oppositional aspects of dual organization by structuring competition and joking. They are also symmetrical. Forsyth's ascription of higher rank to the Sauk *ki·ško·ha* division (Blair 1911-12, 2:193) is unclear and not supported by later studies. The Potawatomi reference to their divisions as senior and junior denotes only birth order—the oldest sibling always being *wšk·aš*—rather than differences in status. While every member of these societies belongs to a division, from the standpoint of dual organization these units are incomplete, with limited functions.

The second system of dual organization, implicit and not openly recognized or described as such, consists of reciprocal services at ceremonies between groups of clans that were formerly patrilineal but are now weakly so among the Fox and hardly unilineal at all among the Sauks and Kickapoos. The Potawatomis lack such a system. It has no connection with marriage. Relations between these clan groups take the form of providing services at ceremonies: issuing invitations, setting out the ritual paraphernalia, killing animals for the feast, cooking, and serving food. Asymmetry is confined to the ceremony itself, reversing when the clans performing these services host their own rituals.

The role of reciprocal clan groups extended beyond ritual into traditional political organization, but in limited ways. The Fox tribal chief belonged to the Bear clan, while their war chief came from the Fox clan in the reciprocal group. A Fish clan provided the Sauk chief; their war chief again belonged to the Fox clan, in the opposite group. Although war-peace dualism was an important feature of traditional Central Algonkian cultures, the reciprocal clan groupings do not seem to have been really associated with this contrast. Rather, each group provided an important chief. Thus, the Oklahoma Kickapoo tribal chief came from the Raccoon clan, while the reciprocal Eagle clan furnished a second chief. In spite of its connection with political structure, this second kind of dual organization is also incomplete, in two respects. First, its tribal role, like that of the dual divisions, contains only part of the usual features of moieties—in this case integration. Second, unlike the divisions, it includes only part of each tribe, even if the greater part. Members of clans without ceremonies are not part of this system.

One could perhaps identify the split between opposed political factions as still a third dual organization (cf. Eggan 1950:303), again limited in function and membership, with the further difference that individuals shift their affiliation.

The Central Algonkians existed under natural conditions that Alfonso Ortiz (1969:132) associates with the existence of dual organizations: a pronounced climatic change between the two halves of the year, a dual subsistence system (in two respects, including not only the seasonal alternation between summer agriculture and winter hunting and trapping, but the distinction between women carrying on agriculture and men hunting) and population movement between the summer village and winter camps. Yet the four tribes examined here consistently fail to carry dual organizations through to completion—whether in function, structure, or both. Even the Kickapoo pseudomoieties, which could unite both the main forms of dual organization, do not, and show the characteristic lack of completion. If the oppositions and alliances in joking among Shawnee name groups are viewed as a form of dual organization, these are also incomplete.

This feature could be interpreted as one diagnostic of systems in decay, yet it has persisted since at least the early nineteenth century and probably long before then, while the more complete dual organizations of related tribes, such as clan-based moieties, disappeared entirely. Either these cultures exist in conditions where this lack of completeness has advantages, or completeness is somehow achieved at another level in their still unexplicated symbolic systems.

## Acknowledgments

This chapter was written in 1981. Following the author's death in 1985 the manuscript was prepared for publication by the editors with the help of Ives Goddard, whose systematization of the writing of the native language terms is gratefully acknowledged.

## References

Blair, Emma H., ed.
  1911-12  The Indian Tribes of the Upper Mississippi Valley and Region of the Great Lakes. 2 vols. Cleveland: Arthur H. Clark.
Callender, Charles
  1955  Fieldnotes of Investigations among the Sauk. Manuscript in Department of Anthropology, University of Chicago.
  1962  Social Organization of the Central Algonkian Indians. Milwaukee Public Museum Publications in Anthropology, no. 7.
  1978a  Great Lakes-Riverine Sociopolitical Organization. In Handbook of North American Indians, vol. 15, edited by Bruce G. Trigger, 610-21. Washington, D.C.: Smithsonian Institution.
  1978b  Shawnee. In Handbook of North American Indians, vol. 15, edited by Bruce G. Trigger, 622-35. Washington, D.C.: Smithsonian Institution.
Callender, Charles, Richard K. Pope, and Susan M. Pope
  1978  Kickapoo. In Handbook of North American Indians, vol. 15, edited by Bruce G. Trigger, 656-67. Washington, D.C.: Smithsonian Institution.

Clifton, James A.
1977       The Prairie People: Continuity and Change in Potawatomi Culture, 1665-
           1965. Lawrence: Regents Press of Kansas.
Dillingham, Betty Ann (Wilder)
1963       The Oklahoma Kickapoo. Ph.D. diss., University of Michigan, Ann Arbor.
Eggan, Fred
1950       Social Organization of the Western Pueblos. Chicago: University of Chicago
           Press.
Fenton, William N.
1978       Northern Iroquoian Culture Patterns. In Handbook of North American Indians,
           vol. 15, edited by Bruce G. Trigger, 296-321. Washington, D.C.: Smithsonian
           Institution.
Fletcher, Alice C., and Francis La Flesche
1911       The Omaha Tribe. Smithsonian Institution, Twenty-Seventh Annual Report
           of the Bureau of American Ethnology. Washington, D.C.
Forsyth, Thomas
1911-12    An Account of the Manners and Customs of the Sauk and Fox Nations of
           Indian Traditions. In The Indian Tribes of the Upper Mississippi Valley and
           Region of the Great Lakes, edited by Emma H. Blair, vol. 2, 183-245.
           Cleveland: Arthur H. Clark.
Galland, Isaac
1869       The Indian Tribes of the West: Their Language, Religion, and Traditions.
           Annals of Iowa 7:347-66.
Goddard, Ives
1975       Fox Social Organization, 1650-1850. In Papers of the 6th Algonquian
           Conference, 1974, edited by William Cowan, 128-40. Canada National
           Museum of Man, Ethnology Division, Mercury Series Paper no. 23. Ottawa.
1978       Mascouten. In Handbook of North American Indians, vol. 15, edited by Bruce
           G. Trigger, 668-72. Washington, D.C.: Smithsonian Institution.
Harrington, Mark R.
1914       Sacred Bundles of the Sac and Fox. University of Pennsylvania Museum
           Anthropological Publications vol. 4. no. 2. Philadelphia.
Hewitt, J. N. B.
1910       Sauk. In Handbook of American Indians North of Mexico, vol. 2, edited by
           Frederick Webb Hodge, 471-80. Smithsonian Institution, Bureau of American
           Ethnology Bulletin 30. Washington, D.C.
Hoffman, Walter J.
1896       The Menomini Indians. In Smithsonian Institution, Fourteenth Annual Report
           of the Bureau of American Ethnology, vol. 1, 3-328. Washington, D.C.
Jones, William
1939       Ethnography of the Fox Indians. Edited by Margaret W. Fisher. Smithsonian
           Institution, Bureau of American Ethnology Bulletin 125. Washington, D.C.
Keesing, Felix M.
1939       The Menomini Indians of Wisconsin: A Study of Three Centuries of Culture
           Contact and Change. American Philosophical Society Memoir 10. Philadel-
           phia.
Kellogg, Louise (Phelps), ed.
1917       Early Narratives of the Northwest, 1634-1699. New York: Charles Scribner's

Sons.

Landes, Ruth
1970    The Prairie Potawatomi: Tradition and Ritual in the Twentieth Century.
        Madison: University of Wisconsin Press.

Latorre, Felipe A., and Dolores L. Latorre
1976    The Mexican Kickapoo Indians. Austin: University of Texas Press.

Lowie, Robert H.
1948    Social Anthropology. New York: Rinehart.

Lurie, Nancy O.
1978    Winnebago. In Handbook of North American Indians, vol. 15, edited by Bruce
        G. Trigger, 670-707. Washington, D.C.: Smithsonian Institution.

Marston, Morrell
1911-12 Letter to Reverend Dr. Jedidiah Morse. In The Indian Tribes of the Upper
        Mississippi Valley and Region of the Great Lakes, edited by Emma H. Blair,
        vol 2, 137-82. Cleveland: Arthur H. Clark.

Michelson, Truman
1925    Notes on the Fox Society Known as "Those Who Worship the Little Spotted
        Buffalo." Smithsonian Institution, Fortieth Annual Report of the Bureau of
        American Ethnology, 497-539. Washington, D.C.
1927    Contributions to Fox Ethnology. Smithsonian Institution, Bureau of American
        Ethnology Bulletin 85. Washington, D.C.
n.d.a   Sauk Linguistic Notes. National Anthropological Archives, Manuscript no.
        1432, Smithsonian Institution, Washington, D.C.
n.d.b   Sauk Linguistic Notes. National Anthropological Archives, Manuscript no.
        2803. Smithsonian Institution, Washington, D.C..

Morgan, Lewis H.
1959    The Indian Journals 1859-1862. Edited by Leslie A. White. Ann Arbor:
        University of Michigan Press.

Ortiz, Alfonso
1965    Dual Organization as an Operational Concept in the Pueblo Southwest.
        Ethnology 4:389-96.
1969    The Tewa World: Space, Time, Being, and Becoming in a Pueblo Society.
        Chicago: University of Chicago Press.

Perrot, Nicolas
1911-12 Memoir on the Manners, Customs, and Religions of the Savages of North
        America. In The Indian Tribes of the Upper Mississippi Valley and Region
        of the Great Lakes, edited by Emma H. Blair, vol. 1, 23-272. Cleveland:
        Arthur H. Clark.

Pratt, G. Michael
1981    The Western Basin Tradition. Ph.D. diss., Case Western Reserve University,
        Cleveland.

Radin, Paul
1923    The Winnebago Tribe. Smithsonian Institution, Thirty-Seventh Annual
        Report of the Bureau of American Ethnology. Washington, D.C.

Skinner, Alanson B.
1923-25 Observations on the Ethnology of the Sauk Indians. Public Museum of the City
        of Milwaukee Bulletin 5.
1924-27 The Mascoutens or Prairie Potawatomi Indians. Public Museum of the City

of Milwaukee Bulletin 6.

Speck, Frank G.
   1909      Ethnology of the Yuchi Indians. University of Pennsylvania Museum
             Anthropological Publications, vol. 1, no. 1. Philadelphia.

Spindler, Louise S.
   1978      Menominee. *In* Handbook of North American Indians, vol. 15, edited by Bruce
             G. Trigger, 708-24. Washington, D.C.: Smithsonian Institution.

Tax, Sol
   1955      The Social Organization of the Fox Indians. *In* Social Organization of North
             American Tribes, edited by Fred Eggan, 243-82. Enlarged ed. Chicago:
             University of Chicago Press.

Thwaites, Reuben Gold
   1896-1901 The Jesuit Relations and Allied Documents. 73 vols. Cleveland: Burrows
             Bros.

Trigger, Bruce G.
   1976      The Children of Aataentsic: A History of the Huron People to 1660. 2 vols.
             Montreal: McGill-Queen's University Press.

Trowbridge, Charles C.
   1938      Meearmeear Traditions. Edited by Vernon Kinietz. University of Michigan
             Museum of Anthropology Occasional Contributions, no. 7. Ann Arbor.

Voegelin, Charles F.
   1936      The Shawnee Female Deity. Yale University Publications in Anthropology
             10. New Haven.

Voegelin, Charles F., and Erminie W. Voegelin
   1935      Shawnee Name Groups. American Anthropologist 37:617-35.

White, Marian E.
   1978      Erie. *In* Handbook of North American Indians, vol. 15, edited by Bruce G.
             Trigger, 412-17. Washington, D.C.: Smithsonian Institution.

# 5

# Kinship and Biology in Sioux Culture

RAYMOND J. DEMALLIE

During the nineteenth century the Sioux Indians, who call themselves *dak'ota* and *lak'ota,* lived in an area that stretched from western Minnesota through North and South Dakota to Montana and Wyoming; they spoke three distinct dialects and were organized into politically autonomous groups.[1] Nonetheless, from the Santee groups in the east, through the intermediate Yankton-Yanktonai groups, to the Teton groups in the west, all the Sioux shared a common system of kin relationship. In the literature on North American Indian kinship systems, that of the Sioux has received an extraordinary degree of attention. Lewis Henry Morgan collected kin terms from eight different Sioux groups in the mid-nineteenth century and since then there have been at least ten other studies of Sioux kinship (see DeMallie 1979). Most notable among them is the work of Alexander Lesser (1930, 1958), who collected and compiled kin terminologies not only for each of the Sioux groups, but for all the tribes of the Siouan linguistic family, and provided a comparative analysis that is one of the most significant empirical studies of large-scale kinship change. Complementing Lesser's study, Ella Deloria (forthcoming) completed in about 1950 a detailed account of Sioux kinship based on personal experience, field study, and historical documents. Fred Eggan (1937, 1955, 1966) placed the work on Sioux kinship in comparative perspective with that on other North American Indian societies and suggested a variety of unsolved problems for further research.

Kinship is a particularly appropriate topic to study among the Sioux because their culture emphasizes the significance of kin relationship in much the same way that social anthropology has emphasized the importance of kinship systems. Eggan noted that for many societies, kinship has proven "the most useful index of social structure. In many societies the kinship system represents practically the entire social structure" (1950:10). For the Sioux, kinship provided what Deloria characterized as "a scheme of life that worked" (1944:24). Far from a scholarly abstraction, in Sioux society kinship provided the driving force of everyday life.

Most studies of the Sioux kinship system have been premised on a genealogical definition of relationship. Again quoting Eggan, "The kinship system consists of socially recognized relations between individuals who are genealogically and affinally connected, plus the set of social usages which normally prevails among them" (1950:10). Following A. R. Radcliffe-Brown, Eggan characterized the totality of these "socially recognized relations" as comprising the social structure, and the "social usages" as culturally defined patterns of behavior.

The forms of social structure are limited in number and each is necessarily well integrated since it provides for the orderly arrangement of society. In contrast, cultural patterns of social relations take a greater variety and require much less integration; or, rather, integration takes place at the individual level rather than that of the group. Importantly, social structures and cultural patterns may vary independently of one another, and therefore they must be analyzed separately (Eggan 1955:492-94).

The social structure of the Sioux has been amply documented (see bibliographical discussion in Walker 1982:8-13). Historically, Sioux society was organized in loose, bilateral bands. The kinship system was of the Iroquois (bifurcate merging) type, with Dakota-type cousin terms (classifying parallel cousins with siblings and differentiating them from cross cousins). Building on the foundation of previous social-structural studies, the present essay explores cultural perspectives: the definition of kinship in Sioux culture, its boundaries, origins, and uses.

Such a cultural analysis requires a relativistic stance; for the Sioux, kinship is not confined to the classification of relationship through links of marriage and descent, but is more broadly defined to embrace all significant social interaction. Schneider (1968, 1972, 1976, 1984) advocated using the concept of *symbols* to designate the building blocks of culture. As units of meaning, symbols embody cultural definitions and relationships; they describe the universe in a unique way, distinctive of a particular social group.

The symbols abstracted for the study of culture are based on analysis of the units and construction of the native language; analysis of native statements of belief and maxim; observation of behavior; and discussion with members of the group to clarify and expand understanding. Because culture as a symbol system is not observable directly, cultural descriptions are analytical and composite; they are models that attempt to account as fully as possible for all available data. They are also comparative by definition, since cultural description is necessarily a process of translation, explaining another culture's symbols in terms of our own—as Clifford Geertz expresses it, enlarging "the universe of human discourse" (1973:14).

# The Gift of Kinship

Like all other fundamentals of Sioux culture, kinship was the gift of *wak'aŋ t'áŋka,* the "great spirits," brought by the White Buffalo Cow Woman, their messenger. The following is an extract from the sacred story as told in 1914 to James R. Walker by Finger, an Oglala shaman:

> In the long ago the Lakotas were in camp and two young men lay upon a hill watching for signs. They saw a long way in the distance a lone person coming . . . When the person came close, they saw that it was a woman and when she came nearer that she was without clothing of any kind except that her hair was very long and fell over her body like a robe. One young man said to the other that he would go and meet the woman and embrace her . . . His companion cautioned him to be careful for this might be a buffalo woman who could enchant him . . . But the young man would not be persuaded and met the woman on the hill . . . His companion saw him attempt to embrace her and there was a cloud closed about them . . . In a short time the cloud disappeared and the woman was alone. She beckoned to the other young man . . .
>
> When he got there, she showed him the bare bones of his companion and told him that the Crazy Buffalo had caused his companion to try to do her harm and that she had destroyed him . . . she told him that if he would do as she directed, no harm would come to him and he should get any girl he wished for his woman. [Walker 1980:109-110]

The symbolism of this story invites interpretation. The sacred woman came bearing the gift of the pipe, the foundation of the Sioux way of life. Before this event, as Left Heron told Scudder Mekeel in 1931, nothing was sacred, there was no social order, and "the people ran around the prairies like so many wild animals." For the Sioux, the control of sexuality was an important aspect of the symbolic duality between animals and humans. Symbolically, animal behavior connoted promiscuous sexual intercourse, represented in the story by the man who tried to rape the sacred woman. The other man, as a reward for controlling his passions and for recognizing the woman as a sacred being, was told that in obeying her commands he could have any wife he wished. In a symbolic sense this part of the story may represent the establishment of marriage as a social institution, the foundation of social order for the Sioux people. It might also be interpreted as restricting appropriate sexual activity to the camp (taking it out of the wilderness) and directing it in ways beneficial to society.

When the sacred woman arrived in the Sioux camp, she gave the people the sacred pipe and tobacco, with the instructions that they be used for prayer. In a linguistic sense, prayer invokes kinship with the universal

powers; to pray and to address someone by a kin term are the same action
*(wac'ekiya).* This is a subtle identification, one that is not necessarily recognized in a conscious manner by Sioux people. Ella Deloria, whose native
language was *Lak'ota,* commented that it was not until she was deeply
engaged in linguistic study that she recognized the identity between these
two uses of the same word (1944:28–29). In the context of the story of the
gift of the pipe, this identity is symbolically clear. The smoke from the pipe
was to be the sacred woman herself, another manifestation of her role as
intermediary between humans and *wak'aŋ t'áŋka.* With the first smoking
of the pipe, she established kin relationship as well as prayer.

The kinship created by smoking the pipe and symbolized thereafter by
the pipe itself is complex. From one perspective it signifies a compact
between *wak'aŋ t'áŋka* and mankind; quoting the words of the sacred
woman from Lone Man's telling of the story, "The tribe shall depend upon
it for their necessary needs. . . . By this pipe the tribe shall live" (Densmore
1918:66). The sacred woman is said to have stayed in the camp for many
days, teaching the rituals—all based on the foundation of the pipe—by
which the people would send their prayers to *wak'aŋ t'áŋka.* From a second
perspective, the pipe signifies the relationship established between the
buffalo and mankind. "I represent the Buffalo tribe," the woman said.
"When you are in need of buffalo meat, smoke this pipe and ask for what
you need and it shall be granted you" (Densmore 1918:65–66). This
compact reverses the original antagonistic relationship between buffalos
and humans that is the subject of various Sioux myths. From a third
perspective, the pipe provided a means for the different tribes of humankind
to establish relationship with one another. "This pipe shall be used as a
peacemaker. The time will come when you shall cease hostilities against
other nations. Whenever peace is agreed upon between two tribes or parties
this pipe shall be a binding instrument" (Densmore 1918:65). Finally, from
a fourth perspective, the pipe signifies kin relationship. When the sacred
woman came, she addressed the people as "brothers" and "sisters." She
said: "I am proud to become a member of your family—a sister to you all"
(Densmore 1918:65). As she spoke, she outlined the kinship obligations
of men, women, and children. Symbolically, the story may be interpreted
as establishing the kinship system itself. Since the pipe is considered to
represent the union of male and female, and since the gift of the pipe is
understood as establishing the Sioux way of life, the story may be
interpreted as transforming natural relations resulting from sexual
intercourse and birth into a culturally defined system of relationship. In a
symbolic sense, this may be the meaning of Left Heron's comment that
before the gift of the pipe, the people were like "wild animals."

Black Elk, an Oglala Sioux religious leader, told a variant story of the origin of kin relationship. According to his account, kinship predated the gift of the pipe by hundreds of years. At that distant time all the Indians lived in a single camp. Slow Buffalo, their chief—who functions in the story as a culture hero—called the people together for a great council. On that occasion he announced that because they had become so numerous, they would disperse in seven groups to various areas of the country. Black Elk told about that council meeting:

> At that time relationships were not known among the people. Slow Buffalo mentioned his father's father, great grandfather, and the mother, and brothers and sisters. He said, "All this, we are going to go on with these relations. Remember, they are the ones you are going to depend upon. Up in the heavens, the Mysterious One, that is your grandfather. In between the earth and the heavens, that is your father. This earth is your grandmother. The dirt is your grandmother. Whatever grows on the earth is your mother. [DeMallie 1984:312]

Although the setting of the story is different, the message is the same as that of the gift of the pipe. Kinship is created by naming the relationships; the kin system is given for the people to understand and to depend upon. This relationship system is not limited to, or necessarily focussed on, human beings, but embraces all the universe.

Use of the pipe symbolizes acceptance of and participation in the system of relatedness that comprises the universe. The pipe itself is the symbol of kinship. The bowl is made of red pipestone, the flesh of the earth, while the stem is of wood that grows from the earth. The (re)union of the female bowl with the phallic stem is a ceremony celebrating relationship; some Sioux people today explicitly say that the pipe is like a man and a woman and that use of the pipe insures the perpetuation of the generations. The ritual of filling the pipebowl with pinches of tobacco offered to the seven directions (the four winds, up, down, and center) symbolizes the universal relatedness. Offering the filled pipe back to the seven directions incorporates the wholeness of the universe in the ritual smoking. George Sword, an Oglala shaman, told Walker in 1896 that the shared smoking of the pipe soothes the spirits of each man who smokes, and as the smoke rises to the *wak'aŋ t'áŋka*, it soothes their spirits as well, joining all in harmonious relationship. "The spirit in the smoke will soothe the spirits of all who thus smoke together and all will be as friends and all think alike" (Walker 1980:82-83).

The pipe was used in many contexts as a tangible symbol of relationship. As a symbol of a leader's office, it was used on all occasions when good will was to be assured. In the case of quarrels between two Sioux men, a leader could physically thrust a pipe between the combatants and enjoin them to smoke it and settle their dispute. A unique kind of pipestem was used in the ritual adoption called *huŋka,* which created kinship between two individuals and among all the members of their families. A shaman's consecrated pipe symbolized his special kinship to the *wak'aŋ t'áŋka.* A pipe smoked by those who had been enemies related them by bonds of friendship normatively as binding as all other kin relationships in Sioux culture. Use of the pipe thus both established and asserted kinship in every context of Sioux life.

## Kinship in Sioux Society

The Sioux considered themselves *ikce wic'aša* 'common men'. In the western or Teton dialect, all who were related were called *lak'ota* 'allied', which by extension included the Cheyennes and Arapahos, with whom the Sioux had established permanent bonds of peace *(wólak'ota).* All other Indians were *t'óka* 'enemies', outside the circle of kinship. Acts of hostility and violence against enemies were sanctioned by the White Buffalo Cow Woman. According to Sword, the sacred woman told the people: "Those who were enemies *(t'ókakic'iyapi)* were not to be friends *(k'olakic'iyapi),* but enemies; and so as enemies they will remain" (Sword n.d.). Short Feather, an Oglala, told Walker in 1898 that "the Sioux are more like the Great Spirits than any other of mankind" (Walker 1980:115), expressing a sense of superiority that may perhaps have served as justification for warfare against tribal enemies. Between the Sioux and their enemies, war was the accepted state. Edgar Fire Thunder, also an Oglala, told Deloria, "Only within the limits of kinship was there safety; beyond it life was as if spent in a danger zone where the enemy might strike from a hidden source" (Deloria 1937).

In contradistinction to all other peoples, the Sioux were a single kindred, *tákukic'iyapi* 'related to each other'. As Deloria wrote, "Kinship was the all-important matter. . . . By kinship all Dakota people were held together in a great relationship that was theoretically all-inclusive and co-extensive with the Dakota domain" (Deloria 1944:24). The unity of the Sioux as a people was symbolized by sharing common language and customs. They also considered themselves to have common ancestors (Walker 1982:3). Women captured from other tribes were considered as Sioux when they learned to speak the language and act according to Sioux ways. Their children were not distinguished in any way from other Sioux children (Walker 1982:54–55).

Sioux people speak of kinship in terms of attitudes and behavior, not genealogical connections. Even so, Ella Deloria mentioned that genealogical connections were important to the Sioux; they were "assiduously traced and remembered, no matter how far back" (1944:27). But in addition, Sioux people shared kinship with all individuals with whom they interacted. Deloria referred to this as "social kinship" and pointed out that while it is distinguished from "legitimate" (i.e., genealogical) kinship by anthropologists, for the Sioux it was no less legitimate a form of kinship. All kin relationships were "real," whether or not they were based on genealogy. Deloria wrote, "through this social system even real outsiders became relatives" (1944:27). The adoption ceremony, *huŋka,* was a ritual mechanism for formalizing such relationship. Deloria reported a case in which a murderer was adopted by the family of the man he had slain, thereby incorporating the ultimate outsider into the kinship network as a means of atonement (1944:34–36).

The consequences of using the kinship system as the basis for organizing social action are twofold. On the one hand, each individual addressed every other by a kin term and any two people stood in a mutually recognized and accepted relationship to one other; on the other hand, these relationships entailed specific attitudinal and behavioral patterns that provided real structure and organization to daily life. Semantically, the reciprocal use of kin terms implied consent to act according to the patterns of shared rights and duties symbolized by each of the kin terms. As Deloria phrased it, "You must assume the correct mental attitude due the particular relative addressed, and you must express that attitude in its fitting outward behavior and mien, according to the accepted conventions" (1944:30).

Kin terms were used instead of personal names for both address and reference. Standing Bear wrote, "It was not customary to call anyone by name" (1933:148); Deloria noted that it was considered rude to use personal names too freely (1944:28). When personal names were used it was with the intention of honoring the individual (since names embodied some deed or attribute of a person or of his relatives) or of teasing someone (i.e., nicknames). Personal names accentuate the individual's uniqueness; kin terms deemphasize individuality by stressing patterns of responsibility to the social group.

The Sioux considered strangers to be potentially dangerous; a person without relatives in the community was an unknown outsider and therefore was suspect. It was essential to make relatives of strangers in order to have a means of dealing with them and a basis for trusting them (Deloria 1944:29). Thus, a man moving into a community in which he had no relatives would soon be addressed, usually by an old woman, as son or grandson. He replied by calling her mother or grandmother, and in this way a kin relationship was established and the pattern for social interaction set. Moreover, since the woman as a community member was related to everyone who lived there, the newcomer simultaneously gained relationship through her to them all, as if the kin relationship had existed since birth. In recounting genealogies, such "adoptive" relationships are rarely mentioned; to point them out would imply some breach of faith or moral failing on the part of the one adopted.

One contemporary Yanktonai consultant, whom I asked (in English) whether the Sioux think about their relatives in terms of biological connections, commented in the affirmative. She suggested one expression that is used to designate such relations: "*Húte etaŋhaŋ waŋži uŋkupi* ('We come from one root')," referring to the descendants of a single ancestor. But then she said:

> Relatives are anyone who depends upon us for anything, and so we respect them. Like if someone comes here and eats with us, maybe stays here out of the cold, he depended on us, and so we are related. We respect one another, have established relationship. We become relatives like that. Sometimes we adopt somebody to replace a relative we have lost. . . . Sometimes there is a ritual adoption, called *huŋka kágapi*. . . Other people just adopt one another in private, without ceremony. . . . For example, a lady came to see me and said, "*T'aŋkec'iyekte* ('You're going to be my younger sister', or, 'I'm relating to you as a younger sister')." This is how one person establishes relationship; he doesn't say, "I want to adopt you as a sister." But you can say that of a child, "I want to adopt him."

For the Sioux, kinship is an active force, the act of relating. They understand their own kinship system to be in striking contrast to the static nature of American kinship, an ascribed system of roles whose behavioral content tends always to be minimized.

Yet it is apparent that some concept of "blood" does underlay the thinking of many contemporary Sioux about kinship. In discussing kinship, Teton consultants frequently mention the term *wic'owe,* variously translated as "family," "siblings," "generation" or "family line." They give the etymology as *wic'o* 'man' + *we* 'blood', "people of blood." However, the historical etymology is *wic'a* 'human' + *owe* 'class', "human class." In the Santee and Yankton-Yanktonai dialects the term is *wic'obe,* "a company," from *wic'a* 'human' + *obe* "a litter, brood; a division, class, sort" (Riggs 1890). It is likely therefore that the conscious recognition of blood as a symbol of kinship is a relatively recent development, bolstered by a folk etymology. The use of blood as a metaphor for kinship may reflect the influence of American culture and the innovation of a system of inheritance based on genealogy that was imposed by the Bureau of Indian Affairs and that has become an important focus of reservation life. Such an emphasis on genealogy was also bolstered by the introduction of standardized surnames around the turn of the century, another significant innovation fostered by the Bureau of Indian Affairs.

The emphasis on blood connection is never the exclusive defining criterion for kinship in Sioux culture. The undeniable fact is that Sioux people continue to make relatives throughout their lives who are classed with, and not differentiated from, those they had at birth. The traditional emphasis on orderliness and social control underscores the importance of making relatives to provide for the harmonious interaction patterns of daily life. Given the nomadic lifeway of the Sioux in historical times, families were continually moving back and forth, and social groups combining and recombining in both large and small camps that closely paralleled the yearly progression of aggregation and dispersal of the buffalo herds. In every new camp there were social relationships to sort out, solidify, or establish. Deloria summarizes the matter very well:

> I don't mean that a Dakota could not rest until he had feverishly gone round the entire camp-circle establishing relationships. After all, the sphere of kith and kin is limited for even a Dakota. When I say that kinship was all-inclusive and co-extensive with the tribe, I mean it was that potentially. It was true that everyone was related to all the people within his own circle of acquaintances. But all those people also had other circles of acquaintance within the large tribe. All such circles overlapped and interlocked. Any Dakota could legitimately find his way to any other, if he wished or needed to do so. And thus, with relatives scattered over the many camp-circles and communities, anyone could go visiting anywhere, and be at home. [1944:37-38]

Since all Sioux recognized themselves as part of a common kindred, all were related. The kinship system itself provided the foundation for social unity and moral order. The norms of kinship were the most basic cultural structures patterning the social system; they formed a network that potentially embraced all members of society and related them as well to the sacred powers of the world at large. Kinship in Sioux culture had no prescribed boundaries; as a system of potentialities it structured and made sense of all human interactions and provided a comforting sense of orderliness to the universe.

## Sioux Concepts of Sexuality and Procreation

Understanding culturally defined concepts of sexuality is essential in order
to assess the significance of biological reproduction for the definition of
kinship in Sioux culture (see DeMallie 1982 for a more extended discussion). The Sioux believed that everything relating to sexuality was imbued
with great power *(wak'aŋ)* and was therefore to be treated circumspectly.
For Sioux men, engaging in sexual relations was at odds with the culturally
defined warrior ethos. Men valued continence as proof of their bravery, and
if a woman became pregnant too frequently, both she and her husband were
considered irresponsible. In cultural terms, sexual desires were believed
to be stronger in women, who were seen as seducing men to have intercourse with them. On the other hand, young men, in particular, made a sport
of seducing women, and those triumphs were recounted as though they
were coups against the enemy. Adultery was a common theme in oral
literature and bore harsh penalties for both parties involved. Adulterous
intercourse was symbolized by the dog. The epithet *dog* was the strongest
possible in Sioux culture and implied promiscuity and lack of self-control.
The dog was also symbolic of men going to war. An early-nineteenth-
century account mentions a ceremony in which, before leaving camp on
an expedition, warriors danced in the nude, exposing their genitals, singing
a song: "This is of dogs!" (DeMallie 1976:274).

Ordinarily, Sioux people were circumspect about all matters relating
to sex, and sexual intercourse was never a proper subject for discussion.
Sexual banter between joking relatives was prescribed behavior, but the
jokes centered on anatomical speculations and teasing propositions, rather
than on sexual acts.

A woman's blood was said to be a very powerful substance, and, during
menstruation, harmful to men—not because it was polluting but because
it was a specifically female power, at odds with or "blocked" by the power
of men. A menstruating woman absented herself from the household and
stayed alone in a small dome-shaped structure apart from the camp circle.
Men's belongings were zealously guarded against contact with menstruating women. In general, sexual relations were considered detrimental to
a man's power. Therefore, sexual intercourse was not engaged in immediately before ceremonial activities, warrior society meetings, or war
expeditions, for it could render a man's sacred power temporarily impotent.
A man was not even supposed to smoke his pipe after sexual intercourse
without first cleansing his genitals; otherwise he might be blinded or hurt
in some other way (Walker 1982:96).

Lakota culture prescribed that sexual intercourse be engaged in sparingly, for the procreation of children. Cultural norms gave precedence to the welfare of children over all else. Robert P. Higheagle, a Hunkpapa, told Densmore:

> It is strictly believed and understood by the Sioux that a child is the greatest gift from Wakaŋ'taŋka, in response to many devout prayers, sacrifices, and promises. Therefore the child is considered "sent by Wakaŋ'taŋka," through some element—namely, the element of human being. [1918:70]

The Sioux believed that conception was caused by the father's seed, nurtured in the mother's womb. According to Deloria (forthcoming) there was no recognition of the ovum, but the body of the developing child was evidently considered to be created out of the mother's blood. Conception resulted from this union of male and female powers, although life was not given to the body until birth, when *škaŋ,* one of the *wak'aŋ t'áŋka,* imparted to each newborn a *šic'uŋ,* a kind of spirit (Walker 1917:156). The emphasis in conception, however, was clearly placed on the male role. As one Teton Sioux chief said in 1865, explaining polygyny, "We want to increase our people, and when we sleep with our women we sleep with them for good" (Board of Commissioners 1866:44).

Such an understanding of procreation implies biological relatedness as a sharing of physical substance. Writing a description of Sioux kinship in 1911, Thomas Tyon, an Oglala, began with the marriage of a man and woman: "From this beginning relationships proceed" (Walker 1982:44). This statement seems to root the Sioux concept of kinship firmly in biology, although it should be noted that Tyon was familiar with American concepts of kinship and may have been trying to pattern his description of Sioux kinship after his understanding of the American system. It is significant that linguistic forms existed that differentiated between one's biological parents and other mothers and fathers, as well as between stepchildren and other children. However, these were descriptive terms for use in reference; to use any of them for address was extremely impolite. The Sioux were sanctioned to treat all relatives called by the same term in a like manner, without favoring any merely because of biological relationship.

It may be concluded that the Sioux explicitly recognized the biological basis for procreation; however, it was not the defining criterion for kinship. Biological relationship was only one of several ways of becoming related in Sioux culture, and there is no evidence that it was accorded primacy or preeminence in the definition of relatedness either in theory or in daily life.

## The Organization of Kinship in Sioux Culture

Among the Sioux, the semantic domain *wótakuye* 'kinship' is designated for any individual by the term *mitakuyepi,* 'my relatives'. As indicated above, this category embraces almost everyone with whom an individual comes into contact; theoretically, it is an infinitely expandable category. All who fall within it are addressed and referred to by a series of kin terms, called *wówahec'uŋ.* Walker gave what is likely a folk etymology for this term as *wówa,* 'marks' + *hec'uŋ,* 'to do', "do marks," or indicators of proper behavior (Walker 1914:101). Though undoubtedly historically inaccurate, this etymology vividly expresses the underlying meaning: kin terms are signals for culturally prescribed behavior patterns. Small children were always enjoined to use kin terms when addressing anyone; this was a responsibility children had to learn as soon as possible. One Yanktonai consultant said that when a child was sent to visit a relative, he was told: *"Yai kiŋhaŋ wówahec'uŋ eya* ('When you get there, say your kin term')." And she added: "When a child is old enough to talk, he knows his relationship—he doesn't have to be told."

The same consultant, asked for her opinion concerning the etymology of *wówahec'uŋ,* replied:

> It means "relationships." [After some thought, she continued.] *Wóohoda,* 'respect'; *wówahec'uŋ* comes from that respect—*wóohoda ec'uŋ,* 'putting respect into action'. They showed their respect for one another by using these terms of respect; they hardly ever called anyone by a personal name. Everyone was related to everyone else and used these terms of respect. *Mitakuyepi,* 'my relatives'—everyone and everything, not only people but the animals and plants, everything is all related because we are all made by one.

The system of kin terms classifies all who are relatives. From an individual's perspective, the general category is *mitakuyepi* 'my relatives'. The domain of relatives is restricted by use of the term *mit'itakuyepi* 'my relatives with whom I live', or "my close relatives" (from *t'i* 'to live' + *takuye* 'relatives'). This term can be used to specify one's personal relations as opposed to relatives in general, or in context it can be used to differentiate one's immediate family from other relatives. Consultants usually agree that the term was originally used to designate all the members of an individual's *t'iyošpaye* 'band' or 'extended family' (from *t'i* 'to live' + *ošpaye* 'a bunch'). Historically, the word doubtlessly referred to the usual residential group and may be freely translated "band relatives." The term also marked the normal limits of exogamy; anyone who married an individual already related as a "band relative" was considered insane *(witko)*.

A semantic analysis of Sioux kin terms can start from the distinction between the all-embracing category of "relatives" and the narrower category of "band relatives" to divide the entire domain into two general classes on the basis of closeness. Most of the kin terms designate "band relatives" and their use reflects a close relationship between the individuals involved. The residual category—for which there is no label—consists of affinal relatives, whose relationship to ego is attenuated by prescribed patterns of conspicuous respect or obligatory joking. It is not surprising that this category is not named; to label it would draw attention to the differences between those more distant relatives and "band relatives," and any such overt suggestion of difference would offend Sioux kinship ethics.

Another pair of concepts is basic to the semantic analysis of Sioux kin terms. *Wic'owe* in one of its senses may be used to designate all of a person's siblings and cousins of both sexes; *hakata* singles out a person's opposite-sex siblings and cousins. According to Deloria (forthcoming), the *wic'owe*—siblings and cross cousins—were spoken of as *owaŋžila* 'one and the same'. She commented that "they belonged together always. There was the logical center of group strength. Consequently they must keep unified through an unremitting insistence on their caring deeply for one another." Between same-sex siblings and cousins there should be friendly cooperation and absence of competition; between *hakata* there was conspicuous respect marked by avoidance. Deloria was told of an old Sioux patriarch who regularly admonished the core group of siblings and cousins of the band: "Children, hold firm together always, for you form the *t'ic'aŋkahu* ['ridgepole'] of the *t'iyošpaye.* "

One more Sioux concept is also essential for semantic analysis of kin terms: *wic'oicaġe*, 'generation' (from *wic'a* 'human' + *oicaġe* 'to grow up'). As a cultural symbol, the Sioux consider a generation to be seventy years, the lifespan of an old man; in organizing time, the generation was an important concept (Mallery 1886:88–89). Likewise, the Sioux system of kin classification emphasizes generation, differentiating relatives in five generational groupings, two above and two below ego's. In order to specify individuals in other generations, either above or below, the term *sam* 'beyond' is used with the words for grandparents and grandchildren.

Starting from those fundamental cultural concepts and adding distinctions based on sex and relative age, a semantic classification of Sioux kin terms can be generated that allows for easy comprehension of its structure from an insider's perspective.

From ego's point of view, relatives in the second ascending generation are classified by four terms:

|  | "band relatives" |  | "relatives" |
|---|---|---|---|
| *t'uŋkašila* | GF | *t'uŋkaši* | F-in-L |
| *uŋci* | GM | *uŋciši* | M-in-L |

These are terms of address. The suffix *-ši* indicates a relationship of conspicuous respect; the suffix *-la* is an endearing one that softens a relationship. Note that there is an ego-centric bias in the definition of "generation"—parents-in-law are classified with the second ascending generation (and, reciprocally, children-in-law are classified with the second descending generation). This identification may be interpreted as reflecting degree of age and status differential between parents-in-law and children-in-law. For purposes of the kin term system, the two sets of defining criteria in the second ascending generation are sex of referent and "band relatives" versus "relatives."

The first ascending generation is also classified by four terms:

|  | "band relatives" | "relatives" |
|---|---|---|
| *ate* | F | — — |
| *ina* | M |  |
| *lekši* | MB |  |
| *t'uŋwiŋ* | FZ |  |

Again two distinctions are operative: sex of referent and parents' *hakata* versus parents' same-sex siblings and cousins; the former are classified as "aunts" and "uncles," while the latter are classified with parents. In the first ascending generation there are no residual affinal relatives (since parents-in-law are classified with the grandparents' generation).

The classification of relatives in ego's generation is the most complex, involving twenty-five terms:

### "band relatives"

| MALE SPEAKER |  | FEMALE SPEAKER |  |
|---|---|---|---|
| *c'iye* | eB | *c'uwe* | eZ |
| *misuŋ* | yB | *mit'aŋ* | yZ |
| *t'aŋhaŋši* | mC-C | *cép'aŋši* | fC-C |
| *maše* | B-in-L; friend | *waše* | Z-in-L; friend |
| *k'ola* | friend | *maške* | friend |
| *kic'uwa* | friend |  |  |

### *hakata* ("cross-sex relatives")

| *t'aŋke* | eZ | *t'iblo* | eB |
|---|---|---|---|
| *t'aŋkši* | yZ | *misuŋ* | yB |
| *haŋkaši* | fC-C | *šic'eši* | mC-C |

## "relatives"

| MALE SPEAKER | | | FEMALE SPEAKER | |
|---|---|---|---|---|
| *mit'awiŋ* | W | | *mihiŋgna* | H |
| | | | *t'éya* | co-W |
| *t'aŋhaŋ* | B-in-L | | *šic'e* | B-in-L |
| *haŋka* | Z-in-L | | *šcép'aŋ* | Z-in-L |

MALE OR FEMALE SPEAKER

*omawahit'uŋ*      co-P-in-L

In ego's generation distinctions are made for "band relatives" versus "relatives," sex of referent, *hakata* versus same-sex siblings and cousins, sex of speaker, relative age, as well as a variety of affective overtones that define the friend relations. For example, the terms *maše* and *waše* are used by men and women respectively for siblings-in-law of the same sex if the speakers are on particularly friendly terms; that is, the relationship is shifted from the category of "relatives" to that of "band relatives"—in this case, converting a joking relationship to one resembling a sibling relationship. Similarly, affective criteria distinguish between *k'ola, kic'uwa,* and *maše* for men and *waše* and *maške* for women. Only one term, that for co-parents-in-law, does not distinguish sex of referent; this term was used by an individual to address his or her son-in-law or daughter-in-law's mothers, fathers, aunts, uncles, and grandparents. Sibling terms are the only ones to mark relative age; variations of those terms occur using prefixes and suffixes to reflect shades of affective meaning.

It is questionable whether the terms for spouses should be included in the category of kinship. Deloria (forthcoming) felt that they should not be; those terms were not used for address and rarely for reference. Instead, individuals referred to their spouses as *iye* 'he/she' and used no term for address; occasionally, according to Deloria, very old couples would address one other as *k'ola,* 'friend'. Apparently, the spouse terms were charged with sexual overtones and their use had the potential to cause tension in the relationship. Co-wives who were not already sisters might adopt one another as such if they shared a harmonious relationship.

The seven terms classifying the first descending generation are:

## "band relatives"

| MALE SPEAKER | | FEMALE SPEAKER | | MALE OR FEMALE SPEAKER | |
|---|---|---|---|---|---|
| *t'uŋška* | Ne | *t'oška* | Ne | *c'iŋkš* | S |
| *t'uŋžaŋ* | Ni | *t'ožaŋ* | Ni | *c'uŋkš* | D |

## "relatives"

MALE OR FEMALE SPEAKER
*t'awaġaŋwaye ciŋ*  step-Ch

In the first descending generation distinctions are again made between "band relatives" and "relatives," sex of referent (except for the term for step-child, which was never used for address), and ego's own children and children of same-sex siblings and cousins versus children of *hakata*.

Finally, the second descending generation is classified by two terms:

| "band relatives" | | "relatives" | |
|---|---|---|---|
| *t'akoža*  GCh | | *t'akoš*  Ch-in-law, GCh-in-law | |

In the second descending generation there is only the single distinction between "band relatives" and "relatives."

The principles of kin classification in the Sioux system are simple and precise. Most importantly they involve a distinction in closeness of relationship and recognition of the unity of the group of same-sex siblings and cousins. Relationships are reckoned systematically within the terms of the system itself, without recourse to supposed biological connections. Terms of address always ignore distinctions between actual biological and nonbiological relationships. The various terms for friends are not specifiable in genealogical terms, but Sioux consultants vigorously defend them as belonging to the kinship system because they are perceived to represent real and enduring bonds of relationship. The overwhelming conclusion is that the kinship classification is a system of symbols based on culturally defined patterns of interaction rather than on any attempt to represent biological connections among individuals.


## The Question of Cross Cousins

Anthropologists have devoted much attention to the Sioux terms for cross cousins, which are composed of the terms for brother-in-law and sister-in-law with the addition of the suffix *–ši*. As Eggan noted (1955:544–45; 1966:98–104), W. H. R. Rivers (1914:69–70) had pointed to this terminological equation to suggest the former practice of cross-cousin marriage by the Sioux. Hassrick (1944) came to the same conclusion based on his study of Brule kinship and suggested that the *–ši* suffix could be translated as "stop" or "go away," a linguistic marker of the change in the nature of the relationship. Eggan analyzed this material together with the extensive data on cross-cousin marriage among northern Algonkian tribes and concluded that the bilateral band based on cross-cousin marriage might be considered a major type of Plains social structure (1955:548). His suggestion served as an alternative to Lesser's hypothesis that the Sioux kinship system was based on the regular operation of the levirate and sororate (1958:295–97).

Semantic analysis of Sioux kin terms sheds further light on the problem. In the first place, the suffix *-ši* appears in a number of other kin terms, always marking relationships of respect. In this sense, Walker (1914:96) had interpreted it to mean that marriage was prohibited between persons who used kin terms for one another that included this suffix. However, such an interpretation fails to account for the use of the suffix between persons of the same sex. For cross cousins, a simpler explanation that fits with the classificatory principles of the system may be suggested. From ego's perspective, cross cousins are children of one's fathers' and mothers' *hakata* (opposite-sex siblings and cousins); fathers and mothers call the spouses of their *hakata* brother-in-law and sister-in-law; ego calls the children of these individuals by the same terms, with the addition of the suffix *-ši,* indicating respect. This is parallel to the use of terms for grandparents + *-ši* and grandchildren + *-ši* for parents-in-law and children-in-law, thus stretching the terms over two generations. Perhaps the siblings-in-law/cross cousin terms should be thought of as generalized "relative-in-law" terms. From this perspective the situation resembles that of the lineally-structured Omaha and Crow systems, which classify individuals by the same term across generations to indicate their structural equivalence. A similar principle may be at work in the Sioux case.

Such an explanation has the value of accounting for the suffix *-ši* as a marker of respect in all cases where it appears, of not requiring conjecture of a prior marriage pattern, and of suggesting a structural parallel to the lineal systems of neighboring, related tribes. Although it does not rule out the hypothesis of the former practice of cross-cousin marriage, it fits well with Lesser's explanation of Sioux kinship as based on the levirate and sororate; by emphasizing the division between cross cousins on the one hand and siblings and parallel cousins on the other hand, it underscores the distinction between children of "mothers" and "fathers" (parents' potential spouses under the levirate and sororate), and "aunts" and "uncles" (who are not parents' potential spouses under the levirate and sororate).

## Conclusion

A cultural approach to Sioux kinship offers a different understanding than does a social-structural approach. Most previous studies of Sioux kinship limited the field of inquiry to terms of address and reference used to designate genealogically specified kin relationships. Such studies reveal the basic structural principles of the kin term system and show the broad extension of kin relationship to genealogically specified individuals. Further, they demonstrate that by extending basic kin terms to distant relatives, the system provides the medium for social interaction as well as for the fundamental organization of the band system, which provided social and political integration. In this sense a social-structural study presents sufficient data to differentiate the Sioux from some of their neighbors (e.g., the lineally structured, clan-organized, semisedentary village tribes such as the Omahas and Hidatsas) and to classify them with others (e.g., the generationally structured, band-organized, nomadic tribes such as the Cheyennes and Arapahos) (see Eggan 1937:89-95). From a perspective of social anthropology, the method accomplishes its goals of providing a basis for the classification of societies and suggesting how the kinship system functions within society to provide social integration.

However, understanding kinship as the Sioux themselves understand it is more impeded than aided by the social-structural approach. By ignoring the religious dimensions of Sioux culture, a social-structural approach misses what is to the Sioux the heart of the kinship system—its basis in a contract with *wak'aŋ t'áŋka,* which thereby unites all forms of being into an unbroken network of relationship. It also misses the understanding of kinship as the foundation for morality. The social-structural approach excludes consideration of all nonhuman relations. Moreover, it artificially limits even the domain of human kinship by excluding nongenealogically specifiable relationships—"friends"—that from the Sioux perspective are a very important component of kinship. By restricting kinship to genealogy, the social-structural approach fails to note that the Sioux define relationship in terms of a set of conceptual categories and the logical relationships among them based on proper "feeling" and behavior, rather than on concrete links of marriage and birth. Although those biological factors are at the basis of Sioux kinship, they are in fact deemphasized by the system, both in terms of classification and behavior. Biological relatedness is frequently overridden by a plethora of adoptive mechanisms; although anthropologists generally relegate adoption to the category of fictive kin, for the Sioux, adoption constitutes genuine kinship. Through those mechanisms the tenuous network of genealogical relatedness is developed into a stronger, more secure system of relationship. For the Sioux, this is the proper perspective on kinship, and if the message of the story of the gift of the pipe is taken at face value, this transformation of natural relatedness into cultural relationship is an important criterion that distinguishes human life from mere animal existence.

Rather than conceptualize the two anthropological approaches as competing for validity, they are better viewed as complementary methods, each valuable for specific purposes. The social-structural approach, by imposing a grid of consanguinity and affinity on the study of kinship, provides a framework for cross-cultural comparison. Such an approach simplifies the facts of kinship for any society and provides a structural model that may bear little relationship to native conceptions. Yet Eggan's work shows clearly the value of such an approach for classifying and tracing distributions of kinship systems cross-culturally. His analyses of the Plains tribes, the Pueblos, and the Southeast have provided examples of the range of understandings and fruitful hypotheses for further study that such an approach can generate.

The cultural or symbolic approach provides entirely different kinds of understandings of kinship systems, although the end products are equally simplified models designed to reveal the structure of the system. In this case, however, the aim is to define the boundaries and contours from a particularistic standpoint, avoiding to the extent that it is possible any imposition of an outside framework. The results are somewhat more difficult to use for cross-cultural comparison, yet such comparisons are the ultimate goal. The great potential of the cultural approach is to provide a basis for cross-cultural comparison of native understandings of kinship. For example, it may be possible to classify North American tribes according to the extent to which they use kinship as the means for organizing social life. How many Plains tribes use kinship exclusively for the purpose of organizing social interaction? How many completely merge religious and social systems such that prayer is the act of invoking relationship? How many generalize relationship as the means for interacting with outsiders? Cross-cultural study from these perspectives may reveal entirely other sets of distributional patterns that could help to develop more sophisticated understandings of historical interactions among the Plains tribes.

The significance of the Sioux case lies in the fact that so much material has been recorded relating to the kinship system that it provides an extraordinarily sound basis for study. From Morgan to Rivers to Radcliffe-Brown to Eggan, Sioux examples have been used to suggest how social anthropological study of kin terminology can reveal patterns of social change. Cultural approaches can further our understanding of those changes and suggest previously unexplored means for reconstructing the historical development of kinship systems.

## Acknowledgments

I would like to thank Karen I. Blu, Raymond Bucko, S.J., John Gizzi, Michael Herzfeld, Elaine A. Jahner, Harvey J. Markowitz, and Douglas R. Parks, each of whom provided helpful and much-appreciated commentary on drafts of this paper.

## Notes

1. For the classification and interrelationships of Sioux dialects, see Parks and DeMallie (1992). The transcription system for Sioux words used in this chapter follows Boas and Deloria (1941), substituting ŋ for subscript hooks to represent nasalization of vowels. All words are stressed on the second syllable except where indicated.

## References

Board of Commissioners
    1866     Proceedings of a Board of Commissioners to Negotiate a Treaty or Treaties with the Hostile Indians of the Upper Missouri. Washington, D.C.: Government Printing Office.

Boas, Franz, and Ella Deloria
    1941     Dakota Grammar. Memoirs of the National Academy of Sciences, vol. 23, no. 2. Washington, D.C.

Deloria, Ella
    1937     Dakota Commentary on Walker's Texts. Boas Collection, American Philosophical Society Library, Philadelphia.
    1944     Speaking of Indians. New York: Friendship Press.
    forthcoming  The Dakota Way of Life. Edited by Raymond J. DeMallie. Lincoln: University of Nebraska Press.

DeMallie, Raymond J.
    1976     Nicollet's Notes on the Dakota. In Joseph N. Nicollet on the Plains and Prairies: The Expeditions of 1838–39 with Journals, Letters, and Notes on the Dakota Indians, edited by Edmund C. Bray and Martha Coleman Bray, 250–81. St. Paul: Minnesota Historical Society Press.
    1979     Change in American Indian Kinship Systems: The Dakota. In Currents in Anthropology: Essays in Honor of Sol Tax, edited by Robert Hinshaw, 221–41. The Hague: Mouton.
    1982     Male and Female in Traditional Lakota Culture. In The Hidden Half: Studies of Plains Indian Women, edited by Patricia C. Albers and Beatrice Medicine, 237–65. Washington, D.C.: University Press of America.

DeMallie, Raymond J., ed.
    1984     The Sixth Grandfather: Black Elk's Teachings Given to John G. Neihardt. Lincoln: University of Nebraska Press.

Densmore, Frances
    1918     Teton Sioux Music. Smithsonian Institution, Bureau of American Ethnology Bulletin 61. Washington, D.C.

Eggan, Fred
    1937    The Cheyenne and Arapaho Kinship System. *In* Social Anthropology of North
            American Tribes, edited by Fred Eggan, 31-95. Chicago: University of
            Chicago Press.
    1950    Social Organization of the Western Pueblos. Chicago: University of Chicago
            Press.
    1955    Social Anthropology: Methods and Results. *In* Social Anthropology of North
            American Tribes, edited by Fred Eggan, 483-551. Enlarged ed. Chicago:
            University of Chicago Press.
    1966    The American Indian: Perspectives for the Study of Social Change. Chicago:
            Aldine Publishing.
Geertz, Clifford
    1973    The Interpretation of Cultures. New York: Basic Books.
Hassrick, Royal B.
    1944    Teton Dakota Kinship System. American Anthropologist 46:338-47.
Lesser, Alexander
    1930    Some Aspects of Siouan Kinship. *In* Proceedings of the Twenty-third
            International Congress of Americanists, 1928, 563-71. New York.
    1958    Siouan Kinship. Ph. D. diss., Columbia University.
Mallery, Garrick
    1886    Pictographs of the North American Indians. *In* Smithsonian Institution, Fourth
            Annual Report of the Bureau of American Ethnology, 3-256. Washington,
            D.C.
Mekeel, Haviland Scudder
    1931    Field Notes, Summer of 1931, White Clay District, Pine Ridge Reservation,
            South Dakota. Typescript in Department of Anthropology, American Museum
            of Natural History, New York.
Parks, Douglas R., and Raymond J. DeMallie
    1992    Sioux, Assiniboine, and Stoney Dialects: A Classification. Anthropological
            Linguistics 34:233-55.
Riggs, Stephen Return, ed.
    1890    A Dakota-English Dictionary. Edited by James Owen Dorsey. Contributions
            to North American Ethnology, vol. 7. Washington, D.C.
Rivers, W. H. R.
    1914    Kinship and Social Organization. New ed., London School of Economics
            Monographs on Social Anthropology no. 34. New York: Humanities Press,
            1968.
Schneider, David M.
    1968    American Kinship: A Cultural Account. Englewood Cliffs: Prentice-Hall.
    1972    What Is Kinship All About? *In* Kinship Studies in the Morgan Centennial
            Year, edited by Priscilla Reining, 32-63. Washington, D.C.: Anthropological
            Society of Washington.
    1976    Notes toward a Theory of Culture. *In* Meaning in Anthropology, edited by
            Keith H. Basso and Henry A. Selby, 197-220. Albuquerque: University of
            New Mexico Press.
    1984    A Critique of the Study of Kinship. Ann Arbor: University of Michigan Press.

Standing Bear, Luther
    1933      Land of the Spotted Eagle. Boston: Houghton Mifflin.
Sword, George
    n.d.      Lakota texts. Transcribed and translated by Ella Deloria. Boas Collection,
              American Philosophical Society Library, Philadelphia.
Walker, James R.
    1914      Oglala Kinship Terms. American Anthropologist 16:96–109.
    1917      The Sun Dance and other Ceremonies of the Oglala Division of the Teton
              Dakota. American Museum of Natural History Anthropological Papers, vol.
              16, pt. 2. New York.
    1980      Lakota Belief and Ritual. Edited by Raymond J. DeMallie and Elaine A.
              Jahner. Lincoln: University of Nebraska Press.
    1982      Lakota Society. Edited by Raymond J. DeMallie. Lincoln: University of
              Nebraska Press.

# 6

## Northern Cheyenne Kinship Reconsidered

ANNE S. STRAUS

In 1933 Fred Eggan went to Oklahoma to study kinship and social organization among the Southern Cheyennes and Arapahos. His "Cheyenne and Arapaho Kinship System" (1937) remains the most thorough and most important consideration of Cheyenne kinship in the literature. His Morgan Lecture, "The Cheyenne and Arapaho in the Perspective of the Plains: Ecology and Society" (1966), reiterates and expands the conclusions of the earlier article.

Based on his fieldwork, Eggan (1937) provided a list of Cheyenne kin terms and described the general patterns of behavior between particular relatives. He further set those relationships in the context of the life cycle—chronicling their development, management, and change. He noted the similarity of Cheyenne and other kinship systems on the High Plains: "tribes coming into the Plains with *different* backgrounds and social systems ended up with *similar* kinship systems" (1937:93) and "a common pattern of social structure" (1966:72).

This common social structure consisted of a "series of social units—the elementary family, the extended household, the band, the society, and the tribe" (1937:82). Among the Cheyennes, the elementary family occupied a single tipi within the matrilocal extended family camp, which Eggan called the household. The household group was the basic economic unit; it included several hunters and enough women to prepare the meat and hides in the event of a large kill. However, it was not large enough to provide adequate defense in an environment of continual warfare. Households related by kinship or friendship joined together in bands that were large enough to provide the necessary protection and flexible enough to adjust to the ever-changing conditions of Plains life. Children usually took their band affiliation from their mothers, in accordance with the preferential matrilocal residence: a man often joined the band of his wife after marriage, but might return to his own band or join a new one if it became expedient. Band affiliation shifted; household bonds remained firm. In the summer, the ten bands came together in a great camp circle,

147

during which time the Council of Forty-Four peace chiefs and the military societies were activated.

In reconstructing Cheyenne history, Eggan tentatively accepted Grinnell's (1923,1:91–92) assessment that Cheyenne bands were once matrilineal. The early pre-Plains Cheyennes are pictured as semisedentary village horticulturalists, much like their Mandan, Hidatsa, and Arikara neighbors along the Missouri River. As Eggan wrote, "all the tribes of the Prairie Areas using earth lodges had a complex social organization centering around the village, with a formal clan organization and kinship systems of a 'lineage' type" (1952:42). As they moved from their earth-lodge villages into the nomadic lifeway of the High Plains, they are presumed to have given up the more rigid matrilineal system for the flexible bilateral bands described above. According to Eggan, "the uncertainties of Plains existence were great, compared with those of the village dwellers, and a flexible type of social structure was required" (1952:40). Kin terminology then changed in relationship to the new circumstances and new social organization.

Eggan saw the convergent social systems and kin terminologies of the Plains not simply as the product of diffusion but as the result of common adaptation to the exigencies of Plains life. Fundamental to that adjustment was the great importance of the relationship between "brothers," a term used for cousins as well as siblings. This essential solidarity of young men was understood to underlie the generation terminology in ego's generation.

Reconsidering Eggan's Cheyenne material, this essay provides some additional data and analysis of the terms themselves, expands on the relevance of the life cycle to the relationship between brothers and the generation terminology, and discusses certain changes in the terminology, social behavior, and social organization during the half-century since Eggan's fieldwork.

## Kin Terminology

Eggan (1937:43–45) listed Cheyenne kin terms (table 1) and provided genealogical charts summarizing the kin terminology (figs. 1–2).

### Inherent Possession and Possessive Prefixes

Eggan did not study the Cheyenne language, nor did he provide linguistic data relevant to the terms he collected. He was apparently unaware of the work of Rodolphe Petter, a Mennonite missionary trained in classical languages and fluent in Cheyenne. His *English-Cheyenne Dictionary* (1913–15) provided important lexical and ethnographic data but was

**Table 1.** Cheyenne Kin Terms

| Kin Type | Eggan's List | Modern Transcription[*] |
|---|---|---|
| GF | *namciḿ* | *námèšeme* |
| GM | *nicji''* | *néške'e* |
| F | *nihu''* | *ného'e* |
| M | *na'go'* | *náhko'e* |
| FZ | *nahán* | *nàháa'e* |
| MB | *naxaṅ* | *nàxāne* |
| OB | *na'níha* | *na'nèha* |
| OZ | *namhan* | *namèhāne* |
| YSib | *na·'sima* | *násemáhe* |
| S | *na·'; na·ᵃha'* | *náe'ha* |
| D | *na'ts;* | *náhtse;* |
| | *na·'tona* | *nàhtòna* (ref., 'my D') |
| Ne | *nats;* | *natse;* |
| | *natsínut* | *natsénota* (ref., 'my Ne') |
| Ni | *na'ᵃham* | *ná'hame* |
| GCh | *nixa* | *néxahe* |
| F-in-L | *namciḿ;* | *námèšeme;* |
| | *tséhemcímit* | *tséhemèšéméto* (ref., 'the one who is my GF/F-in-L') |
| M-in-L | *nicji'ɛ·'* | *néške'e* |
| | *tséheɣisjimiTU* | *tséhevéškeméto* (ref., 'the one who is my GM/M-in-L) |
| S-in-L | *nixa;* | *néxahe* (ref., 'my GCh/Ch-in-L'); |
| | *tséheɣixahaiTU* | *tséhevéxahéto* (ref., 'the one who is my GCh/Ch-in-L) |
| D-in-L | *nixa* | *néxahe* (ref., 'my GCh/Ch-in-L') |
| B-in-L (ms) | *nitówI* | *né'tóve* (ref., 'my B-in-L' [ms]) |
| B-in-L (fs); Z-in-L (ms) | *nitäm* | *nétame* (ref., 'my cross-sex Sib-in-L') |
| Z-in-L (fs); Z (ms) | *naxa'ɛm* | *naaxaa'éhéme* (ref., 'my Z-in-L' [fs]; 'my Z' [ms]) |
| CoP-in-L | *na'Dowaḿ* | *nàhtováme* (ref., 'my CoP-in-L') |
| H | *nạihäm* | *naéhame* (ref., 'my H') |
| W | *na'si'im* | *nàhtse'ème* (ref., 'my wife' [crude]) |
| Friend (ms) | *ni'sima* | *nésemáhe[†]; néséne* |

---

[*]Modern transcriptions are from Glenmore and Leman (1985); Eggan recorded kin terms as vocatives except where referential forms are noted. Throughout this chapter, Cheyenne forms are given as modern transcriptions following Leman (1981).

[†]Conjectural phonemic form based on Eggan's recording; not attested in contemporary Northern Cheyenne speech. However, cf. the form *nis'en* recorded by Petter (1913–15:502).

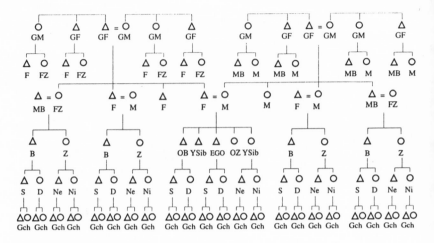

**Figure 1.** Cheyenne kin terms: consanguineal.

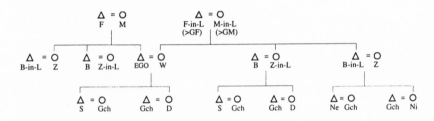

**Figure 2.** Cheyenne kin terms: affinal.

unrecognized at the time Eggan worked on Cheyenne social organization. (Although Petter's preliminary "Sketch of Cheyenne Grammar" appeared in 1901, his *Cheyenne Grammar* was not published until 1952.)

Most of the kin terms given above are in the first person possessive form. In Cheyenne, all kin terms are inherently or inalienably possessed: they occur always and only as possessives and do not require the addition of the usual possessive suffix *-ame/-eme*. Inherent possession applies to terms for relatives and for body parts, but not, for example, to an individual's sacred power (*ma'heo'o* 'sacred power', *nama'heóname* 'my sacred power'). Culturally, relatives, like body parts, are integral to the human being and to being human. (And, as Robert K. Thomas once remarked at a Newberry Library seminar, to American Indians generally an abstract concept of *mother* makes no sense: you must know specifically whose mother in order to interpret the meaning of the term.)

With the intuition of a fluent speaker, Petter considered kin terms as a distinct category of inalienably possessed nouns and suggested semantic implications of the different forms of possession in Cheyenne. He distinguished inherent from artificial possession on the basis of the presence ("artifical") or absence ("inherent") of the possessive suffix. Within the class of inalienably possessed nouns, he distinguished two categories on the basis of the different form of the pronominal prefix (1952:7–19). Petter's analysis of possessives is rejected by contemporary linguists, but nonetheless provides a cultural perspective on kin terms that agrees in part with folk etymologies. Of particular interest is his discussion of the different forms of the possessive pronominal prefix.

In Eggan's list of Cheyenne kin terms, eight take the *né–* form of the possessive pronominal prefix:

| | | | |
|---|---|---|---|
| *néške'e* | GM | *néxahe* | S/D-in-L |
| *ného'e* | F | *né'tóve* | B-in-L (ms) |
| *néxahe* | GCh | *nétame* | cross-sex Sib-in-L |
| *néške'e* | M-in-L | *nésemáhe* | friend |

All terms for affinal kin, except those with multiple referents including consanguineals, are terms with the *né–* prefix. The *né–* also occurs in *ného'e* 'my F'; otherwise, all terms for consanguineals except those with multiple referents including affinals, take the *na–* prefix.

The basic exceptions to the observation that consanguineal relatives are labeled by terms that take the *na–* prefix are *ného'e* 'my F', *néške'e* 'my GM/M-in-L', and *néxahe* 'my GCh/Ch-in-L'. These three are linguistically patterned exceptions. They are the only kin terms with the *\*no:–* prefix in Proto-Algonquian: *\*no:hoa, \*no:hka,* and *\*no:sisema,* respectively. The long vowel that obscures the true morpheme boundary between prefix and stem-initial vowel probably comes from *\*\*ni–o* in pre-Proto-Algonquian. The coalescence of prefix vowel and stem-initial vowel in pre-Proto-Algonquian may explain the regular form in Proto-Algonquian and also in Cheyenne (see Alford 1974).

There is, of course, a further interesting feature of grandmother, grandfather, and grandchild terms: they refer also to the affinal mother-in-law, father-in-law, and child-in-law. The double reference of these terms may also be relevant to the semantic inconsistency of their possessive forms. Eggan gave certain clarification terms he mistakenly thought were used to distinguish father-in-law from grandfather, mother-in-law from grandmother, and child-in-law from grandchild. However, these reference terms (actually participles—*tséhemèšéméto, tséhevéškeméto,* and *tséhevéxahéto)* are not specific to the affinal relatives; they can also be used for consanguineal relatives. In reference as well as in address, grandmother and mother-in-law, grandfather and father-in-law, and grandchild and child-in-law are equated.

As Raymond DeMallie (1979) has pointed out in his analysis of generation-skipping terminology among the Teton Sioux, at the time of his life when ego would be getting married, his future parents-in-law would be getting old. (Ideally, marriages were late, offspring widely spaced.) *Grandfather* thus would be an appropriate term for father-in-law since it was, generally, a term of respect for older men who had some particular relationship to ego. In Cheyenne today, moreover, a young child (presumably with a young grandfather) does not use *námėšeme* in addressing his grandfather, but uses instead the baby talk form *mémééhe*. Only when both individuals are older does *námėšeme* become appropriate. Use of the term *námėšeme* generally extended beyond these specific relationships to ceremonial instructors and to spirit-persons as well. Old men in general were addressed and referred to as *ma'háhkéso* (old women as *máhta-máháahe*), but those with whom a close relationship had been established became *námėšéme* (and *néške'éehe*). A young man might make tactical use of the term *námėšeme* to encourage or establish a relationship where none existed, or, in the case of his father-in-law, to soften a difficult one. Such tactical use of *námėšeme* 'grandfather' is supported by the fact that an older man would avoid a young man he did not respect if he knew that younger man was seeking a ceremonial instructor; if the young man offered him the pipe or called him *námėšeme*, he was in some sense obliged to comply with the request. A Cheyenne did well to have as many grandfathers as possible.

Beyond the argument concerning actual age there is, of course, teknonymy. The relationship with one's parents-in-law is always strengthened by offspring who are understood as consanguineally related to all parents and grandparents in this bilateral society. Teknonymy may well account for the generation-skipping terminology: from the point of view of ego's child, the terms do not skip generations, and a man might commonly assume his child's perspective (e.g., calling his father-in-law "father") since his own relationship with his parents-in-law requires avoidance. As he may address his sister only through her children, so he may address his mother-in-law through his wife or his own children.

A further and important explanation of the terminological equations was offered by a contemporary Northern Cheyenne consultant speaking of his brother and his brother's wife and addressing the (conscious) equation of grandfather with father-in-law, and grandmother with mother-in-law. Within his own family, argued the consultant, a man seeks out his grandfathers as the authority on family relationships and family history and lore. He learns about his wife's family from his father-in-law. Similarly, the man's wife learns the traditions of her own family from her grandmothers, while she learns the traditions of her husband's family from her mother-in-law. There is then a parallel relationship between one's grandmothers and one's mother-in-law, one's grandfathers and one's father-in-law, a relationship that supports the terminological equation.

Similarity of relationship, teknonymy, avoidance, and relative age all support the generation-skipping in-law terminology. Reduction of tension between in-laws is certainly a function of this terminology, as Eggan pointed out. But in order to understand why this particular way might be chosen to reduce tension in this particular culture, one must understand the context within which what Eggan called the "assimilation" of parents-in-law into consanguineal relationship occurs. Generation-skipping consanguineal terms may be used to make the in-law relationship closer; and, conversely, generation-skipping in-law terms were used to make the consanguineal relationship itself closer. A grandmother, that is, might address her grandson as "my little husband," her granddaughter as "my sister-in-law"; a grandfather may jokingly refer to his granddaughter as "my youngest wife" and his grandson as "my brother-in-law." As Eggan suggested, "These terms do not refer to marriage but are terms of affection; they likewise emphasize equality in terms of generation" (1937:54).

## Discussion

Two important points emerge from these prominent exceptions to the semantic distribution of the pronominal prefixes *na-* and *né-* and the cultural context of their use. In the first place, it is clear that native classification distinguishes consanguineal from affinal kin. *Navóohestoto,* a named category, refers to 'my blood relatives', distinguished in behavior and attitudes from kin by marriage or contract. Folk etymology relates the term *navóohestoto* to the term *hēsta* 'heart'. The heart, symbolic center of the body and of personal motivation, was and is understood as the seat of personal relationships, with shared blood as the physical link. Greater or lesser amounts of blood might be shared; but all Cheyennes are understood to share in the Cheyenne substance, the Cheyenne blood.

Within *navóohestoto*, there is a gradient of what contemporary consultants describe as "closeness." Those who share the most 'blood' are the "closest" and serve as a kind of model for relationships with those who are less "close." Those who share the most substance have the greatest obligations to each other and the strictest prohibition of sexual contact. Traditionally, postpubescent opposite-sex siblings avoided and did not speak directly to each other: Cheyennes today interpret this behavior as showing mutual respect. A man might arrange his sister's marriage and develop a close relationship with her husband and her children, but he was obliged to continue to "respect" her even after her marriage.

Relatives by marriage or contract *(nàhtovàmo)* constitute a different category of relations. The stronger the contract, the more reliable; members of one family tended to marry into the same other family, siblings from one family marrying siblings from the other or one male marrying two or more sisters (sororal polygyny was common among those who could afford it). The relationship between siblings-in-law of opposite sex *(nétame,* used reciprocally) was, in contrast to that between siblings of opposite sex, one of sexual joking and license.

Making relatives was a central and a critical activity for Cheyennes. The most respected or powerful people were always the most related (see Straus 1976). Marriage was not the only way of making relatives, but it was a good way. Adoption was another good way of making relatives, as was making "friends." In the case of a death of a child, the family sometimes adopted the child's "friend," the latter assuming kinship roles and terminology previously used by the deceased. "Friends" were of the same sex and about the same age. They were not consanguineally related, but they depended on each other like siblings. Members of the same military society called each other *néséne* 'friend' or used a brother term and probably members of the women's quilling society called each other *nésé'e* 'friend' or used a sister term.

Eggan's terms na·´sima *(násemáhe)* 'my younger sibling' and ni'sima *(nésemahe)* 'my friend' form a minimal pair in which the distinctive feature is the pronominal prefix. Culturally, the two relationships are very similar, implying essentially the same attitudes and behaviors; one, however, is consanguineal, the other contractual. The semantic contrast parallels the linguistic one: the older pronominal prefix *né-* denoting the contractual; *na-*, the consanguineal. In fact, as a linguistic strategy to secure the relationship with a good friend, an individual might switch from *nésemahe* to *násemáhe* in reference or address. The similarity in terms and the strategy of securing friendship by labeling it as a siblingship *(né-* to *ná-)* probably accounts for the statement by Rubie Sooktis, a Northern Cheyenne, that "the term for a brother from a brother does not exist . . . they refer to each other as 'friend.'" The same tactic is used today in Cheyenne-English, where individuals shift from "my friend" to "my sister" or "my brother" in reference, and sometimes in address as well.

In modern Cheyenne, Wayne Leman has argued (personal communication, 1990), speakers tend to regularize the old pronominal prefix, using *né* and *na(vé)* with no difference in meaning. However, the evidence from Petter and Eggan does suggest a difference in meaning, specifically with regard to the *násemáhe/nésemahe* (younger sibling/friend) pair. It is possible that a once meaningful shift has lost meaning over time.

The second major point that emerges from consideration of the pronominal prefixes is the variance evident in Cheyenne kin terms. Variability is also emphasized in John Moore's recent work (1987, 1988) on Cheyenne kinship, though it is there derived from a divergent interpretation of linguistic and historical data. Moore criticizes Eggan for obscuring variability by overdependence on structural-functional theory. My analysis of Cheyenne kin term usage, however, is entirely consistent with Eggan's focus on the "solidarity of brothers." Thus, variance in the use of possessive prefixes in the terms for the critical friend relationship reflects the speaker's tactical intent to enhance and encourage closeness, transforming friends into siblings.

Other alternatives were also clear. Concerning the sibling relationship, ego sometimes had a choice between alternatives for address and reference. Although Eggan reported *na'nèha* 'my older brother' and *namèhāne* 'my older sister' (terms used both for address and reference), Petter also listed the reference terms *nàhtatánéme* 'my older brother' (f.s.) and *naaxaa'éhéme* 'my older sister' (m.s.). The latter is also the term for 'my sister-in-law' (f.s.) and can be used by a grandmother addressing her granddaughter, as mentioned above. Petter (1952:12) noted that *namèhāne* was formerly used only by females, but had come to be used also by males, suggesting that the single term given by Eggan was only one of the choices a man had in addressing his older sister, although we do not know the basis for selection between them. Similarly, a female ego apparently had a choice between *na'nèha* and *nàhtatánéme* for 'my older brother'. Again, the basis for selection cannot be determined, but the linguistic status of the alternative terms, reflecting artifical rather than inherent possession (requiring the *–eme* suffix), should be noted.

Referential kin terms (participles) associated with *na'nèha* and *nàhtatánéme,* as given by Eggan for both male and female speakers, are *tséhe'néhéto* 'the one who is my older brother' and *tséhemèhéto* 'the one who is my older sister'. These terms were also used by both male and female speakers. However, the reference forms *tséhestatanéméto* 'the one who is my older brother' (f.s) and *tséheaxaa'éhéméto* 'the one who is my older sister' (m.s.), which are still used today, depend on the sex of speaker.

Eggan did not record alternative terms for address and for reference used by opposite-sex siblings.[1] Further consideration of the context of use of the alternative terms today would allow a better understanding of the meaning of the terms and of speaker selection between them. The existence of alternative sibling/friend terms in Cheyenne suggests a flexibility in use of kin terms that is also not evident in Eggan's analysis. However, this very terminological focus on the sibling/friend relationship supports his valuable hypothesis concerning the "solidarity of brothers."

## Life Cycle and the Solidarity of Brothers

The solidarity of related young men in hunting, raiding, and defense was essential to Northern Cheyenne survival. As a young man, ego sought to enhance and extend his relationships with his male peers, to establish a broad network of trusted and dependable brothers. The more brothers a man had, the more successful he was. Brotherhood was the most important feature of the relationship between young men, more important than consanguineal or spatial relationships. Consanguineal relationship could, of course, be specified. Ego, for example, recognized the difference between his mother's brother's son and his mother's sister's son, and had lexical modifiers that could be used to specify the particular relationships. But more important to him was his ability to call upon them as brothers and his interdependence with them both in various endeavors. Indeed, he made "brothers" out of "friends" with whom he had no consanguineal relationship but had established trust and cooperation. He had other ways of addressing male relatives—nicknames or even no-naming, both of which are still common today—but when he used the kinship term *brother*, he called upon the solidarity described by Eggan.

At the time in his life when he depended most heavily on a broad network of brothers, ego's spatial orientation was *outside* the camp. He spent most of his energy on and was recognized for his achievements in hunting, fighting, and sex, all of which were appropriately pursued only beyond the limits of the camp circle. He was, in a sense, "centrifugal," as Erik Erikson suggested for young Sioux males (1963). His place was the open prairie, not the domestic circle: the focal place for all young men was beyond the camp boundaries and camp identity. (Berdaches, young men who assumed women's dress and women's roles, remained in camp. Contraries, prohibited from marriage or maturity, lived almost entirely outside the camp circle.) "Brothers" could be found in many camps; the cooperative activities of "brotherhood" mostly took place beyond the limits of those camps.

Hawaiian ("generation") terminology in ego's generation was most important at this time in ego's life cycle, and was entirely consistent with his relationships at this time.

To Eggan, it seemed inconsistent that the parents of "brothers" and "sisters" were not, in Cheyenne terminology, all "mothers" and "fathers," and that there were "nephews" and "nieces" as well as "sons" and "daughters." In explanation, he suggested a prior behavioral and terminological differentiation of cross cousins from parallel cousins and siblings, "consistent" with the aunt-uncle terminology and typical of the riverine groups. As riverine groups moved out onto the High Plains, this differentiation disappeared in the new environment and new "flexible" social organization. In the case of the Teton Sioux, although the terminology did not change, the behavior patterns did, all cousins depending on each other like siblings and no cousins being marriageable. Although the cognate Ojibwa term *ní'nam* for 'marriageable relative' includes cross cousins of opposite sex as well as siblings-in-law of opposite sex (Hallowell 1937: 105), there is no evidence that the Cheyenne *nétame* 'sibling-in-law of opposite sex' (marriageable relative) ever applied to cross cousins or that cross-cousin marriage ever existed. The assumption of prior cross-cousin marriage is associated with the assumption of prior unilineality and is equally questionable.

The structure of Cheyenne kin terminology does not, of course, seem inconsistent to Cheyennes. The equivalence of same-sex siblings and the separation of opposite-sex siblings are clear in the terminology for each generation. The same principles produce different results in the different generations, but they are comprehensible results if proper account is taken of life cycle and context.

As ego first learned and named his relatives in his parents' generation, he called "father" all those who were "brother" to his father, and "mother" all those who were "sister" to his mother. These siblings/cousins/friends of his parents might also live in his own extended family camp. Parental siblings of opposite sex did not, however, and they were terminologically distinguished as "aunts" and "uncles." As a child, ego lived in and focused on his home camp. The old people there were all "grandfather" and "grandmother," the other adults were all "father" and "mother." He had other "fathers" and other "mothers" elsewhere but they were not important in the same way. In another camp he had "aunts" and "uncles" with whom he had special relationships, different from his relationships with "mothers" and "fathers." (The "brothers" and "sisters" in those other camps might have been called "far brothers" and "far sisters"; see Eggan 1937:46 n. 20.)

Camp identity and orientation declined in importance to the young man as he sought to accomplish and be recognized for the proper activities of his age group outside the camp. But he returned again to a camp—usually that of his wife's family—and eventually established his maturity by fathering a child. In the new camp, as in the old, the focal tipi was that of "grandfather" and "grandmother" (in this case, specifically, father-in-law and mother-in-law). In his own generation, he had "brothers" (sometimes siblings or cousins, but all who married sisters became "brothers") and wives, potential *(nétame)* or actual. (Unmarried brothers-in-law might also live in the camp temporarily.) As a father, looking at his child's generation, he classified his own children with those of his potential wives and distinguished them from those of his unmarriageable "sisters," consistent with the separation of opposite-sex siblings and the equivalence of same-sex siblings. Returning to the camp circle, then, he also separated the children of his new camp (all "sons" and "daughters") from the children of his natal camp (all "nephews" and "nieces"). Even if he were to adopt his sister's child, he would continue to call the child "nephew" or "niece," "to keep the relationship right" (Eggan 1937:47 n. 25, quoting a Cheyenne consultant).

To understand the Cheyenne kinship system, each generation must be considered separately. Cheyennes conceptualized kinship as "just like three horizontal lines" (Eggan 1937:67 n. 72). Calling the children of "aunts" and "uncles" "brother" and "sister" is inconsistent only if the system is conceptualized in terms of vertical lines linking generations or if the relationship between camp identity and life cycle is ignored. From the point of view of the individual ego, the solidarity of brothers and the respect of sisters in social behavior is consistent with the terms *father* and *mother*, *uncle* and *aunt*, *son* and *daughter*, *nephew* and *niece,* as well as the terms *brother* and *sister*. But this is evident only when life cycle, domestic cycle, and the varying context of ego's relationships are recognized. Such contextualization of kin term usage may also allow resolution of issues raised by Moore (1988), whose response has been to develop what he calls a "filiocentric" representation of Cheyenne kin terminology.

## Changes in Cheyenne Kinship

In assessing changes in Cheyenne kinship in the fifty years since Eggan's fieldwork, I have drawn on Northern Cheyenne data only. Some discrepancies might be expected, then, since Eggan's work was with Southern Cheyennes in Oklahoma. Kin terms in Eggan's list, however, are all used by Northern Cheyennes today, although certain of them are used differently. The assertion of change is supported by Northern Cheyenne perception, not assumed on the basis of difference from Eggan's Southern Cheyenne list. Eggan asserted his terminology as Cheyenne, not as Southern Cheyenne, and he intended the terminology to apply to Northern Cheyenne as well. There is no reason to dispute his claim. The changes described below for Northern Cheyenne may be considered hypotheses to be tested for Southern Cheyenne, where social and political change has been more extreme and reservation life began earlier.

Just as Eggan described in 1937, sex and generation remain today the fundamental principles organizing Cheyenne kin relationships and kin terminology. That these principles are consistent with native intuition is clear from Ms. Sooktis's discussion of her own Northern Cheyenne terminology ("family terms," as she calls them). In listing kin terms as data for this paper, she rejected a genealogical chart because "the chart repeats itself too much." Instead, she organized the terms in two sections, one dealing with male relatives, the other with female relatives. ("The family terms are divided into the Cheyenne male and female roles of the tribe.") Each section was subdivided according to generation. Where Eggan gave only the first person form of address, Ms. Sooktis, sensitive to the special status of relatives and their "inherent possession," gave three reference terms for each relationship: *my father*, *your father*, and *our father*, for example. The sense of kinship as "three horizontal lines" is still very much there, but there is no indication of a shift toward a consistent generation terminology in either the first ascending or first descending generation.

In the first ascending generation, terms of address for males are the same as reported by Eggan: *ného'e* 'father' (including father's brothers and father's male cousins) and *náxāne* 'uncle' (including mother's brother and mother's male cousins). Eggan did not supply reference terms for these relationships, but they are, today, *ného'éehe* 'my father' and *tséhéhéto* 'the one who is my father', and *nèxāne* 'my uncle' and *tséhešéhéto* 'the one who is my uncle'. Since Petter supplied identical terms (in his own orthography) it is safe to assume that at the time of Eggan's fieldwork the terms were still used, and with the same meanings. Petter specified that the terms of reference apply specifically to "father" and to "uncle" (mother's brothers, mother's male cousins). A third reference term also noted by Petter (1913–15) and used today is *tséhehamóoneto* 'the one who is my second father', 'the one who is my father figure', or 'the one who is my stepfather'. This term specifies, in reference, father's brother or male cousin, distinguishing him from father. Thus, while father and father's brothers and male cousins are classified in address as *ného'e*, in reference they can be terminologically distinguished and apparently have been at least since Petter's time.

Today, the term *tséhešéhéto* 'the one who is my uncle' is used by some speakers for father's brother as well as for mother's brother. This usage represents a change from the situation described by Petter, where this reference term applied only to mother's brother and mother's male cousins (see Alford and Leman 1976:117). Eggan's chart indicates that the same term was also used for father's sister's husband, a male relative on the father's side (like father's brother), albeit a relative by marriage and, in practice, often a brother or male cousin of the mother. My own consultants today deny this usage, insisting that the term applies "only to close relatives," and that such a relative by marriage is not a "close relative." Today, brother-sister exchange is uncommon and father's sister's husband is usually not a "brother" to ego's mother, but "just a relative by marriage." Without a consanguineal connection, apparently still common fifty years ago, *tséhešéhéto* has become inappropriate for father's sister's husband.

While the latter change reduces its extension, the former change increases it. The contemporary use of *tséhešéhéto* to include father's brothers is additionally important because it suggests a structural change in the terminology, classifying all male relatives in the first ascending generation except for ego's father, who remains distinct in address and in reference. However, it is only a very limited shift, one denied by Ms. Sooktis, who insists that *tséhešéhéto* "is used only by the male's sister's and female relative's children" (i.e., only for mother's brother and mother's male cousins). Variance is clear. Some Cheyennes today use *tséhešéhéto* for father's brother as well as for mother's brother, some do not; but no one uses the terms of address in this way.

A parallel shift for some speakers has occurred in the use of "aunt" terms. While father's sister is always called *náháa'e* when a kin term is selected for address, and mother's sister is never addressed in this way, both mother's sister and father's sister are referred to by some speakers as *tséhehaehéto*. Today, as fifty years ago, mother's sister is distinguished from mother by the term *tséheškamóonéto* 'the one who is my step-mother, my second mother' (Petter 1913–15:720). However, classifying mother's sister with father's sister is new. Paralleling the uncle terms, the same "aunt" term was used for mother's brother's wife, a relative on the mother's side of the family as Eggan (but not Petter) reported it. Here too, the consanguineal link took precedence over the affinal link such that the affinal relative, mother's brother's wife, is not called aunt unless she is also father's sister or father's female cousin. Mother's brother's wife, like father's sister's husband, is usually addressed and referred to today by personal name. Again, the shift is limited, and Ms. Sooktis denies the extension of the reference of *tséhehaehéto* to include mother's sister.

The sex of the speaker may be relevant to understanding this variance. Ms. Sooktis's brother, Andy, suggested that a male ego might refer to his mother's sister as *tséhehaehéto*, while he would not call his father's brother *tséhešéhéto*. A female speaker might call her father's brother *tséhešéhéto*, but would not call her mother's sister *tséhehaehéto*. That is, the speaker differentiates those relatives (of same sex) most important to him or her but may lump together those (of opposite sex) who are less important.

Of course, even that limited shift is consistent with American English terminology. All Cheyennes today understand English and know the English use of the terms *uncle* and *aunt*. Interference from these English patterns might account for the shift in aunt-uncle reference in Cheyenne. But most Cheyennes know and use both systems appropriately, distinguishing clearly between them and using each in its particular context. In my experience, Cheyenne terms are used only in speaking to other Cheyennes and only according to the appropriate Cheyenne paradigm. English terms used in speaking to non-Cheyennes are generally used in the appropriate English-speaking paradigm. Whereas there are no "mistakes" made in speaking Cheyenne, there are numerous examples of "mistakes" in English: for example, *sister* in English may refer to a female cousin, *brother* to a male cousin. English terms are also used by Cheyennes speaking to other Cheyennes who do not know the native language. In these cases, the English terms are often given Cheyenne meanings: *brother* and *sister* are as above; *grandfather* and *grandmother* include brothers and sisters of the child's grandparents; and *daddy* may be used for father's brother as well as for father, reciprocally with *my kid* or *my little girl*, and so forth. What interference there is between the two systems, then, seems to affect English usage but not Cheyenne use of Cheyenne terms when speaking to other Cheyennes. Something else must account for the shift suggested above.

The decreasing importance of the localized extended family *household* or *camp* and associated increasing importance of the nuclear family must be considered here. Polygyny is no longer practiced and the levirate and sororate no longer sustain the extended family as they used to (though the children still remain with the mother's family in the case of her death). Matrilocal residence, strongly preferred fifty years ago, is considerably less common today. Young couples go where the houses, the resources, and the jobs are, and that often means living apart from the wife's family. Paved roads and automobiles have radically altered the significance of the local community since intercommunity visiting is now both easy and constant. Neolocal residence and increased mobility have accelerated the decline of the extended family as the focal economic unit. Individuals now support themselves and their families primarily through jobs and federal monies issued to individuals or to nuclear families, though the jobs available depend heavily on jobs held by one's relatives, and monies paid are always shared. The cooperative subsistence activities of the extended family household and cooperative preparation of food still occur and are symbolically important (particularly in the context of major ceremonies), but contribute only minimally to actual subsistence.

The nuclear family, once a mere subdivision of the focal household unit, is today both economically and emotionally more important. This change is probably related to the limited shift in aunt-uncle terminology toward a lineal system, distinguishing nuclear family members—father and mother—from all others.

Also relevant to the terminological shift may be the increasing association between brothers and sisters. Brothers and sisters now seldom observe strict avoidance, even in the "best," most "traditional" families. With increased opportunity for direct expression of support and affection between siblings of opposite sex, the emotional focus on each other's children and the need to use them as "go-betweens" in verbal communication have diminished. (It should be recalled that the reduction of avoidance has not been associated with any shift toward common kin terms for each other. For male and female speakers, kin terms for "my older brother" and "my older sister" show the same variance today as they did fifty years ago, some terms being distinguished according to sex of speaker, some not.) Furthermore, the occasions for actualizing a special relationship with mother's brother or with father's sister are minimized in contemporary Northern Cheyenne life. Many of the traditional responsibilities of these relatives pertained to ceremonial contexts that are no longer relevant to many Northern Cheyennes, though it is still, for example, the father's sister who should and usually does make the cradleboard for her brother's child, and it is still the mother's brother who is the disciplinary threat. From the point of view of the younger relative, there may be no special advantage in distinguishing mother's brother from father's brother or any other "uncles" who might be called upon for social and financial support.

It is common today in some families for a child to have one special "second parent," one of the same sex as the child, with whom he or she has a special relationship. That is, rather than all of ego's father's brothers and male cousins activating their parental relationship to a particular male ego, one is selected as the closest "second father." The others, then, may become more like "uncles" and more reasonably might be classified with them as *tséhešéhéto*.

There are several reasons, then, why we might expect to find the kind of shift that has been noticed in aunt-uncle terminology, and in the relationships named by those terms. But the changes themselves must not be exaggerated. The shift is minimal, apparently limited to reference and to certain speakers and perhaps to certain contexts.

There has been no parallel shift in nephew-niece terms. A male ego today still addresses his sister's children as *natse* 'my nephew' and *ná'hame* 'my niece'; a female ego still uses those terms for her brother's children. The terms *tséhetsénotàhéto* 'the one who is my nephew' and *tséhe'hamèhéto* 'the one who is my niece' apply only to the son or daughter of a man's sister or a woman's brother; the children of a man's brother or a woman's sister are never so named in address or reference. (In one exceptional instance where his sister's child was raised with him like a sibling, a male consultant addresses that child as *násemáhe* 'my younger sibling'—a further example of contextual definition of that term as discussed above.) A male considers himself a "second father," to teach and guide his brother's children; he considers himself a disciplinary aid and a provider to his sister's children. Behavior as well as terminology is understood as differentiated from his point of view. The general reference term *nanéso* 'my child' may be used for all children in the family as differentiated from *naka'éškónèhame* 'my (nonbiological) child'. It is loosely used in this way, however, and does not influence proper use of nephew and niece terms or their differentiation from "son" and "daughter"—one's own or those of one's same-sex sibling.

The shift, albeit minimal, in aunt-uncle terms suggests a parallel shift in niece-nephew terms, but such a shift has not occurred. The stability of the kinship terminology is again underlined. Perhaps if we attend to the perspective of the individual ego, the disparity may be comprehensible. Whereas a young girl may not distinguish her mother's brother from her father's brother in the context of discussing their support of her, her mother's brother, being older and more versed in tribal tradition, may be significantly more concerned with his traditional social and ceremonial obligations to her.

Another shift, again minimal, has occurred for some speakers in the use of *námèšeme* 'grandfather'. Ceremonial instructors, those who paint dancers in the Sun Dance, for example, are not invariably addressed or referred to as "grandfather" today by those whom they paint and instruct. The relationship between dancer and painter remains much like that between "grandson" and "grandfather" (great respect but also familiarity and teasing), yet kin terms are not always used between them. Within the family, moreover, *námèšeme* seems to apply "only to your close relatives" as one consultant describes it—one's grandfather and his brothers, certainly—and the brothers of one's grandmother as well. Tactical use of the term *námèšeme* is perhaps not as extensive today as it was fifty years ago, though use of the term in prayer to address spirit-beings is still common. Old men, generally, are addressed and referred to as *ma'háhkéso* 'old man'.

There is a slight reduction in the extension of the term *brother* today as well. Specifically, two men who have been married to the same woman no longer call each other 'brother' or behave as brothers to each other. With the overall demise of the levirate and sororate, the second husband of a woman or second wife of a man whose spouse has died is seldom the brother- or sister-in-law, respectively. That is, in the case of the levirate, when a man died in battle, his brother or male cousin (also called 'brother') might marry his wife to maintain family relationships. Today, in the absence of that custom, the terminology has changed. Furthermore, men who marry sisters today may not themselves be brothers or male cousins; if they are not, they do not call each other brother.

Personal names are now frequently and often preferably used in addressing one's cousins and other relatives. Traditionally, before English names were given, personal names were not used in address for the norms concerning personal names restricted their use almost entirely. Such names were known but not uttered or sometimes not even known between two people. Today, "Indian names" are occasionally used in address and reference between close friends or relatives; but English names, always profane, are consistently used in this way between relatives and non-relatives alike. Sisters, brothers, cousins, friends, brothers-in-law, and sisters-in-law are commonly addressed and referred to by English name. Older relatives, especially parents and grandparents, are more often addressed by kin terms consistent with American use of English names and kin terms. Younger relatives are addressed and referred to by English name or by what have been called "pet names"—nicknames given to young children and usually abandoned sometime during high school. The new use of personal names in social interaction emphasizes the tactical use of kin terms evident both today and in prereservation times. As the use of personal names has become so common, the use of kin terms assumes a new meaning. When kin terms are used today, it is because that relationship is being called forth for some context-dependent purpose.

Concerning brother/cousin terms more generally, there is no further change in the reported terminology. Younger sibling is still distinguished from older brother and older sister, and the terms for siblings are also the terms for cousins on both sides of the family with no distinction of cross and parallel cousins.

An interesting shift seems to have occurred in the use of the term *navóohestoto*. In Petter's time, it was used to mean 'my blood relatives' as discussed above. Today, according to Ms. Sooktis, the same term is used to mean 'all my cousins and other relatives who are not part of my immediate family'. That is, use today isolates and reiterates the importance of the nuclear family and allows for a classification of other relatives. In so doing, it also allows for a differentiation between *sibling* and *cousin*, the former excluded, the latter belonging.

The solidarity of brothers and cousins still obtains, though the particulars have changed with the reservation context. "Brothers" support each other, look out for each other, share with each other, play basketball together, avoid competing with each other for jobs, and often try to find work for each other. They also still dance together, fight together, and hunt together, though those activities do not have the same critical importance they formerly did. The central position of young men in Northern Cheyenne society has been severely disturbed in the reservation period. Young men find little work, little opportunity to engage in traditionally valued activities. Today, their solidarity is more self-serving, less integrated into tribal purpose.

The young women today do not suffer the same disorientation and difficulties. As Margaret Mead (1932) pointed out (also about fifty years ago), women on the Plains were considerably less disrupted by the reservation experience than men. Women were still the mothers, still responsible for holding families together, raising children, sewing clothing, preparing food, telling children's stories, moving the home, furnishing the house, curing minor ills, and so on. Their activities, consistent with prereservation lifeways, were and are valued. The crafts movement further strengthened the position of women by providing remuneration and recognition for quillwork, beadwork, and other native crafts practiced by women, allowing them to support families when the men were unable to do so. Young women often took better to federal boarding schools and gained a certain measure of success in and through them as well, contributing to the increasingly public and political role that women play in Plains tribes today.

The solidarity of siblings, cousins, and friends is still fundamental to Northern Cheyenne social organization, but it is more notably the solidarity of young women. Despite changes in postmarital residence, women's strongest and most enduring bonds are still with other women—their "sisters" and their "mothers." This is not a society in which a woman looks forward to leaving her mother to establish the central relationship of her life—her marriage. A woman seldom marries a man unacceptable to her parents or her siblings; the man is still understood to join her family, and his place is still tenuous within it. Divorce is common, as it was in prereservation days, and children generally remain with the mother or her close relatives. Today the "solidarity of sisters" holds things together. Perhaps it did so fifty years ago and even before that, but it is more obvious today as reservation life exacts its bitter toll on the young men.

The overall conceptualization of kinship has changed somewhat in recent years. Blood has become the paramount symbol of kinship and tribal identity, with amount of blood representing degree of closeness. Blood relationships are in some sense more rigidly opposed to relationships of marriage since certain occasions for their acceptable overlap (e.g., when ego's mother's brother marries ego's father's sister in brother-sister exchange marriage such that his father's sister's husband is also his mother's brother, a consanguineal relative) have essentially disappeared. At the same time, however, the boundaries of the categories *navóohestoto* 'my blood relatives' and *náhtovàmo* 'my relatives by marriage' have become less clear. Third-cousin marriage, once clearly forbidden, has become acceptable to some who argue that the only alternative is to marry outside the tribe and suffer the losses which that entails.

Blood, already an important symbol in the old days, has become now divisible, dilutable, and quantifiable. Adoption does not now make full relatives out of aliens, since blood can be lost but never acquired. Marriage outside the tribe represents a loss of "blood" and a confusion of identity for the children of the marriage. Where this "blood" comes from is not entirely clear: Cheyenne theory of conception has many variants, some of which include blood coming from the mother as the primal substance from which the body is formed. But the father contributes equally to conception in Cheyenne understanding, and he contributes equally in the computation of blood quantum.

Descent is understood as bilateral today, just as it was fifty years ago. Recent terminological changes are entirely consistent with bilateral descent, though they are not to be understood as direct reflections of it. Grinnell suggested an historical shift from matrilineal to patrilineal descent:

> Such young people positively assert today that the tribal descent is in the male line, and it cannot be doubted that present-day investigation would lead people to that conclusion. The old men up to twenty or twenty-five years ago, however, were unanimous in saying that the children belonged to the mother's group. [1923, 1:91]

Other ethnographers (e.g., Mooney 1907:408–9) have disputed or failed to confirm Grinnell's interpretation. Eggan himself, while arguing for a "less amorphous" and probably matrilineal organization for pre-Plains Cheyennes, remarked that "there is no strong evidence for a former clan system [with strict exogamy and an ideology of descent from a common ancestor], however, and it is possible that his [Grinnell's] informants were rationalizing the past" (1937:85 n. 98). Even Moore (1987, 1988), who posits a historical shift from matrilocal to patrilocal affiliation with the increasing importance of the Dog Soldiers and other military societies, has moved from earlier (1974) assertions of unilineal descent to a focus on patterns of residence.

The evidence for early matrilineal descent is unclear and unconvincing. Consultants' statements such as the one above, obviously elicited in directed questioning through an interpreter, can be accounted for without postulating an ideology of matrilineal descent. Band exogamy (also postulated by Grinnell) might well have described the experience of particular informants, since the ten to fifteen families in a band were generally related by kinship or friendship. The children in the band may have been nearly all related, some through their mothers, some through their fathers. In this case, the prohibition on "cousin" marriage could have meant a de facto band exogamy without unilineality. Preferential cross-cousin marriage, moreover, as discussed above, also postulated by Eggan for the earlier period, has never been reported by any informant in Grinnell or elsewhere. All cousins—at least through third cousins—were un-marriageable.

The claim that children "belong to the mother's group," as described above by Grinnell, is fully explicable in terms of the preferential matrilocal residence of the prereservation Cheyennes. Matrilocal extended family camps were certainly the focal units in prereservation Cheyenne society. But such units were not constituted on an ideology of matrilineal descent. They resulted, rather, from the culturally defined nature of males and females, the inheritance of domestic property, and the strength of bonds between women.

Women have always been the stable domestic core of Cheyenne society—those who stand in the center, as one older woman put it, and "pull in the reins from the Four Directions," straining to orient and domesticate the mobile, "centrifugal" young men. The domestic arena was their special province. They made major decisions; they owned all domestic property including the tipi. The tipi, cooking utensils, and blankets passed down from a woman to her daughters, to those in the family who would use and care for them. Sharing equipment and labor among the women in the camp was not only more efficient, it was more pleasant. Women who lived in the same camp gathered and prepared food together, tanned and sewed and beaded or quilled together. Many belonged to quilling societies which, like the military societies of the men, celebrated their achievements and supported the solidarity of the "sisters" who belonged. What women knew they passed on to their daughters, whose training and behavior they scrutinized with utmost concern. When daughters joined the female work group, they, too, became part of the domestic center; only matrilocality made sense.

The boys, however, went with their fathers, who taught them to hunt and to fight, taught them about life beyond the camp circle and instructed them in the great ceremonies, the special province of the men whose greater spirituality (symbolized by a larger larynx and thus greater breath-spirit, *omotome*) so qualified them. Personal property might pass from father to son, as domestic property passed from mother to daughter. Military society membership also depended heavily on the special relationship between father and son; a young man usually joined his father's society, if the other members deemed him worthy. The military society provided another aspect of the young man's training and the father could attend to it most carefully when both belonged to the same society. Eggan pointed out that "the integrative effect of the [military] society system is very much like that of a nonlocalized patrilineal clan system, as far as the males are concerned" (1937:85 n. 99).

This misleading similarity probably led to Grinnell's statement concerning the later patrilineality of Plains Cheyennes and perhaps to Eggan's assessment that "the feeling concerning descent is bilateral, or even slightly patrilineal at present" (1937:37). Military society membership, "very much like . . . a nonlocalized patrilineal clan," was critical to John Moore's (1974) argument for a historical shift from matrilineal to patrilineal organization. Moore holds that matrilineal ideology and organization prevailed during the period before intense military conflict with whites, arguing that the Council of Forty-Four ("Peace Chiefs"), associated with a matrilineal and domestic ideology, was the dominant political force at that time. Later, during the wars with the federal government, the Council of Forty-Four is seen to have declined, and the military societies, with patrilineal ideology and organization, became more powerful.

E. Adamson Hoebel (1980) reviewed in detail Moore's historical data, distinguished Northern from Southern Cheyenne history, and decisively reaffirmed the bilateral character of Cheyenne descent, which he first described in 1960. In Montana, the Council of Forty-Four persists today and membership generally passes from father to son, as it did in the past. In the case of the death of a council member, the older people, men and women, of the family of the deceased will deliberate and choose the most qualified successor—a son, a brother's son, or even a sister's son, depending upon his personal qualifications. Military society membership, moreover, was always based on relationships among men learning and doing men's work; but military societies neither practiced nor promoted a patrilineal ideology.

Neither matrilineality nor patrilineality has been convincingly demonstrated for Cheyennes at any stage of their history. Inheritance, instruction, and transfer of power and of affiliation have always gone from father to son and from mother to daughter, respecting the division of the sexes discussed at some length by Eggan (1937). The cultural definition of male and female has been misread as unilineal ideology. Male and female domains were strictly defined and distinguished but clearly and continually interdependent. Male and female are understood to contribute differently but equally to the conception and growth of a new life. The direction of that new life is dependent from the very start upon sexual identity, but its descent is understood as bilateral, its membership in a kin group equally dependent upon and equally inclusive of relationships through both parents. This is true today as it was fifty years ago during Eggan's fieldwork, and indeed throughout the historic period.

## Summary

Most Northern Cheyennes today who speak Cheyenne use Cheyenne kin terms consistent with those outlined in Eggan (1937). All the terms Eggan identified are still known and used as he explained, but there are other forms and other uses as well. Alternative codes, alternative terminology, alternative prefixes (in the case of sibling/friend), and the tactical use of kin terms emphasize the importance of considering context of use—including features of life cycle and domestic cycle—in interpreting those terms.

Variant use of kin terms also renders especially difficult the assessment of change in terminology over time. What seems to be a change may be more accurately accounted for by the increased analytical attention to alternatives. But native intuition confirms certain minimal changes in the use of kin terms (*tséhešèhéto* may now refer to father's brother as well as mother's brother; *tséhehaehéto* may now refer to mother's sister as well as father's sister; *námèšeme* 'grandfather', *na'nèha* 'older brother', and probably *namèhāne* 'older sister', are somewhat reduced in extension) and the behavior between kinsmen (brother-sister exchange marriage is uncommon; levirate, sororate, and polygyny are essentially nonexistent; brother-sister avoidance is seldom strictly observed; matrilocal residence and extended family ties have diminished). These changes are consistent with and related to the increasing importance of the nuclear family in contemporary reservation society. The primary kin group today is clearly and consistently bilateral, though reduced in extension, and there is no clear evidence that the Cheyennes had a unilineal descent system during their residence on the High Plains or before.

Changes in behavior have been more pronounced than changes in terminology. Northern Cheyenne kin terminology has changed little in the fifty years since Eggan's fieldwork. There continues to be a "high degree of stability for the basic kinship structures of the Cheyenne . . . over a considerable period of time, extending back into the pre-reservation period" (Eggan 1937:47).

## Acknowledgments

The author wishes to thank Wayne Leman for providing the phonemic transcriptions of Cheyenne words, and for his helpful comments on a draft of this chapter.

## Notes

1. A man would always use the woman's terms when speaking to (*náhtatánéme*) or about (*hestatanèmo*) a woman concerning her brother. Similarly, a woman would always use the man's terms when speaking to or about a man concerning his sister.

## References

Alford, Dan K.
  1974    Linguistic Speculation on the Pre-history of the Cheyenne People. Papers of
          the Sixth Algonquian Conference, edited by William Cowan, 10-29. National
          Museum of Man, Mercury Series, Canadian Ethnology Service Paper no. 23.
          Ottawa.
Alford, Dan K., and Wayne E. Leman
  1976    English-Cheyenne Student Dictionary. Language Research Department of the
          Northern Cheyenne Title VII ESEA Bilingual Education Program. Lame
          Deer, Mont.
DeMallie, Raymond J.
  1979    Change in American Indian Kinship Systems: The Dakota. *In* Currents in
          Anthropology: Essays in Honor of Sol Tax, edited by Robert Hinshaw,
          221-41. The Hague: Mouton.
Eggan, Fred
  1937    The Cheyenne and Arapaho Kinship System. *In* Social Anthropology of North
          American Tribes, edited by Fred Eggan, 35-95. Chicago: University of
          Chicago Press.
  1952    The Ethnological Cultures and Their Archeological Backgrounds. *In*
          Archeology of the Eastern United States, edited by James B. Griffin, 35-45.
          Chicago: University of Chicago Press.

1966      The American Indian: Perspectives for the Study of Social Change. Chicago:
          Aldine Publishing.
Erikson, Erik
1963      Childhood and Society. 2d ed. New York: W. W. Norton.
Glenmore, Josephine Stands In Timber, and Wayne Leman
1985      Cheyenne Topical Dictionary. Rev. ed. Busby, Mont.: Cheyenne Translation
          Project.
Grinnell, George Bird
1923      The Cheyenne Indians: Their History and Ways of Life. 2 vols. New Haven:
          Yale University Press.
Hallowell, A. Irving
1937      Cross-Cousin Marriage in the Lake Winnipeg Area. *In* Philadelphia Anthropo-
          logical Society Publications no. 1, Twenty-Fifth Anniversary Studies, edited
          by D. S. Davidson, 95-110. Philadelphia: University of Pennsylvania Press.
Hoebel, E. Adamson
1960      The Cheyennes. New York: Holt, Rinehart and Winston.
1980      On Cheyenne Sociopolitical Organization. Plains Anthropologist 25:161-69.
Leman, Wayne
1981      Cheyenne Pitch Rules. International Journal of American Linguistics
          47:283-309.
Mead, Margaret
1932      The Changing Culture of an American Indian Tribe. New York: Columbia
          University Press.
Mooney, James
1907      The Cheyenne Indians. American Anthropological Association Memoirs, vol.
          1, 357-442. Washington, D.C.
Moore, John H.
1974      Cheyenne Political History, 1820-1894. Ethnohistory 21:329-59.
1987      The Cheyenne Nation: A Social and Demographic History. Lincoln:
          University of Nebraska Press.
1988      The Dialects of Cheyenne Kinship: Variability and Change. Ethnology
          27:253-69.
Petter, Rodolphe C.
1901      Sketch of the Cheyenne Grammar. American Anthropological Association
          Memoirs, vol. 1, 443-78. Washington, D.C.
1913-15   English-Cheyenne Dictionary. Kettle Falls, Wash.
1952      Cheyenne Grammar. Newton, Kans.: Mennonite Publication Office.
Straus, Anne S.
1976      Being Human in the Cheyenne Way. Ph.D. diss., University of Chicago.
1977      Northern Cheyenne Ethnopsychology. Ethos 5:326-57.

# 7

# The Social Organizations of the Southeast

GREG URBAN

John R. Swanton opined that cultures of the Southeast were everywhere "basically the same" (1946:812). So also for him were the social organizations, and that monolithic model has become the received view. Creek social organization was taken as typical, with the Natchez class system subtype taken as paradigmatic for the Lower Mississippi Valley and Gulf Coast region. There thus emerged for Swanton a Southeastern-type social organization, built around matrilineal clans, matrilocal residence rules, and Crow-type kin terminologies, reflecting in some measure a common adaptation to the southeastern woodland environment.

Over the years, dissenting opinions have been registered. Frank Speck, for instance, in reopening "The Question of Matrilineal Descent in the Southeastern Siouan Area," concluded:

> The results of any attempt to find evidence in *Catawba* institutions and traditions of a unilineal pattern of descent are simply *nil*. The value of evidence hitherto accepted in regard to original Tutelo social organization may be pronounced unstable.... If, on the grounds established by any critical examination of sources, the Catawba and the Tutelo are to be removed from the social companionship of the Creek and Cherokee, i.e., from the grouping which includes the tribes having mother-sibs in the Southeast, a change in the social configuration of tribes of the Southeast must henceforth be mapped out. [1938:10–12]

Similarly, Mary Haas (1939) argued convincingly for the absence of matrilineal clans in former Natchez and Chitimacha society.[1]

From such dissenting opinions can be culled an alternative model of the Southeastern culture area. This chapter reviews developments in the post-Swanton, multiparadigm model. In contrast to the monolithic view, the multiparadigm model emphasizes social organizational diversity. The Southeast appears in that model as a complex culture area, harboring an array of basically distinct social organizations, of which perhaps half lack anything resembling matriclans, and among which Crow-type skewing of cousin terms is probably confined to core-Muskhogean groups (e.g., Creeks, Seminoles, Choctaws, and Chickasaws) and the Cherokees. While

172

our knowledge of many Southeastern social organizations remains sketchy—and this was, in the first instance, what made the monolithic model seem plausible—it is nonetheless often sufficient to suggest divergence from the so-called Southeastern type. In any case, the positive task confronting Southeastern social organizational studies must be to develop and test the multiparadigm model.

## The Comparative Method

Shifting from a monolithic to a multiparadigm model of the Southeast requires a simultaneous shift in comparative method. Consequently, the previous comparative studies of Southeastern social organizations must be mentioned—John R. Swanton (1928a, 1946), Fred Eggan (1937, 1966), and Alexander Spoehr (1947)—in order to contrast their methods with those employed here.

Swanton's method was primarily diffusionist, with a focus on the trait as the unit of analysis. That method dovetailed nicely with his monolithic view of Southeastern culture. Traits, such as matrilineal clans or mother-in-law avoidance, were seen as largely independent of one another, and as diffusing in piecemeal fashion more or less readily from one tribe to another. Consequently, comparison for Swanton consisted in analyzing the distribution of traits. Moreover, because traits tended to cluster geographically, subdivisions of the Southeast for him were usually geographically defined (e.g., Gulf area, Northeastern section). The Southeast itself was one such geographical cluster, with its characteristic type of social organization having resulted from diffusions.

The subsequent comparative efforts of Eggan (1937, 1966) and Spoehr (1947) can be seen as transitional to the multiparadigm point of view. They abandoned traits in favor of a focus on systems, but they retained a view of the Southeast as having once had a single, homogenous type of social organization. As Spoehr stated, the hypothesis was that "kinship systems of pure Crow type were formerly widespread in the Southeast" (1947:159).

That twofold hypothesis is most apparent in Eggan's (1966:33–35) analysis of Yuchi kinship terminology. He focuses primarily on the Choctaws, Chickasaws, Creeks, and Cherokees, where it is abundantly clear that he views social organizations as systematically interconnected wholes rather than as more or less random clusters of traits. He demonstrates that the kinship terminologies of those tribes (approximating in varying degrees a Crow-type skewing pattern) systematically covary in structure with other social institutions, principally the family. For the Yuchis, however, his most complete data (Wagner 1934:339–40) unambiguously indicate an Omaha-type skewing pattern, which was highly anomalous. The monolithic assumption would have led him to hypothesize that the Yuchi system had arisen from a prior system that had conformed to the Southeastern type. And that was precisely the hypothesis for which he argued. Using Speck's (1909:68–70) incomplete data, and the knowledge that Yuchis had been intermarrying with the patrilineal Shawnees, Eggan reached the remarkable conclusion that Yuchis had "gone through the whole sequence of changes from a Crow to an Omaha type of kinship system" (1966:34).

From a multiparadigm perspective, however, it is significant that the Yuchis had *patrilineal* men's moieties, and that from all appearances they were of great antiquity (cf. Swanton 1946:664). Of course, a patrilineal emphasis correlates nicely with Omaha-type skewing of cousin terms. Consequently, judging from the general principles of systematicity, it would appear that Omaha skewing was the more aboriginal form, and that Speck's data were probably collected from informants among whom the aboriginal system was no longer functioning. If so, Yuchi social organization would emerge as highly distinctive.

It is not surprising that the Southeast should exhibit diversity of social organization. From the research of Mary Haas (1973) it is now suspected that the Southeast was an area of considerable linguistic complexity. Insofar as that linguistic complexity mirrors the historico-genetic diversity of tribes themselves, and insofar as social organizations as systems tend to persist over time, it would follow that the Southeast should contain a multiplicity of distinct social organizational systems. At any rate, that has been the guiding postulate of the present research. Of course, tribes do interact and traits do in some measure diffuse. The Mississippian period of pre-Columbian Southeastern history seems incomprehensible without some such assumption. Still, borrowed traits are integrated into ongoing systems, and those systems maintain, in spite of borrowings, their integrity as systems, at least in some measure.

From a methodological point of view, there is a salient difficulty in comparing whole systems. In diffusionism, one can speak simply of the presence versus absence of traits. Understanding a system, however, means gaining insight into the interconnections among its component parts. Comparison therefore consists of an assessment of overall similarities with regard to how the components are put together. It has been the goal of the present research to assess those similarities.

Tentatively, I have concluded that the classification of Southeastern social organizations as systems, at least for the better-known groups, resembles the classification of Southeastern languages (Haas 1973). For the tribes chosen as representative for the present comparison, that classification is as follows:

| MUSKHOGEAN | IROQUOIAN | SIOUAN | CADDOAN | ISOLATED |
|---|---|---|---|---|
| Creek | Cherokee | Catawba | Caddo | Yuchi |
| Seminole | | Tutelo | | Natchez |
| Choctaw | | Biloxi | | Tunica |
| Chickasaw | | | | Timucua |

A corollary of my conclusion is the following: We may use linguistic classification as a guide in classifying the social organizations of lesser-known groups. Hopefully, that rule of thumb will come to replace the monolithic assumption that little-known social organizations must have conformed to the generic Southeastern type.

## Moieties, Clans, and Classes

### Core-Muskhogean Systems

MOIETIES. The diagnostic feature setting apart core-Muskhogean systems is the presence of matrilineal moieties. Such moieties have been reported for the Creeks (Swanton 1928c:156-66), Seminoles (Spoehr 1941:15), Chickasaws (Swanton 1928b:191-95; Speck 1907:51-54), and Choctaws (Swanton 1931:76-79), that is, all of the core-Muskhogean groups sampled here. They are reported nowhere else in the Southeast except among Yuchis, where they are known to be a recent borrowing from the Creeks (Speck 1909:70-78; Swanton 1946:664).

There is, however, a diversity among these moiety systems themselves, especially in regard to their marriage-regulating functions, although this may be due to faulty information. Choctaw moieties were unquestionably exogamous. For the Creeks, the issue is less clear-cut. While their moieties were said to be agamic, some evidence suggests a prior exogamy (Swanton 1928c:165). Markedly anomalous, however, are the Chickasaws, who Swanton (1928b:198-99) claims had actual endogamous matrimoieties (cf. Lévi-Strauss 1963). Here is a problem ripe for further research. While endogamous moieties would seem wholly improbable, it should be observed that endogamous "castes" are reported for the Chitimachas (Swanton 1911:348-49), and that among the Yuchis the patrilineal men's moieties showed a preference for a kind of endogamy (Speck 1909:77).

Marriage regulation was not the only function served by moieties in core-Muskhogean societies. They functioned as well in the ceremonial name transmission process (Seminoles), the organizing of intratown ball games (Creeks and perhaps Choctaws), the channeling of suspicions of sorcery (Creeks and Chickasaws), and the structuring of reciprocal burial obligations (Choctaws). They may have played some role as well in intra-town politics. In any event, the matrimoieties emerge as a focal institution in core-Muskhogean societies, alongside the kindred matrilineal clan.

CLANS. Most Muskhogean systems (except Choctaw) had totemically named matrilineal clans. Nonetheless, those clans are not diagnostic of the Muskhogean-type system, since they are reported as well for the Chero-kees, Timucuas, and Yuchis, and less certainly for the Biloxis. Still, the Muskhogean clan may be set apart from other Southeastern varieties of the matrilineal clan by virtue of its characteristic size and its segmentary (as opposed to structural) nature. These characteristics may themselves be connected.

Clan size has been calculated in table 1 by comparing total tribal population estimates with the number of clans reported per tribe. The results, even though computed by a crude technique, are nonetheless suggestive. From a comparative perspective, the Muskhogean clan is small, probably having ranged aboriginally between 100 and 300 persons.

The segmentary nature of Muskhogean clans may be inferred from ethnographic accounts. New clans were added, old clans died out, without affecting the underlying social structure. Hence, clans were not structural units. Insofar as persistence of the structure is concerned, the specific number of clans was of no significance. Indeed, one suspects that there were demographic limits on clan size, such that change in population size affected not so much clan size as the number of clans. This may be appreciated in some measure from table 1. Whereas average clan size fluctuated maximally within a tenfold range (Florida Seminole to Chicka-saw), population fluctuated within a nearly hundredfold range (Florida Seminole to Creek). The difference was absorbed by variance in the number of clans.

**Table 1.** Average Size of Muskhogean Clans

|                        | Creek   | Chickasaw | Florida Seminole | Oklahoma Seminole |
|------------------------|---------|-----------|------------------|-------------------|
| POP. (IN THOUSANDS)    | 7–15    | 4–5       | 0.175–.5         | 3–5               |
| NO. OF CLANS           | 50      | 15        | 5                | 28                |
| AVERAGE CLAN SIZE      | 140-300 | 267-333   | 35-100           | 107-78            |

With respect to clanship, the Choctaws appear as anomalous, for they seem to have lacked the characteristic "totemically" named, matrilineal grouping. Swanton (1931:79–84) claimed that they had instead nontotemically named house groups, the means for recruitment to which remained unknown. He reported similar local groups for the Chickasaws (1928c: 203–7), who, however, also had matrilineal clans. Unfortunately, the number of Choctaw house groups has not been established. If the groups were comparable in size to those of the Muskhogean clan, we would expect them to have had some fifty to a hundred such groups. Swanton's incomplete and probably inexact list, however, includes only some twenty names.

The possible occurrence of local groups, just where we should find clans among the Choctaws, is of some theoretical interest. For the demographic constraints on Muskhogean clans discussed above may prove to be the product of local constraints. That is, size limits may have had something to do with effective limits on collective interaction, resulting perhaps from the geographical proximity of clan members. If so, then the Muskhogean clan may itself be something of a "local group," with expansion beyond local constraints resulting in fission. Here is another problem clearly in need of further research.

In any case, the principal functions served by Muskhogean clans were: (1) exogamic marriage regulation (Creek, Seminole, and Choctaw)— Chickasaw data (Swanton 1928c:198–99) again suggest the possibility of endogamy; (2) responsibility for conducting blood-feud revenge (Creek); (3) responsibility for punishing an adulterer or adulteress who has wronged a clan member (Creek); (4) collective activity in ceremonies such as the Busk, or Green Corn festival (Creek and Seminole). More extensive discussion of clan functions can be found in Spoehr (1947:204–9).

PHRATRIES. Each Creek, Chickasaw, and Seminole clan was aligned uniquely with one of the moieties. Clans thus subdivided the moieties. Swanton (1928c:120–56), however, provided copious data on Creek social organization for yet a third level—the phratry—coming between clan and moiety. According to him, a phratry was a grouping of allied clans. However, first, it is evident that phratries were not a basic feature of core-Muskhogean systems since they were found only among the Creeks. Second, the phratry appears not to be a component even of Creek social organization equivalent in importance to the clan or moiety, for it appears to have had no functions aside from exogamy. Consequently, such interclan alliances may have been only stages in the formation or disintegration of clans, correlated with demographic shifts.

RANKING. Core-Muskhogean social organizations lacked anything resembling true class systems, such as were found among the Natchez, Chitimachas, and Calusas. Evidence for some sort of hierarchical ordering, however, is found in (1) the ceremonial ranking of Chickasaw clans (Swanton 1928b:197–98), (2) the tendency for chieftainships to remain within the clan, so that there were certain chiefly clans, and (3) the ordering of what appear to have been age grades—stages of warriorhood to elder-hood (Creek and Choctaw)—into a hierarchy of control, an issue requiring further research. On balance, however, the core-Muskhogean systems were strongly egalitarian.

## The Cherokee System

The Cherokees have for so long been considered nearly identical in social organization to the Creeks (cf. Spoehr 1947) that it is surprising just how distinct a fine-grained analysis shows the two groups to be. While the Cherokees had matrilineal clans, they lacked matrimoieties, which are a hallmark of core-Muskhogean systems. Furthermore, their clans were considerably larger, averaging nearly two thousand individuals per clan, an almost tenfold increase over core-Muskhogean, and their clans were structural units. The latter two features are, again, probably linked.

The Cherokees had seven clans, and that number could not be changed without radically affecting the social structure. Indeed, seven was a "sacred number" for the Cherokees. Mooney (1900:212–13) reported the Cherokee belief that there had been originally fourteen clans, but that these were reduced to seven by pairing. While this appears to belie the numerical fixity, in fact it confirms the significance of the number seven, for the belief is probably a variety of origin myth, explaining why there should be seven and only seven clans. In any case, the Cherokee clan exhibits none of the demographic constraints associated with core-Muskhogean clans, and it was undoubtedly not a local grouping. Population changes correlate only with changes in clan size, not in clan number.

The Cherokee clan is most reminiscent of the Iroquois clan, at least in its structural character. Theoretically, this is of interest because of the historico-genetic linkage involved, with the Cherokee language a member of the Iroquois family. However, Cherokee social organization appears to diverge from the Northern Iroquoian social organizations, insofar as the latter have, in common with core-Muskhogean systems, matrilineal moieties (Fenton 1978:310–11). In this regard, however, Cherokee social organization has not evolved toward some Southeastern (i.e., Muskhogean) type, but has undergone an independent evolution.

## The Natchez Class System

Natchez social organization has become the paradigmatic case of a Southeastern class system, largely owing to the rich documentation left by early-eighteenth-century French travelers and missionaries. However, the class system model sketched by Swanton (1911:107), based on these accounts, has given rise to a knotty problem known in the literature as the Natchez paradox (Brain 1971; Fischer 1964; Hart 1943; Josselin de Jong 1930; MacLeod 1924, 1926; Quimby 1946; Tooker 1963; and White, Murdock, and Scaglion 1971). The Natchez system as described by Swanton was demographically unstable. Owing to the marriage and descent rules, the noble class would have tended to mushroom in size, with the lowest stratum being depleted, so that after approximately nine generations a crisis would have ensued. These deductions have been used in turn as evidence that Swanton's model was inadequate. Consequently, whether or not the alleged instability casts doubt on the model, some caution is called for in approaching Natchez social organization. For purposes of situating Natchez social organization within the broader comparative framework, however, Swanton's model is probably more or less adequate.

As described by Swanton (1911:107), the Natchez system was built around two fundamental classes, Nobility and Stinkards. Moreover, the Noble class (but not the Stinkard class) was strictly exogamous. The system thus looks like an asymmetrical version of a Muskhogean moiety system, a resemblance possibly of some comparative significance. In any case, the operative principle of descent was of a complex bilineal nature. The Noble class was further partitioned into three subclasses or ranks (in hierarchical order, Suns, Nobles, and Honored People), recruitment into which was determined by two rules:

(i)   Children of a high-class mother belonged to the mother's subclass.
(ii)  Children of a high-class father belonged to a subclass one rank below that of the father.

Such a bilineal descent principle was probably unique in the Southeast—certainly, anyway, it was distinct from simple matriliny—although Caddo may have had some sort of nonunilineal rule. From a comparative perspective, however, it is interesting that, without rule (ii), the subclass system strongly resembles a matrilineal clan system. It is thus possible to imagine how Natchez and Muskhogean social organizations could be transformations of one another.

A cumbersome but accurate diagrammatic representation of Natchez social organization is given in figure 1. Much of the modern Natchez literature (e.g., see White, Murdock, and Scaglion 1971) has been devoted to demographics and to the patching-up of Swanton's model. The functions of the Natchez class system, however, require more careful scrutiny. Judging from the ethnographic evidence, classes probably did not organize the economic division of labor, since we hear about agricultural work being "done in common," with the "entire village assembled" (Swanton 1911: 75). Sexual division of labor instead predominated (Swanton 1911:89). Nor do the classes seem to have determined in any simple fashion the distribution of wealth. The classes do appear to have had organized relations of respect and authority, with the Stinkards considering themselves socially inferior, and to have correlated with sociolinguistic differences (Swanton 1911:105), although the latter is somewhat puzzling in light of the exogamic marriage rule. Overall, the class system seems to have resembled most closely a shifting warrior aristocracy, perhaps paralleling the gradations of warriorhood found in Muskhogean societies.

## The Lesser-Known Systems

Of the lesser-known systems with "classes," the Chitimachas appear to have had endogamous castes (Swanton 1911:348), a marriage rule clearly distinguishing them from the exogamous Natchez. While Chitimachas were formerly thought to have had clans (Swanton 1911:349), it now seems probable that they did not (Haas 1939). The Calusas as well, according to

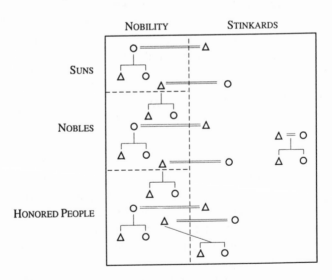

**Figure 1.** The Natchez class system.

the description of Goggin and Sturtevant (1964), had some sort of class system, but the data are insufficient for situating them more precisely. Judging from chiefly succession (Goggin and Sturtevant 1964:192-94), however, descent may not have been matrilineal. Of the Tunicas simply too little is known to assess even whether their social organization included a class system.

From a comparative perspective, Timucua social organization is most interesting. Gatschet (1876:628) affirmed that the Timucuas had a class system that distinguished "nobility" and "common people," and Swanton (1916:451) echoed this claim. Yet they had a clan system as well (Gatschet 1877), for which Swanton (1916:451) claimed, without citing the reference, that descent was matrilineal. If so, the Timucuas would have had the only Southeastern social organization combining a class and clan system.

Descriptions by the missionary Pareja (in Gatschet 1877:492-93), however, suggest a clan system in which the chieftancy was held by one clan, a situation found among both Cherokee and core-Muskhogean systems. It is just possible that the classlike characteristics are a byproduct of Pareja's description of this system in terms of sixteenth-century European class categories.

In any case, Swanton (1928c:156) analyzed the clan system as organized into six phratries. There were nine or ten totemically named clans, and possibly as many as twenty-five clans in all, though it becomes hard to distinguish clans from what may have been local lineages. If either figure proves valid, clans were intermediate in size between Muskhogean and Cherokee clans, averaging between 560 and 1,400 per clan. In all, because of its possible comparative significance, Timucua social organization merits more careful study.

None of the remaining systems sampled here shows evidence of true classes. However, owing to their patrilineal men's moieties (Speck 1909:74-78), labeled Chiefs and Warriors, the Yuchis emerge as unique. This is the only solidly patrilineal system in the Southeast, although Shawnees and Quapaws, tribes that bordered on the Southeastern area, had patrilineal systems. However, the Yuchis are reported as well to have had matrilineal clans (Speck 1909:70-73), which would make their social organization doubly interesting, especially if the clans were aboriginal. The clan system may possibly have been borrowed from the Creeks, among whom the Yuchis have resided since removal to Oklahoma. Almost all of the twenty Yuchi clans reported by Speck are found also among the Creeks, and the average clan size—50 to 150 per clan—falls into the core-Muskhogean range. One clan, however, the Opossum clan, is unique in the

Southeast, perhaps suggesting some historical depth to the Yuchi clan system.

As discussed earlier, Southeastern Siouan social organizations remain a considerable mystery. Indeed, within that category itself it seems preferable to distinguish eastern (e.g., Catawba and Tutelo) from southern (e.g., Biloxi and Ofo) Siouan groups. Speck (1942) argued convincingly that the Catawbas and Tutelos probably lacked matrilineal clans, and he proposed—on the basis, unfortunately, of evidence that is too flimsy—that they might have had bilateral sibs. For the southern Siouan Biloxis, however, Dorsey's (1893, 1894) salvage ethnography turned up a matrilineal clan system. Just how solidly based these results are is difficult to assess, but they are nonetheless of comparative significance. Dorsey reported three clans, Deer, Grizzly Bear, and Alligator, of which Grizzly Bear is found among no other Southeastern tribe. Instead, it is found among the neighboring Quapaws, a patrilineal Siouan tribe, and as well out on the Plains among the Omahas. Since no Alligator clan is reported for the Quapaws, however, it is unlikely that the Biloxi system was borrowed from them in any simple fashion. In any case, we should look to the Plains for parallels with the Biloxi system.

Caddos were somewhat marginal to the Southeast geographically, but their social organization is of great comparative interest. Swanton (1942:163–66) reported that they had a system of *ranked*, totemically named clans, recruitment to which was based on a bilineal principle. Moreover, that principle resembles strikingly that found in the Natchez class system. It may be summarized as follows:

(i)   Children of a higher-clan mother belonged to the mother's clan.
(ii)  Sons of a higher-clan father belonged to the father's clan, but daughters belonged to the mother's clan.

Rule (i) is virtually identical to the Natchez rule (i). Rule (ii) differs in distinguishing the statuses of sons and daughters, but it is very similar in spirit, emphasizing patrilineal connections. Indeed, from it emerges a "Caddo paradox" analogous to the Natchez paradox, with higher clans mushrooming in size while lower clans are depleted.

Among Southeastern social organizations, Caddo thus emerges as most closely parallel to Natchez, suggesting perhaps that we search in the Caddo area, rather than the Gulf Coast zone, for the origin and development of Natchez-like stratification systems. Simultaneously, the Caddo system emerges as transitional between a true class system, such as that of the Natchez, and a true clan system, such as that found among Cherokee and core-Muskhogean groups. Moreover, Caddo clans were probably similar in average size (300-400 per clan, given the figure of ten clans) to core-Muskhogean clans, while their names are a mixture of Siouan, Algonkian, and Muskhogean names. All this suggests that Caddo social organization may play a key role in the comparative picture.

## Kin Classification Systems

Swanton (1928c:80-97) gathered together basic material on kin terminologies for the Creeks and Natchez; the Natchez data, along with Chitimacha data, are reassessed in Haas (1939). Choctaw data are summarized in Swanton (1931:84-90), Chickasaw data in Swanton (1928b:180-86), Cherokee data in Gilbert (1943:216-34), Yuchi data in Speck (1909:68-70) and, perhaps more importantly, in Wagner (1934:339-40), Caddo data in Parsons (1941:11-24) and Swanton (1942:166-69), and Timucua data in Gatschet (1877:493-97) and Swanton (1916). The little we know of Catawba and Tutelo kinship is covered in Speck (1942). For Biloxi data we must rely on dictionary entries (Dorsey and Swanton 1912), supplemented by general discussions in Dorsey (1893:270-71, 1894:244). Haas's (1953) *Tunica Dictionary* provides our only access to the Tunica kin classification system, and on the Calusa system we have nothing.

As these materials are more or less readily available, no attempt has been made here to present basic data in a systematic fashion. Instead, the following discussion is strictly comparative. It is organized in terms of features—cross-cousin skewing patterns, first and second ascending generation classification, and so forth—that serve to differentiate the various Southeastern kin classification systems.

### Skewing Patterns

Crow-type skewing of cousin terms has been considered to be characteristic of the Southeastern type of social organization (Eggan 1937, 1966; Spoehr 1947). Because its principal distinguishing feature—the equation of FZD with FZ and FZS with F—represents a merging of matrilineally connected kinsmen, Crow-type skewing seemed to systematically mesh with another Southeastern-type social organizational feature, namely, the principle of matriliny. In light of this convincing Southeastern type, it is surprising to discover that Southeastern kin classification systems in fact range over the spectrum of possible cross-cousin classification types (Crow, Omaha, Dakota, and Eskimoan), an observation that would seem to support the multiparadigm model.

Core-Muskhogean systems (Choctaw, Chickasaw, Creek, and Seminole) all conform to the Crow type. However, they all (except

Choctaw) display an additional feature. FZD and FZ are themselves further equated with FM and MM. Skewing here thus cuts across all generations, from second ascending on down. This Muskhogean-type skewing is illustrated by the Creek terminology (fig. 2). The Choctaws diverge from the basic Muskhogean pattern, but their term for FZ *(hukni)* seems derivative of the FM term *(pokni)*, perhaps indicating historical conformity to the basic Muskhogean type.[2]

Cherokee cross-cousin terminology also conforms to the Crow type (FZD=FZ and FZS=F), but the Cherokees lack the supplementary Muskhogean-type feature. In Cherokee, the term for FZ *(giłoki)* is distinct from the term for FM *(gilisi)*, and these terms do not seem genetically linked. The Cherokee system is thus distinct from, albeit closely related to, the core-Muskhogean systems.

Timucuas are considerably more divergent yet; their terminology, according to Pareja (in Swanton 1916), shows only a single similarity with the basic Crow type: MBCh are classed with Ch, a merger reciprocal to the FZD=FZ and FZS=F equations. However, skewing is absent on the paternal side. Separate terms distinguish FZCh, which are unrelated to the terms for FZ and F. The Timucua system thus emerges as unique in the Southeast, although once again the sources merit a thorough reexamination.

The Yuchis, according to Wagner's data (1934:339–40), exhibit the wholly distinct Omaha-type skewing usually associated with patrilineal systems. Here it is the patrilineally related kinsmen who are classed together; MBS with MB and MBD with MZ, where the term for MZ is a diminutive of the term for M. This skewing pattern is illustrated in figure 3. If the Yuchi system were a true mirror image of the Muskhogean type, we would expect supplementary skewing into the second ascending

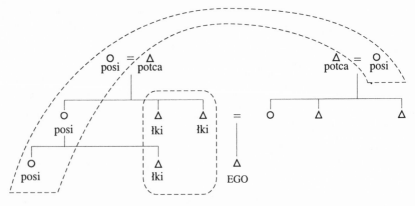

**Figure 2.** Muskhogean-type skewing with Creek terms.

generation (MBS=MB=MF). That does not in fact occur.

Caddo kin classification evidently lacked generational skewing altogether, with cousin classification conforming to the so-called Dakota type (Parsons 1941:13). Cross-cousins (MBCh and FZCh) were grouped under one term *(shahat')*, and differentiated from parallel cousins, who were classed with siblings. The Caddos thus had, like the Yuchis, a system of kin classification highly distinct from the Muskhogean type.

Catawba and Tutelo cousin classification, according to Speck (1942), was of yet another type, known in the literature as Eskimoan. All first cousins are classed together under a single term and differentiated from siblings. This was indeed Speck's principal evidence for the bilateral nature of Southeastern Siouan kinship. Regrettably, we cannot be certain in what measure those data reflect aboriginal patterns, since the systems may have accommodated to Anglo-American usage.

No data on cousin classification are available for the Biloxis, Chitimachas, Natchez, and Tunicas. Nevertheless, even from this limited sample, Southeastern kin classification systems may be seen to exhibit considerable diversity. Certainly, Crow-type skewing was far from a universal feature in the Southeast, probably being confined to core-Muskhogean groups, Cherokees, and perhaps Timucuas. Outside this nucleus, we find a multiplicity of distinct types.

## Second Ascending Generation

A similar diversity is encountered in second ascending generation classification, where the Southeastern systems may be sorted into three classes, for convenience labelled one-term systems, two-term systems, and three-term systems. Of these, two-term systems are the most common—they are found in all core-Muskhogean groups and in the Yuchi, Caddo, Timucua, and possibly Natchez systems. Here we find two terms,

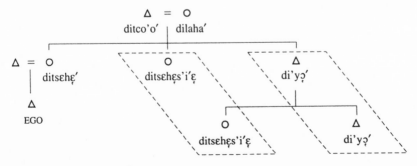

**Figure 3.** Yuchi skewing pattern (Omaha type).

which may be glossed as 'grandmother' and 'grandfather', distinguishing second ascending generation kinsmen only according to sex.

Given the wide distribution of these systems, it is noteworthy that the Cherokees were unique in employing a three-term system. In Cherokee, MM and FM *(gilisi)* are classed together, while MF *(giDuDu)* and FF *(ginisi)* are distinguished by separate terms (Gilbert 1943:218). It is true that Morgan's (1871) schedules indicate a two-term system for the Eastern Cherokees, but this is probably an artifact of the elicitation procedure, since his schedules call for terms for 'grandmother' and 'grandfather'. His Oklahoma Cherokee data show a one-term *(e-ni-si)* system, which, if correct, would suggest that western Cherokees were resisting acculturation to the Muskhogean type, and undergoing instead a separate evolution. Nor does the three-term system itself appear to have roots in Northern Iroquoian usage. From all appearances, Cherokee kin classification forms a distinct system in its own right.

From Haas's (1953) *Tunica Dictionary* it may be inferred that Tunica had a one-term system, with a single stem form *('-hča)* being used for all kin in the second ascending generation. Moreover, a single (derivative) term *('-hčatóhku)* was used as well for 'grandchild'. This is some of our most important evidence regarding Tunica kin classification. It is also critical in regard to the alignment of Tunicas with Chitimachas, where the aboriginal system seems as well to have contained a single term *('a'tipu)* for the second ascending generation (Haas 1939:610).

*First Ascending Generation*

In the first ascending generation bifurcate merging classification (F=FB≠MB and M=MZ≠FZ) was widespread in the Southeast. It was found in all core-Muskhogean systems, in Cherokee, Yuchi, Timucua, and Caddo, and probably as well in Biloxi, since here the term for 'father's elder brother' is derivative of the term for 'father', although age distinctions obscure the pattern. In any case, bifurcate merging classification is known to correlate in some measure with unilineal recruitment to descent groups, and this is true as well in the Southeast. Of the tribes with bifurcate merging terminologies, only the Caddos—with their bilineal recruitment principle—fail to conform to this generalization.

In the Southeast, however, there are also a number of bifurcate collateral systems, in which F, FB, and MB are distinguished by separate terms. Such a system seems to have been the aboriginal form of the Natchez system (Haas 1939:607-8), the Chitimacha system (Haas 1939:609-10), and probably the Tunica system (Haas 1953), although here there is some doubt about the latter, since, while F≠FB≠MB, it appears that M=MZ≠FZ.

Since these systems are so little known, this feature supplies important evidence regarding their classification in the Southeast.

Speck (1942) reported yet another type of system, known in the literature as the lineal type (F≠FB=MB), for the Catawbas and Tutelos. Were this system aboriginal, of course, the Catawbas and Tutelos would emerge as highly distinct within the Southeast. As in the case of cousin terms, however, this pattern for the first ascending generation may simply reflect acculturation to Anglo-American usage.

### Supplementary Features

A highly distinctive characteristic of Timucua kin classification, as described by Pareja (Swanton 1916), is the remarkable elaboration of kin terms based on the feature "living/deceased." Not only are numerous kinsmen referred to by distinct terms subsequent to their death, but terminological usage may be conditioned by the living or deceased status of some other relative. Thus, 'father' is referred to by one term *(iti)* while he is alive, by another term *(siqino)* following his death, and by yet a third term *(itora)* if ego's mother is also dead. Indeed, the living/deceased status of ego's parents affects the terms used for numerous kinsmen, including F, FB, FZ, M, MZ, MB, eB, yB, eZ, yZ, and BCh. So far as is known, this aspect of the Timucua system is without parallel anywhere in the Southeast.

Two supplementary features distinguishing the Biloxi system are a proliferation of age distinctions and a proliferation of kin terms generally. Dorsey himself sums up this distinction:

> The kinship system of the Biloxi is more complicated than that of any other tribe of the [Siouan] stock . . . The names of 53 kinship groups are still remembered, but there are at least a dozen others whose names have been forgotten. Where the Ȼegiha language, for example, has but one term for grandchild and one grandchild group, the Biloxi has at least fourteen. In the ascending series the Dakota and Ȼegiha do not have any terms beyond grandfather and grandmother. But for each sex the Biloxi has distinct terms for at least three degrees beyond the grandparent. . . .
> The Biloxi has distinct terms (and groups) for father's elder sister, father's younger sister, father's elder brother, father's younger brother, and so on for the mother's elder and younger brothers and sisters. The Biloxi distinguishes between an elder sister's son and the son of a younger sister, and so between the daughter of an elder sister and a younger sister's daughter. [1894:213-14]

Unfortunately, Dorsey and Swanton's (1912) *A Dictionary of the Biloxi and Ofo Languages* fails to provide all this seemingly rich material.

However, it may not have offered up all its secrets.

## Summary

The kin classification systems have been presented in a somewhat piecemeal fashion. That deficiency may be remedied by brief summations of the individual systems:

Core-Muskhogean: bifurcate merging; two terms in second ascending generation; Crow-type skewing with supplementary FZ=FM=MM equation (except Choctaw).

Cherokee: bifurcate merging; three terms in second ascending generation (Oklahoma Cherokee: one term); Crow-type skewing, but without supplementary equation.

Yuchi: bifurcate merging; two terms in second ascending generation; Omaha-type skewing.

Caddo: bifurcate merging; two terms in second ascending generation; Dakota-type cousin terms.

Timucua: bifurcate merging; two terms in second ascending generation; MBCh=Ch the only Crow-type feature; FZD≠FZ; prominent use of living/deceased feature.

Biloxi: bifurcate merging; two terms in second ascending generation; proliferation of age distinctions; proliferation of kin terms generally.

Catawba and Tutelo: lineal; Eskimoan cousin terms.

Natchez: bifurcate collateral; two (?) terms in second ascending generation.

Chitimacha and Tunica: bifurcate collateral; one term in second ascending generation.

## Implications for Future Research

I have argued for a pluralistic or multiparadigm model of the Southeast, an area seen as internally complex (rather than homogeneous), including numerous different kinds of social organization. My focus has been primarily on social groupings (moieties, clans, and classes) and on kinship terminology, which have been regarded traditionally as the main elements of social organization.

Space does not permit consideration of settlement patterns and political relations—a consideration that may ultimately prove most important in linking comparative social organizational research to the archeological record. In fact, considerable variation emerges in these areas as well in the Southeast, ranging from isolated villages (Siouans) to autonomous towns fused into loosely knit confederacies (core-Muskhogeans and Cherokees) to centralized states (Natchez). We find as well varying degrees and qualitatively distinct types of centralization: the Natchez show political-mixed-with-ceremonial centralization based on a village system, the Calusas and possibly the Timucuas show political centralization based on a hamlet system, and the Caddos show loose ceremonial (without corresponding political) centralization.

Concerning domestic group processes in Southeastern societies, outside of core-Muskhogean groups and Cherokees, we know little, and so must be prepared to entertain highly tentative hypotheses, based on fragmentary data. The Muskhogean and Cherokee domestic groups were probably matrilocally extended, with approximately five to ten persons per domestic group. In contrast with Iroquois patterns, this extension is minimal, and suggests that domestic groups were probably formed around a mother and her daughters. Natchez domestic groups were similar in size, but appear to have been either patrilocal or neolocal. While the Caddo data may be unreliable, there is the suggestion that domestic group processes may be quite distinct from the Muskhogean pattern, with households averaging possibly thirty persons each. The residence rule, however, was probably also matrilocal. No clear picture has emerged yet for other Southeastern societies, though there is a hint of avunculocality (at least for Orphan Boy) in one Tunica myth (Haas 1950:31).

Some comparative social organization issues that suggest themselves as logical foci for future research are the following: (1) age grading; here we want to study dictionary entries for the purpose of developing models of age classification schemes, as well as life-cycle data and passage rite phenomena; it is suggestive that eastern Siouan groups had an Algonkian-like Huskanaw for boys' initiation (Swanton 1946:815), indicating a sharp child/adult distinction, while lacking the Green Corn ceremony (Swanton 1946:816), wherein gradations of post-adolescent warrior status were emphasized in Muskhogean societies; (2) succession rules; here we find further support for the multiparadigm model, since succession was patrilineal (F to S) among the Caddos (Swanton 1942:170-71), matrilineal (MB to ZS) among Natchez (Swanton 1911:103) and possibly eastern Siouan groups (Swanton 1946:647), with chieftancy tending to remain within the matrilineal clan among core-Muskhogeans and the Cherokees, although there was no explicit matrilineal succession rule; (3) marriage rules; Lévi-Strauss (1969:xxxvi-xxxix) has already drawn attention to the difficulties in applying prescriptive marriage models to the Cherokee (and by implication core-Muskhogean) systems, and Zuidema (1965:112-13) has developed an intricate model of Cherokee marriage rules,[3] but the

Southeast has much more to offer; Natchez class exogamy generates an especially complex system of marriage possibilities, and the same is probably true of Caddo marriage rules; fragmentary Biloxi data on kin-affine terminological equations, and the explicit prohibition of WBD and WFZ marriage, possibly suggest a prescriptive alliance system (cf. Dorsey 1894:244).

Owing to the perhaps imminent linkup of Southeastern archeological results with the historical Southeastern systems, Southeastern social organizational research may be entering a new era. We are beginning to perceive a diachronic picture of these social organizations spanning from pre-Columbian times to the "golden age" (seventeenth and eighteenth centuries) and through the period of Euro-American contact up to the present. By means of comparative reconstruction, attuned to archeological information—on spatial shapes (e.g., the Muskhogean town square) and sizes, on social composition of local groups (e.g., number of households per community), on intercommunity interactions, and so forth—a picture may be developing of social organizations of varying levels of complexity, interacting and evolving over long periods of time. The elaboration of that picture would seem to be a major goal for Southeastern social organizational research.

## Notes

1. Actually, Swanton (1911:107-8) himself declined to impute to the Natchez of "ancient times" a clan system, arguing for a lack of positive evidence. He was a more cautious analyst of the ethnohistorical documents than his generalizations would lead one to suspect. It was principally due to his lifelong efforts that the Southeast came into focus as a culture area, and he was responsible for much of the information we now have on Southeastern social organizations.

2. Eggan (1937, 1966) and Spoehr (1947) account convincingly for the microvariations in the Crow-type skewing of Muskhogean terminologies by positing correlations with the degrees of acculturation of the tribes in question. It is only the extension of their analysis to Yuchi that comes into conflict with the multiparadigm model.

3. Zuidema's (1965:113) analysis of Natchez is incorrect, insofar as he means the classical Natchez system, because the latter almost certainly lacked the clan system on which his analysis is based.

# References

Brain, J. P.
   1971      The Natchez Paradox. Ethnology 10:215-22.
Dorsey, James Owen
   1893      The Biloxi Indians of Louisiana. American Association for the Advancement
             of Science Proceedings, vol. 42, 267-87. Salem, Mass.
   1894      Siouan Sociology. Smithsonian Institution, Fifteenth Annual Report of the
             Bureau of American Ethnology, 207-44. Washington, D.C.
Dorsey, James Owen, and J. R. Swanton
   1912      A Dictionary of the Biloxi and Ofo Languages. Smithsonian Institution,
             Bureau of American Ethnology Bulletin 47. Washington, D.C.
Eggan, Fred
   1937      Historical Changes in the Choctaw Kinship System. American Anthropologist
             39:34-52.
   1966      The Choctaw and Their Neighbors in the Southeast: Acculturation under
             Pressure. In The American Indian, by Fred Eggan, 15-44. Chicago: Aldine
             Publishing.
Fenton, William N.
   1978      Northern Iroquoian Culture Patterns. In Handbook of North American Indians,
             vol. 15, Northeast, edited by Bruce G. Trigger, 296-322. Washington, D.C.:
             Smithsonian Institution.
Fischer, J. L.
   1964      Solutions for the Natchez Paradox. Ethnology 3:53-65.
Gatschet, Albert S.
   1876      The Timucua Language (1). Proceedings of the American Philosophical
             Society, vol. 16, 626-42.
   1877      The Timucua Language (2). Proceedings of the American Philosophical
             Society, vol. 17, 490-504.
Gilbert, William H.
   1943      The Eastern Cherokees. Anthropological Papers no. 23, in Smithsonian
             Institution, Bureau of American Ethnology Bulletin 133, 169-413. Washing-
             ton, D.C.
Goggin, John M., and William C. Sturtevant
   1964      The Calusa: A Stratified, Non-agricultural Society (with Notes on Sibling
             Marriage). In Explorations in Cultural Anthropology: Essays in Honor of
             George Peter Murdock, edited by Ward H. Goodenough, 179-219. New York:
             McGraw-Hill.
Haas, Mary R.
   1939      Natchez and Chitimacha Clans and Kinship Terminology. American
             Anthropologist 41:597-610.
   1950      Tunica Texts. University of California Publications in Linguistics, vol. 6, no.
             1. Berkeley and Los Angeles: University of California Press.
   1953      Tunica Dictionary. University of California Publications in Linguistics vol.
             6, no. 2. Berkeley and Los Angeles: University of California Press.
   1973      The Southeast. In Linguistics in North America. Part 2, Current Trends in
             Linguistics, vol. 10, 1210-49. The Hague: Mouton.

Hart, C. M. W.
    1943    A Reconsideration of the Natchez Social Structure. American Anthropologist
            45:374–86.
Josselin de Jong, J. P. S.
    1930    The Natchez Social Class System. Proceedings of the Twenty-third Interna-
            tional Congress of Americanists, 1928, 553–62. New York.
Lévi-Strauss, Claude
    1963    The Bear and the Barber. Journal of the Royal Anthropological Institute 93:
            1–11.
    1969    The Elementary Structures of Kinship. Boston: Beacon Press. (Original
            French ed., 1949.)
MacLeod, W. C.
    1924    Natchez Political Evolution. American Anthropologist 26:201–29.
    1926    On Natchez Cultural Origins. American Anthropologist 28:409–13.
Mooney, James
    1900    Myths of the Cherokee. Smithsonian Institution, Nineteenth Annual Report
            of the Bureau of American Ethnology, pt. 1. Washington, D.C.
Morgan, Lewis Henry
    1871    Systems of Consanguinity and Affinity of the Human Family. Smithsonian
            Contributions to Knowledge, vol. 17. Washington, D.C.
Parsons, Elsie Clews
    1941    Notes on the Caddo. American Anthropological Association Memoir 57.
            Menasha, Wisc.
Quimby, G. I.
    1946    Natchez Social Structure as an Instrument of Assimilation. American
            Anthropologist 48:134–37.
Speck, Frank G.
    1907a   Notes on Chickasaw Ethnology and Folk-Lore. Journal of American Folk-
            Lore 20:50–58.
    1909    Ethnology of the Yuchi Indians. Anthropological Publications of the
            University Museum, University of Pennsylvania, vol. 1, no. 1. Philadelphia.
    1938    The Question of Matrilineal Descent in the Southeastern Siouan Area.
            American Anthropologist 40:1–12.
Speck, Frank G., and Claude E. Schaeffer
    1942    Catawba Kinship and Social Organization with a Resume of Tutelo Kinship
            Terms. American Anthropologist 44:555–75.
Spoehr, Alexander
    1941    Camp, Clan, and Kin among the Cow Creek Seminole. Field Museum of
            Natural History Anthropology Series, vol. 33, no. 1. Chicago.
    1947    Changing Kinship Systems. Field Museum of Natural History Anthropology
            Series, vol. 33, no. 4. Chicago.
Swanton, John R.
    1911    Indian Tribes of the Lower Mississippi Valley and Adjacent Coast of the Gulf
            of Mexico. Smithsonian Institution, Bureau of American Ethnology Bulletin
            43. Washington, D.C.
    1916    Terms of Relationship in Timucua. In Anthropological Essays Presented to
            William Henry Holmes (Holmes Anniversary Volume), 451–63. Washington,
            D.C.

1928a    Aboriginal Culture of the Southeast. Smithsonian Institution, Forty-Second
         Annual Report of the Bureau of American Ethnology, 673-726. Washington,
         D.C.
1928b    Social and Religious Beliefs and Usages of the Chickasaw Indians. Smithsoni-
         an Institution, Forty-fourth Annual Report of the Bureau of American
         Ethnology, 169-273. Washington, D.C.
1928c    Social Organization and Social Usages of the Indians of the Creek Confeder-
         acy. Smithsonian Institution, Forty-second Annual Report of the Bureau of
         American Ethnology, 23-472. Washington, D.C.
1931     Source Material for the Social and Ceremonial Life of the Choctaw Indians.
         Smithsonian Institution, Bureau of American Ethnology Bulletin 103.
         Washington, D.C.
1942     Source Material on the History and Ethnology of the Caddo Indians.
         Smithsonian Institution, Bureau of American Ethnology Bulletin 132.
         Washington, D.C.
1946     The Indians of the Southeastern United States. Smithsonian Institution,
         Bureau of American Ethnology Bulletin 137. Washington, D.C.
Tooker, Elisabeth
1963     Natchez Social Organization: Fact or Anthropological Folklore? Ethnohistory
         10:358-72.
Wagner, Günter
1934     Yuchi. *Extract from* Handbook of American Indian Languages, vol. 3,
         293-384. New York: J. J. Augustin.
White, Douglas R., George P. Murdock, and Richard Scaglion
1971     Natchez Class and Rank Reconsidered. Ethnology 10:369-88.
Zuidema, R. T.
1965     American Social Systems and Their Mutual Similarity. Bijdragen tot de taal-,
         land- En volkenkunde, Deel 121, le Aflevering, 103-19. The Hague: Martinus
         Nijhoff.

# PART II

# Culture History

# 8

## Fur Trade as Centrifuge: Familial Dispersal and Offspring Identity in Two Company Contexts

JENNIFER S. H. BROWN

The fur trader in northern North America has a history of being treated as a social type. In Canadian popular literature he is the hearty, singing voyageur; in the United States, the macho explorer and mountain man. To anthropologists before the 1970s, he and his records were mainly means to an end—bridges, however inadequate, to Indian worlds lying beyond; he himself did not stir much interest except, sometimes, as biased observer and suspect white man exploiting native groups (e.g., Hickerson 1966). Just as colonial historians tended to lump Indians together with little attention to differences, so anthropologists, having Indian communities as their major focus, usually looked through and beyond the fur traders, treating that "tribe" as a rather inert, homogeneous mass.

When, therefore, I began serious work on British fur traders in the Canadian northwest in 1971, that field of study was refreshingly open. I was soon convinced that the traders themselves were intrinsically interesting, that they were dynamic forces in Indian-white relations, and that they themselves needed to be studied in detail if the full scope of their social and cultural roles and the implications of those roles for the social history of the north were to be understood. It was soon evident that I was not alone in developing that perspective. The 1970s proved fruitful in anthropological studies in this area (e.g., Paine 1971; Savishinsky 1972; Jarvenpa and Zenner 1979). Historians too were beginning to examine fur trade social life from new angles (e.g., Van Kirk 1976; Foster 1976).

I at first shared older assumptions in one respect, however. I tended to assume homogeneity, considering the Britishers on whom my studies were to focus as partakers of the same cultural traditions, woven into the same social fabric, and members of essentially the same economic enterprise, although segmented into the Hudson's Bay Company (HBC) and the North West Company (or its Montreal antecedents) before those two firms merged in 1821. I thus expected to concentrate more on the study of social change during the eighteenth and early nineteenth centuries than on comparison and contrast.

## Controlling Comparisons

My data soon led me into the true heterogeneity of the situation, and it was at this point that a particular methodological contribution of Fred Eggan provided direction and encouragement as well as a certain legitimation of what I undertook to do. I had first read Eggan's discussion of the method of controlled comparison in a seminar with John W. M. Whiting at Harvard University, and my choice of the University of Chicago to pursue my doctoral studies led to a greater exposure to and appreciation of his approach. Perhaps because it became embedded in my mind at an early stage, the value of that approach to me has not been properly acknowledged until now. In 1955 Eggan advocated

> the utilization of the comparative method on a smaller scale and with as much control over the frame of comparison as it is possible to secure. . . . It has seemed natural to utilize regions of relatively homogeneous culture or to work within social or cultural types and further to control the ecological factors so far as it is possible to do so. Above all, it is important to control the historical framework. . . .Comparative study of social phenomena should be made, in the first instance, between phenomena which belong to the same class or type or, alternatively, between phenomena derived from the same historical source. . . . the historical framework which we develop is both a legitimate end in itself—as a portion of culture history—and a means to more adequate comparison. [1955:499–500]

The reference point of the above was of course Eggan's landmark studies of American Indian groups. But his text had a resonance for a beginning student of the northern fur trade. The Hudson's Bay Company and its archrivals, the largely Highland Scottish Montreal partnerships that coalesced into the North West Company between the 1770s and 1804, were two phenomena of "the same class or type" with common roots in the British Isles. Comparative studies indicated that these two organizations—originating from the same nation-state, closely alike in their occupation and aims, and coexisting in the same social and geographic environment in northern Canada—rang interesting changes on common themes. Their dual presence made it clear that fur trade social and economic relations varied in response to differences among European trading companies as well as among Indian communities. The fur trade, rather than being a unitary mode of interaction and mutual adaptation between Indian and white trader, revealed considerable variability, reflecting the social environment that each company itself created through its recruitment procedures, policies, and organizational structure and networks. Traders, then, needed to be viewed not only as actors in Indian-white encounters but also "in the contexts of the restricted and distinctive environments of the companies that hired them" (Brown 1980a:xx–xxi).

## Two Company Contexts

In origins and structure, the rival companies differed greatly. The Hudson's Bay Company was chartered as a royal monopoly in London in 1670. In the following decades its shareholding directors devised a management structure that fostered the longterm survival of the company (Mancke 1988). They held themselves quite separate, however, from the salaried personnel whom they sent to man their Hudson Bay posts; the shareholders never traveled to the bay and the field officers were typically never shareholders. Most field employees were young apprentices and laborers of humble origins. They were English, Lowland Scottish, and increasingly by the late 1700s, of Orkney Islands birth. Having few prospects at home, many accepted long terms of employment in the company. Some, finding in Rupert's Land (the HBC Territory—see map 1) an upward mobility much beyond what they could otherwise expect, became officers or chief factors in charge of posts or districts and accepted Rupert's Land as the permanent focus of their lives and careers.

In so doing, they came under a rather rigid regimen of codes and controls—some more enforceable than others—governing most facets of their existence, and faced long periods of austere living and isolation in their remote outposts. Passage between England and Hudson Bay was restricted by both fiat and physical conditions; one small yearly ship could not transport employees at will, and sometimes the ship itself was lost at sea or winterbound in the bay until the following spring. The company attempted to regulate social and economic relations both within the posts and with Indians. Its ideal, eventually modified by circumstances but persistent through much of the eighteenth century, was a kind of military monasticism intended to ensure security and an unimpeded concentration on commercial objectives (Brown 1980a:24–32).

The Montreal-based North West Company had its roots in several British-dominated fur trade partnerships that arose after the conquest of New France in 1763. Drawing on French *(canadien)* and *métis* labor and expertise, these "Nor'Westers" formed spreading business networks that

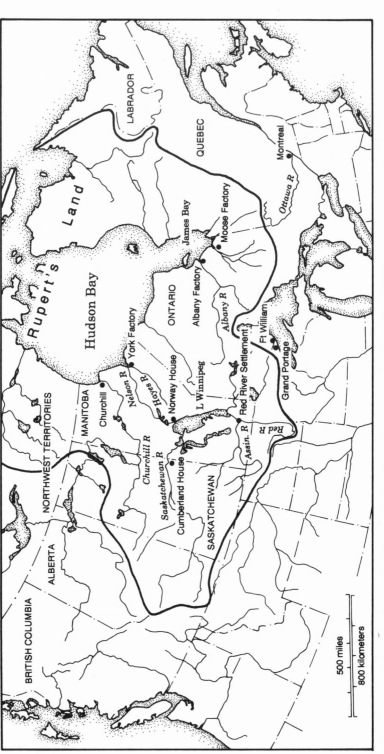

Map 1. Rupert's Land, or the original Hudson's Bay Company territories (from 1670 to 1870), and some major fur trade settlements.

linked Montreal and the Indian country in a flexible organizational framework. Company shareholders included numbers of "wintering partners" who had stature and experience in the worlds of both Montreal and the northwest and who brought to each a knowledge of the other; the social distance that separated the Hudson's Bay Company's officers from "their Honors" in London was much less a characteristic of the Nor'Westers.

Recruitment for leadership also followed distinctive patterns among the Montreal British. Most conspicuous were the numerous Highland Scottish partners who used their mutual familial, clan, and friendship ties to draw into the business younger men both known and personally acceptable to them. Their social controls over their juniors were not so much the formalistic regulations of a transatlantic directorate as the personalized constraints of kinship and mutual acquaintance that operated in both Montreal and the northwest. These ties also served to keep the wintering officers oriented to Montreal as the ultimate center of their lives, even if they were absent from it for many years. There, most of them had status, friends, and kinsmen—advantages that London offered to very few Hudson's Bay field officers (cf. Brown 1980a:35–45).

## Company Families in Indian Country

The social and organizational contrasts between these firms had a variety of implications for the history and anthropology of the fur trade and for the Europeans and Indians (primarily Crees and Ojibwas) whom it brought together. The company traders' personal ties with each other and their employers, with Indian women, and with the mixed-descent offspring of trader-Indian marriages and liaisons have been explored in several books and articles (e.g., Brown 1980a; Van Kirk 1980; and other references in Peterson and Anfinson 1984). This paper examines in greater detail one phase common to many traders' domestic cycles as they developed in two company contexts—the early separations and dispersals that typified so many fur trade families in the late eighteenth and early nineteenth centuries.

By the 1790s, it was commonplace for traders from both the London and Montreal companies to form unions with women in the Indian country. No white colonists had yet penetrated the Canadian northwest; and white men isolated from their homelands were often receptive to accepting Indian women as companions or wives, in marriages "according to the custom of the country," as they came to be called. For their part, Indians fostered such alliances as means of cementing trade ties and friendship. The companies themselves viewed such ties in rather contrasting ways. The Hudson's Bay

Company had long legislated against them, but with increasing ineffectiveness; by the late 1700s, HBC traders were referring to their native families with increasing openness in their journals and correspondence. The Nor'Westers, like their older French counterparts, accepted them as part of the trade, although they gradually became concerned about the growing numbers of dependents around their posts. In 1806 they laid down a rule, often disobeyed, against further unions between their men and Indian women (Brown 1980a:97). The Nor'Westers never, however, laid down a prohibition against alliances with women of mixed descent.

The companies were alike in one respect. Neither gave formal recognition to these unions or, for the most part, considered providing for the education or long-term maintenance of the families that resulted. Only in about 1810 did the Hudson's Bay Company undertake a short-lived enterprise of establishing little schools at a few of its major posts (Brown 1977). Certain North West Company partners and clerks began a fund for a school a decade later (Lamb 1957:6), a plan cut short by the 1821 coalition of the companies. For both firms before 1821, however, the exigencies of the fur trade and of their increasing rivalry for its control were dominant concerns.

These and other factors exerted centrifugal forces on the families of both companies—effects that tended to vary along company lines. Rather frequently, long separations occurred between spouses or between a parent and his or her children, and often families experienced permanent dispersal before their offspring had matured, owing most commonly to an assortment of social and economic pressures brought to bear on the father himself. The actions, expectations, and values of a man's relatives, patrons, company directors, or Indian associates guided and sometimes specified his behavior and options in his familial life, as he acquired attachments and fathered children in the northwest. And his responses and decisions, along with those of his colleagues, formed patterns that constrained the lives of those who followed after—notably, younger traders new to his company, as they in turn became fathers.

Families of all the newcomers' ethnic backgrounds—English, Scottish, French, and of mixed descent—were more or less subject to such constraints. This paper, however, focuses on the offspring of British clerks and officers in the two companies as being the best documented at present, and as being especially subject to centrifugal forces because of their fathers' leadership roles or, at least, aspirations to high standing in their respective companies between the 1780s and 1821.

## HBC Families and Identity Formation

In the Hudson's Bay Company, the London directors' policies were commonly the major force that severed their men's native family ties. During the 1700s, the company censured a number of its employees, such as officers Richard Norton and James Isham, for their alliances with Indian women. Ship's passage to England was usually refused to a trader's native dependents when he went on leave or retired; only a few sons of officers, such as those of Isham and Ferdinand Jacobs, were allowed transport. Eighteenth- and early-nineteenth-century HBC families who sought to remain together had few means of avoiding dispersal; unlike its Canadian counterparts, the company did not allow ex-servants to accumulate with their families as "freemen" around its posts. After 1810, a few retiring HBC families found their way south from James Bay to settle as units on the Ottawa River or in the Montreal area; the John Hodgsons, Robert Longmoors, Halcros, and some branches of the John Thomas family are examples (Brown 1982). But most former employees were required to break their family ties; and no provision for settlement in Britain was made for dependents of men who died while employed or who were dismissed. An incipient HBC fur trade society was thus continually beheaded by the removal of its British husband-fathers.

Around the major posts on Hudson Bay itself, most HBC descendants were reassimilated among their Indian maternal relatives and were classed among the local Cree hunters and traders who were known in company records as Home or Homeguard Indians. (For a recent detailed study of some of these descendants, see Beaumont 1992.) Some sons, if their fathers had been able to give them a little education, found employment in the company as "natives of Hudson's Bay," usually at low ranks, and became permanent residents around Moose or Albany or one of the other large coastal "factories" (the term that from the late 1700s on was used to describe those large centers where resident factors traded).

The statuses and identities assigned to HBC native children at the inland posts seemed to parallel what happened on the bayside; some sons made their way into regular company employment, and others became "Indians" trading at centers such as Cumberland House or Norway House. Definitions of these people in terms of blood or race mixture were decidedly rare before 1821, and if they occurred, they were overshadowed by socioeconomic and cultural criteria. Specifically, the following factors determined whether individuals were Indian: Did they have active ties with a white father or not? Were they employed in post occupations, or did they travel with the Indians, bring in furs, and trade for goods? If they lived with and acted as Indians, then they were Indian, regardless of whether they still bore their fathers' surnames.

In 1821, at Big Point House west of Lake Winnipeg (Manitoba), the fifty-two Indians who had accounts there included Hugh Linkletter, David Sanders, Humphrey Favil (originally Favel), and John Lyons (Hudson's Bay Company Archives [hereafter HBCA] B.51/e/2, fo. 5, Peter Fidler's report on the Manetoba [sic] District). They came by these names through paternal genealogy; this was before missionaries had arrived to baptize native converts with European names, which often bore no relation to their ancestry (on some complexities of Ojibwa surname adoption patterns in the region, see Rogers and Rogers 1978). The list of HBC men in the same report included the district officer, Peter Fidler, and two of his native-born sons, Thomas and George. George was described as a boatman, and "active, a moose hunter, has been with Indians these 17 years" (HBCA, B.51/e/2, fo.4). If his father had not been an officer on the scene fairly consistently, George would almost certainly have been "Indian." Only one person was described in Fidler's report as a "halfbreed," and he was an Indian first. The list of "Indians" trading at Fort Dauphin in 1821 included one Eappeskenet, who was described as "a Halfbreed, rather indolent" (HBCA, B.51/e/2, fo. 5).

Examples of people of mixed ancestry becoming HBC Indians also came from the more northerly post of Cumberland House in the same period. Three such Indians bore the Orkney surname of Twatt—Robert, Willcock, and Mansack. They were almost certainly sons of the former Cumberland district employee, Magnus Twatt. On 1 July 1818, the Twatts arrived at Cumberland "with their mother and families," bringing 100 muskrat skins. They were "very noisy because we have no rum for them" (HBCA, B.49/a/34, fo. 5). They, along with Tomie Humpherville, a "York Factory Home Indian" probably descended from the late-eighteenth-century HBC man Edward Umfreville, who later joined the Nor'Westers, made regular appearances in the Cumberland journals as Indians. For the Twatts, their continuing maternal tie would have reinforced their Indianness—especially given the apparent frequency of matrilocal residence patterns among their kin (e.g., Bishop and Krech 1980:35).

Similarly, at Norway House (Manitoba) in 1822–23, Thomas, grandson of James Isham, the York Fort factor of the 1740s and 1750s, was listed as an Indian of the Pelican band with hunting grounds at Jack River; his father, Charles Isham, one of the first native-born offspring to receive an English education and attain officer status, had retired to England in 1814. In a secondary column of the Norway House list under the heading "Family," however, Thomas was described as "halfbreed" (HBCA,

B.154/e/2, fo. 13). In effect, in the cultural and social context of the Hudson's Bay Company of about 1820, one could say, "this Indian is a halfbreed" and make perfectly good sense. Before 1814 or so, HBC men had not used the word *halfbreed* in their vocabulary; it was a borrowed and subsidiary term referring to parentage, and was evidently picked up from the Nor'Westers, among whom both the category and the distinctive social group whom it described were earlier more visible (Brown 1980b).

## Nor'Wester Families and Diverging Identities

The North West Company (with its main older rival, the XY Company, before their coalition in 1804) presents interesting comparisons to the Hudson's Bay Company. Patterns of familial dispersal were rather more complex. Controls over traders' family formation were not consistent among HBC personnel; but for the Montrealers, they were even less strict and formal, and more personalized. When in 1806 the North West Company partners laid down their rule against further alliances between traders and Indian women, it was unevenly enforced (Brown 1980a:97–98). Questions of local expediency loomed large, as when Duncan McDougall made a commercially useful marriage with the Chinook chief Concomly's daughter on the Pacific coast in 1813. The Montrealers sometimes applied pressures to keep their youngest employees from taking native wives; Sir Alexander Mackenzie's censure of his junior clerk, George Nelson, at Grand Portage (Lake Superior) in 1804 led Nelson to cast off, rather awkwardly, the daughter of his Ojibwa guide of the previous winter (Brown and Brightman 1988:10). But once an employee became established, few barriers to unions with native women were visible.

In fact, in 1808, two years after the North West Company issued its rule against Indian alliances, Nelson's bourgeois (district officer), Duncan Cameron, bullied his clerk into marrying an orphan cousin of his own Ojibwa wife, in order to reduce the number of his dependents. Nelson consented, allowing that "the sex had charms for me as it had for others." But he still had compunctions about what had happened to his first Indian marriage; and he had seen, by then, enough bad results of his colleagues' native alliances to suffer apprehensions over his own. Too many others, he wrote, "to serve craving lusts, thought nothing, and cared nothing for the consequences, of the poor creatures who they took ... with whom they would pass their lives with their children & families, to cast them off afterwards with those to whom they had given birth to linger in want and wretchedness" (Reminiscences: 206, 207).

The variability of the Nor'Westers' handling of these relationships was increased by the fact that more options were open to them than to the Hudson's Bay men. The relative lack of formal moral strictures emanating from a central (if remote) directorate allowed more local flexibility; and the North West wintering partners certainly had more discretionary authority in all domains than did their HBC inland counterparts, who were always clearly subordinate to their bayside chief factors. What might be called the socio-geographic distribution of power varied conspicuously between the two companies.

Given their discretionary powers, North West Company bourgeois in charge of inland departments could guide their own and their employees' family relationships in several different directions. Some bourgeois and clerks were evidently models of consistency and devotion—for example, William Morrison, James Hughes, Daniel Harmon, Charles O. Ermatinger, George Keith, and George Nelson with his second Ojibwa wife and family. Others, to judge by the varied mothers of their children and other evidence, were less consistent in their attachments—Alexander Fraser, Duncan McDougall, James Keith, John Stuart. And some were not above trafficking in women and using them as bargaining chips with their men, as when an engagé was in debt over his woman and needed to trade her away (cf. Masson 1960, 2:385).

The reasons for these variable patterns must be sought in both the Indian country and eastern Canada. For Indians, economic relations were largely coterminous with actual or potential kinship links, and the establishment of marital ties with their white associates was a natural priority, as the young clerk George Nelson quickly found out in the winter of 1803-4. When Northern Algonkian Indian fathers offered their daughters to white men, they hoped for both trade advantages and a lasting commitment to their families. Their widespread practice of at least temporary matrilocal residence (Bishop and Krech 1980) dictated that a new husband remain with and contribute to his wife's family, as Nelson came to understand. Looking back on his brief alliance with his Indian guide's daughter, he wrote of the father, "He thought no doubt that it would be the means of rendering him happy & comfortable in his old days. What a cruel disappointment!" (Reminiscences: 36). These hopes and concerns could lead Indian fathers into urging premature alliances on young white traders, who were sometimes inclined to exploit them in the short term, or who were simply lonely, easily tempted, and without the means of maintaining the commitment. Changed fur trade circumstances or a new company assignment, particularly by a bourgeois who himself did not give high priority to these ties, could abruptly end such unions, and further, communicate a message to a young employee that he was not required to take such alliances seriously.

This message was likely to be reinforced from eastern Canada and Scotland, where many Montreal traders had strong familial and friendship ties. White Canadian society, whether ethnic French or British, conferred no automatic legitimacy on marriages "according to the custom of the country," and it was regarded as acceptable for a trader to sever such ties upon leaving the Indian country, and to take a white wife if he wished, without impediment.

When in 1803, Nor'Wester Daniel W. Harmon took a native wife (whom he was later to retire with and marry), he knew the relationship could be temporary according to his colleagues' norms (Lamb 1957:194), and that at its end he could meet their standards of respectable behavior by leaving the woman with some other party:

> It is customary for all the Gentlemen who come in this Country to remain any length of time to have a *fair* Partner. . . . my intentions now are to keep her as long as I remain in this uncivilized part of the world, but when I return to my native land shall endeavour to place her into the hands of some good honest Man. [Lamb 1957:105]

## Women and Children, Status and Legitimacy

In Harmon's time, those Nor'Westers who thus severed their ties with native women faced no challenge. But in the later nineteenth century, as some mixed-descent offspring attained sufficient education and position to have a place in white society, or at least to have their own patron there, court battles flared over the legitimacy of such marriages and their progeny, as lawyers argued over the estates claimed by native and white heirs. William Connolly's act of separating from his Cree wife of long standing to marry his Montreal cousin in 1832 led to bitter litigation three decades later. The Cree marriage was ultimately vindicated, but a dissenting judge vividly portrayed the challenge this decision posed to deep-rooted Montreal attitudes. Noting the white wife's "good faith" in her marriage despite her knowledge of the Cree liaison, he wrote,

> sharing the belief of public opinion which considered so-called Indian marriages to be null, she contracted with him a marriage ratified by religious and civil authority and under the protection of public law. How could she be removed from her place, deprived of her station and see her children disgraced as bastards and replaced by those who had always been considered illegitimate; and see her own place occupied by the

Indian woman, it is this that appears unjustifiable to me. [quoted with
further detail in Brown 1980a:95]

The prevalence of similar attitudes among old Nor'Westers' white kin
in Scotland occasionally led to protracted litigation in British courts, even
if a father had demonstrated loyalty to his native family. The 1835 will of
Samuel Black listed as heirs both his collateral relatives in Aberdeenshire
and his children born in the Indian country. His sudden death in 1841,
without his having modified the will to include the younger children or
having formally married their mother, touched off two decades of legal and
epistolary disputes, principally between Black's old Nor'Wester colleague,
James Keith, who served as his executor and the deceased's nephew, a
Scottish minister. Pleas to the latter regarding "the destitute condition and
cheerless prospects" of the native offspring (HBCA, A.38/24, fo. 63, 17
Oct. 1850) failed to stir the Scottish kin to sympathy for cousins whom they
viewed as illegitimates, and many years passed before the legacies were
apportioned among the white and native heirs. Several comparable cases
arose among other old Nor'Westers' kin, reflecting the tensions of the
traders' double attachments at home and in the Indian country. In contrast,
the estates of officers of pre-1821 HBC background, with their greater
remoteness from British society, their lack of eastern Canadian ties, and
perhaps also their lesser wealth, evidently were not subject to such
conflicts.

The standing of a trader's native wife and children was thus often
uncertain, even if he consistently affirmed their position. If he died or
departed, they might, especially if they had maintained ties with a viable
Indian community, be reassimilated among the wife's relatives. But that
was not always possible or allowed to happen. When George Nelson cast
off his first Indian wife at Grand Portage in 1804, having brought her there
from Wisconsin, she did not rejoin her family; instead, "an interpreter took
her" (Nelson Journals: Letter journal 1811:34). As Daniel Harmon noted,
some Nor'Westers seriously tried to place their native wives with a
respectable successor. But a woman who had been passed on more than
once could lose standing at each step and come to be viewed as a prostitute.
Old Nor'Wester Peter Warren Dease described one such case, perhaps
exaggerated, in 1825, noting that one of his colleagues had been "on a
Matrimonial Jaunt with the Amiable Cidevant [former] Madam Schiller
dit Trepagner, dit LeMalice dit Landry dit Pain dit La Rance dit Cadieu dit
Turcotte dit Mademoiselle Censols" (to Robert McVicar, 19 July 1825).

George Nelson recorded that in the Indians' view too, a woman could
eventually be ruined by a series of alliances with the Canadian traders, to

the point that her own people rejected her. On the west side of Lake Winnipeg around 1810, an Ojibwa friend of his, La Bezette, proposed to take a second wife. His first wife's father entreated La Bezette to accept his younger daughter, sororal polygyny being a preferred form of marriage. La Bezette resisted for a long time because of her reputation for promiscuity, telling his father-in-law, "She will not do for me nor for any indian. . . . She is only good for the white—they take women not for wives,—to use them as Sluts—to satisfy the animal lust, & when they are satiated, they cast them off, and another one takes her for the same purpose, & by & by casts her off again." La Bezette finally accepted the woman for her father's sake. Of his remarks, however, Nelson wrote, "there was too much truth in this for me either to like it or make a reply to suit my feelings" (Reminiscences: 225; on La Bezette's kin ties, see Brown 1991:169).

Like their mothers, native children of the Montrealers faced a variety of prospects. The Nor'Westers had more opportunities to transport some of their offspring down to Canada than HBC men did to send theirs on the annual company ship to England. But since both their familial commitments and their financial resources varied, they took only limited advantage of that option. Sons were favored; a sampling of church registers recording the baptisms and burials of such children suggests that about twice as many males as females were sent down, to achieve formal recognition of their paternity and perhaps to live and be educated among their father's white relatives (Brown 1985). Their coming to Canada for baptism, however, did not in itself confer legitimacy, and indeed baptism could serve to place these children on record as illegitimate. In Williamstown, Glengarry, Canada, the Reverend John Bethune baptized four sons of "Mr. James Grant Merch[an]t Michilimackina[ck], born in the Indian Country," one boy on 9 March 1786, and three on 8 March 1791. Each name was marked with an asterisk, which was keyed to an endnote in the register: children whose mothers' names were lacking were to be assumed legitimate, "except those marked with an *Astrism" (St. Andrews Presbyterian Church registers, Williamstown, pp. ix, xx).

Other church entries did not raise the question of legitimacy; it never arose explicitly in, for example, the cases of the numerous Nor'Westers' children baptized or buried at the St. Gabriel Street Presbyterian Church in Montreal. But the absence of most native mothers in both person and name cast clouds on the standing of many country marriages, even in instances in which a trader was personally loyal to his children's mother. And only a small minority of Nor'Westers braved the censure (or at least surprise) of Montreal relatives and friends by bringing a native wife down and marrying her in church. In the St. Gabriel Street Church between 1796 and 1835, eighty-nine Montreal traders' offspring were baptized or buried. But only two marriages between their fathers and native mothers occurred (although a few were formalized elsewhere and some endured without formality) and both involved rather marginal characters. On 25 July 1796 Charles Phillips, a trader somewhat on the outs with the North West Company, married "Jenny the Red Bird of the tribe of the Hurons" and presented their three children for baptism. And on 30 October 1812 David Thompson, a Nor'Wester but a former HBC employee of English origin, married the part-Cree Charlotte Small; his relative marginality to North West Company and Montreal social circles and his wife's descent from an early company partner may have insulated him from the pressures other Nor'Westers faced if they formalized their country marriages within eastern Canadian society.

### Fur Trade As Centrifuge: The Duncan McDougall Family

For the fur trade families connected with the St. Gabriel Church, then, as for others, the pattern was one of at least short-term and often long-term dispersals, as some sons and fewer daughters left one or both parents, at an average age of six, for the trip to Montreal. Complete fragmentation did not necessarily occur; some parts of a family might keep in touch and still have strong bonds of sentiment over long distances. A father might visit Montreal for a year and then rejoin his family in the northwest, or he might send down certain of his children for baptism and schooling with the intent of retiring from the fur trade to be with them in a few years. But the frequency of these separations, along with the competing strength of many traders' Montreal attachments, cut deeply into familial lives and sometimes meant that parents and children, once apart, never again managed to become a coresidential unit. If the mother achieved no lasting position as wife, the family's dispersal was the more likely to be permanent, even if a father's attachment to his children persisted.[1]

Duncan McDougall's family history provides an example. McDougall was nephew to two important Nor'Westers, Alexander McDougall on his father's side and Angus Shaw on his mother's, who both surely influenced his choice of career. Between 1803 and 1806, while he was a clerk with the Nor'Westers who were challenging the Hudson's Bay Company's trade in James Bay, he fathered a son and a daughter by one Nancy Hester, native descendant of an eighteenth-century Hudson's Bay Company officer. When the Nor'Westers decamped from the area, he left this infant family behind; they were known to be at the HBC post of Eastmain in 1808. Sometime between 1808 and 1812, McDougall's son, George, was brought to Montreal, where he was baptized on 26 October 1812 in the St. Gabriel Street Church, with his father's brother, Alexander McDougall, as a witness.

By that time, McDougall himself had taken up service with the Pacific Fur Company at Astoria, at the mouth of the Columbia River; he rejoined the North West Company after the sale of that post to his old company. In 1813, he married the daughter of the local Chinook chief, Concomly. On 28 March 1817, shortly before leaving the Pacific coast to cross the continent back to Fort William, he made a will that omitted mention of his Chinook connection, but named his "reputed or rather adopted son George McDougall" from James Bay as residual legatee (*reputed* and *adopted* were terms often used for children whose legitimacy was not established). The daughter, Anne, was not mentioned at that time. But on 15 October 1818, ten days before his death at Fort Alexander on Lake Winnipeg, McDougall added a short codicil to the will: "Should there be any means of aiding my little daughter in James Bay I should feel happy" (Brown 1983a).

## Sons, Daughters, and Ethnogenesis

The McDougall story, in which the parental bond ended early and the destinies of the offspring diverged along sex lines, paralleled many other North West Company domestic cycles, as reflected in the St. Gabriel Street church registers and elsewhere. Sons who traveled out of the fur trade country carried on a father's name, and numerous of those sent down to Canada returned to find fur trade employment, at least for a time, after varying amounts of education in Montreal or elsewhere; personnel retrenchments after the merger with the Hudson's Bay Company in 1821 hit this group rather hard. More, however, probably followed a variety of trades outside the Indian country.

Their sisters were about twice as likely to stay in the Indian country, and were also the likeliest family members to remain with their native mothers (Brown 1983b:41–42). Since Indian matrilocal residence patterns in turn often kept a mother in touch with her own parents, daughters of mixed descent could retain a place in their maternal kin group, if their trader fathers had not carried them great distances from their homeland or otherwise alienated their relatives-in-law. Occasionally, native mothers and children formed units apart from both Indian and fur trade households, perhaps because they lacked Indian ties. George Nelson recorded in his journal of 23 September 1818 that among the people who were to winter in his vicinity at Tete au Brochet, Lake Winnipeg, were one "Mother

Beaulieu" and her daughter, and Boisverd's wife and three children (Boisverd was not present).

Matrilocally based ties were significant not only for daughters of such women, but also for the men to whom they became attached. A good many of the men with whom Nelson traded were identified only in terms of their fathers-in-law—whose names were usually Indian, but sometimes European. Between 1808 and 1811, one of Nelson's trading Indians around River Dauphine was a Cree known as Lorrin's [or Laurrain's] son-in-law, or sometimes simply as le Gendre. He and his wife (Lorrin's daughter) had a daughter who by 1819 was married to an Indian who also lived matrilocally, to judge by a Nelson journal entry of 20 January 1819 (see also 20 May): "L'Assiniboane, the son-in-law of Old Laurrain's son-in-law arrived; he is with his father-in-law." The tie was indeed likely a double one. L'Assiniboane had two wives (Nelson Journals: Tete au Brochet journal, 13 May 1819), and since only one father-in-law was mentioned, they were probably sisters.

Native-born daughters of Canadian traders, along with those sons who remained in the northwest, dispersed in other directions, however, as well as back into their maternal communities. Métis settlements of French-Indian extraction had already begun to form around the Great Lakes by the mid-1700s (Peterson 1978). Farther west, families of freemen and Métis formerly connected with the Montreal fur trade or serving it intermittently were emerging as a distinct population by the early 1800s. In the fall of 1804, the clerk George Nelson was taken on his first buffalo hunt by John Sayer, the part-Indian son of the North West Company partner of that name; Nelson wrote that young Sayer "had been frequently on the plains." Later, in the River Dauphine area just west of Lake Winnipeg, Nelson was often in contact with an old freeman, Charles Racette (or Rassette), and his native family. He recorded that Racette had come to the northwest "a common Servant, but having some abilities for trade, he procured an outfit of several hundred pounds from the N.W. Co. at Grand Portage, and finished by ruining himself" (Reminiscences: 82). The numerous offspring of families such as the Racettes formed an important demographic base for later communities such as Red River. Since the fathers had made lasting commitments to the country itself and could settle in one area close to Indian relatives and free of arbitrary company assignments, their families were likely to be among the more durable mixed-descent residents of the northwest.

The dynamics of the early growth of mixed or Métis and "free" populations rooted in the fur trade are still to be fully understood. Certain similarities did exist in the familial configurations of the progeny of the

HBC and Montreal traders. Both groups faced rather strong probabilities of being separated from one or both parents at early ages. Of course, such separations were not unusual in Britain of that period, where many children left home at the age of twelve or so as apprentices (trader fathers, particularly in the Hudson's Bay Company, had in some instances experienced such separations themselves if they had begun their HBC service as apprentices). And the placing of young adolescents in other households than their own, often with nonkin, was a familiar practice to Europeans.

But fur trade separations often seemed more arbitrary, reflective, perhaps, of a more brittle and insecure social setting. In both companies, they could affect children at a variety of ages depending on when a father retired, was dismissed, went on leave, or was shifted to some distant assignment. A father who was committed to educating his son in the "civilized world" might also seize any chance to place the boy in his homeland when a transport possibility offered itself; thus, George, son of Nor'Wester Daniel Harmon, at the early age of three left both parents behind in the far west when an opportunity came to convey him to his father's relatives in Vermont. And HBC fathers might seize whatever rare occasion presented itself to bring some favored child home on the annual ship from the bay.

Maternal familial relations in the two companies also showed similarities. The attachment of native mothers for their children was a subject of frequent comment. Fathers of both companies could rationalize their children's removals in terms of European standards about education or apprenticeship; but such separations for long periods and distant goals were decidedly foreign to the mothers involved, with their backgrounds in small, closely-knit Indian communities. A few sensitive accounts, necessarily secondhand given the mothers' illiteracy, convey clues about the impact of such separations on these women (e.g., MacLeod 1947: 177–78). And Daniel Harmon recorded his native wife's strong bond, as well as his own, to their children (Lamb 1957:166, 195).

## Diverging Ethnicities, Old and New

Within the framework of these broad similarities, however, were the company contrasts that tended to set the families and progeny of the two firms on rather different courses. Contrast was expressed in the fact that terminological usages varied between the companies with regard to people of mixed descent. In the HBC context of about 1815 to 1820, it was possible, as noted before, to say that some Indians were halfbreeds, as the latter biracial term began to penetrate HBC vocabulary. Such a person was

Indian socially, culturally, and economically; if the term *halfbreed* was used, it referred essentially to family and parentage.

In the North West Company of the same period, such a statement would have been unlikely. Terms such as *halfbreed, brulé,* and *métis* were available and established categories in themselves, and their use reflected social realities. It was true that some Nor'Westers' offspring became Indians—perhaps most readily if they had continuing ties with Indian women; Lorrin's son-in-law was the son and husband of Indian women, and his son-in-law, L'Assiniboane, had an Indian mother and half-Indian wife. But the Métis option was a more likely possibility; certainly the journal of HBC man Peter Fidler as he observed his company's rivals at Red River suggests that by about 1814, "halfbreeds" of North West Company origin had become a visible and viable group, both politically and economically, in at least the Red River area. Their distinctive roles—as buffalo hunters helping to provision the fur trade, and as a political entity whose interests in the Red River area could also be cultivated by the Nor'Westers against their HBC rivals—were already evident.

In sum, *métissage* as a social and cultural phenomenon leading to the founding and recognition of a distinct population evidently first developed in the context of the Montreal fur trade. Although a parallel racial intermixing had occurred in the pre-1821 Hudson's Bay Company, it had not, at least not yet, led to the establishment of a category of people admitted to be neither white nor Indian. (See Peterson and Brown 1985 for broader discussions of these comparisons.)

At least in part, the origins of this difference lay in the divergent demographic and familial patterns that developed in two different company traditions. The families of the Hudson's Bay Company of the eighteenth and early nineteenth centuries were more subject to centrifugal forces of fragmentation by formal and arbitrary policy measures. A very few offspring, once granted passage to England, disappeared into British society; most followed the vastly different alternative of absorption into Indian life. Late in the period under discussion, around 1800, a certain centripetal pull occurred, as HBC officers drew into the service certain of their own and other employees' native sons. And from the middle 1700s onward, certain native-born daughters had likewise been drawn into the posts as traders' country wives. But since the company maintained controls on both its servants' and ex-servants' families and their residential patterns, no distinctive communities of "freemen" and people of mixed descent had sprung up, to develop a separate identity as an intermediate category and social group.

The Nor'Westers, however, followed the paths of the old French fur trade both geographically and socially in many respects. Jacqueline Peterson's work on the ethnogenesis and history of the Great Lakes Métis as communities rooted in the French fur trade of the 1600s and early 1700s has traced the demographic and familial patterns that the British Montreal traders found already established when they began to father their own families in the northwest. The records show that, partly as a consequence of that background, when the offspring of the British Canadian fur trade began to proliferate, the centrifugal tendencies of their familial lives pulled them in directions somewhat different from those of their HBC counterparts. Montreal or other eastern Canadian communities were the destinations of some; but others who remained in the northwest became affiliated with already established nuclei of Métis settlement, if they did not return to the lives and communities of their Indian forebears.

There were, as in the Hudson's Bay Company, occasional exceptions to these centrifugal patterns. Certain mixed-descent daughters were brought into a more or less lasting company life as wives of white Nor'Westers; still fewer of these, such as Charlotte (Small) Thompson, completed their lives as married women in eastern Canada. And a few sons such as the part-Cree McGillivray brothers, Simon and Joseph, found lasting employment as officers within their fathers' company. The standing, however, of most native children of the British Nor'Westers was problematic. The essential determinants of their careers and identities were the nature and consistency of a father's attachment to them, the strength of his potentially conflicting loyalties to his white relatives and home society, and the extent of the resources, both financial and social, that he was able and willing to apply to these children's upbringing. Whatever his options and choices, a normal consequence of the ambiguous position of both himself and his family between the Indian country and the "civilized" world was the dispersal of his family members in two or more different directions, not by company fiat but as a result of individuals' decisions, actions, and inactions.

In the longer run, some British Nor'westers became keenly aware of paternal responsibilities or past irresponsibilities, as when Duncan McDougall in his last days of life recollected his daughter in James Bay. Some of their HBC counterparts were equally sensitive. But the HBC men, torn as they may have been by familial fragmentations, could hold a more formalistic company structure responsible for what could or could not be done to preserve family unity, and were spared some of the tensions of making their own decisions. And some, indeed, shared the eighteenth-century company view that Hudson Bay dependents in all kindness should not be brought to the foreign environment of Britain, but rather should simply be trained to survive in the context of native life (Brown 1980a:156).

## Controlled Comparisons and Black Boxes

These comparisons of certain facets of familial life in two fur trade companies and traditions are a sampling from a domain in which much remains to be done. In the fields of the fur trade, and of colonial Indian-white relations generally, there is an important place for controlled comparative studies of the different agencies involved in similar kinds of activity—be it trade, Christian proselytizing, or any other field in which differing organizations of European origin pursued similar enterprises within the same region.

At a general level, the trader was a social type about whose background, behavior, and values some minimal assumptions can be made. But to understand the dynamics of his relations with and impact on the peoples with whom he interacted, and their implications for later developments (such as the appearance or nonappearance of biracial groups distinct in identity and position), he needs to be examined within the structural frameworks that recruited, maintained, directed, and limited him in both his occupational and personal life. In turn, it is useful to compare those frameworks to the others in which his counterparts and rivals were operating, to understand in detail the range and subtle variations of Indian-white interactions in these different settings. The method of controlled comparison, applied in these directions, affords a systematic means of approaching and organizing the complex historical data on interracial encounters and enriching our perspectives on these critical materials.

This essay began by reflecting on the usefulness of Fred Eggan's ideas about comparative studies. For me, his controlled comparison approach was one of a few master keys helping to unlock the particular black box that historians call the fur trade, so that the contents of this entity could be unpacked, aired, and sorted into its diverse and internally complex parts.

Once unlocked and sorted, of course, the contents, genielike, won't go back into the box. So be it. If the fur trade is less unitary than we thought, then recent historians' formulation of a "fur trade society" in turn proves more problematic; and in contemplating the fundamental question of what a fur trade society might be, we are led again (as we should be) to deeper thoughts about our reifications of society itself (see Brown 1990).

Controlled comparison also leads onto other trails with their own windings, multiple vistas, and pitfalls. To grasp the complex texturings of a cultural region or of a set of related historical human entities is also to be drawn into multiple subjectivities, and to be obliged to acknowledge and assimilate a variety of points of view. To become thus absorbed is to become all the more resolutely historical. (As Eggan suggested, "Above all, it is important to control the historical framework.") Comparative study of the British Hudson's Bay and North West Company traders led me not only to macrobiography, the compiling of data on over two hundred individuals' life patterns and family histories; it also meant trying to grasp their varying outlooks and values, seeing into their minds to understand their actions and behavior. It meant, as well, finding more empathy with some of these human subjects than with others, and admitting the researcher's own subjectivity and selectivity as elements in framing the analysis, and even as part of the historical framework one seeks to control.

Efforts toward a more systematic engagement with issues of empathy and subjectivity lead also to engaging with questions of gender, another black box with its own locks and keys, and its own genie who will not neatly repack herself once released. Controlled comparison as a method did not explicitly attend to issues of subjectivity or of gender as factors affecting analysis. If Eggan were proposing it now, it probably would. We may best honor his intellectual legacy by building on the idea of focused comparison and producing studies that demonstrate not only a controlled analysis that he would appreciate and respect, but also a sensitivity to subjectivity and to gender that carry us beyond the disciplinary scientism of past years.

## Notes

1. *Ikwe*, a film from the National Film Board of Canada (Prairie Region), effectively dramatizes the formation and dispersal of a fur trade family in the late 1700s.

## References

### Unpublished Sources

Fidler, Peter.

Red River Journal 1814–15 (transcript from Selkirk Papers). Provincial Archives of Manitoba. Winnipeg.

Hudson's Bay Company Archives, Provincial Archives of Manitoba.

A.38/24, Estate of Samuel Black. B.49/a/34, Cumberland House Journal. B.51/e/2, Report on Manetoba District. B.154/e/2, Norway House. Winnipeg.

McVicar, Robert.

Papers. McCord Museum. Montreal.

Nelson, George.
    Journals and Reminiscences. Metropolitan Toronto Public Library.
St. Andrews Presbyterian Church Registers, Williamstown.
    Archives of Ontario. Toronto.
St. Gabriel Street Presbyterian Church Registers, Montreal.
    Archives of Ontario (microfilm). Toronto.

## Published Sources

Bishop, Charles A., and Shepard Krech, III
    1980    Matriorganization: The Basis of Aboriginal Subarctic Social Organization.
            Arctic Anthropology 17(2):34-45.
Beaumont, Raymond M.
    1992    Origins and Influences: The Family Ties of the Reverend Henry Budd. Prairie
            Forum 17:167-200
Brown, Jennifer S. H.
    1977    A Colony of Very Useful Hands. The Beaver (spring), 39-45.
    1980a   Strangers in Blood: Fur Trade Company Families in Indian Country.
            Vancouver: University of British Columbia Press.
    1980b   Linguistic Solitudes and Changing Social Categories. In Old Trails and New
            Directions: Papers of the Third North American Fur Trade Conference, edited
            by Carol M. Judd and Arthur J. Ray, 147-59. Toronto: University of Toronto
            Press.
    1982    Children of the Early Fur Trades. In Childhood and Family in Canadian
            History, edited by Joy Parr, 44-68. Toronto: McClelland and Stewart.
    1983a   Duncan McDougall. Dictionary of Canadian Biography, vol. 5, 525-27.
            Toronto: University of Toronto Press.
    1983b   Women as Centre and Symbol in the Emergence of Métis Communities.
            Canadian Journal of Native Studies 3:39-46.
    1985    Diverging Identities: the Presbyterian Métis of St. Gabriel Street, Montreal.
            In The New Peoples, edited by Jacqueline Peterson and Jennifer S. H. Brown,
            197-206. Winnipeg: University of Manitoba Press/Lincoln: University of
            Nebraska Press.
    1990    The Blind Men and the Elephant: Fur Trade History Revisited. In Proceedings
            of the Fort Chipewyan and Fort Vermilion Bicentennial Conference, edited
            by Patricia A. McCormack and R. Geoffrey Ironside, 15-19. Edmonton:
            Boreal Institute for Northern Studies, University of Alberta.
    1991    From Sorel to Lake Winnipeg: George Nelson as an Ethnohistorical Source.
            In New Dimensions in Ethnohistory: Papers of the Second Laurier Conference
            on Ethnohistory and Ethnology, edited by Barry Gough and Laird Christie,
            161-74. Canadian Ethnology Service, Mercury Series Paper no. 120. Ottawa:
            Canadian Museum of Civilization.
Brown, Jennifer S.H., and Robert Brightman
    1988    The Orders of the Dreamed: George Nelson on Cree and Northern Ojibwa
            Religion and Myth, 1823. Winnipeg: University of Manitoba Press/St. Paul:
            Minnesota Historical Society Press.
Eggan, Fred
    1955    Social Anthropology: Methods and Results. In Social Anthropology of North
            American Tribes, edited by Fred Eggan, 485-554. Enlarged ed. Chicago:

University of Chicago Press.

Hickerson, Harold
1966    Review of Lewis Saum, *The Fur Trader and the Indian*. American Anthropologist 68:822–24.

Jarvenpa, Robert, and Walter P. Zenner
1979    Scot Trade/Indian Worker Relations and Ethnic Segregation: A Subarctic Example. Ethnos 44:58–77.

Lamb, W. Kaye, ed.
1957    Sixteen Years in the Indian Country: The Journal of Daniel Williams Harmon 1800–1816. Toronto: Macmillan Company of Canada.

MacLeod, Margaret A., ed.
1947    The Letters of Letitia Hargrave. Champlain Society, vol. 28. Toronto.

Mancke, Elizabeth
1988    A Company of Businessmen: The Hudson's Bay Company and Long-Distance Trade, 1670–1730. Winnipeg: Rupert's Land Research Centre, University of Winnipeg.

Masson, Louis F. R.
1960    Les Bourgeois de la Compagnie du Nord-Ouest: Récits de voyages, lettres et rapports inédits relatifs au Nord-Ouest Canadien. 2 vols. (1st published 1889–90.) New York: Antiquarian Press.

Paine, Robert, ed.
1971    Patrons and Brokers in the East Arctic. Newfoundland Social and Economic Papers, no. 2. Institute of Social and Economic Research, Memorial University of Newfoundland. Toronto: University of Toronto Press.

Peterson, Jacqueline
1978    Prelude to Red River: A Social Portrait of the Great Lakes Métis. Ethnohistory 25:41–68.

Peterson, Jacqueline, and John Anfinson
1984    The Indian and the Fur Trade. *In* Scholars and the Indian Experience: Critical Reviews of Recent Writing in the Social Sciences, edited by W. R. Swagerty, 223–57. Bloomington: Indiana University Press.

Peterson, Jacqueline, and Jennifer S. H. Brown, eds.
1985    The New Peoples: Being and Becoming Métis in North America. Winnipeg: University of Manitoba Press/Lincoln: University of Nebraska Press.

Rogers, Edward S., and Mary Black Rogers
1978    Method for Reconstructing Patterns of Change: Surname Adoption by the Weagamow Ojibwa, 1870–1950. Ethnohistory 25:319–45.

Savishinsky, Joel S.
1972    Coping with Feuding: The Missionary, the Fur Trader, and the Ethnographer. Human Organization 31:281–90.

Van Kirk, Sylvia
1976    "The Custom of the Country": An Examination of Fur Trade Marriage Practices. *In* Essays on Western History in Honour of Lewis Gwynne Thomas, edited by Lewis H. Thomas, 49–70. Edmonton: University of Alberta Press.
1980    "Many Tender Ties": Women in Fur-Trade Society, 1670–1870. Winnipeg: Watson and Dwyer Publishing.

# 9

# The Civilization Strategy:
# Gros Ventres, Northern and Southern Arapahos
# Compared

LORETTA FOWLER

Gros Ventres, Northern Arapahoes, and Southern Arapahos impressed federal officials as cooperative with respect to assimilation or "civilization" programs in the late nineteenth and early twentieth centuries. Each group farmed, sent their children to school, accepted Christian missionaries, and generally expressed a willingness to become "civilized" or live "like a white man." Yet, Indian profession of civilization was in large part a political strategy and did not have the same meaning for Euro-Americans as it did for Indians or for one group of Indians as opposed to another. Plains groups other than Gros Ventres and Arapahos also adopted a "friendly" or civilization strategy (see, for example, Calloway 1986 on the Crow), and on some reservations opposing "hostile" and "friendly" strategies were employed by different groups (see Youngkin 1977 on the Cheyenne River Reservation). As yet, however, there are no comparative studies that focus on the diversity of strategies used by native peoples in dealing with reservation constraints, on the reasons why particular strategies of resistance—be they friendly or hostile—were embraced, or on how such choices contributed to different patterns of sociocultural change.

At the turn of the nineteenth century, and probably earlier, the Gros Ventres, Northern Arapahoes, and Southern Arapahos, who were divisions of a larger Arapaho-speaking population, had very similar sociocultural systems. They shared a body of mythological traditions, a religion based on age-graded ceremonial groups and tribal medicine bundles, and a social organization based on bands that were crosscut by age sets. Bands cooperated in a variety of activities at certain times of the year. As equestrian big-game hunters the three peoples made similar adaptations to the Plains ecosystem: the Gros Ventres between the forks of the Saskatchewan in Canada, the Northern Arapahoes on the central plains of southern Wyoming and eastern Colorado, and the Southern Arapahos on

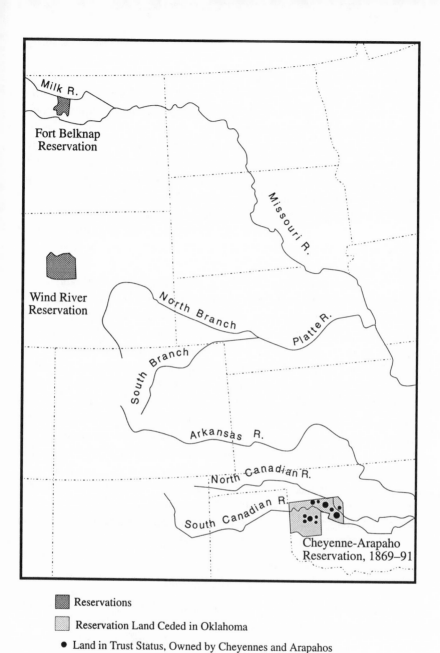

Reservations

Reservation Land Ceded in Oklahoma

● Land in Trust Status, Owned by Cheyennes and Arapahos

**Map 1.** Lands owned by Arapaho peoples, 1935.

the plains of southeastern Colorado and southward (see map 1). All were drawn into but affected differently by the late-eighteenth- and early-nineteenth-century fur trade and, subsequently, had divergent experiences with regard to emigration and the western expansion of the United States. Once the three peoples were on separate reservations in Montana, Wyoming, and Oklahoma, their prior, contrasting patterns of contact with Euro-Americans led to their adopting different strategies in their dealings with the agents of the federal government. Their politico-religious systems diverged further during the reservation years from the 1870s to the 1930s as they coped with contrasting kinds of missionary activity, different sorts of pressures on their land and resources, and variant patterns of coresidency with other native peoples.

This paper uses the controlled comparison method (Eggan 1954) to examine how divergent political strategies evolved among the Gros Ventres, Northern Arapahoes, and Southern Arapahos, consistent with cultural understandings yet responsive to the broader sociopolitical environment, and how those strategies contributed to the reorganization of and sharper contrasts between the politico-religious systems of the three groups. In the broader context of the history of colonial and neocolonial encounters in North America, as well as in the case of the three Arapaho groups, the combined methods of controlled comparison and ethnohistory can lead to hypotheses and eventually to generalizations about factors that precipitated particular responses and initiatives on the part of native peoples as well as differences in the implementation of policies and programs by federal officials. These methods can also provide insights into how cultural continuity persists in the face of major socioeconomic and political transformations, as well as how a commitment to resistance is forged in response to exploitation and domination.

## The Gros Ventres

The fur and robe trade on the northwestern plains led to a far greater development of intrasocietal competitive relations by the Gros Ventres than by other Arapaho divisions on the central and southern plains, where the trade took on different dimensions. Moreover, due to repercussions from the fur trade, the Gros Ventres suffered from population dispersal and loss to a greater extent than did the Northern or Southern Arapahos. These circumstances helped shape Gros Ventre society during the reservation period.

## The Trade Era

When they began to trade directly with the English and the French Canadians in 1779, the Gros Ventres were equestrian hunters. Individuals who owned many horses could attract followers and gain prestige by lending horses to those who owned few and by supporting those unable to hunt. The Gros Ventres became increasingly attracted to the traders' forts along the North and South Saskatchewan rivers, where they could obtain arms and ammunition and the other trade goods on which they had come to depend. The trade goods helped individuals maintain or augment reputations for generosity, expanded the opportunity for competition, and increased the number of competitors. Reputation and competition were formerly based on horse ownership. In fact, those Gros Ventre men with many horses were most successful in trade, for they could sell large quantities of meat as well as horses to the traders. Traders would, however, outfit poorer men, providing them an opportunity for mobility aside from that of raiding for horses (Fowler 1987:26, 34–40).

The expansion of the fur trade into Gros Ventre country brought with it an intensification of intertribal warfare. The Crees and Assiniboines, their own lands hunted out, were attempting to drive the Gros Ventres from their hunting territory. The Gros Ventres suffered terribly from population dispersal and loss. They were gradually driven from the Saskatchewan area into Montana during the first three decades of the nineteenth century. In Montana, they had to fight Crows and Assiniboines, and, later, Western Sioux as they struggled to hold their hunting territory (Fowler 1987:42, 46–52).

Gros Ventre social institutions and ritual life showed the effects of trade relations. The age group system expressed and reinforced competition for prestige through property distribution, as well as bravery. When they reached late adolescence, males joined an age set. The members of this group were roughly the same age and they usually cooperated in economic, military, and ceremonial activities. Males also joined one of two men's organizations (which I shall refer to as moieties, although membership was not based on kinship). If an age set joined one moiety, the next age set to be organized would join the other. The moieties were comprised of men of all ages, and these groups assumed police duties during rituals, such as the Sacrifice Lodge, attended by several bands or during communal hunts. Members of a moiety also jointly participated in dances that not only encouraged individual generosity and bravery but also allowed the moieties to compete with each other for prestige. In addition, Gros Ventre men (and sometimes women) selected "enemy-friends." Men chose their enemy-friends from the opposite moiety. An enemy-friend relationship was initiated when one individual gave property taken in battle to another; thereafter, the two competed to achieve recognition for bravery and for generous distribution of food and property to others.

Age sets also were initiated into a series of age grades or ceremonial statuses. Initiation followed a religious vow, accompanied by sacrifices of property (which was redistributed), and participation in the appropriate ceremony along with one's age set, at which time ritual knowledge was "earned" (i.e., bestowed by older men who had already completed the ceremony). Ritual authority increased with each grade acquired. Much of this ritual also reinforced values of bravery (Fowler 1987:27–30, 34; Flannery 1953:36–43).

There were two tribal medicine bundles, each in the charge of a priest or keeper. Gros Ventre bands tended to devote themselves to one or the other of the bundles, moving in the direction favored by the priest. These positions were transferred frequently and the transfer involved a large property distribution. According to Gros Ventre oral tradition, the bundle keepership was once hereditary in one band. It is possible that epidemics and losses through warfare altered the pattern of succession (Fowler 1987: 27, 34). In any case, trade goods as well as horses figured importantly in the property transfers that were an essential part of all Gros Ventre rituals and in the moiety relations that were the basis of social organization.

Between 1793 and 1794, while they were living in the Saskatchewan country, the Gros Ventres attacked English and French-Canadian trading posts in retaliation for their selling of arms and ammunition to the Crees and Assiniboines. Traders in Montana also were wary of the Gros Ventres and their Blackfeet allies, for they attacked any American trapper they found in the Upper Missouri area, effectively forcing the American Fur Company in 1831 to agree to establish posts where they would buy furs and robes from the Indians rather than send Americans to trap or hunt. Thus, after 1832 the Gros Ventres embarked on a long period of prosperity through the robe trade and of peaceful relations with Americans, never engaging in a military confrontation. In fact, Americans often helped the Gros Ventres against their enemies. Non-Indian settlement in Montana in the 1860s and early 1870s did not directly affect the Gros Ventres in an adverse way, for they occupied an area to the northeast of the settlements (Fowler 1987:42–50). At the time of reservation settlement in 1878, then, the Gros Ventres regarded Americans as allies, not adversaries.

*Becoming Like a White Man: Primacy and Prominence, 1878–1900*

About one thousand Gros Ventres began to camp for most of the year in the vicinity of Fort Belknap Agency in 1878. They had large horse herds; their agent in 1874 noted that they had a larger proportion of horses than most tribes on the northern plains (Fanton 1874). The agency was within the territory that they had been occupying for several generations and, by the terms of an 1855 treaty between the United States and the Gros Ventres and their allies at the time, the Blackfeet tribes, they had a right to settle there. Nearby were several bands of Assiniboines with whom they had been allied since 1869. These and, later, other Upper Assiniboines joined forces with the Gros Ventres against the Tetons, Yanktonais, and Bloods and Piegans (Blackfeet), who were conducting raids, trying to gain control of hunting territory in northern Montana (Fowler 1987:49, 53; Lincoln 1878a).

By 1883 pressure from businessmen and cattlemen in Montana had led to the federal government's determination to eliminate or reduce the size of Indian reservations to accommodate Euro-American settlers. Initially the Gros Ventres were threatened with removal from their land, but they eventually were induced to cede most of it in 1887, retaining only a forty-by-twenty-five-mile tract that today makes up Fort Belknap Reservation (Fowler 1987:66–68). During their struggle to retain a home in Montana, the Gros Ventres developed a strategy they were to use subsequently in their dealings with federal officials during the reservation period. They realized that the policy of the federal government was to introduce the "civilized" life to Indians and that the Assiniboines had impressed government agents as receptive to that aim. It became apparent to the Gros Ventres that they must convince federal officials that they too had embraced the civilization program.

At first their alliance with the Assiniboines was viewed by the Gros Ventres as an asset in the struggle to remain in Montana, for it might be more difficult for the government to remove two tribes than one. Representatives of both tribes claimed during the cession negotiations that the Gros Ventres and Assiniboines were "one people" (Fowler 1987:70). Before the negotiations, the government clearly regarded Fort Belknap as the Gros Ventre agency; when Assiniboines received rations, it was because the Gros Ventres shared their rations with them (Lincoln 1878b, 1878c). Even in 1886 the inspector sent from Washington to investigate conditions at the agency considered it necessary to meet only with Gros Ventre leaders (Minutes of Council 1886).

Within a few years, however, the co-occupation of the reservation had developed into a rivalry or competition for scarce resources and for political dominance. At first the Assiniboines had impressed the Indian agent (the representative of the federal government on the reservation) as more committed to civilization than the Gros Ventres. Agent Wyman

Lincoln noted that the Assiniboines were far more willing than the Gros Ventres to begin farming and to leave the large camps to settle on small family farms: "The Assiniboines show greater adaptability for farming and for work of any kind than the Gros Ventres; they do more farm work, and work more for hire" (quoted in Fowler 1987:70). He also complained that while the Assiniboines stayed near the agency, the Gros Ventres "roamed" (and therefore were less civilized) (Lincoln 1885a). The missionary Father Eberschweiler initially devoted his attentions and the resources of the Catholic church to the Assiniboines, who were settled near the agency complex in 1886 (Fowler 1987:70).

In addition, Assiniboines from Canada and eastern Montana, as well as Crees and French-Chippewas (Métis), whom the Gros Ventres did not recognize as allies, were joining the Assiniboines at Fort Belknap and sharing in the food and supplies issued at the agency (Lincoln 1882, 1885b; Allen 1897). The Gros Ventres bitterly protested, but to no avail. In 1878 the Gros Ventres outnumbered the Assiniboines living at Fort Belknap, but, by 1890, more Assiniboines than Gros Ventres were enrolled there (Fowler 1987:70). Both groups had lost population due to a high death rate, but the Assiniboines had increased their ranks by absorbing people from other groups.

The specter of removal and the perception that the Assiniboines constituted a threat precipitated changes in Gros Ventre society. By 1884 Agent Lincoln noticed a change in the Gros Ventre attitude toward civilization. He remarked that they had undergone an "entire change," showing more interest in "labor." Convincing federal agents in the 1880s that they had embraced civilization was a matter of demonstrating that they could "work," that is, that they could raise livestock and grow crops. The Gros Ventres also sought to demonstrate that they were working better than other tribes, that they were not only deserving of a home in Montana but that to place them with less deserving, more uncivilized Indians would result in their retrogression. When an inspector was sent from Washington, D.C., in 1886 to interview the Gros Ventres, their intermediary chief Under Bull told him, "We are now capable of taking care of our cattle. . . . You have seen our houses that were built by ourselves. . . . You have seen our fields and our fences. We have raised many potatoes, vegetables, and some grain. . . . If we had a boarding school we would send our children." He insisted that his words be written down and shown to the president. In a council held 9 June 1887, Under Bull stated, "I call myself a white man and look upon the white men as my brothers." Running Fisher also remarked, "I call myself a white man." Father Eberschweiler, whose help the Gros Ventres had enlisted, explained what Running Fisher meant: "He likes to be like a white man in farming, educating children." Running Fisher, as a delegate to Washington in 1894, spoke for himself: "I . . . want to be treated like a white man" (quoted in Fowler 1987:62–63, 68, 70–71). He urged the government to.pay Gros Ventres the same wage white men received for the same work.

In return for the aid of the Bureau of Catholic Indian Missions in thwarting the removal of the Gros Ventres from their homeland in Montana, tribal leaders had agreed in 1887 to the establishment of a mission and school in the section of the reservation where most of the Gros Ventres had resettled by 1890. The most prominent men sent their children to the mission school, as they had promised. By 1889 more Gros Ventre than Assiniboine children were attending school and the priests expressed a preference for them as pupils.

In 1896, when Montanans were once again clamoring for an additional cession of land, a federal inspector was persuaded after observing the Gros Ventres to report that they were exceptional among the Indians with whom he was familiar, that they were "doing much better" than the Assiniboines. The Gros Ventres viewed themselves as successful competitors with non-Indians as well. They futilely tried to prevent the 1896 cession of part of the Little Rockies at the southern end of the reservation by arguing that they knew the value of the gold deposits there and had a plan to send their children for training in order to mine the region themselves. Even though they were bitter about the cession, the Gros Ventres continued to work at agriculture. Indian Agents noted in 1896 and 1900 that they were more successful in farming and raising livestock than the Assiniboines (Fowler 1987:71).

The Gros Ventres' civilization strategy was reinforced by the desire of individual Gros Ventres to attain prominence, or high status. For six years after the Gros Ventres settled in the vicinity of the Fort Belknap Agency, they continued to hunt for most of their subsistence and lived without the deprivations suffered by many of the native peoples to the south of Montana, where there were no bison herds. With the end of raiding, horse herds also increased in size. Some trade in robes and furs was still possible as well. Thus, Gros Ventre men were able to continue their pursuit of social prominence. Being prominent meant having sufficient wealth, particularly horses, so that one could be conspicuously generous to others, and so that one could give away property publicly. Public generosity enabled a man to attract followers as well as to earn respect and praise. Young men, born too late to have acquired horse herds before United States and Canadian authorities began to suppress horse raids among Indians on the northern plains, had a difficult time achieving prominence (Fowler 1987:61, 65). For the most part, young men, and to a considerable extent, even older, prominent men, began to depend on the resources of the Indian agent, missionaries, or other non-Indians to acquire the means to be generous.

By convincing the Indian agent of their willingness to embrace civilization, to cooperate with efforts to introduce farming, ranching, and other aspects of an American lifestyle, individuals received various kinds of property, including cattle, which they could generously distribute to others. The agents at Fort Belknap had been given authority by the Commissioner of Indian Affairs and also specifically in the land cession agreements of 1888 and 1896 to issue cattle to "deserving individuals." By retaining an agent's favor, individuals acquired herds which were then gradually sold or butchered for the benefit of others. For the most prominent of the middle-aged headmen, the agent arranged for a large section of land (about 800 acres) to be plowed. The man's followers were assigned small sections within the large field where they planted and harvested vegetables. Part of the produce they gave to the headman, who could then generously feast others or sell the food to a trader.

Gros Ventre and Assiniboine families were issued beef rations at the agency; the hides were issued by the agents to "industrious and deserving Indians." The hides could be sold to a trader. The sale of cowhides was particularly important because by the mid-1880s the numbers of bison in the agency vicinity had decreased so drastically that the buffalo robe trade collapsed, making it difficult for an individual to acquire property to distribute ceremonially, or to buy supplies for his family or the members of his band.

The agent also lent farm machinery (e.g., threshers) to individuals he judged to be cooperative; several headmen acquired the equipment, organized their followers into work groups, and hired out to neighboring ranchers, collecting food and trade goods in payment. Other headmen were employed as freighters to transport supplies to the agency, but the most important position was that of Indian Policeman. In return for enforcing the agent's orders—bringing children to school, for example—several prominent men received salaries, extra rations, cowhides, and other benefits that they used to maintain a following (Fowler 1987:62). In 1893 Agent William McAnaney described how he persuaded ambitious individuals to cooperate: "By a little talking and by judicious occasional issues . . . I have succeeded. . . . Once convince an Indian woman that her husband will stand higher in the social plane . . . the thing is done" (McAnaney 1893).

Gros Ventre men also turned for aid to the Catholic missionaries. By sending their children to the mission boarding school, prominent men obtained "loans," wage work, and a market for wood, grain, and other crops. The mission needed the help of Gros Ventre leaders to fend off the agents' efforts to compete with the mission for students for the agency boarding school. Younger men who supported the mission could obtain wives from the young female pupils under the priests' supervision, thereby avoiding payment of a bride price (Fowler 1987:63-64). Although the Catholics had little success converting adults, in 1889 Father L. Van Gorp noted that there was "less trouble in the management of this school than of any of our schools that I have seen—less interference on the part of the Indians with their children" (Eberschweiler 1888; Van Gorp 1889). In fact, subsequent generations became increasingly drawn to Christianity—in some instances due to vision experiences in which a supernatural helper advised conversion (Fowler 1987:56, 94-95).

In 1886 the Gros Ventres held their last Sacrifice Lodge, a ceremony that necessitated a large camp of several days' duration, and one on which federal officials and missionaries focused their opposition. Yet, subsequently, Gros Ventres who had the means continued to make frequent donations at public events, as well as to provide for people at their camps. Age grade ceremonies ceased to be held, but the Star and Wolf moieties, which claimed most adult males as members, competed in the display of generosity during the 1880s and 1890s. Horses and cattle were donated during the moiety dances and at other rituals, religious and secular, that the Gros Ventres continued to hold despite the federal government's effort to prevent what they perceived as the Indians' tendency to improvidently give away their property (Fowler 1987:57, 65).

## Despair and Revitalization, 1901–34

The cession of the Little Rockies, a low point for the Gros Ventres, helped precipitate political and ritual reorganization. Competition for prominence was channeled into new rituals, and the moiety system was reorganized. The Gros Ventres persisted in their strategy of competing with the Assiniboines, and increasingly with non-Indians. They sought to show federal officials their commitment to civilization or "progress" in order to obtain more control over their own affairs and to put the Assiniboines (and the Métis, who frequently entered the reservation) at a disadvantage.

The inability of the Gros Ventres to prevent the cession of the Little Rockies was extremely traumatic for them. During the council several of the older men, who were moiety leaders, expressed the view that perhaps in the future younger men would be more effective advocates for Gros Ventre interests. The elderly Running Crow commented, "If we should choose a headman out of those young men, I think we would get a good man" (United States 1895:11, 14). In fact, younger, bilingual men increasingly did serve as spokesmen for the Gros Ventres on the "business council." A new agent, W. R. Logan, was appointed in 1902 and he organized a business council of Gros Ventre and Assiniboine leaders in 1904. The Indian Office sanctioned the council by directing that they be asked to consent to the leasing of reservation lands. Before the establishment of the council, agents had often refused to forward leaders' views to Washington, but Logan sent the proceedings of council meetings to the Commissioner of Indian Affairs.

At first Logan and the council were in accord. The Gros Ventres were pleased that he pressed the federal government to obtain a ruling from federal court guaranteeing the tribes' rights to water from the Milk River, on the northern border of the reservation. But they became disenchanted when they realized that he was removing Indian-owned cattle from the reservation to his own ranch. They began complaining about him in 1907 and increasingly asked for more control over reservation affairs. "We want to have something to say ourselves," the Gros Ventre headmen wrote. During the second decade of the century, councilmen were chosen by elderly prominent men at a dance attended by the entire tribe, and those men served on the council until they were elderly (Fowler 1987:79–83, 91; see also pp. 73, 89–90). In 1921 the agent introduced elections by ballot (Marshall 1924). Still, the incumbent councilmen continued to be reelected.

The councilmen were regarded by federal officials as especially progressive, for they promoted ways to improve agricultural production, spoke English, and accepted innovations such as balloting. The Gros Ventres themselves, in correspondence with their agent in 1914, signed themselves "progressive stock raisers." In fact, there were no Gros Ventres who resisted ranching or wage work. Although not everyone was equally successful, all attempted to acquire the means to participate in the cere-monies during which individuals gained prestige by giving away property. A small group of families living in Dodson, Montana, the northeast section of the reservation, were descendants of a few white men who had married Gros Ventre women. Occasionally they participated in council business, but only at the request of council members, and they often attended and participated in the gatherings held in the Gros Ventre community. But no "mixed-blood" faction developed to challenge the Gros Ventre leadership. The Gros Ventre councilmen were no less skilled in farming, ranching, or the use of English than the Dodson Gros Ventres, and they went out of their way to cultivate ties with white politicians, inviting them to attend some of the Gros Ventre celebrations, for example (Fowler 1987:83–85, 89–90, 126).

Beginning in 1911 the Gros Ventre business council embraced the government's program of dividing reservations into individually owned allotments of land. Their support of allotment (in contrast to the opposition of a segment of the Assiniboine population) impressed federal officials as evidence of their progressive bent. The Gros Ventres, aware that one of the results of allotment on other reservations was the loss of land through the sale of any unallotted land, were determined to prevent such loss. In this they succeeded, for no land was sold at the time of allotment in 1922. They also tried to use the allotment of land as a way to prevent those Assiniboines and Métis whom they regarded as not entitled to remain on Fort Belknap from obtaining allotments. At first the Gros Ventres succeeded in convincing the agent and the secretary of interior that the individuals in question were not entitled to allotments and that Gros Ventres could progress faster without them. But eventually the secretary was persuaded to change his mind (Fowler 1987:90-93). Thereafter the Gros Ventre councilmen concentrated on gaining control over the administration of the reservation from federal officials altogether.

When the Indian Reorganization Act (IRA) was proposed in 1934, the Gros Ventres enthusiastically supported it, and Fort Belknap became the first reservation on the Plains to accept its provisions. The IRA provided for conservation and development of Indian land and resources, credit and economic development programs, and home rule. Tribes could decide by majority vote to accept the bill's provisions. The Gros Ventres anticipated that they would gain control over tribal moneys, agency jobs, and management of resources and that they could establish a tribal government separate from the Assiniboines. They were subsequently disillusioned, but at the time of the vote on the IRA, Gros Ventres believed that their strategy of embracing agriculture and formal education had been effective (Fowler 1987:95-97).

During the early twentieth century, the Gros Ventres had a rich ceremonial life that focused on the Grass Dance, newly reorganized moieties, and the Hays Fair. Shortly before 1900 the Grass Dance had become transformed from a ceremony owned and performed by the Wolfmen moiety to one in which the entire tribe participated. The ritual was particularly meaningful to young boarding school alumni, who had not been organized into age sets, for, in their own words, it allowed them to "keep on dancing" and to join their elders in perpetuating "what it [ceremonies] used to be." The modified Grass Dance, held almost weekly before the 1920s, required four directors or "chiefs" and several other office holders, some of whom were women. When each office was transferred, the recipient had to give away large amounts of property, including stock.

During the ritual, officers gave away property to validate their right to take particular actions. For example, the whipman (an officer who compelled people to dance) "paid for" his right to strike nonparticipants in order to make them dance. The officers were among the most prosperous Gros Ventres and their holding of offices served as a leveling mechanism: "If the 'chiefs' happened to be in a good financial condition at the time, they made them 'shell out' in that way," was the way the Gros Ventres explained it. Relatives of officers also gave property away during the ceremony in honor of their kinsmen. Attendance and participation was enforced by heavy fines for those who stayed away—individuals might have their property confiscated until they redeemed it by attending the dance (Flannery 1947:42, 50-52, 61, 64-68; Fowler 1987:76-79, 85-87). A Grass Dance office at once honored a person, bestowed authority on him, and compelled him to share his wealth with others. The emphasis on the ceremony also encouraged agricultural production at the same time it reinforced Gros Ventre ideals and values. While the Assiniboines had their own distinctive ceremonies, the Grass Dance became a primary vehicle for publicly expressing Gros Ventre cultural identity.

Gros Ventres reorganized the moiety structure, as well as the Grass Dance, in the early twentieth century. A group of elderly Gros Ventres organized the community into two divisions, one composed of people settled north of the community hall and one of those settled south. Committees of men and women from the two divisions took turns being in charge of accumulating food and property for Gros Ventre dances. They competed to earn recognition for generosity (Fowler 1987:85, 87). As in the case of the Grass Dance offices, the moieties' activities expressed the Gros Ventre ideal of prestige through competitive distribution of property and served to motivate people to raise grain and cattle.

Logan reported that he introduced the idea of an agricultural fair to the Gros Ventres in 1906 because they were progressive enough to make a success of such a venture. Tribal members today note that the Hays Fair was started by elderly Gros Ventres after they visited the Crow tribe's fair. By 1911 the reservation superintendent complained that the Gros Ventres spent too much money on their fair. The fair committee, comprised of prominent individuals, was expected to donate heavily to the event. The fair featured Gros Ventre games and contests as well as agricultural exhibits and carnival events. There were sham battles between Gros Ventres and Assiniboines and sporting events between Gros Ventres and non-Indians. A Gros Ventre boxer challenged all comers from the neighboring towns. At the close of the fair the Gros Ventres whose exhibits had won prizes gave away their exhibits, thereby earning additional prestige. The fair was a source of pride in that it drew non-Indians from throughout Montana, and it was an expression of the Gros Ventres' feeling that they could best both the Assiniboines and their non-Indian neighbors at anything (Fowler 1987:87–89, 93–94).

## The Northern Arapahoes

The fur trade touched the Northern Arapahoes later and less directly than the Gros Ventres and therefore caused less social disruption. The circumstances of the fur and robe trade on the central and southern plains contributed to an increase in the centralization of authority among the Arapahoes and less emphasis on the individual competition that was so characteristic of the Gros Ventres. Indian-white warfare in the 1860s and 1870s reinforced the centralization of authority.

### Trade Relations and Warfare

Traders on the Missouri River first noted the Arapahoes in 1795. At that time Arapahoes had had no direct contact with them but had traded horses through Cheyenne middlemen for manufactured goods. As a group they had less access to trade goods, and individuals had less opportunity to accumulate goods, than the Gros Ventres did. Arapahoes ranged at least as far northeast as the Black Hills in South Dakota and as far southwest as the Rocky Mountains in Colorado. But as the Sioux began pushing southwest from the Missouri in the early nineteenth century, the Arapahoes retreated toward Wyoming and Colorado to the heart of their hunting territory in the foothills of the Rockies and allied themselves with the Cheyennes, who ranged to the northeast. They avoided large-scale population loss from warfare (although there were losses from epidemics) by a series of tenuous alliances with Sioux and the more southerly Kiowas and Comanches, as well as the Cheyennes. Northern Arapahoes were able to have large bands that combined periodically for ceremonies. The Gros Ventre and Arapahoe populations in 1830 numbered roughly the same—approximately three to four thousand. The Northern Arapahoes were subdivided into four bands. In contrast, there were as many as twelve Gros Ventre bands, some of which were separated from the others for years, largely because of warfare (Fowler 1982a:15–17, 43; 1987:43–48; Flannery 1953:25).

After 1810 fur companies sent trappers into Arapahoe country, rather than establishing a series of forts there. There were occasional clashes; Arapahoes also solicited gifts of trade goods. Between 1834 and 1839 forts were built on the Platte and Arkansas rivers in the heart of Arapahoe and Cheyenne territory and traders began buying buffalo robes. Arapahoes maintained friendly relations with the robe traders. However, fewer robes could be transported overland and down the shallow Platte than down the Missouri by steamboat. So traders bought in larger volume from the Gros Ventres. Also, traders dealt primarily with Arapahoe headmen who served as intermediaries. The importance of those intermediaries increased as a heavy stream of emigrants began moving along the Platte in the 1840s.

The intermediary or "friendly" chief—armed with documents and other symbols attesting to his good reputation—reassured American travelers and officials of the Arapahoes' peaceful intent and, in return, received trade goods. Arapahoes had increasingly come to depend on those goods, as the emigrant traffic and the robe trade led to a decline in the numbers of buffalo. The chief retained the loyalty of his followers because he redistributed the trade goods (Fowler 1982a:17, 21-34).

The Arapahoes were able to attain greater centralization of authority than the Gros Ventres—a situation reflected in and promoted by their age group system and its religious underpinnings, as well as in the institution of intermediary chieftainship. The Arapahoes did not have moieties; the Gros Ventres did. Moreover, a single age grade was occupied by only one age set, which worked to minimize intrasocietal competition, for all those men in the same life stage belonged to the same set of cooperating individuals. At the head of the age group organization were priests who had authority over the intermediary chiefs and all the age grades. The Gros Ventres lacked this priesthood, at least during the nineteenth century. Another priest had custody of the Arapahoes' one tribal medicine bundle. He held his position for life; in fact, the same man held the office throughout the second half of the nineteenth century (Fowler 1982a:26, 54; 1982b:82-83). Centralized and theocratic authority was more developed among the Arapahoes than the Gros Ventres, probably in large part because the Arapahoes were secure enough militarily to hold the ceremonies that were attended by all the bands and that were presided over by the priests.

During the 1860s and 1870s, relations between Arapahoes and Americans deteriorated. In violation of an 1851 treaty, the federal government allowed thousands of settlers into the Arapahoes' hunting territory, which undermined their ability to support themselves. In the 1860s, professional buffalo hunters killed so many animals that Arapahoes had great difficulty subsisting. Open warfare between Americans and Arapahoes, as well as other tribes, occurred during those years. In an effort to avoid being attacked, the Northern Arapahoes withdrew from Colorado, distancing themselves from the Southern Arapahos and thereafter following a political course separate from the bands that hunted on the southern plains. The Northern Arapahoes moved into southeastern Wyoming, where, forming an alliance with Sioux and Cheyennes, they ranged as far north as southern Montana, where there were still large herds of buffalo.

The fighting between Arapahoes and troops and citizens of the United States led to a greater reliance on the intermediary chief. By the 1870s, the position of the Northern Arapahoes had deteriorated; in 1874 an attack by troops left them with only a small portion of their large horse herd. Unable to hunt to meet subsistence needs they began to try to ally themselves with the army. Arapahoes, led by their intermediary chiefs, enlisted as scouts and assisted the army in its campaign against other Indians in 1876 and 1877. Their goal was a reservation in Wyoming, where they hoped to be undisturbed by immigrants and troops. Intermediaries initially were able to obtain military protection for Arapahoe bands, moderate political concessions, and much needed supplies, for the federal government needed Arapahoe assistance. And in 1878 the Arapahoes were permitted to settle in Wyoming on the reservation of the Shoshones, trusted allies of the Americans (Fowler 1982a:34–35, 39, 42–66).

In comparison, Gros Ventre people were not dependent on the diplomatic skills of intermediaries. Gros Ventre relations with the United States were friendly and there was no need to rely on army rations. The Gros Ventres did deal with the government through intermediary chiefs at treaty councils; but, unlike Arapahoe intermediaries, Gros Ventre chiefs were not important to their people's everyday survival, and Gros Ventres other than chiefs could trade robes for manufactured goods (Fowler 1982b:84–86).

## The White Man's Trail: Reassuring Old Enemies, 1878–1905

When the Northern Arapahoes arrived on the Shoshone reservation in 1878, they, like the Shoshones, numbered about one thousand. They expected to stay only temporarily before obtaining their own reservation. The Arapahoes were much less prosperous than the Gros Ventres had been, for their horse herds had been depleted in wars with the U.S. Army, and the buffalo robe trade had collapsed on the central and southern plains. As a result, wealth differentials had been leveled to a great extent. Arapahoes depended on rations of beef and other supplies that were promised them by the government. The intermediary chief was expected to obtain provisions and other benefits from federal officials, then distribute them in an equitable manner. At the time of reservation settlement there were two main intermediary chiefs, Black Coal and Sharp Nose, who worked together to try to convince federal officials to provide the things the Arapahoes needed to survive. Still in place in 1878, the priesthood that directed Arapahoe ceremonies helped mobilize Arapahoe support for the chiefs. The authority of these chiefs also was bolstered by the federal government's reliance on them to counter anticipated attacks on neighboring non-Indians by the Sioux and by the perception on the part of the agents that the chiefs were needed to control the Arapahoes, who only four years earlier, had been "hostiles." In contrast, the Gros Ventres were neither a threat nor a needed ally in northern Montana.

When the Arapahoes came to the Shoshone reservation, the non-Indian settlers in the vicinity of the reservation were fearful of Arapahoe attacks, and the Shoshones, long-standing enemies, were antagonistic toward their arrival. It was important for the Arapahoes to reassure both non-Indians and Shoshones that they could be relied upon as "friendlies" and as allies in case of attack by "hostiles," such as the Sioux.

At Shoshone Agency the intermediary chiefs Black Coal and Sharp Nose worked to convince federal officials that they were at peace with Whites and willing to do agricultural work. In a speech to Governor John Hoyt of the Wyoming Territory, Black Coal stated, "We have come to the place given us and have behaved like good Indians. . . . Once I was wild [a hunter and fighter]. Then at last I found the white man's trail. It is better than the red man's. I hope my people will all find it and stay in it" (quoted in Fowler 1982a). He insisted his speech be transmitted to the president. In their meetings with federal agents, Arapahoe chiefs stressed their records as scouts and "friendlies," displaying peace medals and other gifts from federal officials. Sharp Nose, who often wore his scout uniform, even named his son General Crook. The chiefs also requested that some of their children be sent to Carlisle Indian School, in Pennsylvania, operated by Captain Richard Pratt. Thirteen children went to Carlisle in 1881, each carrying a pipe to be delivered to a federal official, a testament to the Arapahoes' good faith, to assure Americans that they "never more want to go on warpath, but always live in peace," Black Coal said. They also manipulated the Americans' fears of the Sioux, blaming the Sioux for coercing them into hostile acts and stressing that they could be relied on to protect non-Indians from Sioux attack. In actuality, the Sioux were regular visitors and honored guests in the Arapahoe camps (Fowler 1982a:69–74, 79).

The Shoshones already had a well-established reputation as friends of the Americans; thus, Black Coal emphasized that Arapahoes would work like white men to get "a better name [reputation]" for themselves. Agricultural labor was the keystone of the government's civilization program. Arapahoe chiefs realized that they needed to cooperate with the agents in order to reassure officials and also to convince them to allow the chiefs more authority on the reservation. In attempting to cooperate with the agent and raise hay for sale, the large camps dispersed into several smaller encampments along the rivers. The men of each band constructed irrigation ditches. The chiefs had large hay fields and gardens in which their followers worked. The chiefs distributed the produce. The superintendent at the government boarding school wrote in 1897, "We have plenty of tepees and blankets yet in sight, horse racing and gambling and Indian customs still hold sway, but the blanket is laid aside long enough to plow, harrow, build fences and houses, cut wood, make hay, etc." (quoted in Fowler 1982a:89). The chiefs made a favorable impression and, in return for their ability to guarantee peace and cooperation, until the 1890s they were allowed to supervise the slaughter of the beef cattle designated for issue to the tribe and to distribute beef and flour rations to their followers. They also were given the cowhides and received extra rations each week in order to feed their followers (Fowler 1982a:75–76, 80–81, 84–85, 89, 101).

After the government negotiated grazing leases on the northern half of the reservation, to which both the Shoshones and Arapahoes were asked to agree, the chiefs were allowed to keep a copy of the record of leases to cattlemen and to recommend how the lease money would be spent. Arapahoe chiefs also bargained for more provisions by offering to accept allotments, a "progressive" act in the estimation of federal officials. The acceptance of allotments in 1900 also ensured them a place on the reservation despite ongoing efforts on the part of the Shoshones to have them removed. In 1896 the Shoshones and Arapahoes had agreed to cede a small section of land in return for more beef. And, again in 1904, Arapahoe rights on the reservation were established when both tribes, out of economic necessity, ceded the northern half of the reservation. The cession was ratified by Congress in 1905 (Fowler 1982a:91–95, 104).

The bond between the chiefs and the elderly hierarchy of priests remained strong. In fact, influential elders made speeches at public events urging Arapahoes to farm, as well as fulfill ceremonial obligations and avoid quarreling. When the Christian missionaries arrived, the Arapahoe priests did not oppose participation in Christian ritual as long as Arapahoes did not neglect ritual duties in the Sacrifice Lodge and other ceremonies or express disrespect for these traditions. In addition, two groups came to proselytize, the Catholics and the Episcopals, and the Arapahoe chiefs played one group off against the other, accepting mission benefits but able to reject what they found unacceptable. The chiefs, whom the agent relied on to accept employment themselves or to select men to work for the agency in various capacities, chose the leader of the middle-aged men's age grade to head the Indian Police, and that force was never at odds with the priests or chiefs. In fact, as James Mooney learned when he visited the agency, they carefully kept information from the agent that might damage the Arapahoes' reputation for being peaceful and cooperative. The highest-ranking priest, the custodian of the tribal medicine bundle, helped the intermediary chiefs at the 1904 cession council by reassuring Arapahoes that their home was secure. He spoke of a vision experience he had had in which the bundle assured him that the Arapahoes would have a good and secure place to live (Fowler 1982a:77, 85-86, 97, 107, 109, 111-12, 117-18, 122-27).

## Demonstration of "Progress," 1905-34

By the turn of the century, the chiefs' reassurance of peaceful intent no longer influenced federal officials to grant their requests, for the threat of Indian wars had passed. After the cession of the northern half of the reservation, the ceded land, which the federal government had promised to sell on behalf of the Shoshones and Arapahoes, remained unsold to homesteaders, for they could not afford to irrigate. In 1912 the president withdrew the land from sale and restored the reservation (now called Wind River) to an area seventy by fifty-five miles. The northern portion was then leased. The income was expended by federal officials on behalf of the tribes. The Arapahoes still attempted to obtain rations, but the focus of their struggle was on controlling the money the federal government obtained from leasing Indian lands. When the Arapahoe leaders requested rations, they asked for temporary help for those unable to work. They put most of their efforts into attempting to obtain as much of the lease money as possible in per capita payments for each member of the tribe. The land was being leased at unconscionably low rates, and speculators, rather than the tribes, were profiting. Thus, Arapahoe leaders sought to increase the tribe's income from grazing and mineral leases and to influence the way the income was spent (Fowler 1982a:130-34, 140-41).

By stressing their commitment to "progress," Arapahoe leaders hoped to convince federal officials that the tribal members should receive the lease income in per capita payments and that tribal leaders could supervise the leasing process. In 1913 Yellow Calf, who succeeded Sharp Nose, stressed to officials that Arapahoes would enthusiastically engage in agricultural and other work in order to prove their competence to determine how their resources and funds should be used: "in order to obtain a good name for our father [the reservation superintendent Joseph Norris] we must get to work .... When we get him up high where his name will be known all over the world by our work ... we will have a good name as well" (quoted in Fowler 1982a). On another occasion that year he stressed that if Arapahoes worked well each could "be a man someday"; in other words, if Arapahoes proved they were progressive they could gain control over their own financial affairs. Arapahoes had some success with Superintendent Joseph Norris, appointed for 1912-16 by a new administration in Washington. Although he implemented tougher regulations and higher fees, tribal members still received only small, annual per capita payments of from five to twenty dollars (Fowler 1982a:134, 136).

Arapahoe leaders agreed to the federal government's plan to organize a "business council" in lieu of a council of intermediary chiefs. The acceptance of a business council suggested a progressive bent to the federal officials. Actually, chiefs were chosen to serve on the council as spokesmen. And, as in the Gros Ventres' case, the councilmen were selected by elders in a public ceremony. Unlike the Gros Ventre elders, the directors of the ceremony were part of a hierarchy of priests that officiated over native religious rituals. Thus the selection-installation ceremony for Arapahoe councilmen, which involved the use of a kettle drum, was sacred in nature. Even after balloting was imposed in 1930, the ceremony continued to be held to install new leaders. When the drum was struck, prayers were directed to the supernatural by an interlocking set of symbols of mediation, including air in the form of sound, the drum supports, and eagles embroidered on the drumsticks with quills. Air effects communication between humans and the supernatural, for it transcends the division between the world above (heaven) and earth. Prayer-songs resound in the atmosphere. Steam, symbolized by red paint on the drum, propels prayers upward. The drum supports symbolize pipes, from which smoke ascends, carrying prayers upward. The eagle, one of the creatures of the firmament, also soars upward into the heavens. Values of unity and harmony were reaffirmed through the symbolism of the drum lacings, which represented tepees in the camp circle. During the drum ceremony, the drum symbolism served to validate a councilman's leadership position and, at the same time, reinforce his awareness of his obligations to the people and subordinate him to the priests (Fowler 1982a:87, 98-99, 149-51).

To the satisfaction of federal officials, the men's lodges were discontinued at the turn of the century and, in their place, a series of sodalities were organized. The names of the sodalities reflected the Arapahoes' progressive turn (e.g., Christmas Club), but, in fact, they were associated with particular age groups and assumed roles similar in some respects to those of the age grades. Elders continued to occupy the highest positions of authority in the religious sphere; the councilmen were middle-aged; the sodalities included middle-aged men and youths (Fowler 1982a:161).

The most important religious ceremony was the Sacrifice Lodge, in which individuals fulfilled vows with the help of instructors who had previously completed the ceremony. A modest reciprocal exchange of food and gifts occurred between mentor and votary. Arapahoe leaders continued to play the Catholic and Episcopal missions off against each other. In 1910 the Episcopals built a second mission in the midst of a large Arapahoe settlement. In 1917 they established a school there. The Episcopals were not as determined to repress Arapahoe culture as the Catholic school and mission were, and, in fact, even encouraged the Arapahoes to adhere to traditional customs and ceremonies (Fowler 1982a:113-14, 136-37).

In order to keep the support of their constituents, the Arapahoe business councilmen had to continue to distribute resources and provide for the needy. In the early twentieth century the federal policy against furnishing chiefs with extra rations was relaxed in that business councilmen were given large quantities of rations to distribute and were routinely hired to supervise Arapahoe workers on roads, irrigation systems, and other agency projects. The councilmen also frequently received small payments over and above the fee paid to the tribe from persons who leased tribal lands. These resources were used by the councilmen to provide for needy constituents and to help sponsor community celebrations and gatherings. Such generosity was expected of those persons selected as councilmen (Fowler 1982a:138-39, 141).

Still determined to obtain per capita payments, councilmen used a persuasive, persistent approach with federal officials, attempting to convince them that Arapahoe leaders had the business acumen to make decisions about leasing and to make wise use of per capita payments. Some of the Shoshone business councilmen employed a different approach. These "mixed-blood" councilmen (individuals who had grown up in a household with a white parent) were more assertive and aggressive, even at times harassing and threatening or directly accusing officials of incompetence or graft in the management of reservation resources. Arapahoe councilmen were appreciative of the Shoshone advocates, refusing to support the federal government's efforts to censure or silence them. The more conciliatory approach of the Arapahoes was perhaps, at least in part, encouraged by the fact that the Shoshone mixed-bloods were taking a more militant stance (Fowler 1982a:142-48).

Arapahoes did not view themselves as competitive with neighboring non-Indians, as the Gros Ventres seemed to do. Instead they sought patrons from among both local people and groups or individuals with national prominence, attempting to enlist their aid to change federal policies that the Arapahoes disliked. The government's attempt to ban the Sacrifice Lodge was particularly onerous to them. During the early twentieth century tourism was important to the local economy and "Indian" events attracted tourists. At the request of local townspeople Arapahoes appeared in parades and other events during the Fourth of July and Labor Day. Arapahoes invited prominent people to attend their ceremonies, which they characterized as free of offensive or "barbaric" features. They gave their non-Indian visitors Indian names and otherwise tried to persuade them to help. The Sacrifice Lodge was referred to as the Harvest Dance during that time, and groups like the Federated Women's Club and the Red Cross were persuaded to appeal to the government to cease its effort to ban the ritual. In fact, no sanctions against the ceremony were applied and it was allowed to be held openly after 1922 (Fowler 1982a:132, 137-38, 154-55).

By 1934, when federal officials were trying to persuade the Arapahoes to accept the Indian Reorganization Act, the tribe was bitter about the government's refusal to distribute more than a small part of the lease money in per capita payments and they were convinced that their resources were being mismanaged. Elderly ritual leaders spoke against the IRA and so the vast majority voted against accepting the act (Fowler 1982a:172-75).

## The Southern Arapahos

The Southern Arapahos' relations with traders by and large paralleled those of the Northern Arapahoes. Intermediary chieftainship was reinforced by trading and by the troubles that resulted from emigrant traffic and the settlement of Colorado.

### Trade Relations and the Settlement of Colorado

Southern Arapahos, some bands of which lived for a period of time with their Comanche neighbors to the south, were especially rich in horses and were in a good position to trade with Cheyenne middlemen at the turn of the century. They had traded with the Spanish in New Mexico, mostly for textiles and bread, in the eighteenth century. In the 1820s through the 1840s they, and probably some Northern Arapahoes as well, were able to obtain manufactured goods by raiding caravans on the Santa Fe Trail, which gave them some independence from the American traders at the posts on the Arkansas and Platte. Intermediary leadership, based on "friendly" behavior toward Americans, also helped the Southern, as well as the Northern, Arapahos, obtain trade goods in the early nineteenth century. For example, chiefs routinely collected "tolls" from travelers and gifts from government agents upon presentation of the documents of friendly status or good conduct that they obtained from federal officials and emigrants (Whitfield in ARCIA 1855:116).

When their country in west-central Colorado was overrun by miners and settlers beginning in 1859 (Greenwood in ARCIA 1859:21), the Southern Arapahos had to accommodate themselves to this presence in order to remain in their winter camping grounds, and the friendly intermediary chief became even more crucial. Chiefs made regular visits to the settlements to reassure the settlers (Trenholm 1970:154–55).

Arapahos maintained a very close alliance with the Southern Cheyennes during the early nineteenth century—an association that was advantageous for both groups struggling to hold on to hunting territory between the Platte and Arkansas. After the settlement of Colorado that alliance was a potential liability, for the Cheyennes adopted a hostile strategy of resisting American travel and settlement, repeatedly clashing with settlers and federal troops at the same time that the Arapahos were trying to remain friendlies. Arapaho bands tried to stay apart from the Cheyennes and disassociate themselves from Cheyenne actions. At an 1861 treaty council, in which Southern Arapahos ceded some of their land in Colorado in return for a reservation on Sand Creek (which they were never actually able to occupy), they insisted on living separately from the Cheyennes (Kappler 1904, 2:810). Arapahos were drawn into a war with Americans after the Sand Creek massacre in 1864, but after the 1865 peace treaty, even though the Cheyennes resumed raids in 1866, Arapahos tried to avoid the fighting. They helped to ransom non-Indian captives and returned them to the military (see Gordon in ARCIA 1866:277). The importance of intermediary chiefs grew in the context of these hostilities. At the peace council of 1867, Arapahos again tried to separate themselves politically from the Cheyennes (Transcript of the Minutes and Proceedings of the Indian Peace Commission 1867:113). When hostilities resumed in 1868 between Cheyennes and Americans, Arapahos feared with good reason that settlers and troops would attack Indians indiscriminately, and in 1869 the chiefs succeeded in obtaining the assistance of army officers to move south under the protection of troops to the Canadian River country, where they hoped to obtain a reservation.

The age grade system of the Southern Arapahos was virtually identical to that of the Northern Arapahoes. It was headed by tribal priests, although not including the tribal bundle priest after 1859, for he had gone north with the Northern Arapahoes. The Southern Arapahos, who had about the same population size as the Northern Arapahoes in the 1830s, were divided into four bands at mid-century (Hilger 1952:188). But the bands could act together, unified behind the decisions of the priests, who helped the intermediary chiefs build consensus.

Their efforts to present themselves as friendlies or allies appeared to the Arapahos to be successful. They had asked federal officials for a reservation on the Canadian River where they thought they would be safely removed from settlers, and the president had created that reservation by executive order in 1869 (Parker in ARCIA 1869:35). There was sufficient game in the region at that time, and with the protection of the troops the approximately 1,440 to 1,600 Arapahos hoped to live relatively undisturbed, separate from the Cheyennes, who were twice their number (Darlington 1869; Brunot in ARCIA 1869:51). But it was not to be; the Cheyennes began moving onto the reservation in 1870, a few months after the Arapahos.

*Friendly with the Whites: Old Friends and Allies, 1870–1890*

The Arapahos continued, then, to contrast themselves with the Cheyennes and to serve as a buffer and mediator between Cheyennes and Americans. The Arapahos protected agency personnel from hostile Cheyennes, put children in the government boarding school, and worked at agricultural development. To accomplish those ends they relied on the age grades, intermediary chieftainship, and the priesthood.

Arapahos still felt themselves vulnerable to army attack when the Cheyennes came into conflict with settlers and travelers or troops. Clashes between Cheyennes and non-Indians occurred repeatedly throughout the 1870s and 1880s (see Berthrong 1976). The arrival of Northern Cheyennes in 1875 and their subsequent escape from the reservation and return to the northern plains country aggravated the Arapahos' concerns.

Arapaho chiefs assumed responsibility for protecting agency personnel from the Cheyennes and for assisting the government's agents in other ways. Men of the age grades, whom the agent referred to as Dog Soldiers or simply Soldiers, guarded agency grounds and prevented Arapaho war parties from violating the chiefs' and priests' ban on leaving the reservation to raid Pawnees or Utes (see Darlington in ARCIA 1871:470-71; Miles in ARCIA 1874:233). Intermediaries such as Little Raven on several occasions attempted to convince the Cheyennes to refrain from taking military actions against non-Indians who stole from or otherwise abused them (see, for example, War Department 1885).

Arapaho chiefs repeatedly asked for the means to farm in order to set a good example and demonstrate loyalty to the agents on the reservation. Those farms were worked communally, and the chiefs' cattle herds were also cared for by members of their bands. In contrast, the agents perceived the Cheyennes as less willing to commit to agriculture (see, for example Darlington in ARCIA 1871:470; Miles in ARCIA 1873:222; 1877:83; 1883:60-61; Dyer in ARCIA 1884:73). By 1878, the Arapahos reportedly farmed four times more than the Cheyennes and were wealthier in stock, as well (Covington in ARCIA 1878:57-58).

Arapaho chiefs agreed to fill the government school with Arapaho children (although most of the children they placed in school were orphans), while the Cheyennes resisted (Miles 1874; Miles in ARCIA 1874:234-35; Dyer in ARCIA 1884:75). Men of the age grades apparently assumed the responsibility for bringing the children in, and chiefs regularly visited the school and spoke in the camps on behalf of school attendance. In 1879 the leading chiefs made it a point to place their own children at Carlisle Indian School to demonstrate their loyalty to the government (Campbell 1879; Miles 1879), and in subsequent years they sent additional children.

The agents hired Indians to work at the agency, and Arapahos took most of those positions (Lee in ARCIA 1886:116; Williams in ARCIA 1887:78). Men of the age grades were hired as Indian Police. Each Arapaho band organized wagon teams to hire out to bring freight to the agency; the headman was in charge of the freighting outfit (Miles in ARCIA 1877:83). In these ways, the Arapahos impressed the agents as completely loyal, certainly more so than the Cheyennes, although a few Cheyenne bands did try to farm and otherwise cooperate (Berthrong 1976:78, 127-28; also see Moore 1987).

Arapaho chiefs were able to mobilize support among Arapahos for agriculture, wage work and freighting, and boarding schools because chiefs could use those activities to provide for the members of their bands—and because the priests in charge of tribal rituals reaffirmed the chiefs' authority and supported the friendly strategy. The treaty agreements, on which Arapahos based their right to the reservation, were sanctioned by the ritual authorities who validated the right of individual chiefs (e.g., by a smoking ceremony) to represent the Arapaho people in these negotiations. Signing a treaty or "agreement" (or membership in a delegation that met with officials in Washington) generally validated chieftainship. Arapaho chiefs stressed in their orations that they had participated in treaty negotiations and that that participation was a sacred obligation to accept agricultural instruction and schools. As one chief, Powderface, remarked at a council in 1882, "I heard their words and gave them all the country they asked for and in time received this country for our home. Ever since that time I have held fast the promises made and am now living on my own farm, have my own cattle, horses and kind and am still ready to do all that the President may ask. . . . I will always do all I can to keep friendship with the whites but they must not run over us . . ." (Miles 1882). In the 1891 Jerome Agreement, in which Arapahos ceded most of the reservation on the Canadian, the chief

Left Hand remarked, attempting to get the best possible terms, that he had always complied with the wishes of the government by raising corn and stock and sending his children to school (Record of the Meetings of the Cherokee Commission 1890-91).

Local federal officials and missionaries were kept so busy trying to control the Cheyennes, and were so dependent on Arapaho good will as they tried to run the agency, that Arapahos were spared extensive intervention in their ritual life. The Sacrifice Lodge, for example, was vowed and completed regularly during the reservation years. Mennonite missionaries arrived in the 1880s. They operated missions and schools for Arapahos, and Arapahos accepted a Christian education for children in those schools. The Mennonites put most of their resources into their schools and, beset by Cheyenne resistance, courted rather than pressured the Arapahos.

In sum, the Arapaho activity in support of the civilization program both bolstered and was encouraged by the age grades, intermediary chiefs, and priests. Although the beef ration certainly was necessary to Arapaho subsistence, chiefs' authority was linked to their role as organizers of labor and producers of large quantities of food. Unlike the Northern Arapahoe case, their authority did not depend on securing rations from the government.

## Ceding the Reservation: A Well-Disposed Minority, 1891-1902

When the Arapahos and Cheyennes ceded their reservation in 1891, each individual was entitled to receive an allotment of land and the remainder was opened to settlement by non-Indians, who lived in large part by stealing and defrauding Indians of their property. While the federal government gradually withdrew support in the form of rations, equipment, and agricultural assistance, its agents escalated interference in and repression of Arapaho cultural and social institutions (see Berthrong 1976). The economic underpinning of intermediary leadership gradually dissolved and chieftainship became more closely associated with ritual authority.

Some Arapaho leaders accepted allotments because they felt they had no other realistic choice; others, fervent believers in Ghost Dance prophesies that promised the imminent end of white domination and a return to prosperity saw no need to resist the cession (Mooney 1896:899). The intermediary chiefs successfully worked to obtain allotments in clusters, so as to isolate Arapaho bands from non-Indian settlers as much as possible (Ashley in ARCIA 1891:344). They also stressed to federal agents that their cooperative demeanor during the cession negotiations entitled them to expect that the government would keep its promises, with regard to the regular issue of rations, for example. They and the agents also continued to contrast Arapahos, whom they portrayed as "well disposed," loyal and cooperative, with the Cheyennes who, at least some bands of which, persisted in resisting not only allotment but the assimilation program in general (Ashley in ARCIA 1891:341-42, 345; 1892:373-74; Interior Department 1895; Woodson 1898a; Woodson in ARCIA 1899:285). Farming became increasingly difficult because of federal policies that promoted the leasing of Indian land and because Indians and their property did not receive legal protection from non-Indian authorities (see Berthrong 1976).

Arapaho leaders stressed their progress in education, again in contrast to the Cheyennes (Interview with Cheyenne and Arapaho Delegation 1891). Chiefs argued that "education" was a treaty obligation (Ashley 1893); protecting the treaty relationship was important if they were to retain rights to their lands in Oklahoma and to preserve cultural and social integrity as a people. Arapaho intermediaries tried to take advantage of the federal officials' appreciative attitude in order to secure their cooperation, for example, in separating the Arapahos' money (from the 1891 cession) from the Cheyennes'. A division of these moneys would have given the Arapahos more political autonomy. Arapahos also had more success than the Cheyennes in obtaining permission to send delegations to Washington to discuss tribal business and to hold gatherings or ceremonies. In fact, they obtained the agents' and commissioners' consent to a separation of funds, although subsequently Congress did not concur (Woodson 1898b; Talks with Arapahos 1898).

In these difficult times, chiefs had to struggle to counter federal efforts to destroy their ceremonial organization, an organization that also served to support the chiefs' authority, and to politically unify Arapahos, who did not have serious intragroup conflict as did the Cheyennes. As the economic situation deteriorated, chiefs faced eroding confidence, particularly from younger men educated in off-reservation boarding schools (see Proceedings of Talk of Cheyenne and Arapaho Delegates 1898). The intermediary chiefs of the 1890s were leaders in the men's age grade organization, mentors to men in their twenties and thirties and forties, but not yet priests of the highest order. In the 1890s, peyote ritual was introduced to the Arapahos and it was embraced by young men, largely boarding school alumni, among whom were the critics of the chiefs. In part to counter this challenge, age grade ceremonies began to be held, one—the Tomahawk Lodge, for young men—in 1902-03. Other age grade ceremonies followed, though not all men became members. The Sacrifice Lodge (Sun Dance) received more extensive community support, and the

Sun Dance Wheel was refurbished and became an important prayer-sacrifice rite (see Dorsey 1903:24, 98). The emphasis on native religion (including the Ghost Dance, which continued to have strong support, albeit in response to new visions and prophesies) was presented to federal officials as an effort to buttress the assimilation program or was kept hidden from officials to a great extent. The religious ceremonies and secular dances drew the entire Arapaho community together despite allotment and the organization of allotment clusters into farming districts supervised by government farmers.

The role of the chiefs increasingly became that of ritual organizers who were also responsible for intervening with the agents to obtain permits to hold their ceremonies (Fowler 1988). As a consequence of the 1891 cession, there were no tribally owned lands to lease, so there was no need for a business council (as there was at Wind River and Fort Belknap). Chiefs continued to serve as intermediaries, despite the government's disapproval, but they did not have the economic means to help other Arapahos. Part of the payment for the cession of reservation lands was distributed per capita to individuals (and the remainder held in trust by the federal government). Chiefs had no control over those moneys.

The chiefs' role as organizers of secular rituals also received support from local non-Indians. To promote the economy of the new towns that were established as a result of the opening of the reservation, non-Indians encouraged a display of Indian "tradition" at parades and fairs, and town officials publicly acknowledged the chiefs, choosing them to head fair committees.

*Selling the Land: New Definitions of Community and Polity, 1903–1934*

Arapahos continued to cultivate officials' perception of them as "progressives," and especially as more progressive than the Cheyennes (see McConihe 1911). While many Cheyennes continued to resist placing their children in local boarding schools, Arapahos supported the schools and tried to expand the six-year curriculum to eight years (West in SANR, Cantonment 1912; Allen 1916; Bonnin 1926). And, Arapahos pursued non-confrontational strategies in order to dissuade the local federal agent from banning their ceremonies. The goals of Arapaho intermediaries, however, no longer emphasized separation from the Cheyennes, for their problems with the Cheyennes paled in comparison with the consequences of new federal policies—the Dead Indian Act of 1902; the Act of March 2, 1907; and the Competency Commission of 1917.

As intermediaries, the chiefs' primary role was to serve as delegates to meet with officials in Washington; in delegations of 1909, 1911, 1912,

1917, and 1918 they sought to protect their land base by securing an extension of the trust status of the allotted lands beyond the twenty-five-year period provided for in the Jerome Agreement of 1891. In 1917 they obtained a ten-year extension; in 1926 they received another extension until 1937. The delegations also pressed the government not to sell the Fort Reno site and the several agency sites that were reserved at the time of allotment, arguing instead that those lands should be returned to the tribes. The Arapaho delegates successfully pressed for the continuation of the local, federally operated boarding schools and for the relaxation of prohibitions against the Sacrifice Lodge and other ceremonies.

On the other hand, they were unable to defeat the passage of the Dead Indian Act, which encouraged the sale of allotments of deceased Indians, or to prevent the blatant fraud that occurred in connection with the leasing and sale of Indian land. They also struggled unsuccessfully to prevent the per capita distribution (beginning in 1907) of the trust fund the tribes received for the sale of their surplus lands at the time of the Jerome Agreement. As a result, the fund was dissipated by 1927 and only 37 percent of the land remained in Indian ownership in 1928 (Bost in SANR, Cantonment 1927; Berthrong 1985). Nor could they persuade the government to give Arapaho and Cheyenne individuals more control over the money from leasing or sale of their lands or to help equip Indians to farm their lands. They were also unsuccessful in filing a claim against the government for past treaty violations.

The resultant decline in individual income and the erosion of the land base hampered the chiefs' ability to provide for supporters. Rations had been gradually phased out, which ended the chiefs' role in witnessing the issue of and distributing the goods. As individuals, including chiefs, sold land, they had less opportunity to farm and less income from rentals. Arapahos also relied less on sharing and more on individually owned resources.

The chiefs tried to counter their declining economic role by their increased authority and involvement in religious as well as secular rituals. They persuaded agents to permit the Sacrifice Lodge (see Bonnin in SANR, Cheyenne-Arapaho 1922; Bonnin 1923), while the Cheyennes repeatedly came into conflict with agents over this issue. As leaders in their districts, they organized the seasonal dances, which worked to bring the three Arapaho districts together through reciprocal hosting of those gatherings. Most of the chiefs were initiated into the Crazy Lodge in 1906, giving them considerable ritual authority over younger men. By the 1920s the priests who directed the Sacrifice Lodge were all chiefs. Thus, the roles of political intermediary and priest were fused.

For young men, however, the peyote religion increasingly held greater attraction than the lodges. An individual could achieve a leadership position without lengthy, rigorous apprenticeship. Peyotists formed an intertribal network in Oklahoma, as well as a local one, so that by the late 1920s, even the chiefs' ritual authority was of limited use in mobilizing support. In 1908 peyotists successfully countered the agent's efforts to outlaw the religion (Berthrong 1976:323), an action that bolstered the authority of leaders in the movement. In 1919 the Native American Church received a charter from the state of Oklahoma.

In the early twentieth century, the Mennonites began to withdraw, and Baptist missionaries arrived among the Arapahos. The Baptists came as individuals without the support of a local mission community and school. Several of the leaders in Arapaho ceremonies joined the church but continued to participate in the Sun Dance and other ceremonies.

By 1928 the chiefs could not point to accomplishments that could validate their authority. The tribal fund and most of the land were gone (Bost in SANR, Cantonment 1927). The three agencies had been consolidated in 1927, which resulted in the loss of services to the local districts. Two of the three boarding schools that Arapahos had struggled to maintain, and that symbolized treaty obligations, were closed. No progress had been made on legal claims against the government, and the officials in Washington insisted that only "educated," bilingual delegates would be welcome.

In 1928, promoted by the agent and with support from some young Arapaho and Cheyenne men, an elected, forty-eight-member "tribal council" was established. The Arapahos supported the elected council because it focused on the pursuit of Arapaho legal claims. An attorney, in the view of the young Arapaho men, would be more successful than delegations of elderly chiefs. Arapaho intermediary chiefs were elected to the council, along with several younger, bilingual men. The old chiefs accepted the young men as spokesmen for some aspects of the claim matters, such as selection of an attorney. By 1933 the tribal council, now referred to as a business committee, was attending to matters other than claims.

In 1934 the federal government began to encourage the reorganization of tribal governments. Officials made promises of economic aid and more land, indefinite extension of the trust status of Indian land, and help in pursuing the claims. In addition, federal job programs became available. Based on their perception that major change was imminent and that their economic position was continuing to worsen, the Arapahos accepted reorganization under the provisions of the Thomas-Rogers Act, and in 1937 a twenty-eight-member business committee was elected and constitutional government went into effect. Arapahos filled fourteen of the committee positions even though the Cheyenne population was twice that of the Arapaho (Fowler 1988).

## Conclusions

In the early years of reservation life, Gros Ventre and Arapaho leaders adopted what I refer to as a civilization strategy. They convinced federal agents of their commitment to farming, sent children to boarding school, and welcomed missionaries. In all three cases, leaders were motivated to publicly embrace the government's civilization policy because they needed federal help in retaining or acquiring a land base and in protecting their autonomy in relation to other groups. Each was in a position to play on American fears of groups still perceived as hostile and to take advantage of a history (even rather a short history in the Northern Arapahoe case) of friendly relations with the United States.

Acceptance of agriculture, education, and missions was not perceived by native peoples as the adoption of Euro-American values or lifestyle to the exclusion of their own. Nor did Gros Ventres or either Arapaho group deem it unmanly to farm (contrary to the stereotype of the Plains male, whom some anthropologists, as well as officials, often described as temperamentally unsuited to manual labor). In fact, willingness to farm was less a matter of temperament than of political expediency. Each of the three peoples employed the civilization strategy in an attempt to strengthen and revitalize through reorganization their sociopolitical system and ritual life. Native institutions were adapted as much to take advantage of new opportunities as to preserve old values.

The three peoples drew on an age grade tradition and on virtually identical systems of religious belief in responding to conditions on the Plains in the nineteenth century. But, despite a program of assimilation that was intended to have universal application, the circumstances of colonization varied from region to region, reflecting national policies and interests. By the 1930s the Gros Ventres, Northern Arapahoes, and Southern Arapahos had developed different politico-religious systems as they struggled to resist the expropriation of their resources and the assault on their way of life.

By the 1930s the Gros Ventre business council was fully institutionalized and, unopposed, its members worked to obtain economic aid for individual Gros Ventre ranchers and political independence from federal officials, as well as to pursue their rivalry with the Assiniboines. The council leaders' authority was bolstered by their role in revitalizing secular rituals that offered competing individuals and moieties a chance for prestige, unified the community, and contributed to the development of a ranching economy. These developments were the product of a particular history of trade relations, intertribal competition, and American settlement in Montana. By the time the Gros Ventres settled on the reservation, the federal government did not need them as military allies. This made them more vulnerable to cattle interests in Montana and encouraged them to rely heavily on Catholic lobbying. Like themselves, their Assiniboine rivals were perceived as progressive. These factors increased the pressure on the Gros Ventres to cooperate with the assimilation program.

The Northern Arapahoe business council also was fully institutionalized by the 1930s. Councilmen worked for continued federal protection and full rights on the Shoshone reservation and sought to obtain tribal income in per capita payments that contributed to economic leveling among Arapahoes. The councilmen's authority was circumscribed, as well as strengthened, as they cooperated with and deferred to religious leaders. Secular and sacred authority was separate, though mutually reinforcing. Christianity was nominally accepted but, unlike the situation among the Gros Ventres, never replaced native religion. These developments occurred primarily because trade relations and American settlement took a different course on the central plains than in the north, and Northern Arapahoes faced conditions significantly different than those faced by the Gros Ventres at the time of reservation settlement. Federal officials thought that the Northern Arapahoes, formerly "hostile," were held in check and motivated to cooperate by the intermediary chiefs and councilmen; consequently, the intermediaries were supported with extra provisions and other attentions. The Shoshones, who had treaty rights to the reservation, were long-time allies and friends of non-Indians, and officials had much lower expectations of Arapahoes than Shoshones in regard to progress toward civilization. Arapahoes were able to make a good impression on officials with the general appearance of cooperation rather than the kind of universal commitment to ranching and Christianity made by Gros Ventres. Among the Northern Arapahoes, the authority structure became increasingly theocratic and institutions that reinforced economic leveling were strengthened.

The goals of the Gros Ventre and Arapahoe councilmen were different largely because they operated under a different set of external constraints. The large Shoshone reservation in Wyoming (about three million acres) was established in 1868, before cattle interests were strong enough to influence the negotiations. The Shoshones and Northern Arapahoes were able to retain most of that large land base during the early twentieth century, mainly because the area was not well suited to homesteading. Although individual Arapahoes arrived on the reservation horse poor and dependent on rations, Northern Arapahoe intermediaries had a significant resource in the large amount of tribal acreage that generated income. This resource was a major factor in their ability to retain constituents' support and mitigate federal attempts to undermine Arapahoe institutions. The unsold portion of the reservation was leased, which provided an income to the tribes (especially when the lands began to be leased for mineral development in mid-century). Montana was more attractive to cattlemen than homesteaders; allotment was postponed until 1922, by which time the interest in homesteading had waned. On the Gros Ventres' small reservation (about 652,000 acres), which lacked mineral deposits (after the 1896 cession), there was very little tribal land available for leasing. Individuals retained their allotments and subsisted by hay farming and ranching until the 1930s; thus councilmen focused on obtaining maximum individual opportunity.

Until the 1930s chiefs served as the Southern Arapaho intermediaries, for with the cession of the reservation in 1891 there was no tribal land to lease and thus no federal requirement for a business council. The chiefs had few resources with which to aid constituents and the federal government was rapidly disengaging from its responsibilities to the Arapahos and Cheyennes. Chiefs attempted to negotiate for the extension of the trust relationship, which Gros Ventre and Northern Arapahoe intermediaries could take for granted. The chiefs worked with only limited success to protect individual allotments and attempted to shore up their political positions by fusing political and ritual roles and, ultimately, political and religious authority. Increasingly the chiefs were perceived as ineffective in dealing with the federal government and in providing for constituents. The linkage of political and ritual spheres of authority eventually contributed to the undermining of both: a perceived failure in one affected Arapahos' perceptions of the efficacy or legitimacy of the other. Federal policies that resulted in the alienation of resources assured such failures. In western Oklahoma, native groups exchanged ideas, property, and ceremonies, in large part as a way of resisting cultural repression. At the turn of the century, the peyote religion diffused to the Southern Arapahos and gradually attracted considerable numbers of young men, most of whom increasingly were estranged from the Sun Dance ceremonies controlled by the chiefs. An Arapaho version of the peyote ceremony called the Arapaho Way eclipsed the Sun Dance in Arapaho religious life by the 1930s. The peyote religion, in addition to filling spiritual and psychological needs, offered many individuals a chance for leadership positions without as arduous an apprenticeship as in the Sun Dance, and in its pan-tribal aspects probably helped individuals, most of whom were landless, to expand social networks of mutual aid.

The plight of the Arapahos was produced by forces that emanated from outside Oklahoma. In the 1890s western Oklahoma attracted a flood of homesteaders, who expected to farm successfully, as others had in Kansas. The federal government allowed the Arapahos and Cheyennes (and other native peoples in Oklahoma) to keep only a fraction of their reservation acreage and opened the remainder to settlers. The two tribes retained approximately 800,000 out of 4,300,000 acres. During the early twentieth century there was a market for farmland along the Canadian River, and federal legislation facilitated the sale of Indian land. By 1935 allottees were left with about 175,000 acres. Compared to the Gros Ventres and Northern Arapahoes, the Southern Arapahos were the most disadvantaged, for both individual and tribal lands were lost and, with them, the underpinnings of intermediary leadership.

There are general studies of the effects of the world system on native societies in general (Wolf 1982; White 1983, 1991), but they necessarily tend toward overgeneralization. In his excellent social history of the American West, Richard White finds that due to "different traditions of governance" among Native Americans, new political structures that developed in response to conquest varied from tribe to tribe (1991:440). With controlled comparison, we should be better able to explain the nature and extent of that variation. In the Arapaho case, once virtually identical traditions of governance evolved quite differently in response to a host of interconnected factors. Comparison of the three Arapaho subdivisions helps pinpoint those factors.

Plains groups other than the Arapahos separated into several divisions that became situated in different regions and adapted to different socioeconomic and political contexts within the larger American society—Blackfeet, Sioux, Assiniboines, Plains Crees, Cheyennes. Future studies might examine variations in the civilization strategies (as well as the kinds of "hostile" strategies) employed by Native Americans, and might identify factors, such as the size of the tribal land base, that affect the nature and success of resistance. Groups that have been subjected to similar external constraints, as well as divisions of the same group subjected to different sorts of external constraints, can be compared. Such comparisons would shed light on how local and world histories interpenetrate and reveal how those on the periphery of power attempt to shape circumstances they do not fully control.

## Acknowledgments

The research for this study was made possible by grants from the Phillips Fund of the American Philosophical Society, the National Institute on Aging, and the National Endowment for the Humanities. I am indebted to Karen I. Blu for a critical reading of an earlier version of the manuscript and to Regina Flannery Herzfeld for her help with my research on Gros Ventre history. I also wish to thank Steven L. Johnson for assistance with the research on the Southern Arapahos and Cheyennes. The Fort Belknap Community Council and the Gros Ventre and Assiniboine people extended to me every courtesy. I especially wish to thank Elmer Main, Jack Plumage, Preston Stiffarm, and John Capture for their comments on my Gros Ventre research. The Northern Arapahoe Business Council and the people of Wind River Reservation graciously helped me during all phases of my research there. My research on Southern Arapaho and Cheyenne history was greatly facilitated by the cooperation and assistance of the Cheyenne-Arapaho Business Committee and the members of the Arapaho and Cheyenne tribes.

## References

### Unpublished Sources

Allen, E.
  1916    Letter to Commissioner of Indian Affairs, 8 December 1916. Central Files,
          Canton, file 150-127100-1916, Record Group 75, National Archives and
          Records Service, Washington, D.C. [hereafter RG 75, NARS].
Allen, W. J.
  1897    Letter to L. Hays, 7 August 1897. Fort Belknap, RG 75, box 49, Federal
          Archives and Records Center, Seattle, Wash. [hereafter FARC].
Ashley, Charles
  1893    Letter to Commissioner of Indian Affairs, 18 May 1893. Letters Received by
          the Commissioner of Indian Affairs, 1881-1907, file 1893-18546, RG 75,
          NARS.
Bonnin, L.
  1923    Letter to Commissioner of Indian Affairs, 11 June 1923. Central Files,
          Cheyenne-Arapaho, file 062-64212-1921, RG 75, NARS.
  1926    Letter to Commissioner of Indian Affairs, 9 January 1926. Central Files,
          Cheyenne-Arapaho, file 056-1828-1926, RG 75, NARS.
Campbell, C. E.
  1879    Letter to E. A. Hayt, 10 October 1879. Letters Received by the Commissioner
          of Indian Affairs, 1824-81, Cheyenne and Arapaho Agency, RG 75, NARS.
Darlington, Brinton
  1869    Letter to E. Hoag, 2 October 1869. Letters Received by the Commissioner of
          Indian Affairs, 1824-81, Upper Arkansas Agency, RG 75, NARS.
Eberschweiler, F.
  1888    Letter to J. Stephan, June 30, 1888. St. Paul's Mission, Bureau of Catholic
          Indian Missions Records, Marquette University, Milwaukee.
Fanton, William
  1874    Letter to E. Smith, 5 December 1874. Letters Received by the Commissioner
          of Indian Affairs, 1824-81, Montana Superintendency, RG 75, NARS.

Fowler, Loretta
    1988    Oklahoma Arapaho Chieftainship: Rethinking Cultural Perspective in
            Ethnohistory." Paper read at American Society for Ethnohistory meetings,
            11 November 1988, Williamsburg, Va.
Interior Department
    1895    Letter to Commissioner of Indian Affairs, 30 January 1895. Letters Received
            by the Commissioner of Indian Affairs, 1881-1907, file 1895-5001, RG 75,
            NARS.
Interview with Cheyenne and Arapaho Delegation
    1891    Letters Received by the Commissioner of Indian Affairs, 1881-1907, file
            1891-42868, RG 75, NARS.
Lincoln, Wyman
    1878a   Letter to E. A.Hayt, 28 June 1878. Fort Belknap, box 29, RG 75, FARC.
    1878b   Letter to E. A. Hayt, 3 July 1878. Fort Belknap, box 29, RG 75, FARC.
    1878c   Letter to the Commissioner of Indian Affairs, 7 October 1878. Fort Belknap,
            box 29, RG 75, FARC.
    1882    Letter to the Commissioner of Indian Affairs, 18 October 1882. Letters
            Received by the Commissioner of Indian Affairs, 1881-1907, file 19517-1882,
            RG 75, NARS.
    1885a   Letter to the Commissioner of Indian Affairs, 8 February 1885. Fort Belknap,
            box 17, RG 75, FARC.
    1885b   Letter to the Commissioner of Indian Affairs, 18 September 1885. Fort
            Belknap, box 17, RG 75, FARC.
McAnaney, W.
    1893    Letter to the Commissioner of Indian Affairs, 5 May 1893. Fort Belknap, box
            18, RG 75, FARC.
McConihe, W.
    1911    Letter to Commissioner of Indian Affairs, 6 February 1911. Central Files,
            Canton, file 154-15327-1-1911, RG 75, NARS.
Marshall, J. T.
    1924    Annual Narrative Report, 22 July 1924. Fort Belknap, RG 75, NARS.
Miles, John
    1874    Letter to E. P. Smith, 10 November 1874. Letters Received by the
            Commissioner of Indian Affairs, 1824-81, Upper Arkansas Agency, RG 75,
            NARS.
    1879    Letter to E. A. Hayt, 8 October 1879. Letters Received by the Commissioner
            of Indian Affairs, Cheyenne and Arapaho Agency, RG 75, NARS.
    1882    Letter to H. Price, 7 January 1882. Letters Received by the Commissioner of
            Indian Affairs, 1881-1907, file 1882-1024, RG 75, NARS.
Minutes of Council
    1886    Held 24 February 1886 with the Chiefs of the Gros Ventre Tribe of Indians,
            by C. H. Dickson. Letters Received by the Commissioner of Indian Affairs,
            1881-1907, file 7335-1886, RG 75, NARS.
Proceedings of Talk of Cheyenne and Arapaho Delegates
    1898    Transcript of 30 November 1898 meeting. Letters Received by the
            Commissioner of Indian Affairs, 1881-1907, file 1900-502, RG 75, NARS.
Record of the Meetings of the Cherokee Commission
    1890-91 Irregularly Shaped Papers, no. 78, RG 75, NARS.

SANR
1907-38 Superintendents' Annual Narrative Reports. Reports from Field Jurisdictions of the Bureau of Indian Affairs. RG 75, NARS.

Talks with Arapahos
1898 Transcript of 30 March, 4 April, 6 April 1898. Letters Received by the Commissioner of Indian Affairs, 1881-1907, file 1898-14669, RG 75, NARS.

Transcript of the Minutes and Proceedings of the Indian Peace Commission
1867 Records of the Secretary of the Interior, Indian Division. RG 48, NARS.

Van Gorp, L.
1889 Letter to J. Cataldo, 4 July 1889. Oregon Province Archives of the Society of Jesus, St. Paul's Montana Collection, file 1, box 1, Gonzaga University, Spokane.

War Department
1885 Letter to Commissioner of Indian Affairs, 24 February 1885. Letters Received by the Commissioner of Indian Affairs, 1881-1907, file 1885-4459, RG 75, NARS.

Woodson, A. E.
1898a Letter to Commissioner of Indian Affairs, 15 February 1898. Letters Received by the Commissioner of Indian Affairs, 1881-1907, file 1898-7949, RG 75, NARS.
1898b Letter to Commissioner of Indian Affairs, 15 March 1898. Letters Received by the Commissioner of Indian Affairs, 1881-1907, file 1898-12754, RG 75, NARS.

## Published Sources

ARCIA
1846-1906 Annual Reports of the Commissioner of Indian Affairs. Washington, D.C.: Government Printing Office.

Berthrong, Donald J.
1976 The Cheyenne-Arapaho Ordeal: Reservation and Agency Life in the Indian Territory, 1875-1907. Norman: University of Oklahoma Press.
1985 Legacies of the Dawes Act: Bureaucrats and Land Thieves at the Cheyenne-Arapaho Agencies of Oklahoma. Arizona and the West (Winter 1979): 335-54.

Calloway, Collin G.
1986 The Only Way Open to Us: The Crow Struggle for Survival in the Nineteenth Century. North Dakota History 53:25-34.

Dorsey, George A.
1903 The Arapaho Sun Dance: The Ceremony of the Offerings Lodge. Field Columbian Museum Publication no. 75, Anthropological Series no. 4. Chicago.

Eggan, Fred
1954 Social Anthropology and the Method of Controlled Comparison. American Anthropologist 56:743-63.

Flannery, Regina
1947 The Changing Form and Functions of the Gros Ventre Grass Dance. Primitive Man 20:39-70.

1953        The Gros Ventres of Montana. Pt. 1, Social Life. Washington, D.C.: Catholic
            University of America.
Fowler, Loretta
    1982a   Arapahoe Politics, 1851–1978: Symbols in Crises of Authority. Lincoln:
            University of Nebraska Press.
    1982b   "Look at My Hair, It Is Gray": Age Grading, Ritual Authority, and Political
            Change among the Northern Arapahoe and Gros Ventre. *In* Plains Indian
            Studies: A Collection of Essays in Honor of John C. Ewers and Waldo R.
            Wedel, edited by Douglas H. Ubelaker and Herman J. Viola, 73-93.
            Smithsonian Contributions to Anthropology, no. 30. Washington, D.C.
    1987    Shared Symbols, Contested Meanings: Gros Ventre Culture and History,
            1778-1984. Ithaca: Cornell University Press.
Hilger, M. Inez
    1952    Arapaho Child Life and Its Cultural Background. Smithsonian Institution,
            Bureau of American Ethnology Bulletin 142. Washington, D.C.
Kappler, Charles J., ed.
    1904    Indian Affairs: Laws and Treaties. Vol. 2. Washington, D.C.
Mooney, James
    1896    The Ghost-dance Religion and the Sioux Outbreak of 1890. Smithsonian
            Institution, Fourteenth Annual Report of the Bureau of American Ethnology,
            pt. 2. Washington, D.C.
Moore, John H.
    1987    The Cheyenne Nation: A Social and Demographic History. Lincoln:
            University of Nebraska Press.
Trenholm, Virginia Cole
    1970    The Arapahoes, Our People. Norman: University of Oklahoma Press.
United States
    1895    Letter from the Secretary of the Interior, Transmitting an Agreement Made
            and Concluded 9 October 1895, with Indians of the Fort Belknap Reservation.
            54th Cong., 1st sess. S. Doc. 117, vol. 4.
White, Richard
    1983    The Roots of Dependency: Subsistence, Environment, and Social Change
            among the Choctaws, Pawnees, and Navajos. Lincoln: University of Nebraska
            Press.
    1991    "It's Your Misfortune and None of My Own": A History of the American
            West. Norman: University of Oklahoma Press.
Wolf, Eric R.
    1982    Europe and the People without History. Berkeley: University of California
            Press.
Youngkin, S. Douglas
    1977    "Hostile and Friendly": The Pygmalion Effect at Cheyenne River Agency,
            1873-77. South Dakota History 7:402-21.

# 10

# The Roots of Factionalism
# among the Lower Brule Sioux

ERNEST L. SCHUSKY

The first systematic reporting of factions among American Indians occurred in *Acculturation in Seven American Indian Tribes,* edited by Ralph Linton (1940). In touching on Northern Arapahoe factionalism, Henry Elkin described the individuals chosen to serve on the tribe's modern council as characterized by personalities considerably different from the traditional type. Instead of traditional values, councilmen put a premium on an ability to understand and to deal with officials of the Bureau of Indian Affairs. As a result, "every choice of a councilman, and indirectly, every evaluation of an individual, involves conflicting standards of recognition, a perplexity inevitably resulting in social malaise" (Elkin 1940:250-51).

Despite this early emphasis on the process involved in factionalism, later work on the topic defined it largely in structural terms. In *Social Structure,* George Peter Murdock defined factions as "internal divisions, usually two in number" (1949:90). He proceeded to enumerate which functions such groups play, citing ethnographic examples where two such groups are prominent. The *Encyclopedia of the Social Sciences* likewise defined factions as "any constituent group of a larger unit" (Lasswell 1968:49). Most anthropologists accepted the notion that factions, like moieties, were a form of dual division, although Oscar Lewis (1958:113-16) described a village in northern India as crosscut by a multitude of factions. In retrospect, Lewis's data do not differ so much from other ethnographies. Many communities can be seen as crosscut by more than two factions, even while being reported as split by only two of them.

This seeming paradox may be resolved by a closer reading of Lewis's analysis. He noted that the multitude of factions resulted from groups crystallizing around different issues. In effect, at any particular time the Indian village was split into only two factions, dependent on particular issues. Different issues brought different alignments. Lewis's insistence on seeing factions as permanent groups led to considerable confusion. The

258

difficulties arising from analysis of a multitude of factions could have been avoided had Lewis treated factionalism as a process as well as a structure, a perspective advocated by Ted Lewellen (1983:108) and spelled out fully by Edwin Winkler (1969:329–34).

Such an approach to community analysis had been foreseen by Fred Eggan. In his discussion of the methods of social anthropology, he stressed the need to look at societies "in terms of the problems of adjustment or adaptation which they face" (1955:494), indicating that that approach illuminates social structure. His position could serve as a basis for many contemporary factional analyses summarized by Joan Vincent (1978:188). Eggan argued further that some societies adapt better than others because some structures are more efficient than others in solving the problems of adaptation. From his knowledge of the Plains and the Southwest, he advanced an intriguing hypothesis: The flexibility of bilateral structures makes them efficient at adapting to new conditions but handicapped in providing social continuity; in contrast, unilineal structures readily solve problems of continuity but usually have difficulty in adapting to rapidly changing conditions, such as contact with a dominant society. Ramifications of that hypothesis were explored in detail by Loretta Fowler (1982a), in a comparison of Arapahoe and Gros Ventre politics, which suggested that age sets may be a means of providing both flexibility and continuity.

Eggan's early experience in both the Plains and the Southwest doubtless alerted him to the effects of structural differences; years later he returned indirectly to that hypothesis in *The American Indian*. Having watched the Hopis much of his life, he recorded that many modern Hopi problems are dealt with "by factions that explore alternatives in terms of traditional teaching and the realities of the situation" (1966:127). Throughout the twentieth century, the factions were unable to resolve internally the myriad problems facing them and half a dozen new villages had hived off older ones; the Hopis have settled their differences simply by splitting apart.

In contrast, the tribes of the High Plains began with marked flexibility, a requirement for the shifting modes of life between winter and summer. Rapid change was also necessary owing to changes in bison herds and varying threats from neighboring tribes. Eggan noted that as a result, "the amorphous and composite bands were well adapted for such purposes and could change in size and leadership as the situation demanded. A successful leader attracted new members, while those of a poor leader were lost or melted away" (1966:127). Yet, the flexibility allowed factional splits that on occasion paralyzed decision making. Nevertheless, some Plains tribes overcame the problem with ritual and social organization. In his foreword to Loretta Fowler's (1982b) work, Eggan wrote: "The Arapahoes have become experts in the manipulation of political symbols for the benefit of the whole tribe, and her [Fowler's] account may well change many people's minds as to the capacity of American Indian tribes to govern themselves" (1982:xvi).

## Social Organization before Contact

A fluid organization made factions unlikely, because differences over an issue were unlikely to create an opposing structure. Instead, individuals who disagreed separated before a dispute crystallized. This tactic seems to have been particularly important in creating the fluidity of the *t'iyošpaye*, a basic social group among the Sioux. The *t'iyošpaye* had all the features of a band. Leadership was informal, relations were egalitarian, and reciprocity marked relationships. The Sioux and other High Plains tribes would seem to have closely resembled other food collectors, such as Utes and Paiutes, or even African Bushmen, if they were known only from their winter encampments composed of the *t'iyošpaye*.

However, bison hunting during the summer brought many *t'iyošpaye* together. The Sioux and other Plains peoples assumed some of the usual characteristics of tribes at this season. Associations, such as warrior societies, served much as descent groups commonly do in tribes. A complex council of leaders prevailed. Early ethnographic accounts suggest the Sioux were organized in almost statelike fashion. The complexity and rigidity, however, are a result of concentrating on the summer camp and of projecting European models onto a poorly understood organization. Nevertheless, the summer camp certainly changed Sioux society from its winter mode. Probably the process of factionalism was an important but temporary ingredient of the summer camp circle.

Although no ethnographic account records such factionalism, its nature may be inferred from Sioux values and personality. Dorothy Lee captured important elements in analyzing the autobiographical accounts of Sioux before white domination. She emphasized the importance of self-autonomy to the Sioux, noting, "Children learned early to act at their own decision"; "It was a tenet of the society that no man could decide for another" (1959:65). Her conclusions are sustained by almost all contemporary fieldworkers, who report near astonishment at the early age at which children are given autonomy. Indeed, as Lee noted, the Sioux do not recognize that they have any right to "give" autonomy. It is an inalienable right of each individual.

Additionally, young males quickly learned that proper manhood could only be achieved through bravery and self-assertion. What appeared to whites as boasting and vanity was to the Sioux a proper way of asserting oneself and one's exploits. A fully autonomous individual must speak for himself; no one else could assume such a responsibility. With such self-assertiveness, it was inevitable that one man's claims must conflict with another's.

In the summer camp circle this internal conflict caused problems, and various men's associations acted as agents of social control. Not surprisingly, early white observers described these associations as "police." However, the major means of resolving the conflict was either a regrouping of the constituent units— the *t'iyošpaye*—or an individual's exodus. This change of group composition most likely occurred in the winter realignments, but it was also a possibility in the summer camp.

The remarkable flexibility of Sioux social organization is now better understood by anthropologists due to modern changes in conceptualization of kinship. For example, Edmund Leach (1961) vividly showed how kinship and other group relations follow adaptations to subsistence. In effect, it makes much more sense for the villagers of Pul Eliya to rearrange their social ties as they make the best use of their irrigated land rather than attempt to alter their irrigation canals to conform to particular descent and marriage ties. In the same perspective, Sioux must have adjusted their social ties in forming a particular *t'iyošpaye* for a season.

Given that the Sioux kinship system served as a prototype for general kinship studies, it was difficult for anthropologists to see that the system was not based strictly on biological relatedness as among Westerners. Even Lee (1959), who emphasized the importance of relatedness to the Sioux, failed to note explicitly that the kinship system is simply a metaphor for justifying the close relations among members of a *t'iyošpaye*. That is, all its members could make claims on each other as "brother" or "cousin," although relations need not be genealogically traced. The fact that two men lived in the same *t'iyošpaye* made them relatives; they did not live in the same *t'iyošpaye* because they were brothers.

The inherent adaptability of the system is generally assumed to date from the early 1700s, since the conventional wisdom has the Sioux living as forest dwellers in the upper Mississippi Valley in the seventeenth century. Doane Robinson (1904) and most other historians have located the Sioux here—where the first contacts with Europeans occurred. They reason that the Indians must have lived like the ancestors of the Mystic Lake Sioux as described by Ruth Landes (1968). That is, their settlements would have been comparatively permanent, and they might well have had patrilineal descent groups. Clans, or gentes, have persistently been attributed to the Sioux ever since James Owen Dorsey's (1894) survey of their sociology. A bias toward discovery of corporate groups probably occurred because many Siouan speakers, such as the Omahas, did indeed have well developed clans. And, of course, some Sioux were living as settled woodland dwellers in the upper Mississippi region.

However, prairie land in the area was common, and bison were frequent. As early as the mid-1600s the Sioux were known as the "nation of the beef," a detail reported by Pierre Radisson (Adams 1961:148). Radisson's reference to the Sioux is brief but intriguing. He records how he showed them a picture of Joseph and Mary with Jesus, fleeing from the wrath of Herod. The Sioux apparently confused the ass Mary is riding with a white buffalo—the whites seem to have identified the ass as a "buff"— and the Sioux responded to the story with great astonishment. It is tempting to interpret their reaction as based on an origin myth of the Sioux involving a white buffalo and a virgin woman. This origin myth proclaims the bison as a central part of Sioux life. If the myth was well established in the seventeenth century, the Sioux must have been big-game hunters, with summer and winter modes of life, well before the introduction of the horse.

This possibility has occurred to a few historians despite the conventional wisdom. James Bradley located the Yanktons west of the Mississippi Santees, stretching to the Missouri River; the Tetons "roamed generally over the prairie country on its [Missouri River's] south side in Southwestern Dakota and Northern Nebraska." Unfortunately, he claimed not to have had the space to present his evidence, but in the same place he asserted: "I am satisfied that at no time since the Sioux have been known to the whites did the main body of the Yanktons and the Tetons dwell within the limits of the present state of Minnesota." Bradley concluded from their location that most Yanktons and "all the Tetons were nomads of the first order and subsisted entirely by the spoils of the chase" (1922:49–50).

If the Tetons had a prehistoric origin in their present homelands, its nature will have to be determined by archeologists. Presently, the suggestion that they were big-game hunters before the introduction of the horse simply allows more time for development of the flexibility and fluidity in their social organization that Eggan took as their trademark. Even without such an early establishment, historians have the Tetons venturing to the Missouri River early in the 1700s. Even at this later date, they would have had several generations to develop a social life adapted to the High Plains. It is certainly conceivable that they could have made such changes, although a longer period for the development of their cultural values of autonomy and assertiveness, as well as their social organization, would provide desirable support for the hypothesis.

Whether the roots of the cultural values and social organization go deeply into Plains prehistory or originate more recently is a problem for the future. Presently, Sioux society must be understood as one that, in the mid-eighteenth century, held the potential for a high degree of factionalism. Men were always ready to press claims for prestige by infringing on the claims of others; also early reports indicate that disputes over women caused frequent conflict. Since the *t'iyošpaye* often consisted of many alleged relatives, it seems likely that incest rules might be ineffective in preventing illicit sex. Moreover, while men were supposed to ignore their wives' infractions of sexual loyalty, they were allowed to impose severe physical punishment. An origin myth of the Assiniboines claims that their separation from other Sioux was caused by infidelity. In short, cultural values provided a solid foundation for Sioux factionalism, but the process seldom materialized into major disruptions because a fluid social structure allowed protagonists to evade each other easily.

## Contact as a Prelude for Factionalism

For people who could move at will over the High Plains, potential factionalism was easily resolved. However, as soon as Euro-American contact occurred, limits began to be placed on Sioux mobility, and new issues increased the possibility for conflict. Exploration and the fur trade introduced new wealth to the Sioux. While most contacts with whites were friendly, the Sioux quickly found themselves competing with other Indians in the trade. Soon, internal competition grew as well. With the growth of competition and conflict, strong leaders had much more appeal to followers. A man who could establish advantageous ties to a trader built stronger ties to the men around him. The leader who could defeat or drive out other tribes was also a man to be followed. With the new flow of wealth, leaders began to acquire some of the characteristics of Melanesian "big-men." The balanced reciprocity of the traditional giveaway apparently became slightly skewed.

Earlier I recorded initial references to Sioux "chiefs," men renowned for their generosity and an ability to hold followers (Schusky 1971). Elsewhere, I described how the rise of those individuals with more power than usual was a result of contact with Euro-Americans. Government agents looked for Indians who represented others (Schusky 1986:71). Such politics not only resembled their own form of government, but also simplified the agent's work. Early Indian agents along the Missouri who contacted the Teton and Yankton reported negotiating with "chiefs." In retrospect, they exaggerated the power of those individuals, but the more the agents treated them as powerful, the more powerful they became. Since the Indian agents' goal was to reduce warfare among the tribes in order to encourage the fur trade, they distributed goods to the men judged most able to control others. The new wealth increased the power of individuals who could manipulate it; manipulation of the Indian agents, who represented obvious sources of the whites' power, further contributed to the Indians' power. Since the early agents were appointed largely for political reasons and knew little about Indians, many Indians easily used them. Several agents in the early 1800s were honest enough to report humiliating incidents. For instance, sometimes an agent lost goods without concrete promises from the Sioux, which led to his dismissal and the appointment of yet another inexperienced agent.

The most dramatic incident to initiate the drastic changes of the nineteenth century was exposure to epidemic diseases. Several minor outbreaks in the early 1800s warned the Missouri River Indians of what Euro-American contact meant. By 1837, when a smallpox epidemic hit, many Sioux eagerly accepted vaccination; others fled onto the plains, breaking into small groups. The *t'iyošpaye* organization of the Sioux proved invaluable. Village Indians, such as the Mandans and Arikaras, who remained in compact communities, were virtually eliminated. By the 1840s, the Sioux were the only Indians of any power remaining in the Missouri Valley.

However, they faced a new threat: the pioneers. The pressure for land emerged only slowly in the 1850s and ceased temporarily with the Civil War. Yet, even in the early 1860s, farmers left Minnesota and Iowa to claim land in eastern Dakota Territory. The federal government continued efforts to keep the Sioux at peace, while seeking safe passage through their land. Rights to travel through Nebraska along the Platte River were established more or less peacefully; passage up the Missouri to Montana was possible with only minor skirmishes. The federal government secured such rights by making payments to the Sioux. The goods, of course, could not be distributed equally to every *t'iyošpaye*. Government agents looked for chiefs who could make appropriate distributions. While the process began to concentrate power, it must also have led to increasing internal dissension. No precedent could guide the redistribution. More importantly, dissension grew about whether to negotiate with whites or to resist them.

This issue was the major cause of a split among the Brules. They seem to have hunted most often between the Platte and White rivers, ranging westward from the Missouri into the Black Hills. When the fur trade began, some of them remained longer near the Missouri. As permanent white settlements were established, a few *t'iyošpaye* attached themselves.

Probably, the attachment was based on a sexual liaison with the trader, which limited the size of the group. Nevertheless, this shift initiated a new social structure and marked a rift between those aligning with whites and those opposed to them. Some *t'iyošpaye* regularly joined the settlement in the winter and remained there longer in the spring.

By the end of the Civil War, enough Brules were tied to Missouri River traders that they became known as the Lower Brules, while those who remained on the upper reaches of the Platte or White were called the Upper Brules, later to be identified with the Rosebud Reservation. The separation occurred largely over the issue of how to deal with whites.

In 1868 the Lower Brules were officially recognized by Washington when they were assigned to a reservation by executive order. Actually, their reservation was a specified part of an entity designated the Great Sioux Reservation—all the land lying west of the Missouri River to the Wyoming border. The Lower Brules were given special rights to a small part extending up the White River. At the time, the important detail was that they were assigned their own agency, a headquarters for the agent at the mouth of the White River.

Annual reports of the agents tell little about Lower Brule social life. Nine men designated as "chiefs and head men" signed the Treaty of 1865, which was the basis for the Lower Brule agency. Early records refer at various times to nine "bands," no doubt, *t'iyošpaye*. The names on the 1865 treaty are Iron Nation, Medicine Bull, Little Pheasant, One Who Kills The White Buffalo Cow, White Buffalo Cow That Walks, Brave Heart, Wounded Man, Gourd Earrings, and Iron Whip. Only the first three of these men are referred to regularly in later reports. Some of the leaders likely were called by other names; a *t'iyošpaye* organization obviously continued through the 1870s and 1880s, if not later. Agents often complained about the distant location of some groups or about their "hostility." Iron Nation was often singled out because of his "friendliness" and his lack of opposition to farming, although no concrete evidence shows that he himself ever farmed.

It is doubtful that the histories of the various *t'iyošpaye* at Lower Brule can ever be reconstructed in detail. The few written documents do suggest, however, that the Lower Brules were living in bands whose leaders were becoming more prominent. Agents consistently worked through those leaders, and missionaries recognized their importance. Still, it seems likely that individuals could move in and out of different *t'iyošpaye* and even that whole *t'iyošpaye* sometimes left the reservation. When the annual reports mentioned the number of bands, sometimes they exceeded nine, sometimes they were fewer.

Since the annual report form required an estimate of population, such a figure was regularly reported. However, the initial figure of two hundred lodges was so consistently reported, it suggests that agents did not take the census seriously. They always emphasized that the figure was an estimate, and their average of six to a lodge was likewise a guess. Doubtless, the population hovered around 1,200 through the 1870s and 1880s, but *t'iyošpaye* moved back and forth to relatives on the Rosebud or even to the Yankton Reservation down the Missouri. During the summer, there were regularly fewer bands on the reservation. Likely, an agent might count several *t'iyošpaye* as one band, given the flexibility of the social organization.

### Reservation Confinement and Increasing Factionalism

By 1869 the Lower Brule agent began to interfere with social organization to the extent of appointing chiefs for the bands. That step, combined with plans to relocate the agency, led to considerable unrest. Agent William French requested military assistance for the move. The band leader, Medicine Bull, was alleged to have taken a Pawnee scalp, and the army intended to stop such raiding. The agent readily secured the cooperation of Iron Nation in a pledge of peace and cooperation in relocating with his twenty-eight lodges. However, other Lower Brules shot at some of the agency buildings and even shot into the houses that had been built for the chiefs. The army believed Little Pheasant's *t'iyošpaye* was responsible, but their report suggested he was absent at the time. Some of this internal turmoil was a result of hostilities at Fort Laramie, where rumors originated suggesting that some Lower Brule relatives had been killed by whites. It is apparent that the issue over cooperation or resistance to white policy was beginning to shape factional disputes.

Confirmation of this process is supplied by William Welsh, a prominent member of the Board of Indian Commissioners. Welsh prided himself on firsthand visits to the reservations to determine conditions. When he visited the Lower Brules in the summer of 1871, he saw the need for an agency for them separate from the agency at Crow Creek. In his report to the secretary of the interior for that year, he wrote that, "The Brule are very much dissatisfied at not being under the supervision of an Agent having authority. The young men mostly congregate at what is called a hostile camp" (reported in Schusky 1975:82). Very likely, this summer camp was a temporary grouping of those Brules who chose to join other Sioux to hunt in the Black Hills or on the Yellowstone River. The *t'iyošpaye* organization was such that it easily allowed individuals, especially young men, to enter or leave for any length of time.

Pressure to end such easy movement, however, began to build due to policies devised by the whites. Once agencies were established, missionaries with schools soon followed. Initially, the Episcopalians tried to maintain day schools near several of the bands. When they found they could barely keep one school opened, they planned for Indians to settle nearby. The agent had similar hopes. Indians were encouraged to farm under the supervision of an agency farmer, an arrangement that meant far more permanent settlement. The agency also began to provide such services as those of a physician, another motivation for Indians to live close to the agency.

While these local developments were occurring, the federal government began to negotiate further land reductions. Gold had been discovered in the Black Hills, and a series of land commissions appeared among the Sioux to persuade them to sell that territory. Most of the Indians were united against any land sales, but a few could be found who would agree. The issue became a bitter one, increasing the division between those Sioux who accepted whites as necessary and those who chose resistance. In 1875 the Lower Brules met with a land commission at the Spotted Tail (Rosebud) Agency. United with other Brules, they frustrated the commissioners' efforts. It was as if the resistance were a prelude to the Battle of the Little Big Horn the next year. Yet, within a few months of Custer's defeat, another land commission met with only the Lower Brules at their agency and secured their agreement to a land purchase. The nine men who signed were identified as band chiefs: Iron Nation, Medicine Bull, Little Pheasant, White Buffalo Cow, Buffalo Head, Standing Cloud, Useful Heart, Long Bear Claws, and Only Man. At least five of them seem to have been signers of the 1868 treaty, which suggests that band leadership had been fairly stable. It is not clear what pressure faced them; the promise that they would never have to move to Indian Territory if they signed seems to have been an important factor. It also seems apparent that band leaders had not supported Sitting Bull that summer. The reports from the agency throughout the summer were all routine, and the agent was shocked to read in the newspaper about hundreds of Lower Brules leaving the reservation to fight Custer. Clearly, the reporters exaggerated the Lower Brules' participation. On the other hand, some young men who left for the customary summer hunt must have fought in the battle, but the agent had not missed them, nor did the handful of whites living among some 1,500 Lower Brules that summer ever sense any danger.

In short, the Lower Brules were well established as "peaceful"; the coming decades would also make them destitute, a condition that largely confined them to the reservation. With limits on their movement and pressures growing for settlement around the agency, the old tactics of evading conflict became useless. Factionalism began to crystallize into more structured opposition. Dozens of issues from selling land to selling lumber for railroad construction became patterned around cooperation or resistance to the ways of white men.

Nevertheless, there were disruptions in the pattern. Gradually, new jobs were created at the agency. Mixed-bloods or Sioux who knew some English were usually the first employed; but full-bloods were also hired to haul supplies long distances. Besides the pay, workers enjoyed the chance to travel and visit with Indians at other agencies. Moreover, the Lower Brules had more or less made a choice to accept much of the dominant culture when they chose to reside near the first traders and agencies. Thus, the schism between full-bloods and mixed-bloods often fluctuated. This cycle of cooperation and conflict is illustrated by different relations with the agent.

In 1878 the agent appointed a Lower Brule police force, one the agent later found unsatisfactory because it took orders from the chiefs instead of being responsible only to himself. He dismissed the force and the next year reappointed men more loyal to him. When Rosebud Indians invited the Lower Brules to a Sun Dance in the summer of 1879, Agent William E. Dougherty told his police to stop anyone from leaving. A few nights later the police barracks and other agency buildings were fired upon. The police resigned in a body, and the agent wisely forgot his previous order. He noted that, unlike the situation at Crow Creek, only a "few mixed-blood families" lived at Lower Brule and "progress" would be slower (Schusky 1975:106-7).

While most agents at other Sioux reservations regularly described progressive and conservative factions at their agencies, the record at Lower Brule only infrequently refers to such groups. Rather, agents recorded how some individuals took stands on certain issues while opposed by others. During the 1880s Iron Nation and Medicine Bull were often mentioned as leaders, but opposition to them was noted. A contemporary Sioux, Reverend Luke Walker, one of the first to become an ordained minister, exerted considerable influence but never became a dominant power. Whites who married Lower Brules also led on some occasions. As I noted earlier:

> The Dakota simply did not subscribe wholehearted loyalty to anyone. A man could and did move his family to another band or even agency when he disagreed with leaders. No one was in a position to assert great

authority, and agents of course, wavered between delegating and denying authority to the chiefs. The situation was one that made sources of power ambiguous and caused the Indians to employ devious forms of sanctions. [1975:120]

As 1890 drew near, events that united the Lower Brules were countered by divisive forces. The United States finally forced a division of the Great Sioux Nation into half a dozen reservations. At most agencies this threat of division greatly increased the power of emerging chiefs. Likewise, a survey of the reservations and allotment of lands to individual owners united the Sioux in their resistance. At Lower Brule, the unity of opposition was obvious on occasion, but it never lasted long nor did it crystallize around any individual. In 1889 Iron Nation, a likely candidate for chief, reversed his usual position of cooperating with the agent. The reservation was to be moved northward and Iron Nation refused to relocate. Little Pheasant, sometimes described as a "hostile," led the move instead. This disruption was in process when Sioux missionaries of the Ghost Dance religion visited the Lower Brules. The Ghost Dance movement, likewise, divided the Lower Brules. Those who opposed it had little sympathy or support for the twenty or so Lower Brules who were eventually jailed for their participation in the movement.

The suppression of the Ghost Dance and increasing pressure to engage in useless farming caused the turn of the century to be marked by despair. Almost two-thirds of the Lower Brules remained on their old lands along White River rather than move onto the new reservation. The one-third who had moved began to herd cattle on the best land or they secured jobs at the agency. They were regarded by agents as "progressive," while those off the reservation, who hoped to relocate on the Rosebud Reservation, were an embarrassment. In 1893 the confrontation broke into the open. The agent sent his police force to round up bands headed by Medicine Bull, Black Dog, and others. Those Indians were forced to remain at the new agency until they were assigned allotments and scattered over the reservation. Allotment policy, one of whose chief aims was to abolish the power of chiefs, had some effect at Lower Brule. The band structure began to deteriorate in the twentieth century. By the 1950s, the term *t'iyošpaye* was understood only by older Indians, and only one small settlement resembled the old organization.

In addition to the allotment policy, the beginning of the twentieth century saw an ever-increasing number of marriages between Indians and whites. Luke Walker had brought a white wife to the reservation quite early; it was more common, however, for white men to marry Brule women. In a few cases, black men married Brule women. By the 1930s, mixed-bloods usually led in accepting government programs and in adapting innovations from the dominant society. The historical record suggests that membership in factional issues was becoming more stable. A white way of life, even though modified considerably by Brule mothers, was being entrenched among a large segment of the population. Full-bloods, however, continued with entrenched ways of thinking and behaving as Sioux. Raymond DeMallie (1978:260–61) described the process for Pine Ridge, which paralleled the Lower Brule experience.

Most full-bloods never farmed even though residing on an allotment. Those mixed-bloods who did work an allotment subsisted by ranching. Since allotments were too small to support a cattle herd, the Brules never lived as envisioned by the framers of Allotment Policy. By 1930 they were in small communities, usually with a church, sometimes a day school, and occasionally a store. Three of those settlements were in wide flood plains of the Missouri, one was along a tributary, and one on high country at a crossroads. A majority of families were at the agency headquarters on the Missouri, also called Lower Brule. The small ranching communities were composed of mixed-bloods; conservative full-bloods lived along the tributary. The town of Lower Brule included both groups.

With the coming of self-government and the economic programs of the Depression plus the Indian Reorganization Act, factional issues often crossed full-blood and mixed-blood lines. The location of a dam or a road or the question of where land might be purchased by the tribe were issues dividing the Lower Brules along sectional lines rather than the customary conservative-progressive division. In short, factional opposition could be issue-oriented rather than institutionalized by groups.

It is precisely this situation that has made the study of factionalism difficult. On the one hand, social scientists have recognized factions and analyzed events in terms of structured groups. That perspective is useful. When one faction decides a matter, the other faction automatically opposes it, but occasionally some issues are judged on their merits. At Lower Brule, the merits of a particular government program will be overtly discussed, although acceptance or rejection often is along factional lines. Mixed-bloods most often choose something new; full-bloods oppose it, not because they are particularly conservative, but because they oppose the mixed-bloods.

However, issues are not always judged on the basis of factional alignments. During the 1930s, some programs were of more benefit to the outlying population than the people at the agency. These programs led to conflict on a sectional basis, and people crossed over the usual factional lines in taking sides. Thus, some issues are decided on merit; people do take positions that are in their own best interests. On those occasions the conflict may resemble factional strife and be identified with it. An analysis of factionalism must take into account political process, a point made by Harold Lasswell, who noted that factions work to advance the interests of particular people in a "struggle for power." Issues are basic, but some individuals in the struggle simply identify with the causes of their friends. "This primitive alignment rests on no deep calculation of personal interests" (1968:49).

## Factions within Modern Political Processes

Lasswell continued his discussion with an analysis that is appropriately prophetic for the Lower Brule factionalism of the 1950s. He suggested that factionalism frequently occurs with major social changes, noting specifically a sudden increase in wealth. Most appropriate is a comment on the social psychology of factionalism: "When aggressiveness toward the outside world is thwarted it is turned back against the self or against external objects more closely associated with the self" (Lasswell 1968:50).

In 1958, when I began fieldwork among the Lower Brules, they had just lost land to the tailwaters of the Fort Randall Dam, and they faced further loss to the proposed Big Bend Dam. The entire community of Lower Brule was to be flooded and a new community built for them. They felt hopeless to fight against construction of the dam; clearly any aggressiveness toward the dominant outside society was thwarted. Furthermore, they had to deal with a sudden increase in wealth. I expected to find the customary differences between full-bloods and mixed-bloods at their peak and the factions as well crystallized as at any time in the past.

Instead, I found on the reservation a well-developed unity among people who would end my discussions of mixed-blood and full-blood differences largely with a shrug of their shoulders. They admitted past conflicts, but insisted those matters were of no consequence now. Nevertheless, factional strife had occurred. Residents of the reservation spoke with bitterness of nonresident Lower Brules and cast aspersions on them. The nonresidents were all "greedy," had "turned their backs" on Lower Brules, or were "ashamed of being Indian."

As I began to locate and visit Brules in Pierre and elsewhere off the reservation, I found they believed the reservation residents were "shiftless," expected "to live on handouts," and were "greedy." These nonresidents were more likely to have jobs, although often temporary. The housing they had was comparable to that on the reservation, as was the overall standard of living. The greater income of an employed Brule in Pierre or Rapid City was offset by greater expenses required for off-reservation life. Yet, the migrants felt a sense of superiority by being able to claim an independence from the Bureau of Indian Affairs.

Clearly, some general, basic differences split the residents and the migrants, but the fundamental issue at the time was a decision on how to use the money awarded to the tribe for loss of tribal land. The Fort Randall Dam had taken an area worth approximately one million dollars. The tribal council had developed an economic plan calling for investment of that million and a second million to make a sound ranching economy. By playing politics with the federal policy of "termination" current at that time, the Lower Brules had a good chance of acquiring the second million as a kind of investment in independence from the federal government. The plan meant an expenditure of about two million dollars for the hundred reservation families. Even though ranching mixed-bloods would have benefitted the most, full-bloods were convinced they too could prosper if all the money were kept on the reservation.

People who had left the reservation felt they were about to be swindled. They had as much a share in tribal assets as any member, and they felt they had cooperated with the dominant society more than residents had. They were trying to become self-supporting members of the larger society, a goal they had been taught as worthy from their first day in school. Although the migrants were mostly mixed-bloods, some full-bloods had migrated to neighboring towns, such as Pierre; a fair number had also migrated to other reservations. They felt very strongly that the million dollars ought to be divided equally among members or what was commonly spoken of as "per capita." In some effort at compromise, or the appearance of compromise, the tribal council had diverted some funds toward per capita payments. That move largely satisfied the resident full-bloods instead, who saw the payment as getting them out of their immediate debts. Very few migrants saw the limited per capita payments as satisfactory.

Obviously, I was embroiled in a new factional dispute and had the opportunity to study it. Since I have described the issue at length in *The Forgotten Sioux* (1975:211–36), here I turn back to the traditional division between mixed-blood and full-blood factions. In effect, these groups were dormant in 1958, or they might better be understood as one pose of Lower Brule society. Fred Gearing (1958:1148) introduced the term *pose* to indicate how Cherokee society changed at different seasons, and the concept is equally valuable for understanding seasonal changes in the Sioux *t'iyošpaye*. Today, however, with settled reservation life, seasonal poses are negligible, but different poses occur when different political issues arise. My problem was to ascertain if the mixed-blood and full-blood factions continued to exist at Lower Brule and if they were significant parts of the social structure.

While the division was largely dormant, I expected it had a permanence that would be reflected in past practice. The most obvious place for it was in the nuclear family. If people closely aligned on the basis of mixed-blood versus full-blood, marriage choices should coincide. The distribution of marriages readily confirmed the hypothesis. Thirty-two full-blood husbands had full-blood wives; only four full-blood husbands had mixed-blood wives. Of mixed-blood husbands, twenty-eight had mixed-blood wives; only six had full-blood wives.

As I indicated elsewhere (Schusky 1960:61–77) this endogamy was further augmented by language use, church affiliation, religious belief, and similar cultural values. Mixed-bloods were scorned because of their poor ability to speak Lakota or even to understand it. While their ability to comprehend was underrated, they did have difficulty speaking. In turn, they joked about full-bloods' use of English. To the outsider, the differences in language ability seem exaggerated by both sides. Differences in religion were likewise emphasized. The Catholic Church was described as mixed-blood while the Episcopal Church was said to be full-blood. Actually, Episcopal membership was split about equally between mixed-bloods and full-bloods, but hymns were usually sung in Lakota and services were sometimes preached in Lakota or parts translated. Some Episcopals were also identified as believers in traditional religion. They fasted, sought visions, and made use of *yuwipi* or other shamans. Few mixed-bloods ever attended *yuwipi* meetings, but I found that most mixed-bloods still believed *yuwipi* to have extraordinary power. Clearly, they respected parts of traditional religion, although in some contexts they expressed contempt for it. A similar ambiguity occurred for other parts of traditional culture. Mixed-bloods, for instance, joked about how full-bloods could never do anything until all dissent had ended. As a result, supposedly, nothing was ever done. Yet, when meetings of any kind were held, the Brules discussed an issue until it was clear that all agreed. Only then was a formal motion voted on. If it was obvious that a proposal would not get unanimous support, it was sidetracked or delayed. Majority rule remained a white idea.

Adherence to this value was vividly illustrated to me when a Public Health Service (PHS) worker appeared before the Tribal Council to remind members they were to cap a well dug six months earlier by the service. The reservation had a few inconvenient springs; most families used the Missouri River as a water source. People realized the contaminated water could hurt babies and infants or even adult guests so no one actively opposed a clean water source. Everyone I talked to expressed a belief that the PHS ought to dig wells.

It had done so, but under its policy of only "helping people to help themselves," the PHS did not complete the work. It had surveyed, located a source, and even drilled a hole, completing the most costly part of the task. The Tribal Council was supposed to cap the well with an appropriate concrete base and pump as its part of the self-help program. The council had the money necessary to complete work and all the council members spoke favorably to me of the project.

Thus, I was puzzled when the matter was brought before the council and numerous questions were asked of the local Public Health worker. When he left, even more questions were raised, many having little bearing on the issue. It was clear that unanimity could not be expected, and the tribal chair never brought the matter to a vote. Members simply moved to another issue. The chair later told the worker that the motion had been tabled.

In my inquires afterward, I found the full-blood council members suspected the motives of the mixed-bloods in approving a cap for the well. The mixed-blood chair was "up to something"; the one concrete accusation—that the chair intended to use the water for his cattle—was obviously a rationalization. His herd did not use well water nor was it even close to the well. Eventually, I realized the opposition was simply a reaction of full-blood perceptions of mixed-blood interests. Wells were part of the white world; mixed-bloods were the ones who benefited from white innovations. Therefore, the well would be used mostly by mixed-bloods. Full-bloods overlooked their own interests, opposing the issue on the basis of factional alignment. Mixed-bloods, in talking with me, supported the clean water in principle but with little enthusiasm. The chair already had piped water from an artesian well. His conclusion was that he and other mixed-bloods had an obligation to "look out for" the full-bloods; if they did not want the well capped, then he would support their wishes.

In attempting to clarify his position, the chair gave me my initial insight into the processes the Lower Brules used to justify their factional relationships. Only at a superficial level were factions defined as the "bad" and the "good" sides. The ideology of the factions was far more complex than that simple dichotomy. As I focused my interviewing on how individuals felt toward the other faction, I discovered that mixed-bloods generally felt a kind of paternalism toward full-bloods. The full-bloods responded with expressions of dependency. One of the few nonderogatory terms for mixed-bloods is translated as "sons of interpreters." Just as Nancy Hagedorn (1988:60–62) found for the Iroquois, interpreters were essential mediators of the two cultures as well as languages. While mixed-bloods were no longer literally interpreters, they continued to mediate with the white world. Full-bloods approached government representatives and other whites with the aid of a mixed-blood. In turn, mixed-bloods used full-bloods to justify their position in an Indian world. In other words, definitions of Indianness are ambiguous. Some definitions mean knowing the traditional language and culture. Mixed-bloods would not be Indian by such a definition, but they can justify their rights as Indians by asserting their usefulness in supporting the full-bloods. That is, since they have an essential role, they must be rightful community members.

This mutual dependency means the Lower Brules are able to act as a community. Faction fights do cause problems; the alignments do mire political decisions. Yet, people recognize vital relations between full-bloods and mixed-bloods, and they take actions to benefit the whole. I note elsewhere (1977) that the factions can serve as a division of labor for the community to undertake seemingly impossible feats, as when the Lower Brules hosted the Episcopal convocation and cared for several thousand guests. On such an occasion, the factions do not disrupt or prevent action; rather, they are an integral part of a structure for action. Mixed-bloods perform activities requiring interaction with the outside world. Full-bloods work effectively within the community or make ties with other reservations.

In the case of the new well that remained uncapped, it appeared to me at first that the factions had stymied a desirable community goal. After two months of discussion at council meetings as well as outside, the matter seemed unlikely to be resolved. Yet, the case failed to disprove that factions halted decision making because the issue became moot soon afterward when the Corps of Engineers announced definitely that the Big Bend Dam would be built. The land where the well stood would be flooded by its back-waters. The Public Health work had been in vain; the indecision of the Tribal Council had saved the funds that would have been spent for capping.

Nevertheless, the conservative and progressive factions doubtless cause more than delay at times. In the past, attempts to build and maintain a tribal herd have failed, apparently because of factional disputes. The differences have certainly caused many whites to believe that the factions prevent any effective action. However, I found little evidence to support this stereotype. Superficially, the factions appear to be disruptive; feelings of dislike do surface at times and issues are frequently judged on the basis of structure rather than issue. Yet the factions also can serve as a division of labor, and feelings of interdependency produce cooperation. The Lower Brules can work, on occasion, to define and achieve community goals. While well-defined and solidified factions are a result of restricted mobility caused by agency and reservation life, Lower Brule society remains relatively fluid and flexible. As Eggan predicted, High Plains social structure allows for adaptation to changing conditions, even after the original social organization has been altered by the development of factions.

# References

Adams, Arthur T., ed.
    1961    The Explorations of Pierre Esprit Radisson. Minneapolis: Ross and Haines.
Bradley, James H.
    1922    History of the Sioux. Contributions to the Historical Society of Montana, vol. 9, 29-140. Helena.
DeMallie, Raymond
    1978    Pine Ridge Economy: Cultural and Historical Perspectives. In American Indian Economic Development, edited by Sam Stanley, 237-312. The Hague: Mouton.
Dorsey, James Owen
    1894    Siouan Sociology. Smithsonian Institution, Fifteenth Annual Report of the Bureau of American Ethnology, 213-44. Washington, D.C.
Eggan, Fred
    1955    Social Anthropology: Methods and Results. In Social Anthropology of North American Tribes, edited by Fred Eggan, 485-551. Enlarged ed. Chicago: University of Chicago Press.
    1966    The American Indian: Perspectives for the Study of Social Change. Chicago: Aldine Publishing.
    1982    Foreword. In Arapahoe Politics, 1851-1978: Symbols in Crises of Authority, by Loretta Fowler, xv-xvi. Lincoln: University of Nebraska Press.
Elkin, Henry
    1940    The Northern Arapaho of Wyoming. In Acculturation in Seven American Indian Tribes, edited by Ralph Linton, 207-55. New York: D. Appleton-Century Company.
Fowler, Loretta
    1982a   "Look at My Hair, It Is Gray": Age Grading, Ritual Authority, and Political Change among the Northern Arapahoe and Gros Ventre. In Plains Indian Studies: A Collection of Studies in Honor of John C. Ewers and Waldo R. Wedel, edited by Douglas Ubelaker and Herman J. Viola, 73-93. Smithsonian Contributions to Anthropology, no. 30. Washington, D.C.
    1982b   Arapahoe Politics, 1851-1978: Symbols in Crises of Authority. Lincoln: University of Nebraska Press.
Gearing, Fred
    1958    The Structural Poses of 18th Century Cherokee Villages. American Anthropologist 60:1148-57.
Hagedorn, Nancy
    1988    "A Friend to Go Between Them": Interpreters as Cultural Brokers during Anglo-European Councils, 1740-1770. Ethnohistory 35:60-80.

Landes, Ruth
  1968      The Mystic Lake Sioux: Sociology of the Mdewakantonwan Santee. Madison: University of Wisconsin Press.
Lasswell, Harold
  1968      Factions. Encyclopedia of the Social Sciences, vol. 5, 49–51.
Leach, Edmund
  1961      Pul Eliya, a Village in Ceylon. Cambridge: Cambridge University Press.
Lee, Dorothy
  1959      Freedom and Culture. Englewood Cliffs, N.J.: Prentice-Hall.
Lewellen, Ted C.
  1983      Political Anthropology. South Hadley, Mass.: Bergin and Garvey.
Lewis, Oscar
  1958      Village Life in Northern India. New York: Vintage Books.
Linton, Ralph, ed.
  1940      Acculturation in Seven American Indian Tribes. New York: D. Appleton-Century.
Murdock, George Peter
  1949      Social Structure. New York: Macmillan.
Robinson, Doane
  1904      History of Sioux or Sioux Indians. Reprint ed. Minneapolis: Ross and Haines, 1967.
Schusky, Ernest
  1960      The Lower Brule Sioux: The Description of a Distinct Community and the Processes which Keep It Distinct. Ph.D. diss., University of Chicago.
  1971      The Upper Missouri Indian Agency. Missouri Historical Review 65:3:249–69.
  1975      The Forgotten Sioux: An Ethnohistory of the Lower Brule Reservation. Chicago: Nelson-Hall.
  1977      American Indians on Their Own. Christian Century 94:303–6.
  1986      The Evolution of Indian Leadership in the Great Plains, 1750–1950. American Indian Quarterly 10:65–82.
Vincent, Joan
  1978      Political Anthropology: Manipulative Strategies. In Annual Review of Anthropology, 175–94. Palo Alto: Annual Reviews.
Winkler, Edwin
  1969      Political Anthropology. In Biennial Review of Anthropology, 301–86. Palo Alto: Stanford University Press.

# 11

## "Reading Back" to Find Community: Lumbee Ethnohistory

KAREN I. BLU

Like historians, anthropologists read and incorporate documents into their narratives and analyses of events in the past, and the best of each do this with great care. Documents and their authors must be contextualized, just as anthropologists contextualize their informants or consultants for ethnographic sources. But there is a significant difference between the way anthropologists and historians usually approach documents from the past: anthropologists bring to their reading what they know from firsthand experience accumulated while in the field. This bringing-to-bear of contemporary circumstances is usually done quite consciously, although sometimes apologetically. Historians, on the other hand, often see themselves working from the opposite direction—from immersion in the older documents which then leads to a line of connection or comparison with the present. Yet, historians of, for example, France, generally spend a great deal of time in France, in archives and libraries, eating French food, speaking French to the contemporary French, and consciously or unconsciously absorbing current French ways of doing and being.

In what follows, I will suggest, using examples from my own fieldwork and documentary research, some of the virtues of "reading back"—using an analysis of recent conditions to interpret older documents. The idea of using the present to understand the past is, of course, not new. Fenton, in his now classic study of the Iroquois Eagle Dance, looked to archeological methods and borrowed the term "upstreaming" to describe his attempt to reconcile older documentary sources with contemporary ethnographic information. He found that "it works better to begin with the present and work steadily backward," rather than the other way around (Fenton 1953: 1). When Fenton remarks that his method "has the virtue of proceeding from the known to the unknown in a scientific manner" (1953:208), he reflects the dominant orientation in the anthropology of the time toward scientific paradigm in which "the known" and the "unknown" are unproblematically obvious.

Since that time, the epistemological ground has shifted for many researchers from one of absolute and certain knowledge to relative and less confident knowledge. This stems from the position that what we inevitably work with are a variety of interpretations of reality, including our own as researchers, none of which connects unproblematically or simply with that reality. Direct, unmediated access to reality is no longer thought possible. Thus, what we know is always someone's version of reality or knowledge, which must always be problematical. My own term "reading back" owes a debt to Fenton's "upstreaming," but differs in its recognition of the interpretive complexities and deep uncertainties that today constitute any knowledge, including the scientific.

Both Eggan and Fenton insisted on the importance of a thorough integration of historical understanding with the study of culture and society. DeMallie has argued for the centrality of change in this understanding, or, as he succinctly put it, "culture and culture change are, in fact, the same phenomenon" (1993:533). In what follows vast changes in landscape and many aspects of society are outlined at the same time that certain continuities are identified. I believe these continuities would not be seen without "reading back." "Reading back" need not be bound to a strict chronological order (proceeding from present to near past to distant past), but is suited to the more episodic approaches to such postmodern theoretical concerns as how we are to interpret homelands and com—munities.

In the particular case in point I will take an ethnohistorical look at continuities and changes in living circumstances, particularly in community life, for Indians in and around Robeson County, North Carolina, within the last 125 years or so. Given radical changes in the landscape and in their dominion over it, how have Robeson Indians placed themselves upon it and maintained their connection to it? This raises questions about the nature of local communities, their forms, and where in published and unpublished documents we might find out about them. Without an idea of what communities are today, one misses much of what is in the fragmentary references from earlier times. By reading forward only, the senses of what changed and how are thinner, sketchier, and impoverished. At the same time, an ethnohistorical look at these localized communities can add to our general understandings of "community" and of the processes of change and renewal that they make possible.

## Communities

Robeson County, North Carolina, is the symbolic heartland for today's 50-

60,000 Lumbee Indians and for some related people who call themselves Tuscaroras or Cherokees. None has ever had a treaty or a state or federal reservation (see Blu 1980). The Tuscaroras and Cherokees of this area of North Carolina are not identical with the Tuscaroras of New York and Canada or the Cherokees of western North Carolina and Oklahoma. This Robeson heartland or "home(land)" is spatially shared with whites and blacks, who live interspersed, particularly in the countryside, and in a more segregated manner in towns. Towns generally comprise several ethnic communities. For example, Lumberton, the "white" county seat, is home to the Lumberton white community, the Lumberton black community, and the Lumberton Indian community. Symbolically, the county seat is "white" because the power structure there is considered still to be dominated by whites.

The term *community* is used in this region to refer to different levels of inclusion and can therefore be of indeterminate meaning without sufficient context. For example, "the Indian community" at its most encompassing includes Indians in Robeson and surrounding counties in North and South Carolina, as well as those living elsewhere in the diaspora, mostly in urban and suburban areas, both in the North and in the South. In its mid-range use, the term may refer only to Indians who live in the localized Carolina area, not including those in the diaspora, or it may refer only to "the Indian community" within a particular county. Finally, it may be used to refer to the Indians living in or born and reared in any one of a number of localized settlements.

Up to the Civil War, the vast pine forests described so well by Silver (1990) were still in place in this flat, swamp- and river-cut area of the Coastal Plain. To supplement subsistence agriculture practiced on drier patches of swampy land, many Indians worked in the pine woods in turpentine and lumbering industries that made nearby Wilmington a center for national and international trade (Evans 1966:14). After the Civil War, while the South was being "reclaimed" by whites, who then wrote a system of racial segregation into the law and put it into practice, the landscape was transformed. Forests were cut down, many swamps were drained, and the river was tamed by flood control measures. The amount of land under cultivation increased greatly. What had been paths or corduroy roads became a network of more formal paved and unpaved roads, eventually including superhighways, and beginning in the mid-nineteenth century, railroads criss-crossed the county (Thomas 1982:178-85). Today the county is still rural, still farmed, but there are increasing numbers of scattered factories. Towns have grown greatly, and some even have suburbs. Most people are now employed in manufacturing industries.

Whites, not Indians or African Americans, planned and for the most part controlled these changes. Yet the ways in which Indians adapted to them, resisted them, or countered with their own strategies differed from family to family and community to community. This spirit of diversity is reflected today in the localized communities.

As I pored over my field notes and looked through documentary sources, it became clear that *area* was often used interchangeably with *community*, or, especially in older documents, *settlement*. It also emerged that in each case, the territory that the area or community covered was vaguely defined, lacking the sort of firm boundaries that result in lines on a map. These visually unmarked, indistinct areas are an important key to understanding Lumbee persistence.[1]

To recognize where the communities are, a person must possess highly local geographic knowledge, but to grasp the character of each community, a person must have a far deeper and more complex understanding. Each community is deemed to have a separate and distinctive character and to be associated with different families and family names. Individual Indians identify themselves and others by community affiliation. Knowing that tells one about possible kinship connections, political importance, and even economic or social status. All these are rooted in the family, or, as one Indian man put it, "families are the essence of the communities."

Family connections can frequently be seen in the rural countryside, in the form of collections of nearby houses that are owned or rented by relatives of various sorts. In towns this pattern is less common. Understanding this current kin-based pattern of clustered housing has helped me to find evidence of similar patterns in documents from earlier periods, evidence that I would not have been able to piece together without knowing the contemporary situation.

The localized communities are both proud and rivalrous. They often characterize one another in less than flattering terms and have political leaders who jockey for position with each other and who depend on community residents for core support. These leaders are almost always men, and they may or may not occupy formal political offices. They vie informally with one another within a localized community and within the larger countywide Indian community for prominence and influence. Thus, the number, wealth, and social positions of their supporters, centered heavily in their local community, become important factors in their success.

Indians may express their feelings and views about the local communities through storytelling, mild teasing, more serious joking with an edge to it, or outright hostility. Particularly among young males, the matter may come to violence. These rivalries appear from the documents to be persistent, as longstanding perhaps as those reported for North Carolina Cherokee towns or settlements (Gilbert 1943; Kupferer 1966; Fogelson 1975; Wahrhaftig 1975; Kilpatrick 1991; Neely 1992).[2] Certain whole communities, such as Pembroke, have been known for violence in the past, while others, like Union Chapel (sometimes known simply as Chapel), have a more current reputation for it.

Two principal communities are the focus of the old rivalries, each claiming to be the true center of the larger Indian community—Pembroke, a town, and Prospect, a densely populated but rural area. Pembroke town is a relatively recent cultural center for Indian people in Robeson County, having been formally founded in 1892 when a new north-south rail line crossed an older east-west line there. The grid planning and development of the town were carried out by whites in the midst of a dense Indian population. Significantly, the Pembroke community identified by Indians is considerably larger and vaguer than that delineated by the lines drawn by whites on a map that define eligible Pembroke voters. The struggles over formal political control of the town have been resolved in favor of the Indians, who have dominated the town as voters and officeholders at least since the 1950s. In between those times came white hegemony and Indian resistance. Pembroke is now where important institutions that affect all Robeson Indians are located—"the college" (today a branch of the North Carolina State University system), Lumbee Regional Development Association, Lumbee River Legal Services, the Indian newspaper. But in the early years of this century, it was known for violence rather than respectability. As one man whose boyhood was in the 1930s said, "When I was a boy, it wasn't uncommon to see bodies in the street in Pembroke." Currently, violence is not part of the character generally attributed to it. For proud community insiders, Pembroke is an exemplar, a progressive model for others to admire and emulate. Outsiders accuse Pembroke people of being "holier than thou," "stuck up," "people who think they are better," and people who "don't like anybody but themselves."

Pembroke's main rival is Prospect, a community generally acknowledged as the former cultural center, still "the very *heart* of the Lumbee Indian community," as one middle-aged man put it in 1984. "It has the densest Indian population, and in a five mile radius, there are only two parcels of land not owned by Indians," he continued. An older rural community not far from Pembroke, Prospect is today an area with fine farmland and few non-Indians, prosperous and proud. Other Indians say it is conservative, "country," and associated with a distinctive accent, variously called "funny talk," "that Prospect accent," and "that old Elizabethan talk," depending on the perspective of the particular outsider.

Other communities perhaps figure less prominently in Lumbee discourse, coming up less often than others in stories and conversations. One of the more obscure is the Brooks Settlement. One woman told me that when she was growing up (probably in the 1930s), the women there were the only ones she saw who still wore their hair in braids and dressed in long skirts to work in the fields. It was known for its conservative nature, but no one considered it a center like Prospect, which was also known for its cultural conservatism. In contrast to Prospect's prosperity, the Brooks Settlement was not well off.

Some communities cover very large areas, perhaps the largest being Magnolia, an area where more whites live and where travelers through the county pass on the main north-south roads. There, people are said to be more familiar with urban life because of their nearness to Lumberton, the largest town and county seat, and because of encounters with tourists. The differences in wealth associated with communities also varies considerably. One area, Mount Airy, includes at its heart an extremely wealthy church whose grounds, buildings, and recreational facilities are impressive by any standards. The farmland in the area is good, and the people have a reputation for prosperousness, but also for "keeping to themselves," unlike those from Prospect who contend for central recognition. Some from outside the Mount Airy community tease those inside about cousin marriages and about how many marriages involve "Locklears on both sides." Still other communities have been known in the past, at least, for their skills at making and selling "jimmy-john" or "white lightnin'," illegally made liquor. Black Ankle was one of them (Thomas 1982:187; see also three of Joseph Mitchell's stories set in the 1920s [1992:346-63]).

Understanding something about political leadership and disagreements, about family clusters and the visually unmarked communities so important to contemporary Indian life in Robeson County, helps us to interpret the historical documents of earlier periods, providing us with clues, giving us ideas about what to look for, what might be meaningful that we would be unlikely to notice if we depended exclusively on the documents. In this way, ethnography and history can powerfully complement one another, together providing a different, more complex version of how things happened than we would otherwise have. From the foregoing sketch of some contemporary local communities, let us turn to what can be seen of change and continuity by re-reading and reinterpreting some highly selected areas of the documentary record.

## Place and Time: Reading the Historical Records

If we take these current notions of Indian community and settlement and use them to look at the documentary record, we can see both important continuities and many material changes. There is rich documentary evidence for the Civil War and early Reconstruction period because of the widely followed, nationally reported daring and violent deeds of a band of outlawed men led by Henry Berry Lowry,[3] who has become a culture hero for Robeson Indians (Barton 1979; Blu 1980; Dial 1993; Dial and Eliades 1975; Evans 1971; Lucas and Groome 1940). Henry Berry Lowry was a Robeson Indian who took up arms against the white men who had killed his father and brother in what Indians interpreted as an attempt to take their family's land, located in the general area known at the time as "Scuffletown" to whites, and as "The Settlement" to Indians. In the rough-and-tumble period surrounding the end of the Civil War, Henry Berry and several kinsmen and friends managed to avenge the deaths by killing those deemed responsible. Subsequently he and his band were outlawed, and thereafter they were forced to live by their wits, stealing from certain whites and, it is said by Indians, redistributing what they stole to their needy friends and neighbors. They became legends in their own time by staying active over a ten-year span, and Henry Berry Lowry, the leader, was never captured or killed, despite a huge reward offered for him dead or alive. In the end, many gang members were killed or imprisoned, but Henry Berry simply disappeared. People still argue about what really happened to him, the best sort of fate for a legendary hero. He and his men live on in countless stories and in an outdoor drama, "Strike at the Wind," organized and produced by Lumbees since 1976. Because white Democrats (who were Conservatives at that time) raised a local militia, and even called in federal troops in unsuccessful attempts to stop them, the activities of the Lowry band were widely reported in both state and nation.

Materials written at the time provide provocative glimpses of community life in about 1870. They mostly concentrate on the locale whites called Scuffletown, an area that included the place that was to become Pembroke. G. A. Townsend, a Yankee reporter for the *New York Herald* newspaper, was sent to investigate the activities of the band at a time when the national political struggle between Radicals and Conservatives was at its height. His sympathies were strongly Northern and anti-Conservative, to judge from his writings. He compiled a book from the reports sent to the paper from North Carolina (Townsend 1872).

Townsend described Scuffletown as one of two large aggregations of traditionally free and not-white settlements in the state, the other being in

Halifax County (1872:41). He located it astride the main east-west railroad between two station stops, one in the center of the county, the other on the western margin:

> These two stations bound Scuffletown, which spreads besides three or four miles on both sides of the track, and is surrounded on three sides with swamps, which send branches of swamp up through it. . . . These swamps enclose the rivers and their arteries laterally for a few yards, and often, or generally, as the stream winds, there is [sic] swamps on one side and low clay sandbluffs opposite. It is a mean country for troops to trespass upon, but not an impregnable country. [Townsend 1872:42]

Wet weather made the water in the rivers, swamps, and branches rise, so that "this region is almost flooded, and then the only means of inter-communication are small paths, known only to the inhabitants, which connect the island like patches and afford a labyrinthian, mazes for escape to any who keep the clues" (Townsend 1872:43), as the Lowry band did. He goes on to describe the luxuriant undergrowth of summer, hindering visibility, and the winter flooding, hindering movement, together with an abundance of poisonous snakes and wildcats that kill pigs and lambs (Townsend 1872:43).

Within this watery, overgrown area with cleared hummocks, he remarks: "The stranger who expects to see in Scuffletown any approach to a municipal settlement will be disappointed. It is the name of a tract of several miles, covered at wide intervals with hills and log cabins of the rudest and simplest construction, sometime[s] a half dozen of these huts being proximate" (Townsend 1872:43). Here is a vaguely defined space with clusters of houses scattered about, a pattern that can still be seen today, after the clearing and draining of the land, with considerable material improvement in the quality of housing.

Might these clusters be family groupings? A man named Henderson, who also sent reports back to the *Herald,* noted that when he was taken to visit Henry Berry Lowry's mother, he went by Henry Berry's house, which was built "on his father Allen's estate" (Townsend 1872:74), and just before passing Henry Berry's house, he passed the cabin of Andrew Strong, Henry Berry's wife's brother. Henry Berry's brother Sinclair was also living nearby (Townsend 1872:72). As to the association of family with a settlement and degrees of family prominence, Townsend cites a white Robesonian who said: "'The Lowerys and Oxendines were generally accounted the highest families in Scuffletown'" (1872:48). An anonymous handwritten manuscript that discusses the Lowry band and appears to have been composed by a white Robesonian about 1872 refers to Scuffletown as "the centre of the Lowry tribe." The manuscript refers to the inhabitants of Scuffletown as Indians (Anonymous ca. 1872:1, 3).

What the nature of communal life was then is more difficult to delineate, but again there are clues. Townsend remarks that within the Scuffletown settlement, two or three establishments sold "a low character of spirits . . . where the dwellings are densest" (1872:43). The selling and making of liquor is an old and strong tradition in this area of North Carolina. It is a tradition that was still being observed in the late 1960s when alcoholic beverages could only be sold illegally. Bootleggers, some selling legally made but illegally imported and retailed liquor, wine, and beer, and some selling the products of highly illegal local stills, were flourishing. Since the state has allowed local options to sell alcohol, the bootlegging trade has diminished, I understand, but hangs on through after-hours trade and through the patronage of those who do not wish their purchases to be monitored by a wider public, a matter of some importance in a fundamentalist Christian atmosphere.

Townsend and Henderson were both received with great hospitality when they visited the Scuffletown settlement; they were fed and housed with the best that a household could offer. When Henderson stayed at Henry Berry Lowry's house, the household gave him the bed and everyone else slept on the floor. The next morning, he breakfasted on "the same chicken we had tried the night before" (Townsend 1872:79). Chicken for supper would not have been an everyday meal in those difficult post-Civil War times. The anonymous manuscript provides several vignettes of life in that earlier time. Churches were already important aspects of community life, and Henry Berry and his "crowd," despite their being sought by the law, apparently attended New Hope Church in Scuffletown at least occasionally. It also describes the wedding of Rhoda Strong and Henry Berry Lowry, which drew what is estimated at two hundred people, including two white men, and offered supper set up in the yard of Henry Berry's mother's house on a seventy-five-foot table that was "literally groaning under the many good things it supported" (Anonymous ca. 1872:16-17, 20).

Later, in 1885, about a dozen men with Indian surnames petitioned the North Carolina legislature to grant a charter of incorporation for a proposed town of Oxendineville, which would have an Indian mayor (Elias Oxendine) and constable (John V. Oxendine) and at least one Indian commissioner (Angus Chavis). This Indian attempt to create a town predates the founding of Pembroke in 1892 and appears to have been in the same general area (Oxendineville 1885). Section 6 of the petition raises the issue of strong drink:

The mayor and commissioners of said town shall have the power to grant to such person or persons as they see fit a license to sell and retail spirituous liquors within the corporate limits of said town, and all laws and clauses of laws which by enumeration of distances or otherwise prohibit the sale of spirituous, vinous or malt liquors in territory embraced by said town incorporation, are hereby repealed in so far as they relate to said town and no further. [Oxendineville 1885][4]

It appears that spirituous liquors could have been sold within the town by virtue of a waiver of laws that would prevent the sales in other places, if the mayor and commissioners approved. The justification for the waiver is not made manifest, nor do we know whether this was to be a highly special case.

But we do know that Oxendineville never came into being. It is not clear what happened to this would-be town, as the notations on the petition suggest that the committee on corporations considered the bill and recommended its passage. It would have been the only town in the county designated by a distinctively Indian family surname. Many towns and communities were named after whites: Alfordsville, Rowland, Howellsville, Buies, Pates, and many more. But in 1885, Indians were being forced into an increasingly segregated racial system created through a series of Jim Crow laws designed for blacks. The attempt to assert pride of place and the right to name an incorporated town with an unambiguously Indian label occurred at the same time the Indians, after considerable lobbying, were given legal recognition as a separate "race" by the state and granted the right to have schools of their own, separate from both blacks and whites. To this day, there is still no town in Robeson County officially named with one of the local, distinctively Indian, surnames (see Thomas 1982).

By 1888, Hamilton McMillan, a white state legislator and local historian from Robeson County, reported that the Indians owned sixteen churches, both Baptist and Methodist, and that their schoolhouses, "built entirely by private means," were framed and therefore presumably more expensive than log or plank buildings.[5] He further praised their roads, which at that time had to be built and maintained by local residents, as "the best public roads in North Carolina" (McMillan 1888:21). The Reverend J. J. Blanks, a Lumbee, noted in an essay appended to the 1898 republication of McMillan's 1888 work on the history of the Lumbee that "the first places of worship among our people were Hammond Church, Chapel, Prospect and New Hope." By 1898 he counted some twenty-five Indian churches (1898:29, 35). Blanks was both minister and school-teacher, although the way was not easy. To gain those positions, he worked in the local turpentine industry to get through school. He says, initially referring to himself in the third person:

> When the writer's father agreed for him to go to school in order to prepare for [becoming] a teacher, he had to chip boxes morning and evening to pay his way in an entered term of school. And when this two months' term was out his father agreed for him to go . . . and that he would pay board, but that I would have to furnish clothes. So I went into the woods of Dr. S. B. Rozier and dipped turpentine enough to purchase my clothing and then attended school for two months, standing an examination before Prof. J. A. McAllister in 1890, since which time I have been teaching. [Blanks 1898:34][6]

Within a twelve-year period, from 1885 to 1898, the Indians went from having no Indian teachers to fifteen.

Before the disfranchisement of non-whites by the North Carolina constitution of 1835, Robeson Indians could move quite freely through the landscape, physical and social. McMillan, in an 1890 letter to the historian Stephen B. Weeks, stated, "Between 1783 and 1835 they [the Indians] attended the schools along with white people—attended the churches with whites, owned slaves and mustered and voted as white men did. Prior to 1835 they were divided as now between the parties of the day" (1890:34). A Lumbee elder, a man then of more than ninety years, recounted the tradition of schooling and race relations to me in 1973:

> Whites and Indians started schools where they paid teachers, and they all went to school together. These Indians were smart. We went to church together [with whites]. When the Southern states seceded [from the Union], the whites got against the Indians. They were jealous because they [the Indians] were farmers and smart and industrious. When I was a boy I went to Bethel Church, only we called it Dogwood Church on account of it had dogwoods all around it. This was a Southern Methodist church. The church had three rows of pews and two aisles. It had slats between the pews [separating sections]. I asked, "What's this slat here for?" [They told me,] When the [Civil] War came, whites nailed down the slats. Indians were supposed to be on one side and whites on the other. . . . Later on the whites left the Indians the church and built another church and said we weren't supposed to come there.

Schools and churches were both local institutions over which Indians increasingly sought and gained control, partly by using the very system of segregation that they also fought.

Communities and settlements continued to be significant places for political organization. During the pursuit by some Indians of federal recognition as "Cherokee Indians," O. M. McPherson, who had been sent to Robeson County as a special Indian agent to investigate and report on these claims, met with Indians from different settlements. In a letter of August 6, 1914, he reported to the commissioner of Indian affairs:

> On Monday, August 3, I visited the homes of a large number of Indians living southwest of Lumberton in what are known as the Sampson and Hunt settlements. I took notes of their condition and conferred freely with them concerning their history, tribal rights, needs, conditions, and as to what Congress could best do for them. Tuesday, August 4, I conferred with a large number of the Indians in Lumberton, along the same lines, who had come in by arrangement to meet me for such a conference. Yesterday I spent the entire day at Pembroke in a similar conference with the Indians of the Pembroke neighborhood, and conferred with a very large number. I had made arrangements to visit the homes of the Indians of the Pembroke district to-day, but had to postpone the trip on account of rainy weather. [McPherson 1915:245]

He reported that for the academic year 1912-13, there were twenty-seven Indian schools (McPherson 1915:25). The Indians were denied federal recognition as Cherokees, although they already had been so designated by the state.

Undaunted, other Indians mounted a drive for federal recognition as "Siouan Indians" in the 1930s. Included in a typescript "Indian Office Handbook of Information—'Reservation'" compiled by John Pearmain, a federal official in the Indian division of the Resettlement Administration, dated October 1935, are replies to questions Pearmain asked of Joseph Brooks, "Tribal Delegate," in Washington, D.C., on September 9. Brooks's residence is given as Pembroke, and he reportedly told Pearmain:

> There are 10 Siouan communities centered around Pembroke, and averaging about 8 miles from Pembroke, with one community 25 miles away. All are natural communities, with a Day School (public school) in each of the 10 communities. (More schools than that in all.) All are straight Indian schools [schools for Indians only], paid for by the State of North Carolina. [Pearmain 1935:42]

Here again we see the Indian conception of the larger community of Indians being composed of a series of neighborhood communities and the association of schools with local communities.

Pearmain's report and that of Fred A. Baker (1935) both affirm that most Indians at the time were farming, and that although a few were relatively well-off, and some were small farmers, a large majority were landless tenants in need of assistance at that time of the Great Depression.

Baker went to Robeson County in the summer of 1935 to meet with those calling themselves Siouan Indians as a part of a survey of needs and possible tracts of land for a federal resettlement project. His report is eloquent and impassioned in regard to the suffering of tenant farmers and their great need for land to cultivate and control on their own. At that time, less than half the land in Robeson and surrounding counties was under cultivation (Baker 1935:6). He also confirmed the importance of the kind of diffuse rural community already described: "As to the plan of resettlement it was the consensus of opinion among the Indians that the 'neighborhood' plan instead of the village plan should be adopted. All were outspoken in favor of having each home out on the land which is the universal custom among the members of this group" (Baker 1935:10).

When Guy B. Johnson, a sociologist for many years at the University of North Carolina, Chapel Hill, did research in Pembroke in the late 1930s, he reported that Indians ideally desired to own their own farms and not be bossed by anyone else. All the Indians were farmers except for "a handful of teachers, preachers, and small shopkeepers" (Johnson 1939:521). Johnson identified both accomplishments and arenas of struggle for Indians at the time:

> He ["the Indian"] sees his vote count for almost nothing because of the wiles of the County Democratic Machine. [There was a one-party system throughout the South at that time.] He sees his one little town, Pembroke, his social center and seat of his normal school, taken over largely by white merchants. He sees the selection of town officers removed from his own control and placed in the hands of the legislature so that white people can be appointed. He has been, from Reconstruction days until the past year, without representation on any jury in Robeson County. [1939:522]

That the Indians were finally able to sit on juries apparently came about through their own efforts: "The Indians are becoming more group conscious. They have recently demanded the right to serve on juries, they are talking of running for political office, and they are saying among themselves that 'if things don't get better we may have to start killing'" (Johnson 1939:523). This bespeaks an active Indian community aggressively moving forward on a number of fronts, in the fighting spirit of the Henry Berry Lowry era.

Finally, Johnson made some remarks that we can now further interpret: "There are certain families and certain neighborhoods which are known as 'tough', and these produce an unusual amount of drunkenness, assault, and homicide" (1939:522). This characterization sounds much like that given for the Union Chapel community in more recent years, but in any event, the term "neighborhoods" almost certainly refers to what I have called "communities."

Union Chapel, together with eleven other "districts," including Pembroke, Prospect, Magnolia, and Piney Grove, were announced in 1950 as monthly meeting places by the Lumbee Brotherhood, a group "created to bring about a cooperative spirit, regardless of religious affiliations" (Indian Group 1950). The most prominent organizers of the Brotherhood were also men who were the driving forces behind the ultimately successful political move to have their people recognized by the state and federal governments as Lumbee Indians.[7]

## Community and History

Reading older documentary sources in the light of what we know about modern Indian communities in Robeson County shows us the continuing diffuseness of local communities, their lack of clear-cut boundaries (both Scuffletown settlement and Pembroke community). It is also evident that the communities have long been ascribed varied characters that can change over time (Pembroke's goes from wild and violent to progressive, respectable, and culturally central). Our attention is drawn to the increasingly vital roles played by the two institutions most closely linked to local communities—churches and schools. These institutions perhaps were most crucial during the period of legal racial segregation. Communities still have churches, but many have lost their local schools in the rush to consolidation that followed the successes of the Civil Rights Movement in the 1960s. Some Indians have suggested to me that as a result of losing so many local schools, the strength of attachment to local communities is weaker than it was twenty-five years ago. But it seems to me that while the institutions associated with local areas have changed, people nonetheless continue to identify themselves importantly in local community terms, perhaps partly because families still cluster there. Communities also continue to be bases for political mobilization.

If we return to the question of how the Indian community in its wider and more encompassing sense has persisted amidst the vast changes described here in the look and use of the land, in patterns of daily life, and in ways of making a living, one of the answers surely lies in the continuing existence and perhaps proliferation of the *local* Indian communities. There families remain interconnected, by proximity and intermarriage, and local leaders consolidate a power base from which to attempt to influence a wider audience. Here, too, lie the multiple kinds of connectedness (of kin, neighbor, fellow worker, church goer, schoolchild, or parent) that the term community originally conveyed.

Finally, the variety of ways to be Indian expressed by Lumbees in their different characterizations of local communities suggests a moral universe with a range of possibilities for Indian behavior. There are many ways to be legitimately Indian, none of which is unequivocally better than another, and each of which can be a virtue or a problem, depending upon circumstances and point of view. To be "progressive" is to compete effectively with whites but also to fail to conserve valued traditions. To be prosperous and conservative of traditions is to risk being smug and closed minded. To marry one's cousins shows respect and value for family and consolidates landholdings but isolates one from connections with other communities and opens one to accusations of standoffishness. When the set of localized identities is brought into play, boasting is met with teasing, a surfeit of pride with criticism, one exemplary style counterpoised against another. The jostling of local community identities indirectly provides a forum for discussing Indianness, one that helps to account for the flexibility and adaptability present-day Indians and their ancestors have needed to survive in changing circumstances that are often beyond their direct control.

But it must be recalled that the diverse characters of the localized communities are subsumed for some purposes and in some contexts by the more encompassing sense of "the Indian community," which suggests a unity of identity that includes a dialogue about itself in the form of the localized communities. The larger sense of community poses a commonality of identity that contrasts with a national American identity under some circumstances. To a degree, Indians who consider Robeson County to be home have carved out an identity in opposition to a national American identity, but one that is neither nationalist nor separatist in its formulation.

## Acknowledgments

Many people have contributed in different ways to this enterprise. Fred Eggan and Raymond D. Fogelson inspired me to work with American Indians and supported my efforts through the years. The Indian people of Robeson County who spent countless hours over many years trying to help an outsider understand their history, their situation, their desires for the future cannot be named because I promised them anonymity in standard anthropological fashion, but my debt to them is enormous. Raymond J. DeMallie never stopped encouraging me to write, and provided along the way an exemplary model for doing ethnohistory. He read and offered excellent comments on a number of manuscripts. Others have read parts of this piece and made helpful suggestions: Keith Basso, Edward Casey, Steven Feld, Clifford Geertz, Jason Baird Jackson, Joan Lehn, Frank T. Miller. I am deeply obliged to them all.

# Notes

1. The summary of changes in the landscape and of the nature of contemporary communities and their connection to homeplace was developed for a seminar on "Place, Expression, and Experience" organized by Keith Basso and Steven Feld at the School of American Research in 1993. These are detailed and developed differently in Blu (forthcoming).

2. See especially Neely's maps of the mostly dispersed communities (1992:30-31) and her description of the Snowbird Cherokee community living on their own land but dispersed among non-Indian neighbors (1992:40).

3. This is the commonest spelling of the surname Lowry today. However, in various documents, past and present, the name also appears as Lowrie, Lowery, or Lowrey. I have consistently used Lowry, except where original sources used one of the other spellings, and then I have retained the original. The names refer to the same people or set of people, unless otherwise indicated.

4. I am obliged to Geoffrey Mangum, Esq., for the reference and for the trouble he took to locate the original and to send me a photocopy.

5. Michael Ann Williams discusses the differences in older styles of houses in southwestern North Carolina in *Homeplace* (1991). I have assumed that the terminology her informants used would be similar to that used here. All three types of buildings—plank, log, and framed—were present in Robeson County in the nineteenth century.

6. According to Silver (1990:124), one common method of obtaining turpentine (resin) "was to cut large rectangular notches, called 'boxes', on both sides of larger longleaf pines. The valuable sap collected on the flat bottom edge of the box," from where it was "dipped" or ladled out and put into barrels. In Blanks's text, cutting notches is referred to as "chipping boxes."

7. The North Carolina General Assembly designated the people Lumbee Indians in 1953, and the U.S. Congress so designated them in 1956.

# References

Anonymous
   ca. 1872   [Untitled handwritten manuscript relating the origins of the Lowry band.] Location of original unknown, photocopy in possession of author.
Baker, Fred A.
   1935      [Report to the commissioner of Indian affairs, Washington, D.C, July 9.] A Preliminary Survey of Conditions among the Indians of Robeson County to Determine the Feasibility of a Land Purchase-Work Relief Project. Typed manuscript. Location of original unknown, photocopy of carbon quadruplicate copy in possession of author.
Barton, Garry Lewis
   1979      The Life and Times of Henry Berry Lowry. Pembroke, N.C.: Lumbee Publishing.
Blanks, J. J.
   1898      Part Two: The Croatan Indians in the Late War—Their Progress in Education and Religion. *In* The Lost Colony Found: An Historical Sketch of the

Discovery of the Croatan Indians, by Hamilton McMillan, 28-35, Lumberton, N.C.: Robesonian Job Print.

Blu, Karen I.
1980    The Lumbee Problem: The Making of an American Indian People. Cambridge: Cambridge University Press.
forthcoming    "Where Do You Stay At?": Homeplace and Community among the Lumbee. *In* Place, Expression, and Experience, edited by Keith Basso and Steven Feld. Santa Fe, N. Mex.: School of American Research Press.

DeMallie, Raymond J.
1993    "These Have No Ears": Narrative and the Ethnohistorical Method. Ethnohistory 40:515-38.

Dial, Adolph L.
1993    The Lumbee. New York: Chelsea House.

Dial, Adolph L., and David K. Eliades
1975    The Only Land I Know: A History of the Lumbee Indians. San Francisco: Indian Historian Press.

Evans, W. McKee
1966    Ballots and Fence Rails: Reconstruction on the Lower Cape Fear. Chapel Hill: University of North Carolina Press.
1971    To Die Game: The Story of the Lowry Band, Indian Guerrillas of Reconstruction. Baton Rouge: Louisiana State University Press.

Fenton, William N.
1953    The Iroquois Eagle Dance: An Offshoot of the Calumet Dance. Smithsonian Institution, Bureau of American Ethnology Bulletin 156. Washington, D.C.

Fogelson, Raymond D.
1975    An Analysis of Cherokee Sorcery and Witchcraft Beliefs and Practices. *In* Four Centuries of Southern Indians, edited by Charles Hudson, 113-31. Athens: University of Georgia Press.

Gilbert, WIlliam Harlen, Jr.
1943    The Eastern Cherokees. Smithsonian Institution, Anthropological Paper 23, Bureau of American Ethnology Bulletin 133. Washington, D.C.

Indian Group
1950    Indian Group to Hold Meetings on Regular Schedule. Unidentified newspaper clipping, dateline Pembroke, N.C., dated in pencil Nov. 14, 1950, no indication of source. Pembroke State University Archives: 50.

Johnson, Guy B.
1939    Personality in a White-Indian-Negro Community. American Sociological Review 4: 516-23.

Kilpatrick, Alan Edwin
1991    "Going to the Water": A Structural Analysis of Cherokee Purification Rituals. American Indian Culture and Research Journal 15(4):49-58.

Kupferer, Harriet Jane
1966    The "Principal People" 1960: A Study of Cultural and Social Groups of the Eastern Cherokee. Smithsonian Institution, Anthropological Paper 78, Bureau of American Ethnology Bulletin 196. Washington, D.C.

Lucas, John Paul, Jr., and Bailey T. Groome
1940    The King of Scuffletoun: A Croatan Romance. Richmond, Va.: Garrett and Massie.

McMillan, Hamilton
1888    Sir Walter Raleigh's Lost Colony. Wilson, N.C.: Advance Presses.
1890    Letter to Stephen B. Weeks, Dec. 11, 1890. Bound in a copy of McMillan 1888. Stephen B. Weeks Collection, University of North Carolina Library, Chapel Hill.
McPherson, O. M.
1915    Indians of North Carolina: A Report on the Condition and Tribal Rights of the Indians of Robeson and Adjoining Counties of North Carolina. 63rd Cong., 3rd Sess. Sen. Doc. 677.
Mitchell, Joseph
1992    Up in the Old Hotel and Other Stories. New York: Pantheon Books.
Neely, Sharlotte
1992    Adaptation and the Contemporary North Carolina Cherokee Indians. *In* Indians of the Southeastern United States in the Late 20th Century, edited by J. Anthony Paredes, 29-43. Tuscaloosa: University of Alabama Press.
Oxendineville
1885    An Act to Incorporate the Town of Oxendineville in the County of Robeson, Jan. 21, 1885. Legislative Records of General Assembly, Legislative Papers, Engrossed Bills, 1885, Box 1144, North Carolina State Archives, Raleigh.
Pearmain, John D., comp.
1935    Indian Office Handbook of Information—Reservation: Siouan Tribe of Indians of Robeson County, North Carolina. Typed manuscript. Location of original unknown. Photocopy of fifth carbon copy in possession of author.
Silver, Timothy
1990    A New Face on the Countryside: Indians, Colonists, and Slaves in South Atlantic Forests, 1500-1800. Cambridge: Cambridge University Press.
Thomas, Maud
1982    Away Down Home: A History of Robeson County, North Carolina. Lumberton, N.C.: Historic Robeson.
Townsend, George Alfred
1872    The Swamp Outlaws. New York: Robert M. De Witt.
Wahrhaftig, Albert L.
1975    Institution Building Among Oklahoma's Traditional Cherokees. *In* Four Centuries of Southern Indians, edited by Charles Hudson, 132-47. Athens: University of Georgia Press.
Williams, Michael Ann
1991    Homeplace: The Social Use and Meaning of the Folk Dwelling in Southwestern North Carolina. Athens: University of Georgia Press.

# 12

# The Dynamics of Pueblo Cultural Survival

ALFONSO ORTIZ

In confronting any question having to do with the Pueblos of New Mexico and Arizona, considered as a group, we must first ask whether it makes any sense at all to lump them together for any purpose. After all, the term *Pueblos* today encompasses some forty thousand people speaking six mutually unintelligible languages and occupying thirty-odd villages stretched along a rough crescent of more than four hundred miles. In other words, we must consider whether the term *Pueblos,* like the term *Indian,* only denotes an artificial category invented by the Spanish invaders of the sixteenth century for their own purposes and perpetuated in our time by anthropologists and other non-Indians for their own, presumably more exalted, purposes. This question has to be at the heart of any discussion of the survival and persistence of the people presumably encompassed by the term because, at the very least, if the question of specifically Pueblo cultural survival is to be meaningful, there must be some cultural level or levels at which the people knew and know themselves to be different, as a group, from other Indian and non-Indian peoples long in residence near them in the Southwest.

I shall not attempt to sustain any further suspense with my question, because I do indeed believe that we can demonstrate that the peoples called Pueblos, despite their linguistic diversity and wide geographical range, have, at various times reaching far into dim prehistory, shared a sense of cultural similarity, just as they have shared a common homeland. This sense of cultural similarity has probably never settled on any single thing held or believed in common among all Pueblos in their long existence. That this is so might have presented us with a dilemma in the past, when anthropologists were trained to look for some invariant property or properties common to all of the societies being grouped together. This search went on at either the social structural or the cultural level and yielded everything from a common principle of descent to shared symbols of identity.

For the Pueblos, this quest for something universal would be fruitless, at least for the past two thousand years of their existence. The Pueblos, it seems safe to say, have never all shared an institution, nor have they ever had common symbols of cultural identity. Indeed, the institution coming closest to being universal to the Pueblos is the so-called "kachina cult" in its various manifestations, but even this is not found in the northern Tiwa Pueblos of Taos and Picuris.

With the Pueblos we must, indeed, assume a long-term interactionist perspective, one which does not assume that there is a shared property common to all of them, but rather that there have always been shifting clusters of experiences and meanings that have overlapped several groups at the same time, and different groups at other times. Such a long-term interactionist perspective represents an attempt to replicate on the cultural level Fred Eggan's method of controlled comparison, which has proven so successful on the social level (Eggan 1954). It is also similar to Ludwig Wittgenstein's philosophy of language, which he illustrates with the analogy of "family resemblances" (Wittgenstein 1953). Whenever several generations of a large family gather together an external observer is struck by the number of broad physical similarities obtaining among the family members. One knows they are related because of their general physical similarity to one another, yet one cannot point to any single physical characteristic all of them share in common. Instead, there are a multitude of relationships "overlapping and crisscrossing." A second analogy Wittgenstein employs for this concept is that of a thread, in which "the strength of the thread does not reside in the fact that some one fibre runs through its whole length, but in the overlapping of the fibres" (Wittgenstein 1953; Wittgenstein in Edwards 1967:335, 340).

So it is also with the Pueblos; one recognizes enough broad similarities in proceeding from Hopi to Taos (or vice versa) to know that the Pueblos are related to one another culturally and that they belong together conceptually, but one just cannot put a finger on any invariant cultural property held in common throughout the Pueblo crescent at any one time. Such generalizations that are possible to make about the Pueblos—such as that they all have kivas or that they all built multi-story houses—are vacuous in terms of analytical force and explanatory value.

There is, however, one non-social structural and non-cultural factor shared by all of the Pueblos surviving to our time which helps us to understand why and how they survived, and I shall lead into the substance of my discussion with it. I refer to the fact that the Pueblos have never been displaced from their homelands, something almost unique among North American Indian groups. To be sure, they have presided over a steadily shrinking world since late prehistoric times, but the fact remains that, after more than four centuries of European exploration and colonization, most of the Pueblo people still live in places of their own choosing. The importance of this for cultural survival cannot be overemphasized, for, indeed, we might say that the Pueblos only believe in what they see and experience, and in their homeland they can see what they believe. Anthropologists have been inadequately sensitive, I think, to the role a well-established sense of place, of belonging to a space, can play in a people's will to endure. We are just now, in very recent years, beginning to understand how important this sense of place can be. If the Pueblos teach us nothing else, let us learn at least this much from them.

During many long centuries of prehistory the Pueblo people had most of the Southwest to themselves to live in. During this time they imposed their own meanings on the lands and they left quiet monuments to their presence in the form of shrines, many of which are still recognized and visited. There was considerable contact between these prehistoric Pueblo groups. The trails of specific historic Pueblo groups criss-crossed in such maddening patterns during the last centuries preceding European contact that it is still an arena of almost pure conjecture to attempt to state what historic group came from which area of prehistoric occupation. We do know that they traded widely among one another for, among other things, innovations in design or techniques of pottery manufacture quickly became disseminated widely over areas that were otherwise culturally distinguishable from one another. Similarly, there has always been a brisk trade in objects such as crystals and other minerals, materials for tools and weapons such as chert, obsidian and fibrolite, medicines, salt, piñon nuts, and other items too numerous to list here. Hopi mantas and other woven items were prized throughout the Pueblos. Aside from trading expeditions and trade fairs, diverse Pueblo peoples were often brought together by lengthy hunting trips into the mountains and plains, salt-gathering pilgrimages, piñon-gathering encampments, summer farming sites, and even calamities such as warfare, drought, and pestilence. Hence, the Pueblo peoples have always been able to cope in a variety of cultural as well as ecological environments.

In the purely religious realm, strikingly similar kachinas have been known from the Hopi villages to the Rio Grande, and there have long been Zuni and Tewa clowns at Hopi, Keresan clowns and medicine men among the Tewa, and Jemez medicine men also among the Tewa. The initiations for most of these borrowed religious practitioners were and are still conducted only in the Pueblos where they originated. Specialist medicine men also traveled freely through different Pueblos, however far-flung, to treat those who needed them. The Pueblos have also always been known, down through history, to "re-seed" decaying traditions from nearby vital

Pueblos, even across linguistic boundaries. Even priesthoods which have died out in a given Pueblo because of epidemic or other natural disasters are "replanted," to use the native agricultural terminology, by priests from other Pueblos who train and initiate new members for the unfortunate community. This, presumably, is how the borrowed religious specialists originated.

It should come as no surprise, finally, that the various Pueblo linguistic groups mention at least those others adjacent to them in their stories of genesis and other aspects of their traditional histories, something they do not do with any frequency for the Spaniards and the things they introduced, nor for the later Americans and the things that they, in turn, introduced. At the very least, this awareness of other Pueblo groups at the level of their respective genesis traditions speaks of a long, long period of mutual awareness and co-existence, facts that are borne out by the prehistoric evidence.

Prehistoric interaction was not confined to Pueblo groups, but extended to the civilizations of Meso-America as well. Pottery, maize, and, later, parrot feathers, copper bells, some architectural and astronomical knowledge and, perhaps, some religious practices came up from the south over the span of many centuries. How many non-material things actually derived from Meso-America, despite surface similarities between the two areas in many beliefs, is difficult to gauge until much more carefully determinate evidence is in. For our purposes it is sufficient to state that there was a wider awareness through trade, an awareness that, moreover, underscores the mutual pan-Pueblo consciousness during this prehistoric period. As Meso-American traits were adopted by the Pueblos, they became culturally similar in those accretions at least.

On the eve of the Spanish invasion, then, the numerous and superficially diverse Pueblo worlds had already been intersecting and overlapping for centuries in many complex ways. Their adaptability and willingness to aid each other, even across language barriers, had already been demonstrated. Indeed, we might characterize Pueblo existence in general after fifteen hundred years of *in situ* cultural development as being like an accordion. When times were good, the Pueblos expanded, at one time occupying portions of what are now five large Southwestern states. As the land slowly dried up, most of them contracted into the valleys carved by the major watercourses, and here they stayed. Other expansions and contractions, but mainly the latter, were occasioned by warfare and pestilence, but always those seem to have occurred within the context of a common sense of destiny.

The Pueblo traits of adaptability and cultural tenacity were put to a severe test by that rapacious Spanish murderer, Francisco Vásquez de Coronado, whose plundering escapades anthropologists and historians have usually glossed over as acts of exploration. He and his forces rolled into the Pueblo Southwest in 1540-41 and sent shock waves throughout the Pueblos with their murder and plunder at some Tiwa villages near present-day Albuquerque. Then they rolled out again, and the Pueblos had four decades to think about what the Coronado intrusion meant, and what they would do with it when and if it came again. It seems from the historical record since that the seeds for the Pueblos' later pattern of passive but effective resistance were planted at that time.

One specific response to external threat that was to prove characteristic of the Pueblos for at least the next two centuries was already very much in evidence when a group of Coronado's men attempted to visit the ancestral Tewa village of Yunque, on the west bank of the Rio Grande, in 1541. On learning of the approach of the Spaniards, the people of Yunque fled to take refuge in four of their ancestral villages in the mountains. Similar flights to mountain fastnesses or to other places not easily accessible to the Spaniards would be undertaken by various Pueblo groups during the seventeenth and early-eighteenth centuries. The people of present-day Sandia fled to Hopi, the Jemez into the Navajo country, Taos and Picuris to Cuartelejo in the Plains and, most memorably, the southern Tewa to Hopi in 1696. Much cultural exchange likely went on during those periods and many previously clear distinctions among these people blurred.

Following the effective Spanish colonization of their country in 1598, the Pueblos along the Rio Grande and its tributaries settled down to a very difficult eighty-two years of Spanish subjugation. These were years during which the civil and ecclesiastical authorities of the Spaniards alternated with one another in imposing oppressive measures on the Pueblos. By 1680, after many years of repressive measures undertaken to stamp out their aboriginal religions, the Pueblos had taken enough. They arose in righteous revolution and drove the Spaniards back into Mexico, to begin more than a dozen years of relative peace and independence.

The Pueblo Revolt marked the beginning of the most intensive period of cultural revitalization undertaken by the Pueblos thus far in historic times. The period between 1680 and 1696 was also one in which occurred the greatest dislocations and mass movements of Pueblo people in historic times. If the Pueblos by this time still did not share a sense of cultural similarity, they certainly shared at least a sense of common historical destiny. It seems clear that by this time the Spanish oppression had forged among the Pueblos the sense of unity and common purpose necessary to defend Pueblo cultural integrity against Spanish onslaughts. Even the

Hopis, long relatively untouched because of their splendid isolation, began to be drawn into this wider historical consciousness.

The major legacy of interest with regard to cultural survival from the centuries of Spanish rule following the revolution of 1680 is one I discussed in *The Tewa World* (1969:62-72). There I noted that the Spaniards unwittingly gave to all of the Pueblos except the Hopis a set of political institutions that eventually enabled them to cope successfully not only with the Spaniards themselves, but with the Mexicans and, later, the Anglo-Americans as well. Those institutions of Spanish municipal government have enabled the Pueblos to manage and to keep at bay external influences they find threatening. Those institutions and attendant ideas have merely been adapted to adjust to the later American presence, and they are still being adjusted today. In contrast, the Hopis, upon whom was imposed an American-style constitution in 1936, have not yet in more than five decades been able to assimilate it into their inherited perceptions of governance and order. Clearly, it takes time to assimilate and adapt new institutions to a pre-existing order, and the Hopi just have not yet had this time. The remainder of the Pueblos have been able to tinker and to adjust, and so they evolved those originally Spanish concepts into another means of assisting them in their cultural survival and continued revitalization.

It has often been claimed that the Spanish and succeeding Mexican governments both recognized the Pueblos as "civilized," in contrast to the nomadic and semi-nomadic Apache and Navajo bands, and thereby aided in the Pueblos' survival. I am not quite sure what the meaning of this claim is. At best the policy of differential and, presumably, preferential treatment bore mixed results. During the seventeenth century, up until the Pueblo revolution of 1680, this official policy meant very little in terms of how the Pueblos were treated. The Pueblos still suffered such unrelenting pressures to abandon their traditional cultures that they had to rebel to regain their freedom and sense of dignity. After the Spaniards reimposed their domination over them, the Pueblos had certain legal recourses that they were able to use to increasingly better advantage during the eighteenth century, but this was very much an eighteenth-century phenomenon. And, at that, Spanish justice was by no means even-handed with regard to Pueblo rights. In fact, American-style justice has better served the Pueblos in their quest to maintain their cultural sovereignty, at least thus far. (The Mexican period was too short to compare meaningfully with the other two.)

Another historical factor further assisting the Pueblos in their efforts to survive as distinct cultural entities is peculiar to this, the American period. I refer to the emergence, late in the nineteenth century, of the image of the Indians of the Southwest, and most particularly the Pueblos, as artists. This followed upon the entry of the railroads and Fred Harvey hospitality houses into Pueblo country, and it was an image actively promoted by both the Santa Fe Railroad and the Harvey company. This image of the Pueblo peoples as artists has, moreover, survived unto the present time. Indeed, for many people in the Southwest today the only reality the Pueblos have is that of a people who peddle pots and jewelry under the portal of the historic Palace of the Governors in Santa Fe. This image does not permit of the most wholesome of existences for those people caught up in it, but it is far preferable to active racial hate or, worse, genocide. Unfortunately, too little is yet known about the popular image of the Pueblos as artists; perhaps scholars will eventually turn their attention to examining the genesis, elaboration, and long-term practical consequences of this image.

We come now to the ethnographic record to see what additional light it might shed on the question of Pueblo cultural survival. I consider it the most reliable of all the evidence available to us, for the archaeological record is still too full of puzzles with regard to the stubbornly insistent questions of just which historical Pueblo group was where during the critical period of classical Pueblo civilization between 900 and 1300 A.D., and just which group did what, when, where, and why. The historical record, in its turn, is sometimes mute or inadequate for important periods or hopelessly compromised by the observers' biases for anything but the most general of ethnohistorical considerations. We simply cannot get at Pueblo meanings for Pueblo events when most of the people who attempted to represent or interpret Pueblo realities were not only non-Pueblo Indians but were, indeed, individuals who had a vested interest in dismantling traditional Pueblo institutions—such as missionaries and government agents.

Let me pass quickly in review of those items of ethnographic knowledge already mentioned. I have noted that the Pueblos have traveled and traded widely among one another since far back into prehistoric times and that they traded not only material objects but, far more subtly, social institutions and religious knowledge and meanings as well. This pattern of extensive trading and exchange was not so much altered by the Spanish and Americans as it was augmented. They added new trade goods, new means of commerce and travel, and new saints' days for the calendar of commemoration and celebration. I have also noted that the Pueblos shared a mutual awareness in their traditional histories and that they put up an almost solid front of resistance to Spanish persecution when they finally decided to act. All of these factors bespeak a common sense of identity—although it is one that varies in intensity through time—and later, a common sense of destiny as well.

There is one final ethnographic phenomenon of the Pueblos that, in a sense, ties it all together. I refer to the complex ceremonial-festival networks in which all of the Pueblos have been known to participate since the beginning of historic times and probably far back into prehistory as well. From the ethnographic record on these dramatic performances we can now specify clearly what goes on in them on the cultural level, the level of meanings embodied in symbols. There are at least six levels of activity during a major Pueblo religious observance: the public ritual itself, the feeding of visitors from other Pueblos, brisk trade, the exchange of new and other useful information, socializing among young people of different Pueblos, and prayerful meditations and offerings by the priests in the kivas to ensure the success of the whole enterprise. Of these I will focus here only on the first, the public ritual itself, and then only on a very few recurrent themes of interest to us here.

In the grand public rituals around which the whirl of other activity takes place, the Pueblos repeatedly and regularly, through burlesque, caricature, and the occasional parody of clowns, draw a sharp contrast between the self and the not-self, between what is acceptably Pueblo and what is alien. They burlesque not only the government agents, Protestant missionaries, and anthropologists who have bedeviled them in modern times, but the Spaniards and their priests who beset upon them in earlier times as well. In the *Sandaro* of the Rio Grande Keresans and other ceremonies, the Pueblos depict the original coming of the Spaniards in extremely humorous, but also extremely instructive, ways. For example, in Jemez Pueblo each year on November 12, the appearance of a clown in black face wearing a long coat representing Esteban, the first black to enter Pueblo country in 1537, electrifies those onlookers who know what is going on. In such ways as this, throughout the year, the Pueblos take important events of the past that intruded upon them and freeze them into place, as it were, by anchoring the historical events onto symbolic vehicles of expression that are traditional and that, thereby, lock those events comfortably onto their own cultural landscape. This renders what may have begun as a disturbing and disruptive historical intrusion into a permanent, which is to say unvarying, and therefore, unharmful part of their communal experience. In this way they collapse history and, in so doing, they turn time into space as well. To the extent that they have been successful in neutralizing history through these symbolic performances they have avoided getting caught up in it. Again, this should serve as a warning to those who think they are dealing with Pueblo realities when they draw conclusions about what the Pueblos were or are from historical documents alone.

Much has been said of the images whites have of Indians, but the Pueblos, at least, also create images of whites in their mass public ritual dramas, images for their own people to believe in, images that clearly set them apart. They do this not only of Spaniards and other whites, but of other non-Pueblo Indians as well. Rarely, ever so rarely, do they make comic references to the customs of other Pueblo Indians, if we require any more proof at this point of a shared general consciousness operating among all Pueblos at some deep level. Keeping in mind that these are usually occasions during which many other Pueblo people participate as fellow celebrants, these occasions serve to reinforce their image of the self in contrast to the not-self.

Once again, as with the public external image of the Pueblos that exists in the minds of aficionados of Southwestern Indian art, the steadily enlarging, sometimes shifting images the Pueblos have of non-Pueblo peoples need to be studied very carefully, for they are yet other elements contributing to their healthy sense of self and identity and, hence, to their survival. In fact, the dramatic performances and other levels of activity characterizing the ceremonial-festival networks may well constitute the single most important mechanism of cultural survival and revitalization that the Pueblos have, now as well as in the distant past. If anything, it is becoming more vital and widespread in our times because modern modes of transportation enable Pueblo people to travel easily and speedily to religious and festival events occurring anywhere within the Pueblo crescent.

To sum up, then, I have here attempted to demonstrate that we can understand the mechanics of Pueblo cultural adaptability and survival through a careful examination, by means of a dynamic interactionist perspective, of the enduring cultural similarities and shared experiences that have united them through time. That the Pueblos, most of them, have survived is obvious to anyone who knows them. That they can revitalize is also obvious, for revitalization is a way of life for them. It is not just a challenge of the present or recent past, but something that they have had to do regularly for as long as we can trace their presence on the peculiar landscape we know today as the American Southwest. When they came up out of their caves as Basketmakers early in the European Christian era and began to adapt themselves to life as village-building, pottery-making, maize-growers they had to revitalize; when they had to abandon their great towns in Chaco Canyon and Mesa Verde during the thirteenth century and move to areas of more dependable water sources they had to revitalize; when Coronado cut a wide swath through them in the middle of the sixteenth century they had to revitalize; after their great revolution of 1680, when they cast off the yoke of Spanish oppression, they had to revitalize; after a widespread epidemic of smallpox sharply decimated their numbers in 1781-82 they had to revitalize; when there were threats to their remaining land base late in the last century and during the first two decades of this century they had to revitalize; since at least 1960, with renewed threats to their sovereignty and to their land and water rights they have again had to revitalize, and even now they are in the process of doing so. Those numerous revitalization efforts have simply not attracted much attention among scholars because most of their efforts have proceeded quietly and without fanfare.

In this long-demonstrated ability to, as one Tewa metaphor states it, reinvigorate decaying vines from nearby vital ones, lies the strength of the Pueblo people and their prime hope for the future. From my reading of the evidence here I would like to conclude that, for Americans, the Pueblos, like the poor, you shall have always with you. Indeed, shifting to a Pueblo perspective, I do not think that it should be an object of any surprise at all that these mature and sophisticated civilizations have survived two thousand years of *in situ* cultural development; the real wonder lies in the fact that a young and savage American nation has managed to survive over two hundred years.

I would have the temerity to make one final observation. I confess that I find the entire notion of revitalization a trifle culturally hidebound, for I suspect that if we had a comparably rich texture of historical detail for other cultures as we have for the Pueblos we would find that revitalization is not a challenge come uniquely to them under the impact of industrial civilization but, truly, a regularly reoccurring imperative. What we are dealing with here, I believe, are several distinctive manifestations of a universal and noble human aspiration—namely, the will to endure.

# References

Edwards, Paul, ed.
   1967      Encyclopedia of Philosophy, vol. 8. New York: Macmillan.
Eggan, Fred
   1954      Social Anthropology and the Method of Controlled Comparison. American
             Anthropologist 56:743-63.
Ortiz, Alfonso
   1969      The Tewa World: Space, Time, Being and Becoming in a Pueblo Society.
             Chicago: University of Chicago Press.

Wittgenstein, Ludwig
    1953      Philosophical Investigations. New York: Macmillan.

# 13

# Hopi Shamanism: A Reappraisal

JERROLD E. LEVY

The quintessential North American shaman received supernatural power from one or more spirit helpers during a vision experience and effected cures by communicating while in a trance state with those supernaturals. It was the trance that set the true shaman off from the ceremonialist (Underhill 1948:36). Subsequent to the spread of horticulture in the Southwest, shamanism and the vision quest were overlaid by the development of annual fertility and rainmaking ceremonials among those tribes most dependent on farming. The Pueblos organized shamanistic curers into sodalities and vested some curing functions in the hands of the priests of the rainmaking sodalities. The most serious diseases were thought to be of supernatural origin, and, of several supposed causes, witchcraft was the most prominent. The belief that disease was caused by intrusion of a foreign object was ubiquitous. The cure by "sucking" or extracting was the most prevalent shamanistic activity. Second in importance was the belief that disease was caused by soul loss. In such cases it was necessary that the shaman identify the witch, defeat him in combat, kill him, and then restore the stolen heart to the patient. The vision quest was generally absent from Pueblo practice.

The Hopis differed from this pattern in several important respects. Hopi shamans did not use the trance state, did not have spirit quests or confirmations in sodality initiations or group rites, and did not believe in illness caused by soul loss (Jorgensen 1980:500, 564, 569). In addition, the Hopis did not have curing sodalities and believed that breach of taboo was a major cause of disease, perhaps even more important than witchcraft (Underhill 1948:37). The ethnographic literature, however, contains a number of references to shamanistic trances and curing sodalities closely resembling those of other Pueblo groups.

Trance states and public performances of shamanistic powers do not seem consonant with Hopi values, which promote cooperation, conformity, and ordinariness. Exceptional individuals—whether shamans, priests, or innovators—tend to be feared. It is difficult, in consequence, to think of powerful shamans who go into trances as survivals from the preagricultural past. If the references to such practices among the Hopis are valid, either our general descriptions of Hopi healing, values, and world view must be modified or this form of shamanism must be shown to have been introduced to the Hopis at a relatively late date.

Inter-Pueblo differences are often assumed to be the results of divergence from a common Pueblo culture thought to have developed prior to 1300 A.D., and ecological, technological, and acculturational factors have all been invoked to account for them. The great linguistic heterogeneity of the Puebloans encourages me to propose that some inter-Pueblo differences are best explained as due to different origins and histories and that some similarities may be viewed as convergences resulting from diffusion. Fred Eggan (1980) suggested that the Hopis evolved out of a Great Basin Shoshonean past, and Joseph Jorgensen (1980:254) showed that in the domain of ceremonialism the Hopis form a group by themselves at some remove from the rest of the Pueblos, who, in turn, form a distinct cluster of traits. The traits that set the Hopis apart in this instance are those of life cycle events, especially the girls' puberty rituals, and not the more visible community-oriented ceremonies. Hopis also stand apart from the other Pueblos in the realm of spirit quests, shamanism, causes of illness, and magic. The Pueblos were part of a group that included the Apacheans, Pais, Pimas, Patwins, and Valley Maidus, all of whom had 65 percent of traits in common. The Hopis, Pimas, and Western Apaches clustered together (77 percent), while the other Pueblos comprised a subgroup with 70 percent of traits shared (Jorgensen 1980:288).

This paper will attempt, first, to reevaluate the data relevant to the nature and extent of the differences in shamanistic beliefs and practices that existed between the Hopis and the various other Pueblo groups, and second, to explain them by presenting a historical reconstruction that proposes that Hopi shamanism developed independently of the Eastern Pueblos and that the Hopis rejected Keresan influences that were accepted by Zunis and Tanoans.

## Trance States among the Hopis

First-person accounts of Hopi curing practices date from the late nineteenth century. Like other Southwestern tribes, the Hopis distinguished between natural and supernatural causes of disease. The former were treated by herbalists, bonesetters, and a type of healer with a gift for curing internal disorders by means of massage. Stomach swelling and pain were thought to be caused by the patient's own anxieties or bad thoughts. One priest in each ceremonial society had the power to cure the condition thought to be associated with the ceremony in question. The cause might be natural or supernatural. Illness resulting from trespass on the sacred secrets or paraphernalia of the ceremonial societies was supernaturally caused (breach of taboo); but, as in the case of snake bites cured by the Snake society, it might also occur naturally. The illness controlled by a society was known as its whip *(wavata)*. None of these cures even suggests the presence of shamanism. The individual healers used herbal remedies, bone setting, massage, and "talking"; the priests used the medicine of their society, as well as prayer and ritual.

Witchcraft was the other major supernatural cause of disease. Along with most western tribes, the Hopis believed that witches caused illness by shooting foreign objects into the victim, and that the appropriate cure was to suck those objects from the body. The typical cure was performed by a shaman, who diagnosed the cause while in a trance and often went into a trance during the extraction process itself. If, however, Hopi healers did not use trance states, one must question whether they can be thought of as shamans at all.

In 1894 Alexander Stephen (1936:857–63) recorded a sucking cure in which he was the patient. Barbara Aitken (1956) described a similar episode, and Mischa Titiev (1972:20–22, 26, 54, 85) briefly noted several sucking cures he observed between 1933 and 1934. None of these authors mentions trance states. The extraction was performed perfunctorily with little or no attendant ritual. "Exhaling" (of breath) was sometimes a part of the extraction process as well. The whole procedure was concluded with the preparation of a medicine that the patient was instructed to take for four days.

There is also, however, evidence that trance states were sometimes part of the sucking cure. Alfred Whiting (1939:31, 89) reported that medicine men chewed datura (jimsonweed) to induce visions while making a diagnosis, and that two other plants were used in the same manner. Ernest and Pearl Beaglehole (1935:9) stated that members of the *poswimkya,* a medicine society, took medicine that made them stagger as if intoxicated. They went from one person in the audience to another locating and removing "bullets" with the aid of crystals. Emory Sekaquaptewa (p.c.) described a similar public healing ceremony that took place in the late 1930s.

In 1964 Jay Kuwanheptiwa, a healer from Second Mesa, performed a sucking cure for the author and his family. Because a trance state was induced, and because the sequence of events was somewhat unusual, it is recounted here in some detail. I, my wife, and our children sat facing Kuwanheptiwa, who, without preliminaries, pressed a black obsidian projectile point against various parts of my body. Returning the point to his bag, an ordinary woman's black purse, he announced that our blood was bad and that he would draw it out. He then produced a projectile point, some three inches long, of milky white quartz with a slight tint of rose at the tip. This he proceeded to press against various parts of my torso. As he did this, the rose color spread and intensified until the whole blade was a deep, rich, rose color. This process was repeated with my wife, who later told me she had also seen the point change color from white to rose. Kuwanheptiwa then sat back, announcing that the bad blood had been removed and that he must determine what had caused it.

Presenting his profile to us, he proceeded to inhale deeply, inducing a trance state by hyperventilating. There was no agitation; all was deliberate and calm. He remained in this state for only a minute. After regaining consciousness, he announced that he had seen the witch, a Navajo who had placed around our home on the Navajo reservation several arrow points, which he proposed to remove. The illness would be dispelled but the witch would not be harmed. Should this strategy prove ineffective it would be necessary for him to turn the evil back on the witch and kill him. Because the second procedure was dangerous, he preferred to use it only as a last resort.

Kuwanheptiwa then instructed one of our relatives to stand by him with paper towels to catch the arrow points he was going to "suck" from our home. Once again, hyperventilation induced a trance. After only a few seconds, he began to regurgitate convulsively into the towels. From where we sat we could not see the five small black arrow points our relative said she caught and disposed of over the western edge of the village.

Ethnographic data, then, indicate that the Hopis had three kinds of healers: the priests of the ceremonial societies, individual healers who performed the sucking cure without going into a trance, and shamans who used not only trances but also datura.

## Keresan Medicine Societies

Hopi medicine societies were no longer functioning in the nineteenth century, when Stephen made his observations. Because they appear to have been borrowed from the Keresans, the Keresan forms will be described first.

Keresan shamans were referred to as "bears," and the Bear was the most important tutelary spirit. At Cochiti all medicine societies were referred to as Bear societies (Lange 1968:256, 328). According to Edward Dozier (1970:171) the two curing societies of the Tewas were the Cochiti

Bear and the Tewa Bear. Elsie Clews Parsons (1929:119) noted that the Bear was the tutelary spirit of all Tewa shamans but that the mountain lion was also a powerful curer. Parsons also reported that there was once a Bear People society with curing functions at Taos (1936:59). At Acoma the Bear was followed in importance by the Mountain Lion, Eagle, Badger, Snake, and Wolf (White 1930a:110). At Zuni the Bear was the most important tutelary spirit after the Mountain Lion and was followed by Badger, Wolf, Eagle, and Mole (Cushing 1883:16-19). The shamans of the most important Zuni medicine societies had the power to impersonate the bear (Bunzel 1932a:528).

The diseases cured by the Bear shaman societies were those caused by witchcraft, either by means of an intrusive object or by theft of the victim's heart (soul). In addition to performing the sucking cure, these shamans restored stolen hearts by fighting and killing the witch. While in pursuit of witches, shamans could travel immense distances with the aid of the eagle. At Santa Ana the witch, when caught, became a small figure, some twenty inches high (White 1942:321-22).

There were four principle societies of shamans among the Keresans: Flint, *Ci·'k'amε,* Giant, and Fire. These were the oldest and served as the prototypes on which new societies were modeled (White 1930b:604). All told, nine societies have been identified, most appearing in only one, or at most, three of the villages. In addition to the shamans were three types of "doctors" who did not derive their powers from the animal gods, did not combat witchcraft, and who generally functioned as independent curers. Snake doctors cured snake bites. The *shiwanna,* or thunderbird doctors, treated lightning shock and set bones. Ant doctors cured diseases caused by ants with prayer, song, and by "wiping" them off. There was a tendency to organize curers into societies, however. At Cochiti, for example, the snake doctors were a part of the Flint society, while at Santo Domingo they had a society of their own.

The curing methods of the Eastern Keresans were also found at Acoma (White 1930a:107, 121), Isleta (Parsons 1930), and among the Tewas (Parsons 1929:123). The use of crystals and trance states, sometimes induced by the ingestion of a psychoactive plant, were found at Zuni (Bunzel 1932a:489), Acoma (White 1930a:110), Isleta (Parsons 1930:248, 285, 444), and among the Tewas (Ortiz 1969:70). Although trance states are not mentioned by Leslie White for the eastern Keresans, it is unlikely they were absent. Franz Boas's detailed account of Cochiti vision quests quoted by Charles Lange (1968:233, 236) says that men would go out and fast for four days to induce a vision of one of the four great medicine animals, who were also tutelary spirits of the hunt. Power was sought to ensure success in war, the hunt, and even gambling. As the shamans in these accounts are said to have had animal spirit helpers, it is probable that the vision quest and the trance state played some role in the activities of the medicine societies.

The initiation rites of the Keresan societies were kept secret and no shamans ever spoke to anthropologists on the subject. What evidence there is has been summarized by White (1930b). The novice received the supernatural power of the animal patron of the society through instruction, prayer, fasting, coming into contact with the society fetishes, and witnessing demonstrations of the shamans' powers in a concluding public display.

Ruth Bunzel (1932b:795–827) described similar practices at Zuni. Matilda Coxe Stevenson's description of initiation into several of the Zuni curing societies shows that the shaman was thought to be possessed by the Bear. Although the trance state is not specifically mentioned (since it is written by a Victorian), the language is suggestive: "The dancing is more violent"; "he indulges in extravaganza"; "the cries of the women are as wild as the men"; "dance wildly . . . afterward dashing madly about, growling like the beasts they represent"; "as the night wanes and the floor becomes more crowded the scene grows more wild and weird and the excitement is intense"; "A theurgist from the Little Fire fraternity followed by three of his fellows, who appear to be charmed by their leader, enters the chamber"; "This man's actions are so violent that it is remarkable the child [the initiate held on the sponsor's back] retains his position" (1904:495, 563).

Moreover, alcoholic intoxication was compatible with the shamanistic ritual at Zuni:

> One or two of the members of the choir are stimulated with whiskey brought in by the old woman of the house. Shortly after midnight the drinking of whiskey begins in the back room. It is dealt in by both male and female members of the family . . . and those who are not too drunk to stand venture from the back room into the ceremonial chamber and join in drunken revelry. [Stevenson 1904:478]

According to W. W. Hill (1982:310), "possessional shamanism" was not found at the Tewa village of Santa Clara, but Vera Laski's (1959:93–122) detailed description of Tewa initiation and cures indicates otherwise. Initially, a young man received his calling either by sensing a presence and hearing a voice from the darkness that told him, "the bears are waiting for you. Join them," or, having dreamed "powerful things," by finding a fetish, bear claw, or bear necklace. The individual so chosen by the supernaturals would then be instructed in the secrets and rituals of the society. On the final night, in the presence of the chiefs of all the ceremonial societies and the initiate's relatives, the ceremonial sponsor and the initiate would induce a trance by smoking a special medicine. During the trance, the initiate "became" a bear and, in that state, was able to cure. The magic power was lost when the cure wore off. A repeat performance on the following night was open to the general public. On that night the newly initiated shaman demonstrated his power to cure by the sucking method without the assistance of his sponsor (Laski 1959:103-7, 110-11, 115, notes 151-56).

The shaman cured only while in a trance while possessed by Bear. The shaman could cure less serious ailments by himself. In this event the sucking cure was optional and the trance induced was mild. For more serious conditions the society acted as a group. Greater powers were called upon to act through the entranced bodies of the shamans. Herbs were chewed to induce trances during which the shamans became quite wild, impersonated the bear with bear paws and loud cries, diagnosed and removed intrusive objects, and, finally, battled and destroyed the witch (Laski 1959:112-13).

Eastern Keresan medicine societies differed from those of the Western Pueblos in that they wielded great political power (White 1930b:616-17). The medicine societies either appointed officers directly or approved their appointment. In most Keresan villages the caciques were appointed by the Flint society and were most often members of that society themselves. At Cochiti the Flint society also appointed the War Chief and his assistants, while the Giant society appointed the *fiscales*. In political control of the Pueblo the influence of the shamans was paramount.

Although the curing societies were important at Acoma and Zuni, they were not nearly as powerful as they were among the eastern Keresans. The head of the Acoma Antelope clan held all political power in the position of cacique. It was he who appointed the *katsina* and medicine society chiefs for life. The Antelope clan also appointed the War Chief, the second most important official, and the secular officers (Eggan 1950:243-47). The medicine societies then were under the direction of the cacique. Political authority at Zuni was vested in a council of priests from the most important rainmaking (*uwanami*) societies assisted by the Sun Priest and advised by the heads of the *katsina* society (Eggan 1950:210). The Bow priests acted to implement and enforce council decisions. The role of the shamans on this council is not clear.

The Zuni curing societies may have been borrowed from the Keresans (Eggan 1950:209). Only four of the twelve required the head shaman to belong to a specific clan and only those four had origin myths that followed the pattern of the clan origin myths. Zunis thought they were the oldest of the medicine societies. The centralization of political power at Zuni did not completely override the practice of associating each ceremonial society with a controlling clan, as is the case among the Hopis. Although the relationship between clans and the shaman society at Acoma is not well known, they are associated in myth, which suggests that the relationship may be an old one.

Among the Tewas, political control was vested in the chiefs of the moieties, who alternated in governing the village. In that they were assisted by the War Chiefs. New Moiety Chiefs were installed by the chief of the Hunt society. Dozier believed that the clown, *katsina,* and medicine societies were borrowed from the Keresans (Dozier 1970:71-72). In addition to being known as bears, the two Tewa societies were also called Flint and Fire at San Juan (Parsons 1929:117).

In summation, the curing societies of the Tewas, Keresans, and Zunis were very similar and had, perhaps, spread from the Keresans, where they were prominent in political as well as religious life. It is difficult to say whether this political prominence was recent or old. White (1930b) speculated that Keresan shamans were organized into societies very early and that, as agriculture increased in importance, it was the shamans who stood ready to add rainmaking ceremonies to their functions.

## Hopi Medicine Societies and Sucking Shamans

Turning now to the Hopis we find evidence not only of borrowing but also of the absence of several major elements of the Keresan medicine societies. The Hopis had two curing societies, the *yayaat* and the *poswimkya.* The former was a society of wizards who were adept at fire eating, walking on fire, flying, and instantaneously transporting themselves long distances. The name is the Cochiti word for 'mother', used to refer to the corn fetishes of the medicine societies (Lange 1968:258). The magical feats are identical to those performed by the shamans of the Zuni Fire society (Bunzel 1932a:532) and by Keresan and Tanoan shamans generally. The *yayaat* was noted for conducting public ceremonies for the entire community during times of drought or pestilence (Beaglehole and Beaglehole 1935:10; Stephen 1936: xii, xl, xlviii, 1007-8). The society was inactive in 1891, although several of its members were still living. One of them, who was also a member of the *poswimkya,* healed burns. His treatment included swallowing burning embers (Stephen 1936:460). The Hopi origin myth of this society states that the tutelary spirit of the *yayaat* was Hawk and that the shamans had the power to withstand death by fire and falls from heights (Voth 1905:41-46). Hopis of the First Mesa told Stephen that the society was *kahopi*—that is, their practices went against Hopi values and customs (1936:1008). By 1930, some of the society's paraphernalia and ceremony had been incorporated into the First Mesa Tewa *Somaikoli* society (Titiev 1972:289-92). In this context it cured sore eyes.

*Poswimkya* was a society of sucking shamans. It too was inactive by the 1890s. Stephen identified several members from each mesa who still performed cures (1936:857). The fetishes were still kept in Walpi. As with the Keresan societies, *poswimkya* derived its healing powers from various animals, but with an important difference. Instead of the Bear, Badger was the tutelary spirit, even though Bear prayers and medicines were used. Nor were Mountain Lion, Wolf, Eagle, or Mole associated with the Hopi society. In their place were Porcupine, Horned Toad, and the star Aldebaran. These medicine powers were not associated with directional symbolism as at Zuni (Stephen 1936:860). *Poswimkya* was identified with *posaiyanki*, the patron of the Zuni medicine societies (Stephen 1936:281; Cushing 1883:16-18). Although Badger was the tutelary spirit of the *poswimkya*, there is no indication that either Badger or Gray Badger clans had a proprietary interest in the society, and thus no suggestion that the society is very old. Many Hopis believe the society died out because the requirements of fasting and continence were too rigorous.

*Poswimkya* was the only society specializing in the sucking cure, and knowledgeable Hopis of today insist that only members of this society could use datura to induce trances or as a medicine. Several informants were equally insistent that the sucking cure was practiced only by *poswimkya* and that the sucking shamans of today can only practice if they have been taught by a member of the society. According to this view, the individual shaman who goes into a trance and who performs the sucking cure is the last remnant of *poswimkya* and not to be equated with the typical Hopi healer *(tuuhikya)*, who does not belong to a medicine society. Hopis distinguished between curers who were not affiliated with a society *(masong'i'i)* and those who were *(wolokong'i'i)* (Aitken 1956:67). A similar distinction is not made on Third Mesa and it is likely the usage is Tewa (Dozier 1954:348).

The last member of the society died before 1906 (Titiev 1972:69), and Stephen (1936:281, 450, 723) mentioned the members still alive in the 1890s. It is doubtful that those men were the teachers of the shamans who were mentioned by Titiev in the 1930s. At the turn of the century one of the Third Mesa shamans was a stomach specialist. He then became a bone specialist and took up the sucking cure only later in life. Kuwanheptiwa, a sucking shaman in 1964, was not the kind of curer who could do extracting when Titiev knew him (1972:56-57). If apprenticeship to a society member is still important, it can only be done by learning from a nonmember who learned from a society member. Titiev believed that the *tuuhikya* just proclaimed themselves to be curers and then sought to establish a reputation (1972:140).

Neither present-day sucking shamans nor the *poswimkya* ever attained the political power of the Keresan societies, nor did *poswimkya* contribute to solstice and rainmaking ceremonials, as did its counterparts in Zuni, Acoma, and the Tewa and Keresan villages. *Poswimkya* was not associated with any kiva and, although Badger clansmen were thought to have an innate ability to cure, they were not the leaders of this society. Rather, Badger clansmen served as medicine makers and aspersers in the other societies (Stephen 1936:1080).

## Bear Shamanism

We have seen that Keresans, Tanoans, and Zunis had Bear shamans who were organized into sodalities. The Bear shaman impersonated the bear, was thought to be possessed by the spirit of Bear while in a trance, and was the most powerful type of curer, the only one able to cure disease caused by witchcraft. In stark contrast, Badger was the tutelary spirit of the Hopi *poswimkya*. Hopi sucking shamans were not known as bears and, although trance states were induced, there is no evidence that the shaman was thought to be possessed by an animal spirit.

Bear shamanism is an aspect of what many authors have called bear ceremonialism. The term usually refers to rituals connected with hunting the grizzly bear, which has a circumpolar distribution in both the Old and New Worlds (Hallowell 1926). The bear is addressed by a kinship term, told in advance it will be killed, apologized to after being killed, is present at a ceremonial feast, and, often, has its skull preserved. That such a revered and powerful animal should also be an important spirit helper is consistent with the general belief complex. Some tribes of northern North American had elaborate hunt rituals but did not derive shamanistic power from the bear, who was but one among several power animals. Some others believed that the greatest shamans derived their curing powers from the grizzly bear.

The Bear shamans of Central California, especially those of the Penutian-speaking tribes, were the most similar to the Keresan Bear shamans, both in respect of their great supernatural powers and due to their positions as enforcers of the village chiefs' decisions (Park 1938). Not only did these shamans derive their power from the Bear, they were also able to possess the souls of bears and activate them to do the shaman's bidding.

They impersonated bears and could be transformed into bears. They were thought to be very dangerous because they could kill anyone. They were invulnerable and could travel great distances in an instant. Among many of these tribes the dangerous and malevolent aspects of the Bear shamans were more prominent than their curing powers. In this area also Bear shamans were organized into sodalities. Among the Shoshonean-speaking Cupeños, Gabrieleños, and Cahuillas, especially powerful Bear shamans are said to have existed but were not organized into sodalities.

Bear shamanism was an occasional phenomenon among the Great Basin Shoshoneans. Owens Valley Paiute shamans had Bear power, impersonated bears, and could make bears kill people (Steward 1933: 309-10). On the other hand, Bear shamans have not been reported for Utes or Northern and Southern Paiutes, nor was the belief in spirit possession prevalent among the Shoshonean speakers of the eastern Great Basin (Fowler and Fowler 1971; Whiting 1950).

All eastern Shoshoneans practiced a Bear dance, but it was a spring festival that preceded the breaking of winter camps and migrations in search of food and game (Bradfield 1973:218-20). The origin myth specifically linked the dance with the melting of the snow and the emergence of bears from their winter hibernation. Its main purpose was to assist the bears to recover from hibernation and to find food.

The Hopis also associated the bear with the changing of the seasons (Eggan 1950:82). Coming from a Basin Shoshonean background, they may never have had a strong tradition of Bear shamanism. The founding clan was the Bear clan and, in theory, a Bear clansman was village chief, but the clan name referred to the black bear rather than the grizzly (Bradfield 1973:212). Bear, Mountain Lion, Wolf, and Wild Cat were associated with war and were assigned directional positions in Snake, Antelope, and War society ceremonies.

Bear and Mountain Lion were impersonated in ceremonies of the Snake society during which novices and priests sucked Bear medicine from a bowl in which Bear and other fetishes had been submerged (Stephen 1936:578, 645-46, 699-704, 709). In this manner, Bear power was absorbed by the initiated, who were priests rather than shamans. On First Mesa a hunted bear was treated like a dead human enemy. The man who had killed it was called a war chief, beads were placed on the bear's paws, and those who ate the meat painted their faces black (Hallowell 1926:77). This was Tewa practice (Hill 1982:52) and may have been brought to First Mesa by the Hopi-Tewas of Hano village. The practice was not noted on First Mesa by Stephen, however, and there is no trace of it on the other mesas.

In summation, although the bear was recognized as a powerful animal, it was associated with warfare more than with curing. And, although Bear medicines were used by the *poswimkya* society, the Hopis considered Badger the medicine animal.

## Soul Loss

Another feature of Pueblo disease theory not found among the Hopis was soul loss. All other Pueblos and virtually all Shoshoneans believed that soul loss was an important cause of disease. In this regard the Hopis were more like the Pimas and Papagos. Hopis believed that a witch must continually take the life of a relative in order to prolong his own. The witch stole his younger victim's heart, replacing it with his own so that the victim died in his place. Although this was a form of soul loss, it was not thought to be a cause of disease and there was no treatment for it (Titiev 1942:549).

Hopis placed a great emphasis on the patient's responsibility for his own illness. Bad thoughts, improper actions, disbelief, emotional imbalance, and anxiety were all causes of illness. This emphasis, I believe, is related both to the importance accorded to breach of taboo as a cause of illness and the belief that all members of the community must actively promote life by being strong and thinking only good thoughts. The power of witches to cause illness was recognized, but an individual was more susceptible to penetration by foreign objects if his thoughts were not good or if he was depressed or worried. Good thoughts provided considerable resistance to witchcraft. Hopi healers and family members urged the patient to tell his bad thoughts, to put them in the open, and then to throw them away (Aitken 1930:372-73). Spirit helpers appeared to patients not to curers, and patients might be given datura so they could diagnose their own illness (Titiev 1972:20-22, 54). Thus, while a witch may cause an illness, a Hopi must always examine his own actions and mental states to determine the extent of his own responsibility.

This emphasis on the patient's responsibility is incompatible with the idea of soul loss, which implies that the patient is helpless and has no power of his own to resist witchcraft. Hopis recognized that witches may cause insanity and other forms of irrational behavior and that, in such cases, the individual was not responsible for his actions. In practice, however, the madman was feared and shunned just as a witch was feared (Titiev 1942:353-54). Where soul loss is an important cause of illness, the patient places himself in the hands of the all powerful shaman, who assumes responsibility for combating and defeating the witch.

In a study of epilepsy among Navajos, Zunis, Hopis, and Tewas, only Hopis believed that it was a sign of personal weakness to rely on antiepileptic medications to prevent recurrence of seizures (Levy 1987). Young people were told, "Go it alone; you can beat this by yourself." By contrast, Zunis believed that inadvertent contact with improperly killed game animals was the most common cause of seizures among children. Tewas referred to the epileptic as an "unfortunate" and believed that an evil wind, sent by a witch, had entered the body. When medications were not taken properly it was due to poor understanding of physicians' orders and not to any beliefs about the disease or its causes.

Titiev (1942:552) thought that reluctance to seek treatment from a shaman was due to the belief that they were witches. I am convinced that the responsibility of the patient for his own condition was equally important, especially as the same reluctance is found when treatment from other types of Hopi healers and from physicians is at issue. In fact, Hopis I have questioned on this subject believed that older shamans of good reputation were never feared although the younger, less-established healers of all types might be considered incompetent or thought to be charlatans.

## Guardian Spirits and the Acquisition of Power

We have seen that the Tewa shaman first received a "call" from the Bear spirits, that after a period of learning he acquired his power while in a trance during which he "became" a bear as the tutelary spirit entered his body, and that he could only perform the sucking cure while in a trance. All this, I proposed, was probably Keresan and Zuni practice as well. Hopi shamans also used trance states in the sucking cure, although it could be performed successfully without such practice. How the Hopi shaman acquired his power must now be examined.

The shamans, or curers, mentioned by Titiev received their calls in a variety of ways. One was a Badger clansman, potentially able to cure by virtue of his clan membership, who began to practice following a vow made while sick (Titiev 1972:66). Another survived a lightning strike and later dreamed that he had been chosen by the cloud deities, who imbued him with their healing power. A third vowed while seriously ill that he would become a curer if he survived (Titiev 1942:552). Information on learning is lacking. The vow appears sufficient to qualify, and supernatural power may be conferred directly as part of the call. There is no mention in the literature of visions or of the animal spirits of *poswimkya*.

The ascription of supernatural power through birth into the Badger clan is closer to the practice of the ceremonial, nonshamanistic societies, whose leadership was inherited matrilineally. A gift for healing but not for shamanistic power was also thought to be possessed by individuals who were twins in embryo. Don Talayesva (1942:25) related that after examination by a healer, his pregnant mother was told she would bear twins. The birth of twins was avoided by "twisting" the two fetuses into one. When Titiev knew him in the 1930s, Kuwanheptiwa derived his healing power from his status as a prenatal twin (Titiev 1972:54).

The concept of the spirit helper *(itamuytumala'y taqa)*, or one who takes care of us, was known to Hopis. These beings, however, appeared to laymen and not to shamans often telling them the cause of their illness (Titiev 1941, 1972:21). There is no evidence that shamans relied on these helpers or that it was an important element of Hopi religious belief.

The closest Hopi data allow us to come to tutelary spirits is in the domain of witchcraft. Witches were called two hearts, and were thought to possess the heart of an animal whose form they assumed while working their evil as well as the human heart with which they were born (Titiev 1942:549–50). The witch possessed supernatural power derived from his animal familiar. There is, however, no evidence that the witch obtained power from these animal spirits while in a trance. Instead, they were recruited and taught by other witches much as novitiates were initiated into the ceremonial societies.

The idea that one is chosen by supernatural beings to become a curer and that one learns of this in an unsolicited dream is also found among the Paiutes (Steward 1933:308; Whiting 1950:29). Power came to the Paiute shaman early in life, as early as age five or six (Steward 1933:312). By age twenty-five, he or she had learned many songs through recurrent dreaming, but it was not until age thirty or forty that the spirit told him that he was a healer. This absence of a single vision experience followed by formal training and announcement of the newly acquired status is very similar to some of the Hopi accounts that include the sudden announcement later in life and the addition of healing skills over a long period of time.

## The Ambiguous Position of the Hopi Shaman

The Hopis, along with the Shoshonean speakers of the Great Basin, were ambivalent about shamans. The Comanches made no basic distinction between a medicine man and a sorcerer; "medicine was a two edged sword. It could cut for good or evil" (Hoebel 1940:85). Supernatural power—Hopi *powa*, Ute *puwa*, Shoshone *poha*, Paiute *puha*, Comanche *puha*—was neither good nor evil except as it was used by the one who controlled it. The shaman who possessed this power was a *puhakut* (Comanche) or *puha'ga* (Paiute), and to practice witchcraft was *pu'awi* in Ute. Hopis expressed things in much the same way: to cure, to make whole or perfect was *powata*, to use the power for sorcery was *powaka*.

The healing and purifying aspect of *powa* is expressed in the ceremonial sphere controlled by the priestly societies. The Hopi ceremonial year, synchronized with the agricultural cycle, symbolizes the duality of life and death. Winter starts at the time of the summer solstice (about June 22), when crops are growing and close to ripening. In July the benevolent *katsina*s return to the underworld for the winter half of the year. Of the *katsina*s only *Masau'u*, the god of death, walks in the world of the living during this period. Badger clan, whose tutelary spirit is the medicine animal, takes control of the *katsina*s during winter's dangerous months on Third Mesa. After the harvest, in October, the earth appears dead. The most dangerous period is reached in December *(kya müye* 'dangerous moon'). Witches are thought to be especially active at this time, and people curtail their nighttime activities severely. This is the time to call the *katsina*s back to help purify the land. Soyal *katsina,* as an old man still groggy from his long sleep, comes at the beginning of the dangerous month to prepare the way for the return of the *katsina*s. At the end of the month, the *Soyal* ceremony is performed, reaching its climax at the winter solstice (about December 22). The sun is enjoined to continue on its journey bringing summer warmth to the upperworld, thus ensuring continued life. All benevolent spirits are called upon to help purify the land so that humans may plant their crops safely.

During January, the *katsina*s respond to the Hopis' prayers and come to the villages in increasing numbers. But Badger clan cannot relinquish its guardianship until the land has been purified by the *Powamu* ceremony in February. This month, *powamüye,* has been called "exorcising moon" (Parsons 1933:59) to emphasize the fact that dangerous and evil powers are removed at this time. Purification is preferable because it includes both the idea of exorcism and that of making the earth whole again (Emory Sekaquaptewa, p. c.). The *Powamu* ceremony accomplishes this purification by planting and germinating beans in the *kivas*. Thus, the first planting is conducted in the confines of sacred chambers. Once successful germination has taken place in the sacred arena, purification is completed and Badger clan relinquishes its responsibility for the *katsina* ceremonies to the *katsina* clan for the next half year. Even then, however, from mid-April to mid-May, a series of nine sacred plantings of corn are made for the *katsina*s at several sacred places before the people may plant crops for themselves.

The use of *powa* for evil purposes by witches is a persistent notion. Its use for good purposes, however, is completely in the hands of the priests and is denied to the shamans. Other uses of *powa* in the priestly realm are *powalawu* (ritual) and *powatawi* (song). The individual Hopi shaman was called a *tuuhikya* and did not control *powa* for healing purposes. His power was called *tuuhisa,* a term that Titiev believed also referred to the power a witch received from his animal familiar (1942:549). *Tuu* is also used to mean 'to hurt' *(tuuhota)* and 'to dream' or 'to die' *(tuumoki).* One gets the impression that *tuu* has few positive associations while *powa* has many.

The morpheme *tuu* has two distributions within Uto-Aztecan: (1) 'dream' in Tubatulabal, Tarahumara, Yaqui-Mayo; (2) 'supernatural power' in Southern Paiute and the Tacic subfamily—Cupeño, Cahuilla, Serrano, Luiseño, Gabrieleño, and Kitanamuk (David Shaul, p. c.). Hopi shares both meanings—supernatural power and dream. In Uto-Aztecan there is a family-wide connection between 'to die' and 'unconscious'. In the Numic subfamily, for example, *tuu* means 'to die'. *Tuu* is linked to the California Shoshoneans and to the south. The morpheme, *powa,* by contrast, is found only in Numic.

From this it may be inferred that the *tuuhikya* is, as Underhill (1948) believed, a survival of a pre-Pueblo type of curer common to Great Basin and Southern Californian Shoshoneans, and that, as the ceremonial sodalities of the agriculturalist period developed, the *tuuhikya* was relegated to a subordinate position and the change of status reflected in the use of *powa* by the priests and *tuuhisa* by the individual shamans.

## Discussion

Despite considerable sharing of traits within a general Puebloan frame-work, Hopi shamanism exhibits differences both in degree and in kind. The absence of Bear shamanism, spirit helpers, the concept of soul loss, and the idea that an individual's state of mind is an important element in the disease process are salient differences. The weak and short-lived development of shaman societies among the Hopis contrasts with the prominent position they held in the other Pueblos. The question arises whether these differences can be explained by assuming a derivation from a common Puebloan prototype.

The prominence of the shaman societies and the elaborateness of their organization among the Keresans and Zunis led Parsons (1927) to infer that witchcraft played a minor role in everyday Hopi life and that its greater importance in New Mexico was due to Spanish influence. Titiev's (1942, 1972) data show that Hopi concern with witchcraft was pervasive, however, and derivation of Eastern Pueblo beliefs from those of the Spaniards was rejected by Eggan (1966:135). The general pattern of witchcraft belief (including witch trials, confessions, and executions), which might conceivably be attributed to borrowing or to the stresses of

Spanish occupation, is found as far away as the Northwest Coast (de Laguna 1972:728–38, 741).

The organization of shamans into societies and their political dominance among the eastern Keresans might be viewed as a consequence of the development of centralized political control among the New Mexico Pueblos. Eggan (1966) and Dozier (1970) have discussed the lack of centralization among the Hopis, and both have suggested that the Tanoans developed centralized government first to meet the labor demands made by irrigation agriculture, subsequently to satisfy the need for defense against nomads, and, finally, to contend with the pressures of Spanish domination. Zuni and Acoma were affected by the last two pressures. The virtues of the argument notwithstanding, the prominence attained by the Keresan societies cannot be viewed as an inevitable consequence of that development. The Tanoans, who experienced the entire sequence, did not rely on the curing societies as much as did the Keresans, who adopted irrigation agriculture at a later date.

Ultimately, Dozier (1970:152, 172) accepted a diffusionist explanation. The Keresans utilized preexisting shaman societies, elaborated their rituals, and added weather and political control functions. This pattern then diffused up the Rio Grande but fell short of Taos and Picuris. The westward diffusion to Zuni did not quite reach Hopi either. There is, in fact, evidence to support this interpretation. Zunis used Keresan prayers and recognized Zia shamans as more skilled. Tewas called their societies Flint and Fire as well as Tewa Bear and Cochiti Bear. The Hopi shaman societies used Keresan and Zuni terms and the *yayaat* looked very much like a Keresan Fire society, although the Zunis claimed that they borrowed their Little Fire society from the Hopis (Stevenson 1904:411). Both Dozier (1970:172) and Laski (1959:118–22) believed that Bear shamanism was adopted after the full development of the Puebloan agricultural pattern. Dozier thought it did not develop in Taos or Picuris because of their northern location and proximity to the Plains. Laski believed the complex diffused from the Plains but did not identify its source or explain why it was not adopted by the northern Tiwas, had only nominal success among the Tewas, and developed its full complexity among the Keresans and Zunis.

Leaving these questions aside for the moment, it does seem to me that the *poswimkya* and the *yayaat* were introduced to the Hopis relatively late. Bear hunting ceremonialism—and presumably Bear shamanism as well—was probably universal in the northern half of the continent and in much of northern Asia (Driver and Massey 1957:254–55). Its wide distribution suggests considerable antiquity and a strong association with a hunting economy. The Hopis developed out of a Shoshonean Great Basin economy that was based predominantly on gathering. Hunt magic and Bear shamanism in all likelihood did not play as important a role as they did in societies more reliant on medium and large game animals and in areas where the grizzly, or brown, bear was plentiful.

The Hopis never permitted their hunt shamans to retain an important position in their agricultural society. Priestly societies performed weather control functions while shamans continued as individual curers without political power. In a society that demanded cooperation and conformity, the exceptional or powerful individual came to be mistrusted. Trance states and visions came to be disvalued and the *tuuhikya* became a healer who, although frequently called upon, did not have the power or respect accorded the priests of the rainmaking societies who also had the power to heal. The earlier symbols of shamanism, those of the prey animals, were absorbed into the priestly rituals, while ideas of soul loss and the ability of the shaman to send one of his hearts to the spirit world were lost, remaining only vestigially as attributes of witches.

By the time the fully developed shaman societies of the Eastern Pueblos reached them, the Hopis refused to accept the central elements of possession, soul loss, and Bear as tutelary. The adoption of *yayaat* and *poswimkya* must have been after the arrival of the Spaniards, for how could societies called un-Hopi by the Hopis themselves survive for long? That the *yayaat* worked to treat such community disasters as pestilence and famine suggests an introduction after the experience of European epidemics and restriction of Hopi territory by Navajo incursions. It is even possible they were introduced as recently as the nineteenth century. According to Stephen (1936:860-61), the traditions of the *poswimkya* at First Mesa associated the society with the Badger clan even though Badger clan had no proprietary interest in the society. At Third Mesa two Badger clans are mentioned; one with medicine power, the other with the *katsina* cult (Voth 1905:29). There is no mention of *poswimkya.* This association of *poswimkya* with Badger clan, without the usual Hopi practice of assigning to the clan a proprietary interest in the ceremony, raises the possibility that the society was introduced by Zunis of the Badger clan, who are known to have migrated to Walpi during a famine early in the nineteenth century (Kroeber 1917:101).

These borrowed societies were never given political functions, nor were they integrated into the Hopi system of clan ownership of ceremonies. Thus, the contemporary Hopi shaman, or *tuuhikya,* may be viewed both as a vestige of the *poswimkya* society shaman who performed sucking cures and went into a trance and as a continuation of the older individual curing shaman derived from a Great Basin prototype. Whether the *tuuhikya* could induce a trance before the introduction of the *poswimkya* is moot. It is certain, however, that he did not seek his power through a vision quest and that he had no spirit helper. The source of his power was ill-defined and he shared his domain with another healer who had a "gift" derived from his twin origins.

The foregoing reconstruction is, of course, nothing more than speculation. While it fits most of the data, many questions are left unanswered, the most crucial being those raised by postulating an association between Bear shamanism and hunting economies. If Keresan bear shaman societies date from the preagricultural past, why were they more prominent among the eastern than the western Keresans? And if they were introduced to the eastern Keresans after their settlement along the Rio Grande, what was the source of their inspiration and the reasons for its acceptance? Although the task of historical reconstruction can never hope for success, further inquiry into such areas as ceremonial symbolism and mythology using a broad comparative approach may be helpful in suggesting new hypotheses.

## References

Aitken, Barbara (Freire-Marreco)
  1930    Temperament in Native American Religion. Journal of the Royal Anthropological Institute of Great Britain and Ireland 60:363–87.
  1956    A Trance Experience. Plateau 28:67–70.
Beaglehole, Ernest, and Pearl Beaglehole
  1935    Hopi of the Second Mesa. American Anthropological Association Memoir 44. Menasha, Wisc.
Bradfield, Richard Maitland
  1973    A Natural History of Associations: A Study in the Meaning of Community. Vol. 2. London: Duckworth.
Bunzel, Ruth
  1932a   Introduction to Zuni Ceremonialism. *In* Smithsonian Institution, Forty-seventh Annual Report of the Bureau of American Ethnology, 467–544. Washington, D.C.
  1932b   Zuni Ritual Poetry. *In* Smithsonian Institution, Forty-seventh Annual Report of the Bureau of American Ethnology, 611–835. Washington, D.C.
Cushing, Frank Hamilton
  1883    Zuni Fetishes. *In* Smithsonian Institution, Second Annual Report of the Bureau of [American] Ethnology, 9–43. Washington, D.C.
de Laguna, Frederica
  1972    Under Mount Saint Elias: The History and Culture of the Yakutat Tlingit. 3 vols. Smithsonian Contributions to Anthropology, no. 7. Washington, D.C.
Dozier, Edward P.
  1954    The Hopi-Tewa of Arizona. Berkeley and Los Angeles: University of California Press.

1970  The Pueblo Indians of North America. New York: Holt, Rinehart, and Winston.

Driver, Harold E., and William C. Massey
1957  Comparative Studies of North American Indians. American Philosophical Society Transactions, vol. 47, no. 2. Philadelphia.

Eggan, Fred
1950  Social Organization of the Western Pueblos. Chicago: University of Chicago Press.
1966  The American Indian: Perspectives for the Study of Social Change. Chicago: Aldine Publishing.
1980  Shoshone Kinship Structures and Their Significance for Anthropological Theory. Journal of the Steward Anthropological Society 11:165–92.

Fowler, Don D., and Catherine S. Fowler, eds.
1971  Anthropology of the Numa: John Wesley Powell's Manuscripts on the Numic Peoples of Western North America, 1868–1880. Smithsonian Contributions to Anthropology, no. 14. Washington, D.C.

Hallowell, A. I.
1926  Bear Ceremonialism in the Northern Hemisphere. American Anthropologist 28:1–175.

Hill, W. W.
1982  An Ethnography of Santa Clara Pueblo, New Mexico. Edited and annotated by Charles H. Lange. Albuquerque: University of New Mexico Press.

Hoebel, E. Adamson
1940  The Political Organization and Law-ways of the Comanche Indians. American Anthropological Association Memoir 54. Menasha, Wisc.

Jorgensen, Joseph G.
1980  Western Indians. San Francisco: W. H. Freeman.

Kroeber, Alfred L.
1917  Zuni Kin and Clan. American Museum of Natural History Anthropological Papers, vol. 18, no. 2. New York.

Lange, Charles H.
1968  Cochiti: A New Mexico Pueblo Past and Present. (Original ed. 1959.) Revised ed., Carbondale: Southern Illinois University Press.

Laski, Vera
1959  Seeking Life. American Folklore Society Memoir 50. Philadelphia.

Levy, Jerrold E.
1987  Psychological and Social Problems of Epileptic Children in Four Southwestern Indian Tribes. Community Psychology 15:307–15.

Ortiz, Alfonso
1969  The Tewa World: Space, Time, and Becoming in a Pueblo Society. Chicago: University of Chicago Press.

Park, Willard Z.
1938  Shamanism in Western North America. Northwestern University Studies in the Social Sciences, no. 2. Evanston, Ill.

Parsons, Elsie Clews
1927  Witchcraft among the Pueblos: Indian or Spanish? Man 27:106–12, 125–28.
1929  The Social Organization of the Tewa of New Mexico. American Anthropological Association Memoir 36. Menasha, Wisc.

1930      Isleta. *In* Smithsonian Institution, Forty-seventh Annual Report of the Bureau of American Ethnology, 193–466. Washington, D.C.
1933      Hopi and Zuni Ceremonialism. American Anthropological Association Memoir 39. Menasha, Wisc.
1936      Taos Pueblo. General Series in Anthropology 2. Menasha, Wisc.
1939      Pueblo Indian Religion. 2 vols. Chicago: University of Chicago Press.

Stephen, Alexander M.
1936      Hopi Journal of Alexander M. Stephen. Edited by Elsie Clews Parsons. 2 vols. Columbia University Contributions to Anthropology 23. Reprint ed. New York: AMS Press, 1969.

Stevenson, Matilda Coxe
1904      The Zuni Indians. Smithsonian Institution, Twenty-third Annual Report of the Bureau of American Ethnology. Washington, D.C.

Steward, Julian H.
1933      Ethnography of the Owens Valley Paiute. University of California Publications in American Archaeology and Anthropology, vol. 33, no. 3. Berkeley and Los Angeles.

Talayesva, Don C.
1942      Sun Chief: The Autobiography of a Hopi Indian. New Haven: Yale University Press.

Titiev, Mischa
1941      A Hopi Visit to the Afterworld. Papers of the Michigan Academy of Science, Arts, and Letters, vol. 26, 495–504. Ann Arbor: University of Michigan Press.
1942      Notes on Hopi Witchcraft. Papers of the Michigan Academy of Science, Arts, and Letters, vol. 28, 549–57. Ann Arbor: University of Michigan Press. (Published in 1943.)
1944      Old Oraibi. Harvard University, Papers of the Peabody Museum of American Archaeology and Ethnology, vol. 22, no. 1. Cambridge, Mass.
1972      The Hopi Indians of Old Oraibi: Change and Continuity. Ann Arbor: University of Michigan Press.

Underhill, Ruth M.
1948      Ceremonial Patterns in the Greater Southwest. American Ethnological Society Monograph 13. New York: J. J. Augustin.

Voth, Henry R.
1905      The Traditions of the Hopi. Field Columbian Museum Publication no. 96, Anthropological Series no. 8. Chicago.

White, Leslie A.
1930a     The Acoma Indians. *In* Smithsonian Institution, Forty-seventh Annual Report of the Bureau of American Ethnology, 17–192. Washington, D.C.
1930b     A Comparative Study of Keresan Medicine Societies. Proceedings of the Twenty-third International Congress of Americanists, 1928, 604–19. New York.
1942      The Pueblo of Santa Ana, New Mexico. American Anthropological Association Memoir 60. Menasha, Wisc.

Whiting, Alfred F.
1939      Ethnobotany of the Hopi. Museum of Northern Arizona Bulletin 15. Flagstaff.

Whiting, Beatrice Blyth
1950      Paiute Sorcery. Viking Fund Publications in Anthropology, no. 15. New York.

# 14

# Patterns of Leadership In Western Pueblo Society

TRILOKI NATH PANDEY

Introducing a book of popular essays on Native American life, A. L. Kroeber remarked: "On the side of economics and government, the book is underdone . . . because ethnological knowledge on these topics is insufficient." For Kroeber "economic and political institutions are unquestionably difficult to learn about. They are the first to crumble on contact with Anglo-Saxon or Spanish civilization. So they lack the definiteness of ceremonialism, and their reconstruction from native memories is a bafflingly intricate task." He believed that "possibly ethnologists have not become sufficiently interested or trained" to investigate those institutions (Kroeber 1922:14–15).

The Pueblo Southwest is obviously a prime area for the testing of Kroeber's ideas because Pueblo Indians were the first to come in contact with Spanish civilization, and since 1540 they have been forced to adjust to outside pressures provided by Spanish, Mexican, and American governments, as well as by other Indians (see Spicer 1962). Also, few if any other Indian groups have been studied by as many professional anthropologists as the Pueblos of the American Southwest. During the last few decades, large amounts of material have been recorded on Pueblo economics and politics by such scholars as Sophie Aberle (1948), Ruth Bunzel (1938), Edward Dozier (1970), E. Adamson Hoebel (1962), Edward A. Kennard (1966, 1979), Shuichi Nagata (1970), Alfonso Ortiz (1969), Bernard J. Siegel (1949), M. Estellie Smith (1969), Watson Smith and John M. Roberts (1954), Mischa Titiev (1944), Steadman Upham (1982), and Peter Whiteley (1987, 1988), among others. These studies indicate that the Pueblos reacted variously to outside pressures due to differing historical factors and their geographical locations. Thus the Zunis, originally dispersed in six villages at the time of their "discovery" in the early sixteenth century, consolidated themselves into a single community after the Pueblo Rebellion of 1680 and developed a central religious hierarchy and centralized political power to maintain discipline and unity in the face of the Spanish and the Navajo-Apache threat. The Pueblos of the Rio Grande region, on the other hand, maintained their village and cultural autonomy by overtly accepting the separation of church and state introduced by the Spaniards and by compartmentalizing their socioceremonial systems (Dozier 1970). Unlike those Pueblos, however, the Hopis never developed such political mechanisms, nor the patterns of compartmentalization and secrecy necessary to ward off Spanish pressures. Rather, they continued to rely on village dispersal, without centralizing political power or developing the idea of secular government introduced by the Spanish (Eggan 1966; Sekaquaptewa 1972). It is only now that the Hopis have started to see the importance of having a secular government—their Tribal Council—in dealing with their land-claims cases and in distributing the money they have received from land leases to different companies (Kammer 1980).

Scholars looking at economic and political developments among the Pueblos are invariably struck by the differences in their adjustment to outside pressures, but so far no systematic attempt has been made to account for them. It is the primary concern of this paper to examine the recent history and present structure of the political systems of two Western Pueblos, Hopi and Zuni. Against an historical background, and relying on the method of controlled comparison so admirably used by Fred Eggan (1950) in his study of the social organization of the Western Pueblos, this paper will focus on the structure of the Hopi and the Zuni theocracies; the nature, rate, and extent of political and economic changes; and the impact of various factors on the patterns of leadership in these two Pueblos.

The dominant role of religion in Pueblo life has prompted anthropologists and casual visitors alike to cite the Pueblos as theocracies ruled by priests. Thus, Richard Thurnwald describes Zuni "as the extreme example of a sacred state, a theocracy ruled by priests who are the heads of certain preferred or aristocratic families and who govern through civil authorities appointed by them" (quoted in Pauker 1966:196). According to Elsie Clews Parsons, the Hopi theocracy "is strikingly like the theocracy of Zuni," with the exception of "secular offices which, being of Spanish provenience, are missing among the Hopi" (Parsons 1933:53; also Whiteley 1988:14-15).

As David L. Webster (1976) has pointed out in his paper on theocracies, in the anthropological and archeological literature, the term theocracy has been used for both a type of society and a stage of socio-political evolution. What are some of the general characteristics of theocracies? In theocracies, political and religious associations are one and the same. Some specialization of political roles is possible, but they have their significance in a system of religious ideas. Theocracies have a system of kingship or priesthood, although leadership may be shared jointly. Many forms of leadership are thus possible, but leaders have two major qualities. First, they have roles that are both personalized and institutionalized. Second, they are representatives of the deity; their authority derives from that, even if they are selected by the public at large.[1]

Theocracies are communities that are part of both the natural and supernatural order. In them, laws tend to be linked to custom, ritual, or decree. An important part of the sacred element of the community is maintained by the religious practices and special classes of individuals who cater to ritual and custom in efforts to maintain the purity of the society and prevent the defilement of the sacred by the secular.

Those characteristics should be sufficient to indicate the nature of theocracy. To what extent are Zuni and Hopi characterized by them? Can we find these characteristics in Hopi and Zuni social systems? I mentioned earlier that religion plays a central role in Pueblo life. To both Hopis and Zunis, ritual and ceremony are "the paramount religious interests" (Parsons 1933:78). Ruth Bunzel suggested that "all of Zuni life is oriented about religious observance" (1932:509). Similarly, ownership of and participation in a ceremony are major determinants of status in Hopi society. But what about political activities? Are they controlled by religious associations?

The Hopis make no sharp distinction between religious and political domains (Eggan 1950; Whiteley 1988). This is exemplified in some villages by merging the office of village chief with that of leadership in the Soyal (winter solstice) ceremony (Titiev 1944:63). They believe that their form of government was established solely upon religious and traditional grounds (Sekaquaptewa 1972:239–40). The divine plan of life in this land was laid out for them by Great Spirit, *Masau'u*. That plan cannot be changed (Clemmer 1973:29).

There is no central authority for the Hopis as a whole. Within each major village there is a hereditary group of priests or chiefs. In most of the Hopi villages the village chieftainship is associated with the Bear clan, and the chiefs are installed by the Kwan society. That society, which is particularly associated with the dead, was in former times the main protection of the village. It controls the office and person of the village chief and takes care of law and order in the pueblo. As the village chief is supposed to keep a "good heart" in order to protect his people, he takes little interest in mundane affairs. Members of the Kwan society take part in the initiation rites. In some villages there used to be a War Chief who assisted the *kikmongwi*, the village chief, in chastizing disorderly adults and others who presented a threat to the pueblo (see Titiev 1944:65–66; Whiteley 1987:702, 1988:66–69).

Unlike Zuni, there was no council of priests among the Hopis. The nearest thing to a council was the chiefs' assembly that was held in connection with the Soyal ceremony (Levy 1992:24; Whiteley 1987:701). However, this meeting had no legislative significance and was more concerned with the ceremonial cycle of the coming year and how to maintain the Hopi way of life (Eggan 1950:107).

Traditionally the council of priests has been the most important religious-political unit in Zuni life. Its central position has made anthropologists believe that "government in Zuni is *centralized* in [this] . . . priestly hierarchy" (Goldman 1937:313). The membership of this hierarchy has varied from four to eight. During the 1880s, in Frank Cushing's time, there were seven members on the council;[2] now there are only four, representing the four cardinal directions. The head of this hierarchy is the priest of the north, *kiakwemosi*, the 'house chief', who also serves as *pekwin*, the Sun Priest, whose office is vacant at present. The Elder Brother Bow Priest and the heads of the Kachina society and of different dance groups are also consulted on matters of general concern (see Pandey 1977; Ferguson, Hart, and Seciwa 1988).

The Bow Priests act as the executive arm of the council of priests. The Bow Priesthood, composed of warriors who had taken scalps from the enemy, was responsible for protecting the pueblo against both external and internal enemies, but with the decline in warfare, its numbers and prestige also declined, and its primary concern came to be warfare against Zuni witches, who were believed to cause drought, sickness, and death.

The principal matters that come before the council relate to impersonations of the gods, the time of tribal initiations, changes in the ceremonial calendar, and questions of tribal policy. They have the welfare of the pueblo in their hands and are too sacred to be concerned with secular quarrels and problems.

The Zuni Tribal Council in the nineteenth century was composed of the governor, a lieutenant governor, and a number of assistants who were annually selected by the Bow Priests and installed by the council of priests. During the twentieth century the Tribal Council gradually increased in size and importance and came to achieve a dominant position in the political life of Zuni. Though Kroeber (1917) thought the Tribal Council to be a native institution, it originated in a Spanish edict of 1620, and was apparently not applied to Zuni until after the Pueblo Rebellion of 1680. During the nineteenth century the council played a minor role, but the new outside contacts and pressures that were developing, and the new problems resulting from factional divisions, put the Tribal Council in the forefront (see Pandey 1967, 1977).

The Tribal Council is responsible for the health, safety, morals, and welfare of the Zuni community and has the power to negotiate with the federal and state governments with regard to tribal resources and activities. During the past few decades, the Tribal Council has tried to gain control over reservation resources and activities by promoting silver jewelry into a major source of income for the pueblo, by trying to attract industry to the reservation, and by expanding the educational system to approximate that of local white communities (Eggan and Pandey 1979). With money from the land claims settlement in 1990, the Tribal Council has started several programs for improving the economic and social life of the pueblo.

In 1934, the Zunis, as well as the Hopis, accepted the Indian Reorganization Act, which provided, among other things, for the election of a Tribal Council by secret ballot. The Indian agent at Zuni appointed a nominating committee, divided equally between the two factions, to select candidates for governor, lieutenant governor, and five (later six) *tenientes* representing the farming villages and Zuni proper. The resulting Tribal Council was elected by popular vote and installed by the council of priests. The insignia of office are canes—one set originally from the Spanish crown and the second presented by President Lincoln in 1863.[3] In recent times only the Lincoln canes have been used and the authority of the office resides in the cane; when it is taken away the official has no power (see Pandey 1968, 1977).

In complying with the Indian Reorganization Act, the Hopi experience has been considerably different (see Sekaquaptewa 1972). The constitution required that the Tribal Council would be made up of representatives from all the Hopi villages in order to represent the interests of the Hopi Tribe as a whole. But conservative villages refused to participate, thereby resulting in a split and mutual antagonism between the supporters of the new Tribal Council and the upholders of the traditional socio-religious, village-based structure. This aggravated the already existing factional splits between "friendlies" and "hostiles" (Nagata 1970:55). The Hopis remain today with a dual system, two simultaneously operating political structures, each of which claims to represent the people. But with nine different sets of leadership among the thirteen Hopi villages, the Bureau of Indian Affairs and other outside groups have difficulty dealing with the Hopi Tribe as a whole.[4]

With the adoption of an elective form of government under the Indian Reorganization Act, the Hopi and Zuni priests were deprived of the right to select the civil authorities for their pueblos. Officials of the civil government came to be elected by the adult members of the tribes, and their election has become a significant feature of Pueblo political organization. While in the past the secular officers were mainly responsible to the priests who appointed them, after the change in the form of succession to political offices (from appointive to elective) they became responsible to all of the electorate. This tends to force them toward action independent of priests in defense of their own political life.

We have seen that in both the Zuni and Hopi theocracies, church and state were coalesced in order to maintain the "harmonious order" that was the ideal of the society. Symbolic support for this system was provided by myths and the performance of rituals and ceremonies. In such societies, a good man was one who "should without fail cooperate easily with others either in the field or in ritual, never betraying a suspicion of arrogance or a strong emotion" (Benedict 1934:99). But in economic and political domains it is difficult to do that if one is surrounded by people who value competition and individualism. If one follows the American model and tries to take advantage of the opportunities for getting ahead, then he immediately becomes a threat to the status quo of his own society. Thus in Zuni, if an individual became more successful than others in acquiring wealth, a skill, contacts with outsiders, and so forth, then it was expected that for the benefit of the community such individualized power would have to be turned into institutionalized power. Otherwise, in Zuni belief, such people would become "witches" whose "special power" would cause sickness, death, drought, and other calamities. Even the priests were suspected of "conjuring" if they performed any ritual for their personal benefit (Benedict 1934:97). "Poor" Zunis, those without religious knowledge beyond that of the Kachina society, often suspected priests of witchcraft, that is, of using "valuable" religious knowledge for private ends (Parsons 1917:234; also Benedict 1935, 2:86, 153, 160).

In this connection, it should be recalled that when a warrior who had killed an enemy and scalped him returned to Zuni, he was expected to join the Bow Priesthood. By doing that, I believe, he not only saved his own life from the ghost of the enemy, but he also turned his personal trophy into a powerful object that brought benefit to the entire community (cf. Leach 1965:168). Indeed, it was not much different in the case of the secular leaders. The information I have on them suggests that many governors and councilmen have been prosperous stockmen, silversmiths, and successful employees of the Bureau of Indian Affairs. They are the ones who have been most successful in dealing with outsiders and are therefore the best qualified to represent the political and economic interests of their people. I suspect that, by giving such responsibility to them, the Zuni try to use their personal skills and accomplishments to achieve the goals of their society.

Since the acceptance of the Indian Reorganization Act a number of principal bases of power have emerged in the pueblo that are being utilized by some people and not others. However, these people do not have "independent power" (Adams 1970:120) and have to depend upon different sources for their existence. This creates instability in the political life of the Pueblo Indians. In the theocracy the political was subordinate to the religious, but since the separation of church and state it has become increasingly autonomous. Even so, it still lacks an independent principle of legitimacy that would make it strong enough to fill the vacuum left by the shrinking importance of the old mechanisms of social control and political coordination that in the past permeated the whole system (Pauker 1966:201). If the processes of secularization and democratization, which are well underway, succeed in Zuni, perhaps the secular leaders might become emancipated from priestly sources of legitimation.

The Hopi political situation seems to be much more complicated. In addition to factional alliances and the complex relationships between mother and daughter villages, there is a triple system of socio-political control operating simultaneously at Hopi: the traditional (village-based) authority system, the Tribal Council system introduced by the Indian Reorganization Act, and the state-national political organization. Of the two Hopi political structures claiming to represent the Hopi people, the Bureau of Indian Affairs only recognizes the Tribal Council (Nagata 1970:61). Nagata's study of Moenkopi shows that recent years have seen the development of a secular leadership in that pueblo (1970:42–44). Similar developments for Bakavi have been reported by Whiteley (1988:236). Also, New Oraibi *(Kiqötsmovi)* has started to elect officials in annual elections, like the Eastern Pueblos. Perhaps with the settlement of claims cases and with their new resources in coal and other minerals, the Hopis will react differently to the Tribal Council and its leaders who are working hard for the betterment of their future (Kammer 1980; Loftin 1991).

With the Zuni experience in mind, as well as the insights into the political dynamics that Nagata provides for Moenkopi and Whiteley for Bakavi, I suspect that the other Hopi villages will eventually recognize the importance of overall tribal unity in presenting a front to the outside world.

As I said earlier, it was largely due to the Spanish threat, and possibly the Navajo and Apache raids, that the Zuni consolidated themselves in one village in 1696, following the Pueblo Rebellion, and developed a central religious hierarchy and centralized political power. It is unlikely that the Hopi will ever consolidate in this manner so long as they live in dispersed settlements and rely on their strong clan system to regulate political life.[5] But like Zuni, different Hopi villages can participate in creating a political community that can handle the new problems brought by modernity and new economic opportunities. Recent studies of the Navajo-Hopi land disputes, such as Emily Benedek (1992), Catherine Feher-Elston (1988), and Jerry Kammer (1980), suggest that this has already started to happen.[6]

This brief historical and comparative study of the Hopi and Zuni theocracies shows the gradual separation of politics from religion after contact with Spanish and Anglo-American civilization, but (contrary to Kroeber's generalization) not their collapse. This study reveals that while traditional forms of leadership among the Hopis and Zunis were based upon membership in various religious societies, it is one's achieved status depending on entrepreneurial activities, wealth, and success in acquiring new skills through education and modernization that has resulted in a shift to a form of secular leadership provided by members of the elected tribal councils at Zuni and in some Hopi villages.[7] It suggests that the traditional and modern forms of leadership exist side-by-side in Zuni, and in some Hopi villages, sometimes in mutual rivalry but mostly in mutual interpenetration. This situation is not unique, and is reported for several theocratic societies in David L. Webster (1976:816).[8]

I think that the comparative aspects of this study reveal much about the political dynamics of "tribal" societies in the modern world. The relationship between traditional and modern forms of leadership requires serious consideration. There is a growing body of literature that suggests that such a comparative study will prove fruitful to understanding the tension between religion and politics and how it has been used to construct the landscape of religious and political leadership during periods of rapid cultural and social change.

## Acknowledgments

Some of the ideas discussed in this paper were presented in seminars beginning at Chicago (1977), Cambridge (1984), and Santa Barbara (1986). I would like to record my gratitude to Fred Eggan, Jack Goody, and Elvin Hatch for arranging those sessions, and for their thoughtful comments. I would also like to thank the Master and Fellows of St. John's College, Cambridge, for providing hospitality during my visit. My thanks are also due to Raymond J. DeMallie and Eugene Sekaquaptewa for their helpful comments on the manuscript.

## Notes

1. In describing the characteristics of theocracies I have drawn heavily on David J. Apter (1963), Roger Caillois (1959), and Raimundo Panikkar (1978).

2. J. Howard Gore, who visited Zuni in 1881 while Cushing was there, remarked that "seven caciques and one priestess constitute the supreme ecclesiastical tribunal, to whom all disputes and doubted points in religious or ceremonial matters are referred" (1882:87). However, Sylvester Baxter, who also visited Zuni in 1881, spoke only of "the seven great chiefs of Zuni" (1882:85).

3. Ortiz (1969:67) talks of a third set given by the Mexican government in 1821.

4. Kammer (1980) discusses some of these issues as do Sekaquaptewa (1972) and Benedek (1992).

5. Eggan believed that "a strong clan system is correlated with a weak political system" (1950:118). Whiteley (1988) provides a different perspective in his study of Bakavi.

6. This confirms Eggan's hunch that even though the Hopi-Zuni ecological and historical situations differ, "the problems are similar, as is the trend" (quoted in Pandey 1991:108).

7. For details on Zuni see Bunzel (1938:356); Ferguson, Hart, and Seciwa (1988:123); and Ladd (1979:498). For the Hopi situation, see Clemmer (1978:33–35) and Whiteley (1988:66–70).

8. Meyer Fortes drew my attention to a similar situation in several African societies described in Shack and Cohen (1979).

## References

Aberle, Sophie D.
  1948      The Pueblo Indians of New Mexico: Their Land, Economy and Civil Organization. American Anthropological Association Memoir 70. Menasha, Wisc.
Adams, Richard N.
  1970      Crucifixion by Power: Essays on Guatemalan National Social Structure, 1944–1966. Austin, Texas: University of Texas Press.
Apter, David J.
  1963      Political Religion in the New Nations. In Old Societies and New States, edited by Clifford Geertz, 57–104. New York: Free Press.
Baxter, Sylvester
  1882      The Father of the Pueblos. Harper's New Monthly Magazine 65:72–91.
Benedek, Emily
  1992      The Wind Won't Know Me: A History of the Navajo-Hopi Land Dispute. New

York: Alfred A. Knopf.

Benedict, Ruth
1934    Patterns of Culture. Boston: Houghton Mifflin.
1935    Zuni Mythology. 2 vols. Columbia University Contributions to Anthropology 21. New York: Columbia University Press.

Bunzel, Ruth L.
1932    Introduction to Zuni Ceremonialism. Smithsonian Institution, Forty-seventh Annual Report of the Bureau of American Ethnology, 467-544. Washington, D.C.
1938    The Economic Organization of Primitive Peoples. In General Anthropology, edited by Franz Boas, 327-408. New York: D. C. Heath.

Caillois, Roger
1959    Man and the Sacred. New York: Free Press.

Clemmer, Richard O.
1973    Culture Change and the Hopi Nation: The Impact of Federal Jurisdiction. (Mimeographed.)
1978    Continuities of Hopi Culture Change. Ramona, California: Acoma Books.
1979    Hopi History, 1940-1974. In Handbook of North American Indians, vol. 9, Southwest, edited by Alfonso Ortiz, 533-38. Washington, D.C.: Smithsonian Institution.

Dozier, Edward P.
1970    The Pueblo Indians of North America. New York: Holt.

Eggan, Fred
1950    Social Organization of the Western Pueblos. Chicago: University of Chicago Press.
1966    The American Indian: Perspectives for the Study of Social Change. Chicago: Aldine Publishing.

Eggan, Fred, and Triloki Nath Pandey
1979    Zuni History, 1850-1970. In Handbook of North American Indians, vol. 9, Southwest, edited by Alfonso Ortiz, 474-81. Washington, D.C.: Smithsonian Institution.

Feher-Elston, Catherine
1988    Children of Sacred Ground: America's Last Indian War. Flagstaff, Arizona: Northland Publishing.

Ferguson, T. J., E. Richard Hart, and Calbert Seciwa
1988    Twentieth Century Zuni Political and Economic Development in Relation to Federal Indian Policy. In Public Policy Impacts on American Indian Development, edited by C. Matthew Snipp, 113-44. Native American Studies, University of New Mexico. Development Series 4. Albuquerque.

Fortes, Meyer
1980    Review of Politics in Leadership: A Comparative Perspective, edited by William Shack and Percy Cohen. The Jewish Journal of Sociology 22:214-17.

Goldman, Irving
1937    The Zuni of New Mexico. In Cooperation and Competition among Primitive Peoples, edited by Margaret Mead, 313-53. Reprint ed., Boston: Beacon Press, 1961.

Gore, J. Howard
1882    Regulative System of the Zunis. Transactions of the Anthropological Society

of Washington, vol. 1, 68-88.

Hoebel, E. Adamson
1968    The Character of Keresan Pueblo Law. Proceedings of the American Philosophical Society, vol. 112, 127-30. Philadelphia.

Kammer, Jerry
1980    The Second Long Walk: The Navajo-Hopi Land Dispute. Albuquerque: University of New Mexico Press.

Kennard, Edward A.
1966    Post-War Economic Changes among the Hopi. *In* Essays in Economic Anthropology, Proceedings of the 1965 Annual Meetings of the American Ethnological Society, 25-32. Seattle: University of Washington Press.
1979    Hopi Economy and Subsistence. *In* Handbook of North American Indians, vol. 9, Southwest, edited by Alfonso Ortiz, 554-63. Washington, D.C.: Smithsonian Institution.

Kroeber, A. L.
1917    Zuni Kin and Clan. Anthropological Papers of the American Museum of Natural History, vol. 18, no. 2. New York.
1922    Introduction. *In* American Indian Life, edited by Elsie Clews Parsons, 5-16. Reprint ed. Lincoln: University of Nebraska Press, 1967.

Ladd, Edmund J.
1979    Zuni Economy. *In* Handbook of North American Indians, vol. 9, Southwest, edited by Alfonso Ortiz, 492-98. Washington, D.C.: Smithsonian Institution.

Leach, Edmund R.
1965    The Nature of War. Disarmament and Arms Control 3:165-83.

Levy, Jerrold E.
1992    Orayvi Revisited: Social Stratification in an "Egalitarian" Society. Santa Fe: School of American Research Press.

Loftin, John D.
1991    Religion and Hopi Life in the Twentieth Century. Bloomington: Indiana University Press.

Nagata, Shuichi
1970    Modern Transformations of Moenkopi Pueblo. Urbana: University of Illinois Press.

Ortiz, Alfonso
1969    The Tewa World: Space, Time, Being, and Becoming in a Pueblo Society. Chicago: University of Chicago Press.

Pandey, Triloki Nath
1967    Factionalism in a Southwestern Pueblo. Ph.D. diss., University of Chicago.
1968    Tribal Council Elections in a Southwestern Pueblo. Ethnology 7:71-85.
1977    Images of Power in a Southwestern Pueblo. *In* The Anthropology of Power, edited by Raymond D. Fogelson and Richard N. Adams, 195-215. New York: Academic Press.
1991    Fred Eggan. *In* Remembering the University of Chicago: Teachers, Scientists, and Scholars, edited by Edward Shils, 97-109. Chicago: University of Chicago Press.

Panikkar, Raimundo
1978    Non-dualistic Relation between Religion and Politics. Religion and Society 25(3):53-63.

Parsons, Elsie Clews
  1917    Notes on Zuni. Memoirs of the American Anthropological Association, vol.
          4, nos. 3-4. Menasha, Wisc.
  1933    Hopi and Zuni Ceremonialism. Memoirs of the American Anthropological
          Association 39. Menasha, Wisc.
Pauker, Guy J.
  1966    Political Structure. In People of Rimrock, edited by Evon Z. Vogt and Ethel
          M. Albert, 191-226. Cambridge, Massachusetts: Harvard University Press.
Sekaquaptewa, Emory
  1972    Preserving the Good Things of Hopi Life. In Plural Society in the Southwest,
          edited by Edward H. Spicer and Raymond H. Thompson, 239-60. New York:
          Interbook.
Shack, William A. and Percy S. Cohen, eds.
  1979    Politics in Leadership: A Comparative Perspective. Oxford: Clarendon Press.
Siegel, Bernard J.
  1949    Some Observations on the Pueblo Pattern at Taos. American Anthropologist
          51:562-77.
Smith, M. Estellie
  1969    Governing at Taos Pueblo. Eastern New Mexico University Contributions in
          Anthropology, vol. 2, no. 1, edited by C. Irwin-Williams. Portales: Eastern
          New Mexico University Press.
Smith, Watson, and John M. Roberts
  1954    Zuni Law: A Field of Values. Papers of the Peabody Museum of American
          Archaeology and Ethnology, Harvard University, no. 43. Cambridge, Mass.
Spicer, Edward H.
  1962    Cycles of Conquest: The Impact of Spain, Mexico, and the United States on
          the Indians of the Southwest, 1533-1960. Tucson: University of Arizona
          Press.
Tedlock, Barbara
  1992    The Beautiful and the Dangerous: Encounters with the Zuni Indians. New
          York: Viking Penguin.
Titiev, Mischa
  1944    Old Oraibi: A Study of the Hopi Indians of Third Mesa. Papers of the Peabody
          Museum of American Archaeology and Ethnology, Harvard University, no.
          22. Cambridge, Mass.
  1972    The Hopi Indians of Old Oraibi: Change and Continuity. Ann Arbor:
          University of Michigan Press.
Upham, Steadman
  1982    Politics and Power: A Social and Economic History of the Western Pueblo.
          New York: Academic Press.
Webster, David L.
  1976    On Theocracies. American Anthropologist 78:812-28.
Whiteley, Peter M.
  1987    The Interpretation of Politics: A Hopi Conundrum. Man 22:694-714.
  1988    Deliberate Acts: Changing Hopi Culture Through the Oraibi Split. Tucson:
          University of Arizona Press.

# 15

# Indian Law and Puebloan Tribal Law

BRUCE B. MACLACHLAN

In *Social Organization of the Western Pueblos* Fred Eggan (1950) expounded a system of theoretical concepts and a method of controlled comparison, and applied these tools to a rigorous comparison of key elements of social structure among the Hopi, Hano, Zuni, Acoma, and Laguna pueblos, establishing them as a single structural type, Western Pueblo. This he contrasted with a distinct, but related, structural type, Eastern Pueblo, consisting of the rest of the Indian pueblos in the Rio Grande Basin. The result of that application was a middle-range theory of the Puebloan Southwest that (1) accounts for a wider range of the available data more satisfactorily than any previous account, (2) is highly fruitful heuristically, and (3) is, by design, falsifiable and subject to elaboration or amendment. This essay uses Eggan's theory as a foundation for elucidation of processes of social change, a development of his work forecast by Eggan himself. I postulate that the community of Santa Clara Pueblo is representative of a Tewa variant of an Eastern Pueblo-type structure. The approach is significantly constrained by the substantive ethnographic material, which was gathered initially for a different, limited purpose.

Eggan's conceptual scheme distinguishes between structure and culture, which are independent but functionally related to each other. A social structure consists of a set of relationships between persons or sets of persons. Such structures tend to assume a limited number of relatively stable forms (structural types), which transmute by determinable processes. Cultural types, their constituent entities and relationships, and their transformations are, on the other hand, harder to define. Consequently, social structure types more crisply differentiate themselves as objects for analysis by their relative sameness in specific parameters.

A great utility of a theory of structural types is that it gives a basis for identifying specific parameters and critical structural elements for the study of change. Parallel series of types can be compared across different regions. In the Canadian Northwest, for example, appearance of Tlingit kin terminology among peripheral Northern Athapaskan groups suggests transition to a new structural type (Eggan 1955:541–43). Salient forces in this process were exchange and alliance among Indian groups enriched by European trade but not under the political control of Euro-American governments (MacLachlan 1981). In the Southwest there is a comparable series of peripheral Athapaskan groups, probably variants of a single type, adjusting their social relationships to resemble characteristics of one, or both, of the Puebloan structural types identified by Eggan. Comparison of a Puebloan-oriented series of Southern Athapaskan groups led me to look into the Puebloan structural types. There, however, the driving force within the ethnographic present is the political control that has existed for centuries. The critical institutions are not those of exchange, but those that control norms; of the latter institutions, "law" has become preeminent.

Empirical social groups represented by structural types are specific manifestations of persistent, continuously but variously manifested institutions. Thus, for defining a Puebloan structural type a short character-ization of institutions under key rubrics is sufficient: kinship, lineage, sodalities, ceremonial groups, dual division, organization of cultivation and irrigation, householding, land holding. Other institutions, including law, are not significant in specifying structural type. However, this essay focuses on the significance of legal institutions undergoing social change, including transmutation of structural types.

Legal institutions are latent in all polities. A wide variety of them persist and are continuously manifested in modern Western nations. In a tribal or band society, legal institutions are typically few and manifested only occasionally, with participation being adjunct to the actors' roles in other, more structurally significant institutions, such as kindreds or moieties. In a context of culture contact with Euro-American nations, legal institutions become vastly more manifest in the social environment.

Eggan's study yielded two structural types, Western Pueblo and Eastern Pueblo. Communities of the Western Pueblo type, the specific subjects of Eggan's study, were better known ethnographically than the eastern communities. Western Pueblo is today a valid, useful structural type.

The Eastern Pueblo type is more problematic. One reason for this is persistent problems with terminology and the underlying concepts. Even as recently as 1975, whether or not the Santa Clara Tewas are patrilineal was an issue in litigation, and expert anthropological opinion had been adduced on both sides of the issue. The trial judge in the litigation adopted "patrilineal" in his opinion (*Martinez v. Santa Clara* 1975a). The principle of patrilineal descent is a valid one, although its applicability is more limited than once thought. The problem in the present context is that none of the kinship terms "matrilineal," "patrilineal," or "bilateral," was most commonly used to characterize a whole kinship system. None of the three terms as generally defined seems to fit the Tewa system well. Various observers have used whichever of the terms seemed to them to be the closest approximation to Tewa practice. Frequently, but not always, the choice of term was accompanied by explicit, appropriate qualifications. Nevertheless, the Tewa example demonstrates the perils of "backward translation" of anthropological terms into a non-Western culture (Bohannan 1969:410). The term *endogamy* also arises problematically in connection with Santa Clara. That term is a lame contrast to the relatively well defined and understood *exogamy*.

The use of the term *law* in this essay needs brief discussion. A number of significantly different interpretations of law are productively used in anthropology. Some imply that law "in the strict sense" is an institution of developed societies that has evolved from human situations in which at best there existed only prelaw, protolaw, or primitive law. This definition implies that the law of developed societies, of nation-states, is the culmination of a series of developments of lesser values. It begs a multitude of questions that are worth raising. My interest is in a conception of law that is characteristic of all human societies. Law is a brooding omnipresence in human relations.

On the assumption that the nation-state is not merely an institution of a society, but an institution that incorporates all society, to the nation-state is imputed a monopoly on the use of force to compel conformity to law. Thus, if coercive force is a necessary attribute of law, anything not mandated or permitted by the state cannot be law. This definition, too, begs nontrivial questions. To get to those questions, I start by assuming the possibility of multiple, roughly equivalent, systems of law within a society.

In the title of this paper *Indian law* refers to that segment of the formal legal system of the United States that pertains to Native Americans, who, of course, were not "Indians" until Europeans came and started making laws for them. In other words, "Indian law" is an Anglo-American culture trait. Indian law contains assumptions about, and goals for, Indian social life. The assumptions are not necessarily accurate or mutually consistent. Specific goals tend to be consistent with an ultimate goal of orderly and just assimilation of the remnants of the Indian nations into the United States nation-state. Justice is probably insolubly problematic. It is achieved in the large-scale, bureaucratic U.S. society through *formal rationality* (Weber 1954:61–64), using abstract, technical concepts often masked by familiar vernacular terms.

The process is complicated by the existence of at least two major traditions within Indian law. A Whig tradition is the assimilation of Indians in separate local communities; relative tolerance of local custom; relative stress on honoring Indian treaties; and indirect rule through tribal leaders. From the pertinent Utilitarian viewpoints, particularistic groups and customs and old promises have scant relevance until they become important as obstacles to the achievement of Utilitarian agendas. Utilitarians tend to view with greater favor the assimilation of individual Indians into a pan-Indian, nationwide ethnic group, represented by national ethnic Indian leadership and associations unfettered by tribal particularisms. The identity and unity of that ethnic group are symbolized by an eclectic pan-Indian culture. Such Utilitarian viewpoints emphasize the concepts of civil and human rights of individual Indians within their communities.

*Tribal law* is intended to refer to the law of specific Indian polities, which are commonly called tribes. Here legal reasoning tends to be casuistic and substantively irrational in Weber's (1954) sense. Tribal law contains autochthonous elements that may be forbidden, unrecognized, or incomprehensible in Indian law. Inevitably, in a context of centuries of high-intensity acculturation, elements of Euro-American law have been incorporated through imposition, mechanical diffusion, or stimulus diffusion.

Legal elements can belong to more than one distinct system, but diffusion of an element from one legal system to another must be analyzed carefully. A manual of Indian offenses published by the U.S. Interior Department and enforced by Bureau of Indian Affairs (BIA) police or by federal troops is an element of Indian law, but probably not of tribal law. It is, however, a fact of tribal life, and, wholly or in part, the manual may well become assimilated into tribal law. A code drafted by BIA representatives in consultation with tribal members, ratified by popular plebiscite, enforced by tribal police, and interpreted by judges who are members of the tribe, is presumably an element of tribal law, however inconsistent it may be with other elements. This does not mean that the new code has become the totality of tribal law, or even the preeminent form. Within some communities, undoubtedly, there are laws of which outsiders do not even dream.

The Puebloan communities of the Southwest developed very effective tribal organizations in response to Spanish and Mexican hegemony. They continued that policy under the regime of the United States. By evading legal status as Indian for almost a century, they mitigated pressures from federal Indian law toward assimilative standardization of Indian institutions on an Anglo-American model. There were also pressures toward assimilative ethnogenesis (i.e., pan-Indianism), which were mitigated by a parochial exclusionary policy discouraging intertribal marriage and extruding native cultural entrepreneurs. That policy exacerbated endemic factionalism and strains of territorial losses and the internal pressures of making choices under conditions of contact with a vastly different civilization, which became intolerable in some instances.

Three aspects of the centuries of Hispanic dominance bear comment:

(1) On demographic grounds, it is highly likely that many migrated from the Indian pueblos to the Hispanic pueblos. Did the Indian pueblos by their exclusionary policies successfully block all lasting relationships between the emigrants and their stay-behind kin? Whether or not they did certainly has implications for acculturation and—at least indirectly—for social structure. Rules of, or preferences for, endogamy have a place here, but both the history and the functional relationships are unclear.

(2) The Indian pueblos of Arizona and New Mexico developed a set of Spanish-type civil officials. Eggan appropriately does not include those officials in the definition of Western and Eastern Pueblo types, which are designed for the widest possible validity independent of the particulars of specific culture areas. Nonetheless, in diagnostic definition of the structural types found in the Southwest, these officials can not be dismissed out of hand. However responsive they were to the traditional leadership, the new kind of officials had real jobs to do in making things happen in the community. They had access to alien information; they had established relationships with Spanish officials and representatives of other communities, Indian and Spanish. Inevitably they would acquire an independent base of power—as can be documented by nineteenth- and twentieth-century accounts. I suspect that this is an instance in which the structural significance of Spanish acculturation has been underestimated. The effects of Spanish influence upon the diagnostic criteria defining the structural type is not a simple issue with a foregone answer. Puebloan society was held together by energetically inculcated, intensely supported moral ordering supplemented by a hypertrophied apparatus of technical ordering (Hoebel 1962, 1969). Dissidents were quickly identified through gossip and scandal in a concentrated population. They were subject to execution, torture, and exile. Thus, a nominally secular official appointed by ceremonial-political adepts could be well insulated from individualistic temptations. The structural issue can not be resolved on cultural or historical grounds alone.

(3) Dual division is generally a poor mechanism to handle great stress in larger populations. Factionalism was probably inherent in Pueblo culture

before the Spanish Entrada. But in Euro-American times it became epidemic, in some cases causing structural failure. Does factionalism vary with structural type? Are factions diagnostic of structure types? In structures characterized by dual organization, does proliferation of factions regularly result from serial bifurcation of factions or nonfactional groups? In the present context answers to those questions, based on controlled comparison, would be useful. Some structural types are undoubtedly more prone to faction as a cultural epiphenomenon, but when the "factions" seem to be permanent, the nature of the structure needs to be reassessed.

Perhaps since some time in the eighteenth century there existed a schism in Santa Clara that produced a series of crises (Dozier 1966; Parsons 1939:1137; Hill 1982:190-201). In 1894 a conservative faction, which dominated one ceremonial-governmental moiety, and which controlled all but one of the officeholders from the other moiety, staged a coup, seizing the symbols and apparatus of government. Elsewhere, similar situations were resolved by emigration into Indian or Spanish-American communities, or by a collective movement to establish a dissident pueblo on a new site. In this instance the progressives stayed and, sometimes violently, resisted attempts by the conservative regime to enforce its authority.

The conservative faction was apparently dominated by an authoritarian, theocratic viewpoint that ascribed legitimate power to the traditional religious organization, and conceded little independent authority or discretion to the secular officers introduced by the Spanish. This faction retained de facto control of the government, but it never achieved legitimacy as a government of the whole pueblo. By 1934—forty years after the coup—there were four factions, bad times, and poor prospects. Intervention of the U.S. government and reorganization under the newly enacted Indian Reorganization Act offered hope of something better. The leaders of the several factions were persuaded to accept a new, written constitution, which was endorsed by popular plebiscite (Dozier 1966: 180-83; Hill 1982:200-201). The four factions, which were able to come together on a radically new course of action, appear to have been generated by serial bifurcation, moiety-based caucuses gradually emerging within both the conservative and progressive factions.

Within the coalition formed around acceptance of the constitution, the dominant viewpoint was that ultimate authority was embodied in the religious leadership. However, that viewpoint recognized a sphere in which secular officers had discretionary authority that was responsive to religious moral authority, but not directed by religious adepts. The viewpoint was strongly oriented to traditional moral authority, and it was not radically democratic; but it was open to expanded *technical ordering* (Redfield 1953:21) through Anglo-American economic and political techniques.

The Santa Clarans by no means fully understood the implications of adopting this constitution, but the action, according to Dozier, "ended more than 200 years of religious and political conflict within the pueblo." He adds that it brought about a "complete separation of religious and secular affairs in the pueblo" (1966:182). The categorical finality of that statement is weakened by other statements in the same article. It is inconsistent with Hill's (1982) observations made shortly after adoption of the constitution. It is inconsistent also with court testimony given in 1974 *(Martinez v. Santa Clara)*, which was about forty years after the events and eight years after Dozier's assessment was published.

The Santa Clara government appears to have tried in good faith to make the new institutions work as a series of novel situations and problems were addressed.

The balance of population and resources was unfavorable and deteriorating. Real property resources were limited. Per capita cash payments were anticipated as an important source of limited income. Short-run means of expanding the resource base were not evident. Stabilizing or reducing population would improve the situation.

In spite of a normative and relatively normal pattern of endogamy in the recent past, nonenrolled spouses of tribal members were living in the pueblo in significant numbers. By itself, the degree of endogamy does not necessarily affect population size, but, when it is combined with other factors, such as postmarital residence patterns or formal criteria for recognizing population membership, the combination is very likely to be a significant determinant of population size. Additionally, out-marriage is likely to bring in resident outsiders, who not only compete for limited resources, but who also may be regarded as intrinsically undesirable. There was ample normative motivation to try to limit the size or growth rate of the resident alien population. Given the delicate factional balance of the community, the most feasible approach to population control was to limit further increase in the number entitled to the tribal resources.

In 1939 the tribe enacted a membership ordinance abolishing two channels by which people could and did previously become tribal members: enrollment of children of a marriage between a member and an alien, and naturalization of an adult alien. The operative part of the ordinance reads as follows:

1. All children born of marriages between members of the Santa Clara Pueblo shall be members of the Santa Clara Pueblo.

2. All children born of marriage between male members of the Santa Clara Pueblo and non-members shall be members of the Santa Clara Pueblo.

3. Children born of marriage between female members of the Santa Clara Pueblo and non-members shall not be members of the Santa Clara Pueblo.

4. Persons shall not be naturalized as members of the Santa Clara Pueblo under any circumstances. [*Santa Clara v. Martinez* 1978:52]

The four vernacular English sentences plainly state a single principle, which can be restated technically: patrifiliation (Fortes 1959) is the sole basis for membership in the Santa Clara Pueblo. Patrifiliation is also entailed in many other institutions of Santa Clara. Priority of patrifiliation is surely a basic structural feature of Santa Clara. One way in which the Santa Clarans do not manifest the principle of filiation is in the formation of the kind of group that is properly called a lineage. There does not seem to be any way in which the term *patrilineal* can usefully be applied to Santa Clara.

The head of the Santa Clara household was presumed to be a man, and members of the group, including his wife, even if she were native and he alien, were expected to follow his lead and instruction in political and in important ritual matters. Therefore, a substantial number of women marrying aliens would result in significant influence of outsiders in the affairs of the pueblo. Marriage of Santa Clara men to alien women would not have the same effect on Santa Clara. A functionally related expectation was virilocality in intercommunity marriages that could have mitigated the influence of alien husbands, but there was still concern. That concern was intensified by the fact that in the 1930s (and since) the number of resident alien husbands in the pueblo has been significant (Dozier 1960:431).

There is some evidence (*Martinez v. Santa Clara* 1974) that there was current, if not universally accepted, a presumption that females by nature literally *could* not be conduits or vessels of certain sacred, intangible goods, but the scanty evidence requires confirmation. There is stronger evidence that such sacred intangibles, although they morally and legally should not be revealed, could be transmitted to aliens.

On the basis of such considerations the tribal council enacted the ordinance barring the enrollment of children of an alien father.

The events and issues discussed here are merely especially conspicuous incidents in a long-term trend of elaboration and expansion of technical ordering and formal rationality. The trend seems irreversible, and the tempo has accelerated in living memory.

In substantively irrational logic there is no need to reach the same decision or to act in the same way under conditions that are narrowly and abstractly conceived of as the same. In a little community with a simple system of intensively multiplex relationships (Gluckman 1955) it is a great power of substantive irrationality that it tailors action to the full particularity of the given situation and to the social relationships of the participants by exploiting inequalities between situations. All parties to a substantively irrational resolution may feel that they have gained something. However, the efficiency of irrational problem solving declines rapidly with the increasing size and complexity of the social field and the related tendency to simplex relationships.

Formal rationality requires general categories, abstract criteria, and an explicit set of mutually consistent principles upon which to base the criteria of law. With literacy, a characteristic expression of rationality is a systematic written code.

Civilizers and colonial rulers have often attempted to codify in writing a traditional corpus of normative custom that lacks explicit codification, that is highly particularistic and concrete in its conceptions, and that is suffused with substantive irrationality in its case-by-case administration of justice. There are more and less reliable ways of doing this. Pospisil (1971:273–339) has outlined techniques that suggest a promising approach. Less-promising approaches have been the norm—for example, that of Sir Arthur Gordon, which was based on Lewis H. Morgan's anthropology (France 1968). The record of actual cases under a preliterate regime is likely to confound any unrigorous universalistic statement of invariant relationships by many apparent contradictions, exceptions, and inconsistencies. For Euro-Americans it is all too easy to explain the apparent discrepancies as manifestations of primitive ignorance, individual corruption, mystic superstition (MacLachlan 1963, 1979), social disintegration, or elite oppression of the masses. The complexities are compounded when putative traditional principles are applied (even by the natives themselves) to situations for which there is little direct experience and relevant practical wisdom in the tradition. The results will be novel. Any judgment as to the traditional customary basis of the results is subject to many sources of uncertainty (see Equal Protection 1977).

In the specific example of Santa Clara, my opinion is that the 1939 membership ordinance has a traditional basis, and that it is not solely the creation de novo of modern economic interests, the opinion of the United States Tenth Circuit Court to the contrary notwithstanding (MacLachlan 1978; *Martinez v. Santa Clara* 1976). Patrifiliation is institutional in Santa

Clara. The membership ordinance of 1939 seems to have been a reasonable and justifiable measure in its time and circumstances, although not the only such alternative. The considerations in the formulation of the ordinance are documented in the trial testimony *(Martinez v. Santa Clara* 1974, 1975b) or the ethnographic documents in the record, and they are consistent with the facts available to me. Hence, as a matter of methodological principle, the documented considerations are the presumptive motivation of the tribal council. This is not to say that the council corporately and each of its several members did not have other motives as well; nor is it to deny that some of any such motives may have been self-serving or otherwise nonnormative.

Regardless of whether the ordinance was reasonable and justifiable, it created new issues. The number of alien husbands who settled with their Santa Clara wives at Santa Clara was larger than expected. Many of those wives, still members of the tribe, along with relatives and sympathizers in the tribe, sought over the years to have their children enrolled. That endeavor resulted in 1971 in the filing of the lawsuit mentioned here. The suit claimed that the 1939 membership ordinance violated a provision of the Indian Civil Rights Act of 1968. Passage of that act was greeted by most Indian observers with surprise, generally with apathy, and in some cases with open opposition (Schusky 1969, 1970). The act seems to have some mutually inconsistent purposes, and it probably reflects a flawed combination of Whig and Utilitarian viewpoints on Indian law and civil rights law. The present status of Indian law generally seems explicable as a tension between Whig and Utilitarian viewpoints. The field of civil rights law was once dominated by Whig impulses. Now the overwhelming impulse seems to be Utilitarian. Whiggish views are expressed, but may be less influential than a perceptible Anarchist tendency. Had the suit against Santa Clara prevailed, the drift to assimilate Indian law under civil rights law would have reenforced the trend toward assimilating Indians as individual ethnics.

The legal action ended in the Supreme Court of the United States *(Santa Clara v. Martinez* 1978), which found that Congress had not given the federal courts jurisdiction over controversies arising under the Indian Civil Rights Act (ICRA). Possibly that is a decision worthy of Solomon. By keeping the federal courts out of the implementation of the ICRA, the Supreme Court may have advanced both of the partly incompatible purposes of the act—that is, strengthening tribal government *and* assuring certain standards of universal human rights within tribes. Adversarial, zero-sum, formal litigation is no locus for reconciling irreconcilables. Santa Clara and the other federally recognized tribes have been given an opportunity, an implied responsibility under Indian law, and more time, to develop for such cases procedures that are most compatible with the preservation of the cultural integrity, autonomy, and residual sovereignty of each tribe. The ICRA itself provides means. However, adoption of those means would be yet another step of assimilation through standardization to Euro-American criteria.

Assuming that the Santa Clara membership issue is resolved and that procedures for remedying wrongs defined under the ICRA have been developed, there will still be new issues on the same pattern. In the technical ordering of the United States, enacted regulation of human relationships and litigation of controversies are increasingly the modes of first resort. Therefore, competition among disparate viewpoints for dominance in the legal institutions is endemic. The interactions at higher and more encompassing levels of the society have counterpart interactions in the legal institutions of communities like Santa Clara; and stimuli go in both directions. There is both cyclicity and time-boundedness in the flow of these events. Critical time-binding events in Santa Clara were the establishment of a bureaucratic framework for legal ordering in 1935 and the progressive encompassing of Santa Clara tribal law within the Indian law of the United States. Probably also a critical, time-binding, irreversible event was the acceptance of Hispanic-style civil officers centuries before. To the extent that Santa Clarans do not maintain alternative institutions by-passing Indian law in Santa Clara, transactions between moral and technical orders and relationships between persons will be mediated by a Euro-American technical ordering carrying in its interstices Euro-American moral assumptions. Herein, from one perspective, lies one of the greatest promises for orderly assimilation—or, from another perspective, one of the greatest threats to the survival of traditional institutions.

Results of analysis of one pueblo variant of a structural type may have broader significance, especially for other variants of that type within the region. For Native American communities and tribes recognized in Indian law, key to assimilation are the institutions for defining, interpreting, and maintaining norms. Introduction of Spanish-style civil officials in the Southwest established a small, but firm base for the realignment of relationships within the community in the direction of Euro-American structures. Puebloan ceremonial-political functionaries probably overestimated their own capacity to control the new officials, and underestimated the structural implications of the innovation. The Indian Reorganization Act of 1934 had purposes consistent with those of the Spanish policy and built on that base. Both Spanish and U.S. governments had experimented with military conquest and the suppression of native religion. Their experiments had not proved to be cost-effective. Both governments shifted to diplomacy, persuasion, unilateral normative regulation—all sanctioned by force or the threat of force.

As an operative process, stimulus diffusion (Kroeber 1940) has been underrated. The terms *diffusion* and *acculturation* are overly vague as indicators of any specific process. They serve better to identify a state of affairs in which a family of processes is likely at work. *Diffusion* connotes an essential parity between sociocultural systems; *acculturation,* a significant disparity. In relational, as opposed to cultural, terms the disparity is in control of the actions of persons or control over resources and benefits (Nadel 1957). At specific times and places the relationship of, say, neighboring Indian and Hispanic pueblos was near parity. Mechanical diffusion of objects, demonstration of techniques and actions, and face-to-face communication of ideas occurred. The sheer introduction of the novel civil officials fits this formula. But the mere presence of the officials in the perceptual field undoubtedly triggered thought, speculation, and consequences in the minds of members of the pueblo, including the officials themselves and the ceremonial-political functionaries. The result would have been institutions and practices sometimes closely paralleling Hispanic counterparts, but often going in different directions that reflected the pueblo milieu. For the anthropologist, the main problem with the process of stimulus diffusion is that it is hard to document after the fact. Scanty ethnographic observations or casual references in documents will reveal situations of diffusion or acculturation. The actual process must be observed over time and recorded as such. Still, theories or hypothetical reconstructions of development in the Southwest are flawed in omitting or discounting analysis of the probable incidence and significance of stimulus diffusion.

Within the acculturation situation a conspicuous process was premeditated social engineering of assimilation through legalistic forms. Control over the interactions of persons is gained by establishing dependence on resources and benefits controlled by or through the federal government. (At issue in the Santa Clara case, *Martinez v. Santa Clara,* was access to public housing on the reservation, which was contingent on formal tribal membership. Public housing and written membership rolls are federal benefits.)

Discussion of the patrilineality attributed to Santa Clara tells us more about the customs of the anthropological tribe than it does about Tewa social organization. That is a subject in itself (MacLachlan 1978; Paul 1979). The Tewa have been described (often tentatively or equivocally) as patrilineal. They have also been labeled as patriarchical, or as having a patrilineal bias. The Tewa are not patrilineal. But that is not the end of it.

Another, undeservedly neglected concept, *filiation,* is applicable. Patri-filiation is clearly manifest in Santa Clara. It may be justifiable to character-ize Santa Clara as patrifilial, although such terms should probably be used relatively or quantitatively, rather than qualitatively. Further analysis or research may show that manifest patrifiliation is important in Eastern Pueblos generally and even that it is a definitive element in a putative Eastern Pueblo-type structure.

*Endogamy* is a term frequently invoked, but not much analyzed as a concept. It is possible that in normal use it represents a heterogeneous residual category that masks the operation of several distinct processes. It has been used above to characterize Santa Clara practice, but that use is a jargon bandage to cover ignorance. Constraints on the distribution of marriageable partners is an important subject. So also is the actual distribution of marriages against social or cultural boundaries. Both are too important to bury under a set of ill-conceived categories. In the sources of this paper it is not clear what the Santa Clara did about marriage or what they thought they were doing. It is clear that there is, or was, a graded scale of diffusely disapproved categories of marriage outside the community.

Although dual division has long been regarded as an important, if somewhat mysterious, phenomenon, analysis of its significance in the Southwest was long insufficient. Now it is clear that dual organization is basic to the Tewa (Ortiz 1969). It is hard to accept the Tewa being considered representative of a structural type that does not include dual organization as a criterion.

The subject of dual organization, which transcends moieties and emphasizes the cultural aspects of social organization, also arose in the testimony during the Santa Clara case. Santa Clara witnesses were strikingly uninformative or reticent on the subject. Their lack of testimony clearly weakened the pueblo's case. A careful observer would conclude that there was something important about the subject, and that it had something to do with religion or ritual. But there was no clue as to how important it was, why it was important, or of what it consisted. If Indians cannot in good conscience testify concerning the most important things, then their side of the case will not get a fair hearing. Consequently, litigation in Anglo—American courts as a mode of resolution is even more heavily stacked against Indian tribes than might first appear. Even tribal courts set up on the Anglo-American model have had great difficulty administering tribal law in witchcraft cases. Capability to act in such grievances effectively may be a litmus test of the viability of a dependent sovereign nation with borrowed justitial machinery.

## Acknowledgments

The work from which most of this paper is drawn was part of a research project on the representation of Indian cultures in Anglo-American courts done while I was on the faculty of the Department of Anthropology, Southern Illinois University, Carbondale. The department supported the project with released time, a budget, and a graduate research assistant, Keltie-Jean Paul. Her dedicated assembly, organization, and insightful analysis of data were essential to the project.

## References

Bohannan, Paul
  1969    Ethnography and Comparison in Legal Anthropology. *In* Law in Culture and Society, edited by Laura Nader, 401–18. Chicago: Aldine Publishing.
Dozier, Edward P.
  1960    A Comparison of Eastern Keresan and Tewa Kinship Systems. Selected Papers of the Fifth International Congress of Anthropological and Ethnological Sciences, edited by Anthony F. C. Wallace, 430–36. Philadelphia: University of Pennsylvania Press.
  1966    Factionalism at Santa Clara Pueblo. Ethnology 5:172–85.
Equal Protection under the Indian Civil Rights Act: *Martinez v. Santa Clara Pueblo.*
  1977    Harvard Law Review 90:627–36.
Eggan, Fred
  1950    Social Organization of the Western Pueblos. Chicago: University of Chicago Press.
  1955    Methods and Results. *In* Social Anthropology of the North American Tribes, edited by Fred Eggan, 485–551. Enlarged ed. Chicago: University of Chicago Press.
Fortes, Meyer
  1959    Descent, Filiation and Affinity: A Response to Dr. Leach. Man 59:193–97, 206–12.
France, Peter
  1968    The Founding of an Orthodoxy: Sir Arthur Gordon and the Doctrine of the Fijian Way of Life. Journal of the Polynesian Society 77:6–32.
Gluckman, Max
  1955    The Judicial Process among the Barotse of Northern Rhodesia. Manchester: Manchester University Press.
Hill, W. W.
  1982    An Ethnography of Santa Clara Pueblo, New Mexico. Edited by Charles Lange. Albuquerque: University of New Mexico Press.
Hoebel, E. Adamson
  1962    The Authority Systems of the Pueblos of the Southwestern United States. Proceedings of the Thirty-fourth International Congress of Americanists, 555–63. Vienna.
  1969    Keresan Pueblo Law. *In* Law in Culture and Society, edited by Laura Nader, 92–116. Chicago: Aldine Publishing.
Kroeber, A. L.
  1940    Stimulus Diffusion. American Anthropologist 42:1–20.

MacLachlan, Bruce B.
   1963      On "Indian Justice." Plains Anthropologist 8:257-61.
   1978      Cultural Integrity, Individual Rights, the Courts, and Ethnography. Paper
            presented at the annual meeting of the Central States Anthropological Society,
            23 March.
   1979      The Case of the Protracted Pregnancy. In Currents in Anthropology: Essays
            in Honor of Sol Tax, edited by Robert Hinshaw, 363-70. The Hague: Mouton.
   1981      Tahltan. In Handbook of North American Indians. Vol. 6, Subarctic, edited
            by June Helm, 458-68. Washington, D.C.: Smithsonian Institution.
Martinez v. Santa Clara
   1974      Transcript of testimony, United States District Court for the District of New
            Mexico, 25-26 November 1974. Albuquerque.
   1975a     Memorandum Opinion of the Presiding Judge, United States District Court
            for the District of New Mexico. American Indian Law Newsletter:121-39.
   1975b     402 Federal Supplement 5 (District of New Mexico).
   1976      540 Federal Reporter, 2d Series 1039.
Nadel, S. F.
   1957      The Theory of Social Structure. Glencoe: The Free Press.
Ortiz, Alfonso
   1969      The Tewa World: Space, Time, Being, and Becoming in a Pueblo Society.
            Chicago: University of Chicago Press.
Parsons, Elsie C.
   1939      Pueblo Indian Religion. 2 vols. Chicago: University of Chicago Press.
Paul, Keltie-Jean
   1979      The Anthropological Expert Witness and the Courts. Paper presented at the
            annual meeting of the Southern Anthropological Society, 28 February.
Pospisil, Leopold
   1971      Anthropology of Law: A Comparative Theory. New York: Harper & Row.
Redfield, Robert
   1953      The Primitive World and Its Transformations. Ithaca: Cornell University
            Press.
Santa Clara v. Martinez
   1978      436 United States Reports 49.
Schusky, Ernest L.
   1969      American Indians and the 1968 Civil Rights Act. América Indígena
            29:367-75.
   1970      An Indian Dilemma. International Journal of Comparative Sociology
            11:58-66.
Weber, Max
   1954      Max Weber on Law in Economy and Society. Edited by Max Rheinstein.
            Cambridge: Harvard University Press.

# 16

# Cultural Motifs in Navajo Weaving

GARY WITHERSPOON

To discover the cultural import of the design patterns found in Navajo weaving, I explore the depths and details of Navajo oral history, religion, ceremonialism, social structure, military alliance, linguistic labels and classifications, and the Navajo patterns of organizing geometrical space—not to lose sight of Navajo weaving, but to find its roots, its links, and, most of all, its semiotic context. Weaving is part of the collective life of the Navajos. It is part of their history. Moreover, probably as much as anything else, Navajo weaving expresses the essence of being Navajo. It exemplifies the Navajo way of seeing the world and of being a part of the world.

This chapter is about the cultural geometry of Navajo weaving. Unlike many other works, it treats Navajo weaving as a form of art and it places that art in its cultural context. The Navajo aesthetic style can be characterized by what I call holistic symmetry, which finds its cultural basis in the Navajo term *hózhǫ́*. *Hózhǫ́* is an all-inclusive concept of beauty, harmony, and well-being. It derives from the supreme Holy Pair, *Są'ah Naagháí* and *Bik'eh Hózhǫ́*, and it is fully manifested in the profound personality of Changing Woman, who is the inner form of the earth. It is this philosophical and aesthetic theme that is expressed in the holistic and symmetrical patterns and forms of Navajo weaving, and it is to these deities, as well as Born for the Water and Monster Slayer, that the inter-woven motifs of Navajo weaving refer.

The concept of holistic essence—*hózhǫ́*—is found in every aspect of Navajo language, art, and culture, not just in Navajo weaving. It permeates the culture, and its maintenance, celebration, or restoration is the goal of all ritual action. The concept of *hózhǫ́* is too abstract and too contextual to express in simple and autonomous imagery; it must be conveyed in inter-active, symmetrical, and holistic compositions that are presented in one-image formats.

Weaving by its very nature and technique is inherently integrative, holistic, and systemic. Therefore, it does not seem metaphorically insignificant that so many people speak of a cosmic web, nor is it surprising that the ancestors of the Navajos learned to weave from Spider Woman. The description of Spider Woman's loom illustrates the Navajo conception that weaving is an act of universal integration and an art that expresses cosmic holism:

> Spider Woman instructed the Navajo women how to weave on a loom which Spider Man told them how to make. The crosspoles were made of sky and earth cords, the warp sticks of sun rays, the healds of rock crystal and sheet lightning. The batten was a sun halo, white shell made the comb. There were four spindles: one a stick of zigzag lightning with a whorl of cannel coal; one a stick of flash lightning with a whorl of turquoise; a third had a stick of sheet lightning with a whorl of abalone; a rain streamer formed the stick of the fourth and its whorl was white shell. [Reichard 1934:frontispiece]

The loom of Spider Woman represents the Navajo universe in microcosm and in metaphor. In weaving on a loom made of earth and sky cords, sun rays and halos of the sun, lightning in zigzags, flashes, and sheets, and rain streamers and precious jewels, the Navajo weaver unites the Sky Father with the Earth Mother, and this interwoven union brings together all the cosmic forces associated with fertility, fecundity, beauty, and power. The sacred and beautiful jewels associated with the four weaving sticks represent the colors of the four underworlds through which the Holy People traversed on their way to their emergence to the surface of the earth. These four sacred jewels are also metaphorically associated with the cardinal directions, the four sacred mountains that enclose the Navajo universe in the shape of a diamond, and the particular types of animals, plants, winds, and Holy People that are associated with the cardinal directions and the sacred mountains.[1]

The act of weaving on Spider Woman's loom (the prototype of Navajo looms) metaphorically interweaves Navajo history with the male/female essences and forces of the cosmos that come together in woven composi-tions to express the Navajo concept of dynamic and regenerative cycles. These cycles are generated by the most powerful and the most sacred of all beings in the Navajo universe, the male *Sǫ'ah Naagháí* and the female *Bik'eh Hózhǫ́*, about whom much more will be said later. The important point here is that weaving, as taught by Spider Woman, is an act of universal integration and an artistic expression of holistic symmetry. It is not surprising that others have found the same sort of universal metaphors in the act and art of weaving:

> The picture of an interconnected cosmic web which emerges from modern atomic physics has been used extensively in the East to convey

the mystical experience of nature. For the Hindus, *Brahman* is the unifying thread in the cosmic web, the ultimate ground of all being:

*He on whom the sky, the earth, and the atmosphere*
*Are woven, and the wind, together with all life-breaths,*
*Him alone know as the one Soul.*

In Buddhism, the image of the cosmic web plays an even greater role. The core of the *Avatamsaka Sutra*, one of the main scriptures of Mahayana Buddhism, is the description of the world as a perfect network of mutual relations where all things and events interact in an infinitely complicated way. . . . The cosmic web, finally, plays a central role in Tantric Buddhism. . . . The scriptures of this school are called the *Tantras*, a word whose Sanskrit root means '**to weave**' and which refers to the interwovenness and interdependence of all things and events. [Capra 1975: 139; emphasis (in bold) added]

To begin a study of Navajo weaving, we must explore this art form in the context of Navajo culture and from the perspective of the Navajo philosophy of art. In Navajo society the emphasis with regard to art is placed on creation rather than consumption, production rather than preservation, and design rather than display. Correspondingly, nearly everyone in Navajo society is an artist of one sort or of many sorts, but very few Navajos buy or display works of art. They use them in ritual, sell them to non-Navajos, or destroy them. This attitude and practice is not unusual among Native Americans. The Eskimos, for example, act in a similar manner:

When spring comes and igloos melt, the old habitation sites are littered with waste, including beautifully-designed tools and tiny ivory carvings, not deliberately thrown away, but, with even greater indifference, just lost. Eskimo are interested in the artistic act, not in the product of the activity. A carving, like a song, is not a thing, it is an action. When you feel a song within you, you sing it; when you sense a form emerging from ivory, you release it. It's senseless to assume that when we collect these silent, static carvings we have collected Eskimo art, even if we record date and provenience. Measurements of size, diagrams of diffusion, and seriation studies of chronology do nothing to correct the initial error. [Carpenter 1961:362]

In Native American societies, art is not viewed as marginal, unessential, or extracurricular. Instead, art is viewed as a way of seeing the world, and a way of being in the world. Much of Navajo art—song, poetry, dance, sandpainting—occurs in ritual performances. Although the Navajos do not in their society present concerts for spectators, they do perform rituals that Reichard correctly characterized as symphonies of the arts. These rituals contain oral literature, drama, dance, poetry, music, and sandpainting. They are performed to celebrate, maintain, or restore *hózhǫ́*. When a Navajo gets out of harmony with those other beings with whom he or she shares this world, the ceremonies are there to reformulate aboriginal harmony and beauty. They are participant symphonies, and the patient not only participates in the symphony but also becomes the symphony through absorption. The patient becomes the central figure in the story, sings in chorus with the Singer (ritual leader), repeats the poetic prayers, and is placed directly in the sandpainting when it is finished. The sandpainting is not just to be seen but to be absorbed. When absorbed, its beauty and harmony heal mind and body. The patient does not just visualize nature or the environment; the patient becomes absorbed in its reformulated harmony and beauty.

Navajos do not "look" for beauty and harmony; they absorb and immerse themselves in it. When it is disrupted, they reformulate it; when it is lost, they restore it; when it is diminished, they renew it; when it is present, they celebrate it. The Navajo say in their own vernacular: *shił hózhǫ́* 'with me there is beauty'; *shii' hózhǫ́* 'in me there is beauty'; *shaa hózhǫ́* 'from me beauty radiates'. The Navajos express and celebrate this beauty in speech and prayer, in song and dance, in myth and ritual, and in their daily lives and activities, as well as in their graphic arts.

The nature of Navajo weaving as a creative act and the cultural import of the motifs of Navajo weaving are part of a larger historical, social, and cultural context, and cannot be adequately understood outside that context.

## Cultural Motifs

The Navajos as a nation call themselves *Diné*. *Diné* is a linguistic representation of a social, political, and military alliance. Two of the indigenous emblems of that alliance are most commonly known as the emblems of Born for the Water and Monster Slayer (see fig. 1). They have an important history, and a rich set of meanings. They also contain the basic design elements from which many of the patterns of Navajo weaving are derived. Let us first place these emblems in their cultural and historical contexts, and then later we will see how these designs recur in Navajo weaving styles and patterns.

Other than on Navajo rugs and in Navajo sandpaintings, one can find the emblems shown below in four other places:[2] (1) on the staff of the *Diné* in the Enemyway ritual, (2) on the masks, clothing, and attire of the ritual impersonations of Born for the Water and Monster Slayer, (3) in the hair buns of Changing Woman and of ordinary Navajo men and women, and (4) on the rock walls of the area called *Dinétah*. I will start with the latter.

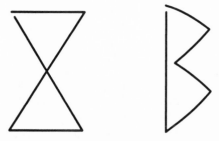

**Figure 1.** Born for the Water and Monster Slayer emblems.

*Dinétah* is a Navajo word that contains the suffix –*tah*, which means 'among', 'through', or 'in the area of'. The usage here designates an area considered special and sacred by the Navajos because it is their place of origin. It is the area from which the Holy People emerged to this world, and the early events of this world mostly took place there. It is the place where Changing Woman (the principal Navajo deity) was found, where she grew up, and where she provided her blessings. It is where her children, the *Diné*, first located after they were created at her home in the West. It therefore represents the sacred homeland of the Navajos.

This sacred homeland is outlined or demarcated by four sacred mountains: Blanca Peak and Hesperus Peak in Colorado, Mount Taylor in New Mexico, and the San Francisco Peaks in Arizona. If connecting lines are drawn between these mountains, the resulting shape is an imperfect diamond. The exact center of this diamond is a few miles east and north of Bloomfield, New Mexico. Near this center point are two more sacred mountains, Gobernador Knob and Huerfano Mesa. These are known to the Navajos as the center or middle mountains. It was in this center area of Gobenador Knob and Huerfano Mesa that the early events of Navajo history took place. On this point, the Navajos are in agreement with archeologists, who have found the earliest traces of Navajo residence in the Southwest in this area.

The emblems of Monster Slayer and Born for the Water are found throughout the petroglyphs of this area. Robert A. Roessel, Jr., an educator and longtime friend and student of the Navajos includes photographs of these designs in his book on the area, *Dinétah* (1983:6, 29, 30, 50, 62, 114, 126, 128, 129). It is clear from these numerous petroglyphs that the Navajos considered the emblems of Born for the Water and Monster Slayer to be theirs. These represented one way the Navajos conveyed their identity and identified their homeland.

The Born for the Water design also has been said to be associated with the bun into which Changing Woman's hair was tied during her Blessing-way and puberty rite. All young Navajo girls have their hair tied in such a bun during their puberty rites. Traditionally, most Navajo men and women wore their hair in this type of bun, and many Navajos still do today. The Navajos are one of the few groups of American Indians to wear their hair in this manner. For contemporary Navajos, the daily re-creation of the hairbun is a strong symbol of traditionalism whose power, importance, and prominence is quite evident. It is hard to imagine any more appropriate or more prominent way to display a national emblem and cultural symbol.

The bow pattern of Monster Slayer's emblem was also with the Navajos almost daily in traditional times. The bow was used extensively, and was proudly displayed when not in use. The distinctive sinew-backed bow of the Navajos was well known among native peoples of the South-west, and it was one of the most powerful and effective weapons of its kind found anywhere in native North America.

The emblems of Born for the Water and Monster Slayer are also found prominently in Navajo ritual. Before these emblems and what they represent can be understood, a brief outline of Navajo history, as told by the Navajos, needs to be presented. This oral history has filled several volumes. All that can be provided here is a brief sketch of some of the principal details.

## The Emergence

The gods and forerunners of the Navajos emerged into this world through four underworlds or previous stages of existence.[3] The place of the emergence is thought to be somewhere near what is now Navajo Lake. The world at the time of the Emergence was without form, shape, or dimension. It was described as mud. The *Diyin Dine'é* ('Holy People') who emerged into this world were called into a great sweathouse wherein they thought, sang, and prayed the world into existence. They were able to do this as a result of their previously gained knowledge and ritual power. An important aspect to this story of creation was the mountain bundle that First Man brought with him from the underworlds. The sacred mountains were said to have existed in the underworlds, and First Man brought with him soil from each of them. From the soil bundles he was able to recreate the sacred mountains in this new world.

Another important part of First Man's sacred bundle was the inner forms—life-giving and animating powers—of various vital dimensions of this world. The world was, in part, organized by controlling and directing these inner forms to take their places and fulfill their roles in the newly prepared world. The inner forms included, among others, those for the sun and moon, the water and the mountains, and the cardinal directions. The world was organized into day and night and into seasons. Birth, growth, decay, and death were set as basic dimensions. Plants and animals, fabrics and jewels also were fundamental aspects of the world as created and organized by the Holy People. The *Diné* or *Nihookáá' Dine'é* ('Earth Surface People') were not yet created. This creation was solely the domain of the *Diyin Dine'é* ('Holy People' or 'Gods').

In the third underworld some of the people abused their capacity to reproduce. These abuses included incest, adultery, masturbation, and immodesty, the consequences of which did not become apparent until the females started to give birth to various monsters that began to terrorize and devour the people. The capacity to reproduce properly was thus lost, and death and despair set in.

To save the world and the people, First Man came up with a plan. There is some suggestion that this plan may have been in the scheme of things from the beginning. The most beautiful and powerful of all inner forms arose from First Man's medicine bundle. This pair was known as *Sạ'ah Naaghái* Boy and *Bik'eh Hózhọ́* Girl (Wyman 1970:126, note 111; Witherspoon 1977:17-40). The pair were the parents of Changing Woman, who was found as a baby on the top of Gobernador Knob (Wyman 1970:139-43). According to First Man's plan, Changing Woman would save the world by first restoring the power of reproduction, and then by giving birth to the Twins who would slay the monsters.

Changing Woman grew to puberty in four days and had the Blessing-way ceremony performed for her as a puberty rite. The Blessingway, its power and its beauty, became hers, as it was given to her at the end of the ceremony. The ceremony prepared her for conjugal union with the inner form of the Sun. That union resulted in the birth of twin boys, known later as Born for the Water and Monster Slayer. The Twins lived only at their mother's home at first. Then, wanting to discover who their father was, they embarked on a journey to find his home. They went through trials and tests along the way. Finally, they found their father, the Sun. From him they got the bow and other weapons with which to kill the monsters.

While the Twins were on their journey to find their father, they noticed smoke coming out of a hole in the ground. They looked in to investigate, and they found an old woman weaving. It was Spider Woman. She invited them in. The Twins descended into the home on a ladder with four rungs. After the Twins told Spider Woman where they were going, she was pessimistic. To insure their success, and to protect them in their battles with the monsters, Spider Woman gave the Twins a bundle of talking prayer sticks (usually called "life feathers") and several protective formulas. These gifts protected the Twins in their travels and prevented them from succumbing to several of the monsters' tricks.

The Twins returned to the home of their mother, showed her the weapons they obtained, and then proceeded to take on and slay each of the monsters. Monster Slayer—or Enemy Slayer—took a more active role in these battles than did Born for the Water. Born for the Water was more of an assistant, a lookout, and an aide who helped protect Monster Slayer. Monster Slayer did the actual killing. When all the monsters were killed, there was relief, but not yet complete joy. The earth was still not purified. The ghosts of the dead monsters still haunted the Twins and contaminated the beauty and purity of the earth. Another ceremony was needed to rid the world and the minds of the Twins from the haunting and contaminating effects of the enemy ghosts. To do this, the Enemyway ceremony was performed over the Twins.

Once the Enemyway was performed and the world was purified of the ghosts of the dead monsters, harmony and beauty—*hózhǫ*—were restored to the world. There was great rejoicing, and Changing Woman was now ready to create the four original Navajo clans. She did this from powers she obtained from the Blessingway and from First Man's medicine bundle, both of which she now controlled. This is the first time the ancestors of the Navajos, as the "Earth Surface People," had come into being. It seems that everything previous to this point had been done in anticipation of or in preparation for the coming of the *Diné* (Navajos). With the creation of the *Diné*, the Holy People all disappeared into their outer forms, and their inner forms were never seen again. The Navajos were told, however, that they would be able to discern the presence of the Holy People in the future when they heard the voice of the wind and the singing of the bluebirds, and observed the growth of the corn. Any living or growing being would indicate the presence of the Gods (Fishler 1953:92). By these, the Navajos would confirm the continued presence of the Gods.

## The Enemyway

The emblems of the Twins are carved on the staff that plays a key role in the symbolism of the Enemyway. The Enemyway has always been a popular ceremony with the Navajo people. It is a ritual of nationalism, and has taken on even greater popularity as the sense and reality of Navajo nationalism increases.

As with nearly all Navajo ceremonies, the Enemyway is designed to cure patients who are ill because they are bothered by the ghosts or the spirits of dead *Ana 'í* (non-Navajos), often considered the result of too much contact with non-Navajos. The Enemyway is an attack on the ghost of the alien that is causing the illness. The victorious attack, dramatized in the ritual, cures the patients.

There are two main symbols in the Enemyway rite. One is the rattlestick, or staff; the other is the scalp. The staff is a symbol of the *Diné*, and the scalp is a symbol of the *Ana 'í.* The term *Diné* signifies a group of Navajos who are bound together by combinations of kinship and non-kinship solidarity (reciprocity). One of the major forms of reciprocity on which Navajo society is built is that of mutual assistance in warfare. *Diné* are not to fight against each other, and are to help each other when attacked by an outsider. The *Diné*, then, are bound together by a military alliance, and the Enemyway enacts and defines that alliance.

The staff is obtained and decorated on the first day of the rite. The first design put on the staff is that of the bow, which symbolizes Monster Slayer and the power he had over his enemies, the monsters. The source of this power is the Sun, the father of the Twins. The second design is that of Born for the Water, patterned after Changing Woman's hair bun. (These two designs were shown earlier in fig. 1.) The staff is then further decorated with materials whose symbolic meanings I have discussed in detail elsewhere (1975:56-64) and which are summarized below:

| STAFF | SCALP |
|---|---|
| *Diné* 'Navajo' | *Ana 'í* 'enemy, foreigner' |
| Life | Death |
| Good | Evil |
| Power | Weakness |
| Moisture | Dryness |
| New pure vegetation | Old, impure vegetation |
| Reproduction of life | End of life |
| Active | Static |
| Purity | Contamination, impurity |
| Beauty | Ugliness |

The nationalism of the *Diné* is symbolized by the staff, and this national identity is ritually opposed to the scalp, the symbol of the *Ana 'í.* During the blackening ceremony, the patient is dressed in the clothes of Monster Slayer and arrayed with the symbols of the life and power of the *Diné*. When this is complete, he or she goes out and attacks the scalp with a crow bill. Others shoot at it, bury it with ashes, and burn it into nonexistence. This experience provides a tremendous bolstering of national pride and solidarity. The power of the *Diné* over its enemies is asserted and demonstrated. This power comes from the vast ceremonial system of the Navajos, and from the military, political, and social alliance represented by the emblems of Monster Slayer and Born for the Water.

As emblems, these designs signify Monster Slayer and Born for the Water, but as polysemic symbols they mean life, beauty, good, power, growth, reproduction, and, most of all, they mean *Diné*. They symbolize the vitality, the integration, and the power of the Navajo Nation. In previous centuries they appear to have been a trademark of the Navajos. They are not just secular symbols or weaving motifs; they are also sacred symbols, whose meanings are deeply embedded and prominently displayed in the religious and ceremonial order of the Navajos.

## Other Occurrences of the Cultural Motifs

The emblems of Monster Slayer and Born for the Water are found on the masks and bodies of those who impersonate these deities in ritual. In *Navajo Legends*, Washington Matthews presents a plate with Born for the Water's ritual representation or impersonation (1897: plate 7; reproduced here as fig. 2). His emblems are prominently displayed on his left leg and arm, on his chest, and on his head mask. Matthews also shows an impersonation of Monster Slayer (1897: plate 4; reproduced here as fig. 3).

The emblems of Monster Slayer and Born for the Water are not the only cultural motifs found in weaving patterns, nor are they the most primary or fundamental of the culturally significant design elements. There is much evidence to indicate that the diamond and the triangle are also important cultural symbols.

The Navajos conceive of the Fifth World as a plane in the shape of a diamond whose outline is demarcated by the sacred mountains. Mother Earth and Father Sky are conceived as anthropomorphic (Pinxten, van Dooren, and Harvey 1983:9) and have been depicted thus in at least one rug (Maxwell 1963:40). In this woven composition based on a sandpainting motif (Wyman 1983:107-8; Newcomb and Reichard 1975:37), Mother Earth is a female who lies on her back with her head to the east. Her torso is shaped like a diamond with four appendages that join to form two Monster Slayer bows. The head is rectangular.

Father Sky possesses the same shape and complementary attributes as Mother Earth. They lie together in the pattern of sexual intercourse. The rain from the sky is analogically associated with semen, and its intrusion into the Earth causes reproduction, birth, and the sprouting of new life. This process is depicted by the images in the bodies of Father Sky and Mother

**Figure 2.** Ritual impersonation of Born for the Water. Drawing by Dolly Spalding (reprinted from Matthews 1897: plate 7).

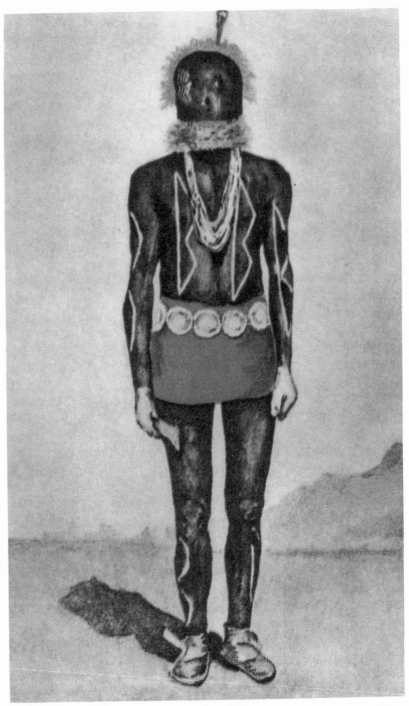

**Figure 3.** Ritual impersonation of Monster Slayer. Drawing by Dolly Spalding (reprinted from Matthews 1897: plate 4).

Earth. Changing Woman is the inner form of the Earth, is often referred to as Earth Woman, and is symbolized by the diamond shape of the Earth.

The present world of the Earth Surface People is based on the number four. There are four cardinal directions, four phases of the day (dawn, daylight, twilight, darkness), four seasons of the year, four sacred mountains, four principal colors, jewels, and food plants, and there are four phases to the cycle of life. It is not surprising, therefore, that this world would then be conceived of as a four-sided figure. Both the square and the diamond have four sides, but the diamond is aesthetically dynamic in comparison to the more static shape of the square.

The face masks used in *Yé'ii* initiation ceremonies also seem to indicate that the Navajo want their initiates to see the world through the shape of a diamond. The masks that the initiates are required to look through all have triangular-shaped eye openings. These triangles have their apexes pointing outward and their bases pointing inward (see fig. 4). Examples of these masks can be found in Stevenson (1891: plate 115), Haile (1947:73, 86) and Matthews (1902:18). The masks with triangulated eyeholes also have been found in the Gobernador region and date to the *Dinétah* period (Hester 1972:121; Carlson 1965:47). All female masks have the triangular eye openings, and it is these masks that are put on the youth during the initiation. When one puts on the mask and looks through the triangular eyes, the resulting view of the world is diamond shaped. Let us explore the initiation process a little more carefully to see how this diamond-shaped view of the world is acquired.

The first ethnographer to observe and undergo the *Yé'ii* initiation was Washington Matthews, whose full account is given in his major work, *The Night Chant* (1902:116-20). I have also undergone this initiation. It normally is performed a couple of hours after sunset on the fifth night of the Night Chant. The initiates enter the ceremonial *hooghan* with their heads bowed and their eyes cast down. After seating themselves, they cover their heads with blankets. Then, one by one, the initiates are called to come out from under their blankets and face the masked Gods. Next, Talking God

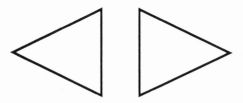

**Figure 4.** Eyeholes of initiation mask.

and Female God administer to the initiate. The Female God applies cornmeal to various parts of the initiate's body, then Talking God symbolically whips the initiate with a yucca leaf. This does not inflict pain, and the female initiates are only touched with the leaf.

After each initiate has been administered to and blessed by the Gods, the candidates again are seated in a row. While the initiates' heads are bowed and their faces covered, the Gods take off their masks and lay them side by side, face up, with the heads to the east. The men and women who impersonated the Gods then stand with uncovered faces before the initiates. The initiates are told to throw back their blankets and look up. When they do so, the secret of the impersonation of the Gods is revealed. Then comes the part of the ceremony that is most relevant to the present discussion:

> The next part of the ceremony is the application of the mask. He who masquerades as a Goddess takes the female mask and applies it in turn to the face of each of the candidates—proceeding along the row from north to south—and adjusts the mask carefully to the face so that the candidate can look out through the eye-holes and understand fully the mechanism of the mask. The mask is then laid in its former position, south of the other masks on the buffalo robe. The actor takes good care that the eyes of the candidate are seen clearly through the eye-holes in the mask. [Matthews 1902:119]

The triangulated eyeholes (bases to the center) provide a diamond-shaped view of the Gods, the other masks, and the world in general. This experience makes a powerful and lasting impression on the initiate. The rite seems to say that there is only one sacred and appropriate way for the Navajo to view their Gods and their universe, and that it is through triangulated eyes that render a diamond-shaped view. It seems clear that this diamond-shaped view is primarily associated with the female. All female masks have triangular-shaped eyeholes, and only female masks are put on the initiates, regardless of whether they are male or female. Males are allowed to impersonate Female Gods, but must wear the masks of the Female Gods. Male masks have variously shaped eyeholes, although square eyeholes may be most common. But the square eyeholes are never used in the initiation ceremony when the mask is placed on the face of the initiates.

Haile gives us a similar version of this rite:

> After seeing who the ye-i are, the female ye-i moves its mask to the face of each candidate and makes sure that the initiated look through the eye

openings of the mask. This manipulation of the female mask appears to
be part of the ceremony of 'seeing the ye-i' if not an essential part of it.
[1947:55]

It is quite obvious from the design of the masks that the Navajos were
cognizant that a diamond consists of two equal triangles. The emblems of
Monster Slayer, Born for the Water, and Changing Woman all incorporate
two triangles in their construction. However, Born for the Water's emblem
turns them "in" and puts them in opposing symmetry, while Monster
Slayer's emblem turns both triangles "out" in the same direction. The
diamond turns both triangles "out" in opposite directions, giving the idea
of infinite extension from a center point. All these key cultural emblems
are based on the triangle. The triangle is the generative basis of Navajo
semiotic geometry.

The two triangles that constitute the diamond are associated with the
parents of Changing Woman, *Sǫ'ah Naagháí* and *Bik'eh Hózhǫ́*. They
represent the ultimate source of life, beauty, harmony, order, good, and
regeneration in the universe. In effect they represent ultimate power,
intelligence, and beauty; as such, they are in part beyond human conception
or representation. Although all the ceremonies are designed to identify the
patient with these deities in order that he or she might absorb their power
and beauty, and although they are invoked in nearly every stanza of every
song and every prayer of every ceremony, they are never portrayed in sandpaintings and are never discussed openly. The meanings of their names and
their ultimate identities are rarely disclosed. Such knowledge is the most
sacred and most valued knowledge of every Singer (ceremonial prac-
titioner), and it is only revealed to very special students or relatives, and
often only on one's deathbed. This secrecy partially explains why a line
dividing the two triangles incorporated in the diamond shape is rarely
marked or shown.

The geometric pattern of the divine triad is what is shown to initiates
in the Night Chant, a rite that is described in the Navajo language as seeing
the Gods. It is no wonder, then, that the Navajos take great care to make sure
the young initiates get the correct "view" of the Gods and of the world they
control. These triangular and diamond shapes and their meanings are
consciously and unconsciously woven into the patterns of Navajo blankets,
rugs, and tapestries.

The four-sided diamond is associated in Navajo conception with the
Earth and, by extension, with Changing Woman. The association with
Changing Woman, however, is not as pronounced or as widely known as
the association of the hairbun pattern with Born for the Water or the bow

pattern with Monster Slayer. The diamond integrates the emblems of Monster Slayer and Born for the Water when they are conjoined in a motif commonly found in Navajo weaving. This combination is also found in the petroglyphs of the *Dinétah* area. When the emblems of these deities are interwoven, the resulting configuration is the motif represented in figure 5.

Viewed vertically, this motif shows a pairing of Born for the Water's design. Viewed horizontally, it shows two of Monster Slayer's bows pointed at each other. In the middle, two triangles are paired to form a diamond. The four-sided diamond links the emblems together into a pattern that can be infinitely reproduced and regenerated. First known to us on the petroglyphs of the *Dinétah* area, the pattern occurs extensively in Navajo weaving, particularly during the latter part of the Classic Period (1820–65). The woven compositions in plate 1 illustrate the use of this motif in textiles. The geometric elements incorporated in this particular motif are deeply rooted in Navajo identity, history, culture, and worldview.

## Conclusions

Navajo women have woven the designs of Monster Slayer, Born for the Water, and the diamond shape of the earth into their blankets and rugs in various combinations and in various alterations for over two centuries. These geometric shapes—modified, combined, multiplied, varied, halved, separated, embellished—have formed the primary motifs of Navajo weaving once it passed the striped-line or banded phase. Navajo culture expresses a particular way of seeing the Gods and seeing the world. The angles, shapes, dimensions, and motifs of this cultural geometry are reflected in the patterns and motifs of Navajo weaving. The most apparent forms and patterns have changed over time, but the underlying motifs remain distinctly Navajo because they are deeply rooted in the archetypal symbols of Navajo society and culture and in the spatial organization of Navajo geometry.

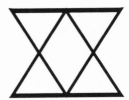

**Figure 5.** Basic Navajo cultural motif.

**Plate 1.** Navajo weavings.

In a previous work (Witherspoon 1987), I discussed the various ways these cultural motifs were incorporated into contemporary regional styles. The triangular motifs of Navajo geometry still provide the format for contemporary Navajo weaving compositions in all their variety. Although experimentation and innovation will continue to exist in Navajo weaving, as they have always existed, important cultural motifs will likely survive and endure, as they have always endured ever since they started to appear on the striped blankets of the nineteenth century. Even though many of the meanings associated with these archetypal symbols are not always consciously apparent to contemporary weavers, these patterns and shapes continue to dominate the way they organize space.

The generation of life and the creation of form involve the transformation of the static condition into the active dimension, but the asymmetry of movement, life, and creation always returns movement to rest, life to death, order to randomness, and beauty to plainness. Therefore, life must be forever regenerated, movement forever rejuvenated, order forever restored, and beauty forever renewed. This infinite process goes from static to active and active to static. It is not surprising, then, that Changing Woman—the very essence and personification of regeneration, rejuvenation, renewal, and dynamic beauty—is the most beautiful and the most revered of all the Holy People. This is the model of creative synthesis and holistic symmetry that is operative in Navajo language, history, and culture. I think it is the same model that underlies the holistic symmetry found in Navajo weaving. Certainly this model is reflected in the principal motifs of Navajo weaving.

Navajo weaving deals with abstract concepts, abstract patterns, abstract relationships, and with holistic essence. The abstractions expressed in Navajo weaving are mostly analogical—just like poetry, dance, music, myth, ritual, and other forms of art. Woven compositions are expressions of *hózhǫ́* ('cosmic concert').

The overall meaning or expression of a woven composition is not to be construed from a symbolic interpretation of individual design elements in the composition. Most individual design elements mean nothing by themselves. They take on their meaning only as a part of a holistic composition. The complete composition is a unique and abstract rendering of *hózhǫ́*. *Hózhǫ́* incorporates and expresses the beauty, the balance, the harmony, and the dynamics of the universe, as constructed by the Holy People in the beginning and as maintained by the People of the Earth's Surface (the Navajos) in the present. The artistic compositions created by Navajo weavers express, accentuate, and celebrate the inherent beauty and magnificence of the universe as conceived in Navajo culture.

To the Indians of the Southwest, religion is not an intellectual exercise of belief; it is a performance—a song, a dance, a prayer, a painting, a story, a concert. Religion is not a matter of allegiance; it is an experience of cosmic concert, a communal song and dance with cosmic dimensions. In the Navajo language, the verb stem –zhíísh refers to the orderly movement of heavenly bodies and to the forms of dance found in ritual. Indians of the Southwest dance to the rhythms of the universe, to the cycles of the earth, to the pulsation of organic life, and to the forms of divine creation and human imagination. From these native peoples, we learn that art is not only a way to understand or represent the world, but also a way to be in the world and to participate in the cosmic concert, which is their imaginative formulation of the world.

As with most origin stories, the world of the Navajos originates in a nameless, formless, meaningless condition. Pattern, dimension, direction, sensibility, order, beauty, and harmony are added to that domain by the ancient and profound personalities called the *Diyin Dine'é* 'Holy People'. Accordingly, the universe comes alive with color, dimension, direction, gender, season, life cycle, and generation. For the traditional Navajo artist, aesthetic creation becomes a celebration and a renewal of this primordial achievement of the Holy People. It is a commemoration or a reenactment of the primordial experience of the Holy People as they creatively thought and sung the world into existence, imbuing it with shape, pattern, dimension, color, beauty, harmony, and meaning.

As noted earlier, the loom is a representation of the universe in microcosm and in metaphor. In each blanket or rug, the Navajo artist experiences in smaller dimensions the primordial achievement of thought and action in re-creating and reordering the world on the loom. *Creation is primordial and transcendental.* In experiencing it, the Navajo artist transcends her ordinary station in life, and assumes the station of the Holy People. Not surprisingly, then, she integrates the symbols of the Holy People into her abstract reformulations of the world.

Weaving is an act of creative transformation. Navajo women transform the wool from the backs of their sheep into abstract compositions that express a universal theme. Through the process of shearing, cleaning, carding, dyeing, spinning, and weaving, weaving becomes an activity with primordial roots and cosmic dimensions. On the loom the weaver seeks to blend fine and bold contrasts in color, feature, and design into a single whole that is harmonious and beautiful, just as the Holy People did when they created the world. I contend this is at the heart of the creative experience in Navajo culture. In each composition, the weaver seeks a personal, unique expression of a universal theme. The personal transformation or reformulation of the world found in weaving is an exhilarating experience, and it is this experience—even in small degrees—that primarily motivates most of the weavers.

*Navajo weaving is abstract art built on cultural motifs.* Navajo cultural motifs are built on the emblems of their principal deities: *Sạ'ah Naaghái, Bik'eh Hózhǫ́*, Changing Woman, Born for the Water, and Monster Slayer. When incorporated into weaving motifs, these emblems express Navajo pride, power, and identity. To the Navajos, weaving is a source of national pride and identity. Weaving demonstrates the complexity, power, and beauty of the Navajo imagination, and it expresses the vitality, strength, and integration of Navajo society.

Whether woven of native cotton, commercial yarn, or wool; whether dyed with vegetal or commercial dyes; whether woven in the eighteenth, nineteenth, or twentieth century; whether woven into blankets, clothing, rugs, or tapestries; whether woven at Ganado, Crystal, or Red Lake— Navajo weavers have nearly always woven the emblems of their Gods and the profound powers and personalities those Gods embody into their creative compositions. These compositions combine symbolism with abstraction to express a universal theme: *hózhǫ́*.

## Notes

1. Gladys Reichard presents the entire picture as a chart of the creation of the Navajo universe in her book, *Navaho Religion* (1950: chart 1).

2. The sign for Born for the Water can also be found on some of the kachinas that are seen in the Chakwaina Dance at Zuni. There are two groups of kachinas who dance: one is known as the Towa or Home Chakwaina, and the other is the Drum Chakwaina, which is thought to be an import from Laguna. It is the Home Chakwaina who wear the sign of Born for the Water. About these, Wright (1985:88) notes: "The kachinas who come in the Towa Chakwaina (Plate 24a) are more dangerous than those of the Drum Chakwaina. They dance in a menacing stooped position (Bunzel 1929:30,1021) using a bundle drum for accompaniment (Parsons 1917a, No. 3:212). . . . These kachinas are also called the Unkind Kachinas." The zigzag of Monster Slayer's bow is also apparent on some of these dancers.

The connection of these warrior kachinas to the Navajos seems unmistakable. The exact nature of this connection and its origin are open to speculation. When the Navajos raided and engaged in warfare, they wore the signs of Born for the Water and Monster Slayer on their bodies and on their clothing. Having seen these signs on the Navajos on such occasions, the Zunis and other Pueblos may have thought they were appropriate for display on an unkind, warrior kachina. There are other possibilities as well, and we have not as yet had a chance to fully explore or confirm any of them. In any case, during the Gobernador period or the *Dinétah* phase, these designs became the national symbols of the *Diné*.

3. Some Navajos telling the emergence story enumerate only three underworlds and make this world the fourth. Other storytellers have four underworlds and make this the fifth. The latter group provides a very minimal account of the fourth world. When the people emerge to the fourth world, they find it uninviting and simply move on to the fifth world.

# References

Capra, Fritjof
1975     The Tao of Physics. Berkeley: Shambhala Publications.
Carlson, Roy L.
1965     Eighteenth Century Navajo Fortresses of the Gobernador District. Earl Morris Papers, no. 2. Boulder: University of Colorado Press.
Carpenter, Edmund
1961     Comments on Hazelberger's "Methods of Studying Ethnological Art." Current Anthropology 2:361-63.
Fishler, Stanley A.
1953     In the Beginning: A Navaho Creation Myth. Anthropology Papers, no. 13. Salt Lake City: University of Utah Press.
Haile, Father Berard
1938     Origin Legend of the Navajo Enemy Way. New Haven: Yale University Press.
1947     Head and Face Masks in Navaho Ceremonialism. St. Michaels, Ariz.: St. Michaels Press.
Hester, James J.
1962     Early Navajo Migrations and Acculturation in the Southwest. Museum of New Mexico Papers in Anthropology, no. 6. Santa Fe.
Matthews, Washington
1897     Navaho Legends. American Folklore Society, Memoirs, vol. 5. New York: G. E. Stechert.
1902     The Night Chant, a Navaho Ceremony. American Museum of Natural History, Memoirs, vol. 6 (Anthropology vol. 5). New York.
Maxwell, Gilbert S.
1963     Navajo Rugs—Past, Present and Future. Palm Desert, Calif.: Best-West Publications. Reprint (rev. ed.). Santa Fe: Heritage Art, 1984.
Newcomb, Franc J., and Gladys A. Reichard
1975     Sandpaintings of the Navajo Shooting Chant. New York: Dover.
Pinxten, R. K., Ingrid van Dooren, and Frank Harvey
1980     The Anthropology of Space: Explorations into the Natural Philosophy and Semantics of the Navajo. Philadelphia: University of Pennsylvania Press.
Reichard, Gladys
1934     Spider Woman: A Story of Navajo Weavers and Chanters. New York: McMillan. Reprint. Glorieta, N. Mex.: Rio Grande Press, 1968.
1950     Navajo Religion: A Study of Symbolism. 2 vols. New York: Bollingen Foundation.
Roessel, Robert A., Jr.
1983     Dinétah. Rough Rock, Ariz.: Navajo Curriculum Center.

of the Bureau of American Ethnology, 229-85. Washington, D.C.

Witherspoon, Gary J.
    1975    Navajo Kinship and Marriage. Chicago: University of Chicago Press.
    1977    Language and Art in the Navajo Universe. Ann Arbor: University of Michigan Press.
    1987    Navajo Weaving: Art in Its Cultural Context. Research Paper no. 36. Flagstaff: Museum of Northern Arizona.

Wright, Barton
    1985    Kachinas of the Zuni. Flagstaff: Northland Press.

Wyman, Leland
    1970    Blessingway. Tucson: University of Arizona Press.
    1983    Southwest Indian Drypainting. Southwest Indian Series, School of American Research. Albuquerque: University of New Mexico Press.

# 17

# On the Application of the Phylogenetic Model
# to the Maya

EVON Z. VOGT

The creative contributions of Fred Eggan to the controlled comparative study of American Indian cultures have stimulated me to engage in comparative research that has been modeled on his pioneering achievements in combining historical and structural approaches (see especially Eggan 1937, 1950, 1952, 1954, 1966, and 1980).

My earlier field research in the Southwest (from 1947 to 1953) resulted in a number of controlled comparative studies (see Adair and Vogt 1949; Vogt and O'Dea 1953; Vogt 1955; Vogt and Albert 1966; Vogt 1961). Since 1957 my work has been focused on the Tzotzil Maya of the highlands of Chiapas in southeastern Mexico (see Vogt 1978), where fundamental ethnographic data gathering had to precede the kind of comparative analysis that has long been possible in the Southwest, with its century-long record of anthropological fieldwork (Basso 1979:14). But some items of controlled comparison in the Eggan model are beginning to appear on highland Chiapas (see especially Bricker 1973; Vogt 1973, 1985, 1992), and I view this comparative work as a small aspect of what will eventually be possible using the phylogenetic model on the Maya.

## The Phylogenetic Model

The phylogenetic model grows out of the work of many linguists, especially Sapir (1916), on the relationships among languages, and of many ethnologists, especially Eggan (1954) on "the method of controlled comparison." The earlier uses of the model appeared in Romney (1957) and Vogt (1963, 1964b, 1971), where the term *genetic* was used to describe the model in these papers, but was an unfortunate choice since "it conjures up a biological image that is misleading" (Flannery and Marcus 1983:8). A brilliant article applying the method to Polynesia has convincingly argued that *phylogenetic* is a more appropriate label because it "places the emphasis on the essential aspect of the model—the delineation of phylogenies or historical sequences of divergence from a common ancestor" (Kirch and Green 1987:9), a critical point that has also been discussed in detail by Flannery and Marcus (1983:xix–xxi, 2, 6, 355-62).

In controlled comparisons, the cultures selected for study are set within a geographic and historical frame. A good example is Eggan's (1950) classic study of the social organization of the western Pueblos, all geographically located in the Colorado Plateau country of the Southwest, and all subjected to approximately the same sequence of historical events.

The phylogenetic model goes a step further and takes as a field of comparative study a group of tribes that are set off from all other groups by sharing a common physical type, possessing common systemic patterns, and speaking phylogenetically related languages. Correspondence among those three factors indicates a common historical tradition for these tribes. This segment of cultural history can be termed a *phylogenetic unit* and it includes the ancestral group and all intermediate groups, as well as the tribes living in the present. It is *not* assumed that all the people in the phylogenetic unit are necessarily descended from the ancestral group in a strict biological sense, for biological mixing always occurs when two different cultural groups come into contact. All that is required is a physical type that converges rather than diverges as we go back in time (Romney 1957:36-37).

Not only does the phylogenetic model maintain the geographical and historical contexts, it also provides a framework for analysis that uses the data of all the branches of anthropology—archeology, linguistics, ethnology, and physical anthropology—as well as the data of the historians. Elsewhere in Mesoamerica, Flannery and Marcus (1983) have applied the model to the divergent evolution of the Zapotec and Mixtec of Oaxaca with very illuminating results (see also Marcus 1983a). In North America the work of Dumond (1987) on Eskimo-Aleut prehistory uses an essentially phylogenetic interpretation. On a smaller regional basis, the model has also been used for an archeological and historical study of an extinct group of Mayan speakers, the Coxoh, who lived in the upper Grijalva valley (Lee 1979; Lee and Markham 1976), and more recently by Lee (1989) for an excellent analysis of the prehistoric cultural history of the Chiapas highlands. On a continental basis, the work of Greenberg, Turner, and Zegura (1986) and Greenberg (1987) on the remarkable correspondence of linguistic, dental, and genetic evidence in North America exemplifies the exciting potential of the model on a large scale as they present their hypothesis that the pre-Columbian inhabitants of the New World were all derived from three migrations from Asia across the Bering Strait: Amerind, Na-Dene, and Aleut-Eskimo. Renfrew (1992) has likewise recently used the essence of the model to take an even longer-range view of human diversity on all of the continents and to analyze the correspondences between mitochondrial DNA and archeological findings.

## Application of the Model to the Maya

The Maya are an ideal case for the application of the phylogenetic model because:

- Except for the Huastec in northern Veracruz and adjacent San Luis Potosi and some areas of the southern Mayan lowlands that are now uninhabited or occupied by non-Indians, the present Mayan cultures have a nearly contiguous distribution in Mexico, Guatemala, Belize, and Honduras (see map 1).
- There is no doubt (Campbell and Kaufman 1985; Kaufman 1976) that all of the thirty-one Mayan languages are traceable—that is, reconstructible—to a single ancestral language, Proto-Mayan, which appears to have been a single unified speech community for some unspecified time before 2200 B.C., when the ancestral community began to break up (Josserand 1975:502). Two of the languages— Chicomuceltec and Cholti—are extinct, but the remaining twenty-nine languages are still spoken by the approximately five million living Mayas.
- There has been a great deal of archeological and linguistic work on the Mayas, and the rate of research in ethnology, ethnohistory, and physical anthropology is increasing, including the study of mitochondrial DNA on both the prehistoric and living Mayas (see, for example, Wallace and Torroni 1992).
- Careful comparative analysis of the marked contrasts in ecological settings and historical experience should eventually account for the present variations in Mayan culture.

In the application of the model, it is theoretically possible to begin with any of the three factors that define the phylogenetic unit—physical type, language, or systemic patterns. In practice, it is more economical to begin with language because we are further along in the definition of phylogenetic units in terms of related languages.

Given that point of departure, there are eight basic steps in the analysis.

*Step 1*. Plotting the distribution of the related languages in the ethnographic present (map 1).

*Step 2*. Calculating the approximate time depths and charting the various divergences of the related languages, using glottochronology.

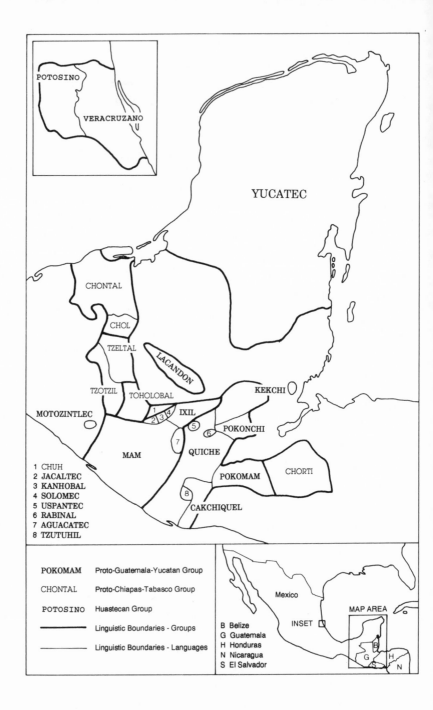

**Map 1.** Schematic map of Maya-speaking Indians (adapted from Vogt 1969b:22).

Although that method has been much criticized, I note that radiocarbon dating (the model on which Swadesh based his thinking about glottochronology) has analogous methodological problems, but continues to be used, often by the same scholars who are critical of glottochronology. The most recent evidence to support the native language retention rate of 86 percent per thousand years calculated by Swadesh (1952) and Lees (1956) is the finding of Luckenbach and Levy (1980:456) that the retention rate for the Nahua language over the four and one-half centuries since the Spanish conquest is 79 percent. That documented case shows a rate of change only slightly more rapid than the 86 percent of Swadesh and the faster rate is probably due to the drastic nature of the Spanish language contact.

Divergence charts on the glottochronology of Mayan (see fig. 1) are based on the work of Kaufman (1964, 1976) and Campbell and Kaufman (1985:189), who provide a more recent version of their views on Mayan diversification, but without estimated time depths.

*Step 3.* Locating the Proto-Mayan homeland and the dispersal of the protogroups, using comparative linguistics and migration theory. The work of the historical linguists in the Maya area has advanced markedly during the last two decades (see Campbell et al. 1978; Campbell and Kaufman 1985). Using these data and the "least moves" model of migration theory (Dyen 1956; Diebold 1960), it is inferred that the Proto-Mayan homeland was in a highland area, not far from the lowlands. That inference is based on the fact that the protolanguage has terms for both highland and lowland flora and fauna. The argument of the linguists: in the Maya area, there are exclusively lowland peoples ignorant of the highland zone; there are no primarily highland peoples ignorant of the lowland zone. Therefore, the Proto-Mayan homeland was in a highland area bordering on the lowlands (Kaufman 1976:105; Josserand 1975:507). But the question is *where* in the highlands?

Inspecting in map 2 the postulated distribution of Mayan languages for the Late Classic period (A.D. 600 to 900), the Huastec (not shown in the map) can be rolled back from the migration to northern Veracruz, and the Yucatec Maya from a lateral spread into the peninsula from the highlands. Chorti, Chol, and Chontal can be put back together as the Cholic (Cholan) languages, which, in turn, have close relationships to the Tzotzilic (Tzeltalan) languages. The result is a closely contiguous series of Mayan languages in the highlands from Chiapas to southeastern Guatemala and El Salvador.

For the homeland Kaufman (1976:104) suggests the Soloma area of the Cuchumatanes of northwest Guatemala, which is both adjacent to the lowlands and near rivers flowing north (the Usumacinta), east (the Rio

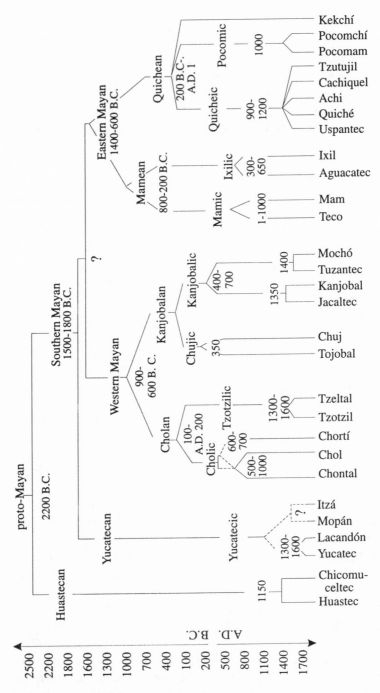

**Figure 1.** Glottochronology of Mayan (after Josserand 1975).

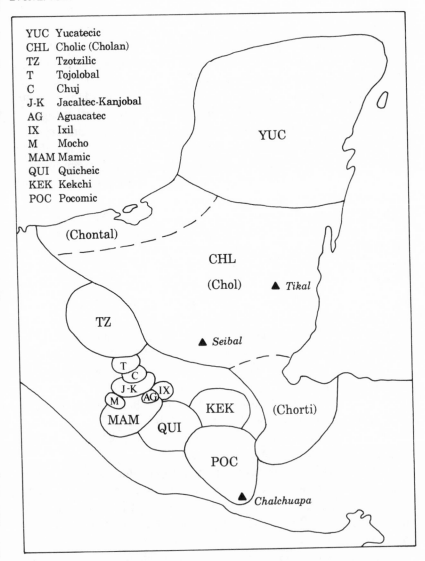

| | |
|---|---|
| YUC | Yucatecic |
| CHL | Cholic (Cholan) |
| TZ | Tzotzilic |
| T | Tojolobal |
| C | Chuj |
| J-K | Jacaltec-Kanjobal |
| AG | Aguacatec |
| IX | Ixil |
| M | Mocho |
| MAM | Mamic |
| QUI | Quicheic |
| KEK | Kekchi |
| POC | Pocomic |

**Map 2.** Late Classic distribution of Mayan languages (after Josserand 1975).

Negro), and west (the Grijalva). In rugged highlands, as Kaufman points out, river valleys facilitate population movements, and it is easier to move downstream than upstream.

Josserand agrees that the homeland was in the highlands, but argues that almost any highland area from Chiapas to Honduras would fit the specifications. She adds that the Cuchumatanes "look much more like a shatter zone of languages created by the convergence of two or more different centers of influence" (1975:507), and on the basis of archeological evidence (see Sharer and Gifford 1970; Sharer 1974, 1978b) she advances the idea of the Chalchuapa area of El Salvador as the homeland. Chalchuapa is located on a tributary of the Lempa, which flows to the Pacific, but it originates near the headwaters of a tributary of the Motagua that flows eastward into the Gulf of Honduras. Josserand further suggests that the earlier pioneering lowland populations (Xe and Mamom) were derived from the Chalchuapa area; the Chicanel Yucatecan population arrived later and in turn gave way to Cholans who carried a more complex cultural tradition and were the catalysts to the homogeneous and conservative Chicanel, producing the new synthesis we call Classic Maya: "The transition was peaceful, and as Cholan replaced Yucatecan in the Peten, Yucatecan strengthened its position in northern Yucatan, thus accounting for the cultural break between the northern and southern Mayan lowlands during the Classic period" (1975:509). She further concludes that the break-up of Greater Cholan into Cholan versus Tzotzilan occurred around A.D. 100–200 with the Tzotzilans moving to the west and the Cholans carrying on in the southern lowlands.

Kaufman's (1976) archeological correlations are somewhat different and the inferences more precise. His stages of dispersion are:

I. Proto-Mayan was spoken in the Soloma area of the Cuchumatan highlands about 2200 B.C.

II. Shortly thereafter Huastecan left the homeland, moved down the Usamacinta, and migrated north along the Gulf Coast.

III. Around 1600 B.C. Eastern Mayan (Mam, Ixil, Quichean, Pocomam, etc.) moved south and east along the Rio Negro.

IV. About 1400 B.C. Eastern Mayan separated into Greater Mamean and Greater Quichean; sometime between 1400 and 1000 B.C. Yucatecan left the homeland and moved toward the Yucatan peninsula, arriving perhaps as early as 1000 B.C. The language remaining in the homeland can be called Western Mayan.

V. About 1000 B.C. Greater Tzeltalan separated from Western Mayan, moved off downriver, and settled along both sides of the Usumacinta.

VI. Around 600 B.C. Greater Quichean split up into Uspantec, Quichean Proper, Pocom, and Kekchi; Greater Mamean divided into Ixilan and Mamean Proper. Before stage VII, Greater Tzeltalan, manifested in the Chicanel archeological horizon, occupied most of the southern Mayan lowlands and spread to the Copan region.

VII. About 100 B.C. Chujean separated from the Kanjobalan proper. The southern Gulf Coast was occupied by Zoqueans; Yucatan by Yucatecans; and the Peten (Holmul I, Matzanel) by Greater Tzeltalan.

VIII. Around A.D. 100 Cholan separated from Tzeltalan Proper, perhaps by crossing the Usumacinta and crowding Tzeltalan Proper westward. Within a century or two the Tzeltalans moved into the Chiapas highlands near Teopisca (Kan phase).

Further separations are postulated during the subsequent Classic Period, including at about A.D. 600, when Cholan broke up into Chorti and Chol-Chontal, Tzeltalan Proper split into Tzeltal and Tzotzil, and Ixilan into Aguacatec and Ixil. Research by Campbell (1988) indicates that Quichean groups expanded into eastern and southern Guatemala after A.D. 1200, and that much of eastern Guatemala below the Motagua was occupied by Xincan speakers until that time.

It is clear that speakers of Mayan languages had a much more limited distribution in earlier times than has often been postulated by archeologists (Campbell and Kaufman 1985:192–93). The archeological Olmecs were Mixe-Zoque speakers (Campbell and Kaufman 1976), as were the bearers of greater Izapan culture, including the site of Izapa itself (Campbell 1985; Justeson et al. 1985).

More research is necessary to permit us to choose between the two sets of hypotheses on the precise location of the proto-Mayan homeland as well as between the varying inferences concerning the dispersal and the archeological correlations with the linguistic divergences. The linguistic inferences about the homeland must also take into account the data of MacNeish (1981; MacNeish, Wilkerson, and Nelken-Turner 1980) on the early preceramic sites in Belize with dates extending from 9000 B.C. to 2000 B.C. Whether or not these very early occupations have connections with the earliest radiocarbon-dated horizons of the Maya in the lowlands is unclear.

*Step 4.* Reconstructing the protolanguage, and as much of the ancestral culture as possible, using the techniques of historical-comparative linguistics. We already know (Kaufman 1964, 1976), for example, that the Proto-Mayans were agriculturalists with domesticated maize; that they also cultivated beans, squashes, avocados, chiles, sweet potatoes, and cotton; and that they kept domesticated dogs and turkeys. They ground maize on metates, but seem not to have had the tortilla cooked on the comal until the Classic period; they ate the maize in other forms, such as roasting ears, atole, *pozol*, or tamales.

The Proto-Mayans also had words for bench, mat, bed, house, road, axe, whetstone, and cord, as well as for writing, paper, tribe, lord, rattle drum, and copal incense which they burned then as now. No Mayanist has yet undertaken a full-scale interpretation of the implications of this Proto-Mayan vocabulary for the culture of the Proto-Mayan community, but the possibilities are exciting.

*Step 5.* Using archeological data to confirm, reject, or modify hypotheses about the location of the homeland and migrations from this dispersal area as well as the reconstruction of the ancestral culture and of the variations that have occurred over time.

To date the earliest demonstrably Mayan evidence of dispersal into the lowlands occurs about 1000 B.C. in the early Middle Pre-Classic Xe ceramic complex at Altar de Sacrificios and the closely related Real complex at Siebal, both on the Pasion River in the southeast Peten (Adams 1971; Sabloff 1975), and in the Swasey phase at the site of Cuello in northern Belize (Andrews and Hammond 1990). This early occupation of lowlands by the Maya is well within the time frame for such movements from the Proto-Mayan community, which the linguists locate in the highlands of Guatemala at approximately 2500 B.C. It is likewise clear from recent archeological work in the northern Mayan highlands of Guatemala (Sharer and Sedat 1987) that the highlands participated fundamentally in the development of Mayan civilization from Pre-Classic times (ca. 800 B.C.) onward. To go beyond our present understanding requires the solution of two critical operational problems: the definition of a series of diagnostic Mayan traits for an early horizon (on the order of 2000 B.C.), and the ability to detect these traits in the postulated homelands in the highlands where not as much archeological work has been done as in the Mayan lowlands.

*Step 6.* Adding physical and biological anthropological data on skeletal materials and on living Mayan populations to check on shared and variable features in physical type within the phylogenetic unit. With reference to the hypothesized common physical type among the Mayas, my most severe critic was the late Juan Comas (1966, 1969), who concluded that both prehistoric skeletal data and measurements on the living indicate

> the nonexistence of a unique somatic type, with definable characteristics representative of the Mayan linguistic family. We are inclined to think that the hypothesis of a genetic unit which E. Z. Vogt used to characterize the people of Mayan civilization lacks objective basis at least in one of the 3 characters (a common physical type). [1966:35]

On the other hand, Frank Saul (1968) concluded that Comas's data were too limited to reject my hypothesis. But from this controversy it was clear that skeletal materials from the Maya area (where preservation is usually poor) were quite limited, and that much more research was needed on the living populations.

More recently, the data and analyses of Carlos Serrano Sanchez and Julieta Arechiga Viramontes (Serrano 1973, 1975, 1976–77; Serrano and

Arechiga 1978, 1979; Arechiga 1979) have been more encouraging. They present exciting dermatoglyph data on the Yucatec Mayas and the Zoques, but also reanalyze data previously collected in the Mayan highlands. As Serrano points out, dermatoglyphs are critically relevant for cultural historical studies because they are polygenetically controlled, probably nonadaptive, and undergo no postnatal modifications—unlike, for example, head form. If a person has whorls, rather than loops or arches on his fingers, he was born with them and will have them all his life, and such patterns have no apparent adaptive significance (fig. 2).

Unlike the earlier findings of Newman (1960), which indicated a marked difference between the Yucatec-Guatemalan-Highland Maya, on the one hand, and the Maya in the Chiapas highlands, on the other, Serrano finds evidence of uniformity in dermatoglyphs among the Maya, and marked differences between the Maya and the Indians of southern and central Mexico. The crucial differences are the relatively different percentages of whorls and loops as displayed in figure 3. In the Yucatec and Chiapas Maya (Tzeltals and Tzotzils) more than 40 percent have whorls (as opposed to loops); in the southern and central Mexican non-Mayan Indian populations fewer than 40 percent have whorls (as opposed to loops). Similarly, in the Cummins Index—a measure of pattern intensity— there is also generally a difference (see table 1) between the Maya and the other Indians in southern and central Mexico. The break here is between those populations with an index of greater than or less than 13.4 percent, the Mayan samples (with the exception of one Tzotzil sample of 12.9 and a Yucatec Maya sample of 11.9) being all greater than 13.4.

Serrano suggests that the above data indicate some kind of common physical type among the Maya, a physical type that converges as one goes back in time and that diverges in later prehistoric and contemporary populations. The divergences are what we observe in measurements made on skeletons and on living bodies. These divergences are most probably due

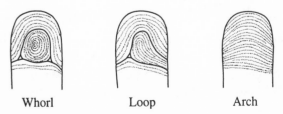

Whorl          Loop          Arch

**Figure 2.** The three basic types of digital dermatoglyphs: whorl, loop, arch (adapted from Serrano 1973:20).

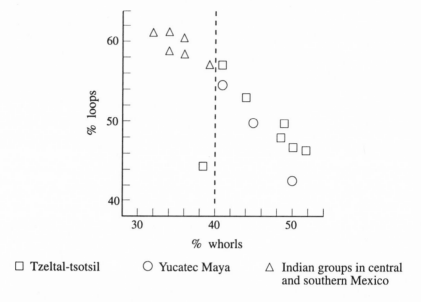

□ Tzeltal-tsotsil          ○ Yucatec Maya          △ Indian groups in central
                                                              and southern Mexico

**Figure 3.** Distribution of the frequency (in percentages) of loops and whorls in Mesoamerican Indian populations (adapted from Serrano 1973:27).

to differences in environmental adaptations and to biological interbreeding, as for example, in the biological mestizoization process that Serrano and Arechiga (1978) have documented in Yucatan.

Finally, Serrano's (1976-77) Zoque data suggest that at a deeper level of time, the Zoques could have been part of a macro-Mayan family of languages and peoples. Recall that the Olmecs, who lived along the Gulf Coast just to the northwest of the Mayas, were almost certainly Mixe-Zoque speakers (Campbell and Kaufman 1976).

The most exciting recent development is the beginning of mitochondrial DNA studies among the Maya, research that should, in the long run, enable us to trace commonalities and divergences in the Mayan population with precision (Wallace and Torroni 1992).

*Step 7.* Using ethnohistorical materials to provide readings on the various branches of the phylogenetic unit between the time of the Spanish conquest and the modern ethnographic studies of living tribes. Here the work of the earlier ethnohistorians, especially Roys and Scholes, is being continued and deepened by the research of many younger scholars, such as Farriss (1984).

*Step 8.* Adding ethnographic data on living Mayan communities to map variations in common systemic patterns that have survived from earlier

**Table 1.** Dermatoglyphic Patterns in Mesoamerican Indian Groups, Males (in Percentages) (adapted from Serrano 1976-77:27)

| Group | n | Arches | Loops | Whorls | Cummins Index |
|---|---|---|---|---|---|
| CHIAPAS | | | | | |
| Tzeltal (Amatenango) | 49 | 1.2 | 46.4 | 52.4 | 15.4 |
| Tzotzil (Zinancantan) | 24 | 2.2 | 48.2 | 49.6 | 14.7 |
| Tzotzil (Huixtan) | 50 | 2.5 | 49.6 | 48.9 | 14.6 |
| Tzotzil (Zinancantan) | 90 | 2.8 | 46.8 | 50.4 | 14.8 |
| Tzotzil (Chamula) | 100 | 3.4 | 52.8 | 43.8 | 14.0 |
| Tzeltal | 62 | 5.0 | 52.6 | 42.4 | 13.7 |
| Tzeltal | 47 | 2.8 | 57.0 | 40.2 | 13.7 |
| Tzotzil | 230 | 7.2 | 57.0 | 35.8 | 12.9 |
| Tzeltal-Tzotzil(S. Cristobal) | 90 | 6.4 | 58.6 | 34.9 | 13.5 |
| Zoques (Copoya) | 74 | 6.6 | 53.0 | 40.3 | 13.5 |
| YUCATAN | | | | | |
| Peto | 160 | 4.9 | 54.8 | 40.3 | 13.5 |
| Chichimila | 72 | 5.6 | 49.7 | 44.7 | 11.9 |
| Hacienda Acu | 25 | 6.4 | 42.4 | 51.2 | 14.5 |
| ZONA CENTRO-SUR | | | | | |
| Tarascos | 116 | 4.2 | 61.6 | 34.2 | 13.0 |
| Nahuas (Cholula, Pue.) | 178 | 5.6 | 58.1 | 35.3 | 13.0 |
| Zapotecos | 50 | 3.0 | 61.0 | 36.0 | 13.3 |
| Zapotecos | 104 | 6.6 | 59.1 | 34.2 | 13.3 |
| Mixtecos | 78 | 3.0 | 57.0 | 40.0 | 13.7 |
| (Mestizos, Mexico, D.F.) | 250 | 3.4 | 61.4 | 32.6 | 31.1 |

time levels and to detect cultural drifts or trends that are still occurring in these living systems (Vogt 1960). In some parts of the Maya area, notably highland Chiapas, parts of Yucatan, and in some zones of highland Guatemala, our data base is finally approaching the quality and size that will make further intensive comparisons possible.

## Mayan Systemic Patterns

The third prong of the phylogenetic model concerns systemic patterns (Kroeber 1948:312-13)—patterns that seem to run deep in time in the

Mayan phylogenetic unit and that may have evolved at the prototime level or shortly thereafter, and with variations, continue to be important in Mayan cultures up to the present time. I now take a new look at a sample of systemic patterns that I have identified for the Maya (Vogt 1971: 435–39, 1983:90–114).

*The subsistence system is based on the cultivation of domesticated maize, supplemented importantly by beans, in a swidden type of agricultural system.*

Data on raised-field agriculture in wetland parts of the lowland Maya area (Puleston 1977; Harrison 1977, 1978; Siemens 1978, 1982; Turner 1974; Harrison and Turner 1978; Hammond 1978; Adams 1983; Turner 1983; Turner and Harrison 1983; Santley, Killion, and Lycett 1986), especially from the Pasion River region of Guatemala and from northern Belize, demonstrate that intensive agriculture was also used extensively. In addition, there is evidence, especially from the Rio Bec region of southern Campeche (Turner 1978), of another important system of intensive agrotechnology, that of terraced fields on sloping land.

On the other hand, the extent of the raised-field system is still unclear. For example, Anabel Ford (1980) surveyed transects from Tikal to Yaxha and from Tikal to Uaxactun in the northeastern Peten and found that the settlement patterns around the largest Mayan center—Tikal—fit better with a system of swidden agriculture than they do with a system of raised fields. Further caution is indicated by Millet Camara (1984), who points out that some of the canal patterns in Campeche are historic logging canals rather than prehistoric agricultural patterns. In any event, it is most likely that swidden agriculture was prior and basic in the Mayan case and that it clearly outlived the ridged-field system of prehistoric times. This conclusion is reinforced by the Marcus study of the plant world of the sixteenth- and seventeenth-century lowland Maya. She concluded that swidden agriculture, with its great species diversity, more closely approximated nature and was the most stable over long periods of time (1982a:269).

*The basic type of Mayan settlement pattern is one of dispersed hamlets (where the bulk of the population lives) in sustaining areas surrounding ceremonial centers.*

Except where there are very special geographical factors (as in towns surrounding Lake Atitlán in Guatemala) or special historical factors (as in nucleated archeological sites constructed on headlands for military protection, in sites such as Mayapan that were participating in a Post-Classic Interaction Sphere that included central Mexican elements, or in post-Conquest towns like Amatenango, Chiapas, or in Yucatan that followed Spanish models) the empirical data still seem to bear out the proposition that the Maya are basically a hamlet-dwelling people (see Vogt 1983).

Data (Fox 1978) from the Guatemalan highlands focus on the nucleated civic centers of the Quiche state. Insufficient data are presented on settlement patterns outside the centers to judge whether the basic pattern was one of centers with outlying hamlets. In any event, the developments occurred late (clearly Post-Classic) and were apparently heavily influenced by peoples from central Mexico.

The nature of lowland Mayan settlement patterns and their variation has been reviewed in detail (Ashmore 1981), but a question still remains: What about the most compact Mayan centers, such as Tikal? Are they ancient Mayan *cities* that disprove my hypothesis? (see especially Haviland 1975; Jones, Coe, and Haviland 1981; Willey 1981b:17; Ashmore 1981:16; Marcus 1983b). Except for the complexes of buildings such as the North and Central Acropoli, the map of Tikal (Carr and Hazard 1961) appears to me to display a series of extended family patio-groups living in hamlets that have been "compressed" together. In a word, the basic pattern is still there; it is just more dense! If Tikal was a "city," it bore little resemblance to the wall-to-wall settlement patterns that characterized Roman, medieval European, southwestern Pueblo, or central Mexican cities like Teotihuacán or Tenochtitlán. According to Willey:

> This is not to deny a number of important urban or civilized functions to Tikal; but its 50,000 persons dispersed over 165 square kilometers . . . makes for not only a quantitatively but a qualitatively different entity than does Teotihuacan's 100,000 to 200,000 residents packed within a zone of 21 square kilometers. [1978:335]

Even if the Tikal population was as high as 72,000 within the 120-square-kilometer zone (Willey 1981a:396, 1981b:18), Willey's earlier comment is still applicable.

MacKinnon's systematic analysis of the Tikal map more than under-scores my conclusion:

> Spatial analysis of the Tikal map supports Vogt's assertion that the Maya remained predominantly small-hamlet dwellers; at Tikal living in housemound clusters regularly spaced and freely and naturally related to the topography, taking advantage of better building sites and avoiding unfavorable ones, but following no rigid plan or social hierarchy. [1981: 245]

A perceptive conclusion was also reached by Koenig and Williams (1985), who, using a "liquid model" of settlement, argue that the numbers of early settlements increased as the residence-to-field commutation made the founding of a new community preferable to enlargement of the old. The new settlements were established "not too far but not too near the original one." Subsequent evolution was "growth in place: increased population now means predominantly increased population (but not site) density, as well as new methods of food production" such as terracing and raised fields (1985:258-59). That image conforms well to my hypothesis that the basic settlement pattern was one of hamlets becoming more and more compressed around Mayan centers as the population increased in the late Classic period.

Our studies of Mayan settlement patterns will be deepened by the more refined data just now being published, especially in the work of Sabloff and Tourtellot (1991) at Sayil, which provide much more detail on the nature of the settlement pattern and the variations found in the prehistoric structures.

*The social structure of the Mayan hamlets was (and continues to be) characterized by patrilocal extended families; by patrilineages composed of groups of extended families; and in some cases by fully developed patrilineal clans.*

This hypothesized systemic pattern has been subjected to several critical reviews, especially by Haviland (1966a, 1966b, 1972). In those papers, Haviland explored various facets of Mayan social organization, but finally concluded that

> most people are prepared to accept the idea that the usual Classic Maya household was a patrilocal extended family. Extended family organization is ultimately dependent on unilocal residence. At Tikal, a number of conditions known to be conducive to patrilocal residence are indicated by the archaeological information. [1972:2-3]

On the other hand, Haviland is less certain from the archeological evidence about patrilineages and patriclans, especially in the later periods of Tikal, where he thinks they may have been breaking down (1972). Later, Haviland (1977) presented an analysis of Tikal dynasty traced through twelve generations (A.D. 376-768) in which he shows that patrilineal succession seems to have been the rule (see also Jones and Satterthwaite 1982; Schele and Freidel 1990). Haviland (1985) has also provided two models of patrilocal household clusters, one elite and one lower class, drawn from the Tikal settlement pattern and glyphic data.

In a review of the settlement pattern data from the lowlands, Willey concludes that patio-groups may be considered as the basic "building block" of the Maya settlement study. They consisted, most usually of from 2 to 6 structures. Some of these were residences, others kitchens or storage places. Patio-groups are, in turn, often found in clusters of from 5 to 12. In such clusters one patio-group, usually in a central location in the cluster, is larger than the others and has one mound or building that is more imposing than any of the others in that patio-group or in the cluster. Where these have been excavated it has been found that this "most imposing" building, frequently situated on the east side of its patio-group, had the functions of a shrine, a little temple, or perhaps an administrative office. [1980:255]

With respect to the social units, Willey adds that

there is ethnohistorical and ethnographic evidence to link the single house or minimal residential unit with the biological family and the larger patio-group unit to the extended family, all in a kin system that was essentially patrilineal and patrilocal. The social correlate of the next largest settlement unit, the cluster of patio-groups, is more uncertain although it seems most likely that it had kin significance. Certainly the presence of the "most imposing" building, the temple, shrine, or office in the clusters suggests a locus for small group authority that is compatible with lineage organization. [1980:257]

Willey's is a nearly perfect description of the settlement patterns and social groupings we find in contemporary Tzotzil Mayan communities like Zinacantan (Vogt 1969a) where the individual houses are residences for the nuclear families, the house compounds of two or more houses arranged around a patio are ordinarily occupied by patrilocal extended families, and the clusters of house compounds that I call *snas* are local patrilineages. Moreover, the house compounds (or patio-groups) that make up the *snas* number from five to twelve in traditional hamlets (Vogt 1983:98-99, esp. fig. 6-4).

An alternative hypothesis concerning royal succession in the Classic Maya period recently advanced by Fox and Justeson (1986) is that rulership was in the hands of a royal matriline and that cross-cousin marriage, first noted in Colonial Yucatec kinship terminology by Eggan (1934), was used in an alliance system practiced by the elite. The analysis employs hiero-glyphic texts as ethnohistorical sources, and the authors present their reconstruction as a working hypothesis to be further explored.

If the Maya had these matrilineal institutions in the Classic period, they had almost certainly disappeared by the Post-Classic period. Edmonson examined these questions by attempting to subtract central Mexican influence from descriptions of the Post-Classic Yucatec Maya, and came to the conclusion that the Classic Maya most probably had patrilineal descent groups, virilocal residence, and hence patricompounds, as well as patrilineal primogeniture in succession and inheritance (1978:9–10). Similarly, Farriss reports that the patrilineal extended family in dispersed hamlets was the preferred residential unit among the Yucatec Maya in colonial times. She adds that the Yucatec had about 250 patronymics, possibly reflecting some kind of lineage division (1984:137).

As one would expect from the marked differences in ecological settings and in historical experiences, the contemporary Maya manifest considerable variations in these patterns of social organization. As Romney (1967) discovered in his survey, most contemporary Mayan systems are "loosely patrilocal," but the solidity and frequency of the patrilocally extended household and of the patrilineage varies. For example, some of the more conservative highland Chiapas communities appear to come the closest to full patrilineal systems; a few—such as Chalchihuitan, studied by Guiteras-Holmes (1966); Oxchuc, studied by Villa Rojas (1947); or Bachajon, studied by Breton (1979)—are even characterized by Omaha kinship terminology. But other systems in Chiapas, such as those of Chamula and Zinacantan (Vogt 1969b), have shifted to bilateral kinship terminology. An orderly progression from Omaha to bilateral terminology can be seen in the following Tzeltal Mayan series: Oxchuc, Tenejapa, Chanal, Aguacatenango.

In the highlands of Guatemala, Hill and Monaghan (1987) have discovered ethnohistorical documents on the Quiche community of Sacapulcas that show continuities between the contemporary *canton* and the pre-Columbian *chinamit* organized as a territorial unit similar to the Aztec *calpulli*, a unit that seems to be more important than the patrilineage. On the other hand, Fox (1987, 1989) shows that, at least among the elite, the lineage was crucial in social structure of the Quiche.

We are just beginning to have enough solid studies of the traditional social organization in contemporary Mayan communities to provide the basis for more fruitful systematic comparisons.

*The social structure of the important ceremonial centers was (and continues to be) characterized by a hierarchy of religious officials (priests) who were (and are) probably of two types: permanent specialists and officials serving shorter periods of time on a rotating basis.*

This hypothesized pattern has, by all odds, triggered the most controversy (Vogt and Ruz 1971:436–38; Vogt 1983; Willey 1989:29-30), and it is now clear that revisions in the statement are necessary as it applies to ancient Mayan social structure.

During the past thirty years archeological work has demonstrated that not only were there rulers with their seats of power in the centers, but there also emerged hereditary elites in the form of dynastic lineages. The work of Proskouriakoff (1963-64), Kelley (1962, 1976), and Coggins (1975, 1979) has been followed by the work of Haviland (1977, 1985) and Jones and Satterthwaite (1982)—which develops Coggins's (1975) proposed dynastic succession at Tikal—and by that of Mathews and Schele (1974) and Robertson (1985) on the ruling dynasty at Palenque. Schele is currently working out the dynastic succession for Copan, and Freidel and Schele (1988) and Schele and Freidel (1990) have recently analyzed the general pattern of Mayan kingship, as has Fash (1991) for Copan.

Many of the Mayan stelae have proved to contain iconographic portraits of living rulers, rather than picturing only ancestral gods, as I had supposed. These data on dynastic rulers are convincing. However, some of the roof combs at sites such as Tikal are probably images of deceased rulers or ancestors, as I shall discuss below.

There remains, however, some question as to what extent these dynastic rulers were political figures and to what extent they were the high priests of their complex ritual and symbolic systems. Judging from the recent interpretations of the iconographic programs of late Classic Palenque, the rulers must have carried very heavy ritual duties, including penis perforation with stingray spines in self-inflicted blood sacrifice, and were probably conceived of as some kind of earthly manifestation of the sun god (Schele 1978; Schele and Miller 1986; Schele and Freidel 1990). As expressed well by Sharer, "The ruler of each Mayan center seems to have served as principal priest, responsible for certain rituals and divinations held to ensure the success and well-being of the state" (Morley, Brainerd, and Sharer 1983:461). Schele (1977) also believes that the particular responsibility of the Palenque rulers was the ritual care of the western gateway to the Underworld.

There is also some question as to how literally we should take the dynastic history recorded in the glyphs. For example, the epigraphers are certain that Lord Pacal was in his fifth *katun* (eighty years, 158 days old) when he died (Mathews and Schele 1974:65). But the archeologist Alberto Ruz, who discovered and excavated the tomb, rejected that interpretation of his age. He reported that physical anthropologists who analyzed (and recently reanalyzed the bones) judge the age of the skeleton to have been forty to fifty years (Ruz Lhuiller 1977). Considering that the hieroglyphic texts were written in couplets, like Mayan myths and prayers (Bricker 1973; Edmonson 1971; Gossen 1974; Laughlin 1977; Vogt and Vogt 1980), and that many of the texts concerning Lord Pacal were written about a hundred years after his death, I would agree with Carlson (1978) that the glyphs record traditional or political, rather than literal, history and that the Maya did not concern themselves with differences between what we regard as history as opposed to myth (see Lounsbury 1976; Clancy 1986; Schele and Miller 1986:321). Carlson adds that "the Maya historiographers who manipulated the numbers and calendrical cycles were essentially providing a divine and cosmic sanction for the ruler by linking the significant rites of passage in his life, and thus his destiny, to those of mythical ancestral beings" (1978:199); see also Marcus (1992).

Further, a "calculated adjustment" on the part of an ancient Palenque calendar priest to make a deceased ruler of greater age fits everything we know about the crucial importance of age, heat, and power in contemporary Mayan society (Vogt 1976:206-7).

However, if the Maya have been, and continue to be, basically hamlet-dwelling around centers, the question still arises as to how the hamlets are socially, economically, and politically related to the center. Many Mayanists have tended to approach this question with only one model in mind: the feudal model derived from our own European cultural background or from Asian or African societies. That model places a king in the ceremonial center, surrounds him by nobles, and pictures the hamlet-dwelling Maya as corn-farming peasants who obediently travel into the center to bring food for the aristocracy to consume and to perform the hard labor of building pyramids.

While there were aristocratic elites in command of the prehistoric Mayan centers, the feudal model still seems naive and simplistic to me (see also Marcus 1982b, 1983a). This does not mean that I am arguing for democracy or egalitarianism among the ancient Maya as Ruz Lhuiller (1964) or many more recent researchers, writing about my views of the cargo model or the egalitarian model (e.g., Becker 1979; Ashmore 1981:14), have incorrectly assumed. On the contrary, my field research among the Zinacantecos in Chiapas demonstrates that the Maya are as conscious of rank as any people I have ever encountered. The Zinacantecos have their important, high-ranking lineages that control many hectares of land and own large houses both in the hamlets and in the ceremonial center; they also have their low-ranking lineages that control smaller amounts of land and own small houses. The members of the low-ranking lineages aspire to only the most lowly posts, if any at all, in the cargo system. Further, Zinacanteco officials (whether religious or political) pay meticulous attention to rank order—they sit on long benches in precise rank order, with the highest official toward the rising sun; they march in precise rank order. At ceremonial banquets, a strict rank order is observed in the seating and in the order of serving food and drinks (Vogt 1976:34–44, 1983:100).

The basic question is not whether the Maya, ancient or modern, have their elites—they clearly did, and do. Rather, the problem concerns whether there was some system of rotation (of residence and religious duty) between the dispersed hamlets and the centers, and I have suggested a "periphery-to-center pulsations model" to describe the relationship between the hamlets and the centers (Vogt 1983:105–10).

Whether or not the rulers resided permanently with their families and retainers in the heart of the ancient Mayan centers is still debatable in spite of *National Geographic Magazine* reconstructions of royal life in the so-called palaces and more speculation than hard data on the part of the archeologists. The presence of trash heaps with broken cooking pots in the heart of the centers does not prove that the rulers lived in the palaces. Food can be cooked in outlying houses and carried into the heart of the center, where it is warmed over fires and fed to groups of religious officials. Trash heaps with charcoal, broken pots, animal bones, and so forth are being accumulated outside the Catholic chapels in contemporary Zinacantan as the religious officials are being fed in the manner I describe.

It also seems quite likely on the basis of the archeological data that there were various lineages competing for top power at different periods in the history of sites such as Tikal or Copan. Some of those powerful lineages may have had their homes and lands in hamlets or neighborhoods near (one to two kilometers from) the ceremonial centers, as for example in unit CV-43 near Copan center (Willey, Leventhal, and Fash 1978) or the 7F-1 architectural complex near Tikal center (Haviland 1981). More details on the complexity of the relationship between centers and hamlets are provided in Bricker (1978), Freidel (1981), and Vogt (1983).

One matter seems clear. By colonial Mayan times in Yucatan

> the *principales* [nobility] lived in somewhat grander versions of the same pitched-roof houses of the *macehuales* [commoners], which are still the standard dwelling of the rural Maya. Either the pre-Columbian structures that archaeologists label as "elite residences" served some other purpose, or else stone houses had gone out of fashion by the time of the conquest. The Maya nobles who experimented with Spanish-style masonry dwellings are reported to have found them uncomfortable and unhealthy . . . their preference for the airier, less substantial house of Maya design seems to have been more a matter of taste than economics. [Farriss 1984:178]

*One of the fundamentally important deity concepts is that of ancestral gods of the various units of Mayan society.*

My hypothesis is that each significant unit in a Mayan social system—the extended family living in a patio group, the patrilineage, or the patriclan—had deified ancestral beings that were given offerings at some kind of ceremonial focus whether it be a small household shrine or a seventy-meter-high pyramid. If that is the case, then the multiple pyramid-temples in the ceremonial centers probably represented the ancestors of the various important lineages (Coggins 1980:738). While it now appears that some of the stelae contain portraits of living rulers, some were of ancestors, and we find ancestral figures on the roof combs of pyramids, and, of course, buried inside the pyramids, such as Lord Pacal at Palenque or Curl Nose at Tikal. The iconography is intricately sophisticated, including carvings at Palenque that depict an already deceased ancestor transmitting the symbols of royal power to his living son (Schele 1978), or a mythological "first father" transmitting the symbols of power to his living descendant (Clancy 1986). Schele correctly concludes that "genealogy and ancestor 'worship' were major concerns of Classic Maya royalty and culture in general" (1978:79) and they appear to be of universal importance in Mayan society (see also Schele and Miller 1986; Miller 1988).

Taking a longer evolutionary view, Marcus (1978, 1983b) sees the ancient Maya as revering their ancestors, with royal ancestors being especially important. From Formative times onward, stingray spines, obsidian blades, shark's teeth, and so on were used to draw blood from various parts of the body to offer to one's ancestors. In the Formative, figurines were used to create scenes of deceased ancestors and the rituals were performed on their behalf. But by Classic times, stelae picturing royal ancestors largely supplanted the use of clay figurines (Marcus 1978).

Looking more broadly at Mayan religion, two distinctive and contrasting symbolic patterns seem to emerge: the cult of the ancestors, and the cult of the sun. Every Mayan system that we know—prehistoric, ethnohistoric, or contemporary—shows some manifestation of those important cults. But the two cults have quite different symbolic and political work to do—they are used by Mayas for different political objectives.

This use of symbolism is exemplified in Coggins's (1979, 1980) analysis in which she hypothesizes that when the Mexicanized Sky Dynasty came to power at Tikal, it instituted a Katun-marking celebration (with erection of twin-temple complexes and stelae) to override and control the power of the ancient Tikal lineages, who were worshipping their various ancestors in lineage temples. The Katun celebration broadened "the role of the ruler to include that of formal interpreter of the shape of time and diviner of its prophecy" (1980:737).

It is possible that a comparable process was under way at Palenque in the late Classic period with the ruling dynasty emphasizing the cult of the sun—in the iconography of the Temples of the Cross, Foliated Cross, and Sun, and on the sarcophagus lid of Lord Pacal's tomb—in order to override and contain the power of various competing lineages.

I have reported on a contemporary case (Vogt 1973) in which there appears a clear-cut interrelationship between the sacred symbol system and the political structure in the two neighboring Tzotzil Maya communities of Zinacantan and Chamula. Although both symbolic systems clearly contain both the cult of the ancestors and the cult of the sun, Zinacantan places relatively more emphasis on the ancestors, while Chamula empha- sizes the cult of the sun (see Gossen 1974). The political system of Zinacantan is characterized by factional struggles among competing lineages, while Chamula has, in recent decades, been controlled by two important caciques (political bosses). As political power is dispersed in Zinacantan, sacred power is likewise dispersed, not only among family and lineage ancestors, but also among a series of outlying hamlet chapels, each with its own collection of saints and its own cargo officials. On the other hand, Chamula has only one central church in the ceremonial center where the patron saint, San Juan, is viewed as a manifestation of the sun god, and the most powerful political cacique often serves as *Presidente del Templo*—the caretaker of the saints! Even the construction of a chapel in any outlying hamlet is forbidden by the political leaders.

*Mountains and pyramids function as conceptual and structural equiva- lents in the Mayan religious system in that they both serve as dwelling places for the ancestral gods.*

This hypothesis, which I first advanced in Paris in 1960 (Vogt 1964a), merits continuing investigation. All the Mayan ethnographic data indicate a close relationship between sacred places—whether they be mountains, caves, waterholes, or churches with Catholic saints—and segments of the social structure. Every patio-group has its shrine; every localized lineage its sacred cave, waterhole, or small mountain; every ceremonial center its churches, waterhole, or larger sacred mountains. These data led me to suggest that there must be some conceptual relationship between mountains as homes of ancestral gods and the pyramids, many of which have ancestral figures on their roof combs, carved on panels inside their temples, and/or entombed inside.

In Zinacantan, shamans and cargoholders go in procession from their hamlets to the mountain shrines to pray to the ancestral gods who live inside the mountains. They first light candles, burn copal incense, and pray at the shrine at the foot of the mountains; then they climb to the summit to pray to another shrine that is said to be the patio shrine of the ancestral god who lives inside (Vogt 1976). One can imagine groups of ritualists coming to a site like Tikal to pray at the foot of the pyramid and then climbing the steps to pray again to the ancestral deity at the top.

That this inference is not merely a product of my imagination is suggested by a survey of Palenque region incensarios by Rands, Bishop, and Harbottle (1978). Chemical analysis showed that while the incensario supports were made in Palenque itself, the incensarios found at Palenque were made both at Palenque and elsewhere. Since the incensario supports would appear to be prehistoric forerunners of the cross shrines now used for worship with copal incense by the contemporary highland Chiapas Maya, these data strongly suggest that ritual movements into Palenque center from outlying areas for incense-burning rites did occur (Rands, Bishop, and Harbottle 1978:28-29).

The conceptual relationship of "lineage mountains" to "lineage pyramids" has also been discussed by Coe (1965:110-11) and is becoming even clearer in recent archeological studies of dedication and termination rituals in ancient Mayan sites (Freidel and Schele 1990). The relationship has also been confirmed by the work of David Stuart at Copan, where a glyph on the hieroglyphic stairway has been decoded as *witz*, the Mayan word for mountain (Stuart 1987; Schele and Freidel 1990:65–66). Schele and Freidel have likewise added an important innovative insight to the manner in which Mayan monuments are symbolically modeled on nature. They point out that "the slab-shaped monuments they carved with the images of kings were called *te-tun*, 'tree-stone'. Plazas with these tree-stones [stelae] then represented the earth covered by a tropical forest" (1990:71-72). Alternatively, a new theory proposed by Bassie-Sweet (1991:120-21) suggests that stalagmites in sacred caves—the portals to the supernatural world—provide the natural model for the Mayan stelae.

When a Zinacanteco was taken on a journey to Palenque for the first time a number of years ago, he immediately drew a parallel in his own mind between the sacred mountains housing the sacred gods in Zinacantan and the pyramids he climbed. In fact, he immediately conceptualized the tunnel inside the pyramid of the inscriptions as a cave of the type that penetrates deep into the sacred mountains of Zinacantan (Robert M. Laughlin, p.c.).

## Discussion

Since my first attempt to apply the phylogenetic model to the Maya (Vogt 1964b), there have been significant advances in Mayan linguistics, archeology, and ethnography, and the physical anthropologists and ethno-historians are beginning to increase the pace of their researches as well. The linguists have produced an impressive corpus on individual Mayan languages (Campbell et al. 1978; Campbell and Kaufman 1985), which has aided the process of decoding the glyphs, provided better data on the diversification of the Mayan languages, and increased our knowledge of the protolanguage. Using what is known of the protolanguage, we are now in position to begin to reconstruct the ancestral Mayan society. In such a reconstruction Mayanists can learn much from following the example of the Polynesianists, who have published a list of 3,000 Proto-Polynesian lexical items (Biggs 1979), as well as a smaller list bearing on the main outlines of the protoculture (Pawley and Green 1971), and have made impressive progress in reconstructing the ancestral Polynesian society (Kirch 1984; Green 1986.)

The location of the Mayan homeland is still in doubt; the linguists favor the highlands, but do not yet agree on the precise location of the proto-community in the highlands (Morley, Brainerd, and Sharer 1983:501-2). The possibility that the Mayan homeland in the highlands was a somewhat larger *region*, as the Polynesianists are now discovering in the case of the Polynesian homeland (Green 1981; Kirch 1986), rather than a precisely located small area, should be explored. The solution to the homeland problem will require more research in comparative and historical linguistics, as well as much-needed archeological work on early horizons in the highlands.

In the study of later prehistoric horizons we have had an explosion of archeological knowledge on the Maya: the discovery and analysis of raised-field and other systems of intensive agriculture; the detailed studies of settlement patterns; the amazing progress in the decoding of the glyphs (Schele 1982; Bricker 1986; Schele and Freidel 1990; Coe 1992; Marcus 1992) and in the interpreting of the iconographic programs (Schele and Miller 1986). Much of that progress in the study of the glyphs and the iconography has been based on the pioneering work of Proskouriakoff, who first documented the rise and fall of rulers, lineages, and dynasties (1963-64). Out of her research other studies have documented the development of territorial organization from the inscriptions and dynastic histories of many sites such as Copan, Quirigua, Palenque, and Tikal (e.g., Marcus 1976; Jones 1977; Sharer 1978a; Schele and Freidel 1990). I have described some of those developments, but much more needs to be done in using those data to explore the basic, systemic patterns of the Maya and their variations in space and evolution in time (see also Danien and Sharer 1992).

In Maya ethnography the field research of clearest relevance to the phylogenetic model in the past twenty-five years has been concentrated in the Chiapas highlands (Vogt 1978), and secondarily in the Guatemalan highlands (see especially Tedlock 1982; Warren 1992; Watanabe 1983, 1992). Less progress has been made in the lowlands, apart from the research of Boremanse (1981, 1984, 1986) and McGee (1990) on the Lacandon and a few field studies among the Yucatec Maya (e.g., Thompson 1974; Bricker 1981; Hanks 1990; Kintz 1990). We have just begun to use ethnographic data to explore systemic patterns by comparative studies of the contemporary Maya and by working back and forth from the present to the past (see especially Aveni 1992; Freidel, Schele, and Parker 1993; Vogt 1994).

While the work of Serrano and his colleagues on dermatoglyphs has been an important step in the physical anthropology of the Maya, especially in its implications for our understanding of the Parental Mayan Population that carried the ancestral Mayan culture, it is obvious that we need much more research on the Maya, especially on the order of the work of Greenberg and his colleagues (Greenberg, Turner, and Zegura 1986; Greenberg 1987) on indigenous populations in the New World. The latter work has demonstrated an amazing correspondence among language groups, dental traits, and genetic patterns in North American indigenous populations, and it forms a model of the research that is now called for in Mesoamerica. In Oceania, genetic studies (e.g., Blake et al. 1983) likewise exhibit remarkable correspondences with the findings from archeology and linguistics and offer independent confirmation of cultural-historical interpretations using the phylogenetic model (Kirch 1985).

After a long drought in published research on the history of the Maya, a number of works have recently appeared (e.g. Wauchope 1964-76, vols. 12-15; Calnek 1962; Bricker 1981; Clendinnen 1987; Farriss 1984; MacLeod 1973; Carmack 1973; Fox 1978, 1987; Wasserstrom 1983) that add immeasurably to this essential step in the application of the phylogenetic model.

In addition to studying divergences within and among Mayan populations, we should also have as one of our long-range goals the study of divergences between Mixe-Zoque and Mayan, between Otomanguean and Mayan, and so on. For those analyses we still need to know more precisely what aspects of Mayan culture are pan-Mesoamerican and a legacy from the remote preceramic past, which aspects are specifically Mayan, and which are unique to the Tzotzil Maya, the Quiche Maya, the Yucatec Maya, or even to the contemporary municipios of Zinacantan, Chamula, or Chichicastenango. Has the process of divergence been merely a question of when each group diverged from another, or has each group in turn evolved in the context of still other groups and in a different ecological microniche?

In conclusion, I predict we are on the verge of exciting developments in the understanding of Mayan divergence from the ancestral Mayan culture and of the processes of cultural history and evolution that have led to the presently observed variations in Mayan communities.

## Acknowledgments

This paper has benefited from comments and criticisms by Stephen Black, Joyce Marcus, Jeremy A. Sabloff, John M. Watanabe, and Gordon R. Willey.

## References

Adair, John, and Evon Vogt
  1949    Navaho and Zuni Veterans: A Study of Contrasting Modes of Culture Change. American Anthropologist 51:547-61.
Adams, R. E. W.
  1971    The Ceramics of Altar de Sacrificios. Papers of the Peabody Museum of American Archaeology and Ethnology, vol. 63, no. 1. Harvard University.
  1983    Ancient Land Use and Culture History in the Pasion River Region. In Prehistoric Settlement Patterns: Essays in Honor of Gordon R. Willey, edited by Evon Z. Vogt and Richard M. Leventhal, 319-36. Albuquerque: University of New Mexico Press.
Andrews, E. Wyllys, and Norman Hammond
  1990    Redefinition of the Swazey Phase at Cuello, Belize. American Antiquity 55:570-84.
Arechiga Viramontes, Julieta
  1979    Algunos aspectos de la antropologia fisica de los Tojolobales. Master's thesis, Escuela Nacional de Antropologia y Historia, Mexico.
Ashmore, Wendy, ed.
  1981    Lowland Maya Settlement Patterns. Albuquerque: University of New Mexico Press.
Aveni, Anthony F., ed.
  1992    The Sky in Mayan Literature. New York: Oxford University Press.
Bassie-Sweet, Karen
  1991    From the Mouth of the Dark Cave: Commemorative Sculpture of the Late Classic Maya. Norman: University of Oklahoma Press.
Basso, Keith H.
  1979    History of Ethnological Research. In Handbook of North American Indians. Vol. 9, edited by Alfonso Ortiz, 14-23. Washington, D.C.: Smithsonian Institution.
Becker, Marshall Joseph
  1979    Priests, Peasants, and Ceremonial Centers: The Intellectual History of a Model. In Maya Archaeology and Ethnohistory, edited by Norman Hammond and Gordon R. Willey, 3-20. Austin: University of Texas Press.
Biggs, B.
  1979    Proto-Polynesian Word List II. Working Papers in Anthropology, no. 53. Department of Anthropology, University of Auckland.

Blake, N. M., B. R. Hawkins, R. L. Kirk, K. Bhatia, P. Brown, R. M. Garruto, and D. C. Gajdusek.
1983      A Population Genetic Study of the Banks and Torres Islands (Vanuatu) and of the Santa Cruz Islands and Polynesian Outliers (Solomon Islands). American Journal of Physical Anthropology 62:343-61.
Boremanse, Didier
1981      A Comparative Study of Two Maya Kinship Systems. Sociologus 31:1-37.
1984      Mitologia y organizacion social entre los 'Lacandones' (Hach Winik) de la Selva Chiapaneca. Estudios de Cultura Maya 15:225-50.
1986      Contes et mythologie des indiens lacandones. Paris: Editions L'Harmattan.
Breton, Alain
1979      Les Tzeltal de Bachajon. Recherches americaines, no. 3. Nanterre: Laboratoire d'Ethnologie.
Bricker, Victoria Reifler
1973      Ritual Humor in Highland Chiapas. Austin: University of Texas Press.
1978      Symbolic Representations of Protohistoric Social Stratification and Religious Organization in a Modern Maya Community. In Codex Wauchope, edited by Marco Biardino, Barbara Edmonson, and Winifred Creamer, 39-54. New Orleans: Human Mosaic, Tulane University.
1981      The Indian Christ, the Indian King: The Historical Substrate of Maya Myth and Ritual. Austin: University of Texas Press.
1986      A Grammar of Mayan Hieroglyphs. Middle American Research Institute, Publication no. 56. Tulane University.
Calnek, Edward E.
1962      Highland Chiapas before the Spanish Conquest. Papers of the New World Archaeological Foundation, no. 55. Provo: Brigham Young University Press.
Campbell, Lyle
1988      The Linguistics of Southeast Chiapas, Mexico. Papers of the New World Archaeological Foundation, no. 50. Provo: Brigham Young University Press.
Campbell, Lyle, and Terrence Kaufman
1976      A Linguistic Look at the Olmecs. American Antiquity 41:80-89.
1985      Maya Linguistics: Where Are We Now? Annual Reviews in Anthropology, vol. 14, 187-98.
Campbell, Lyle, Pierre Ventur, Russell Stewart, and Brant Gardner
1978      Bibliography of Mayan Linguistics and Languages. Institute for Mesoamerican Studies Publication no. 3. State University of New York, Albany.
Carlson, John B.
1978      On Classic Maya Monumental Recorded History. In Third Palenque Round Table, edited by Merle Greene Robertson, 199-203. Austin: University of Texas Press.
Carmack, Robert M.
1973      Quichean Civilization. Berkeley and Los Angeles: University of California Press.
Carr, Robert P., and James E. Hazard
1961      Map of the Ruins of Tikal, El Peten, Guatemala. Tikal Reports, no 11. University Museum, University of Pennsylvania.
Clancy, Flora S.
1986      Text and Image in the Tablets of the Cross Group at Palenque. Res 11:17-32.

Clendinnen, Inga
    1987    Ambivalent Conquests: Maya and Spaniard in Yucatan, 1515-1570.
            Cambridge: Cambridge University Press.
Coe, Michael D.
    1965    A Model of Ancient Community Structure in the Maya Lowlands. South-
            western Journal of Anthropology 21:97-114.
    1992    Breaking the Maya Code. London: Thames Hudson.
Coggins, Clemency
    1975    Painting and Drawing Styles at Tikal. Ph.D. diss., Harvard University. Ann
            Arbor: University Microfilms.
    1979    A New Order and the Role of the Calendar: Some Characteristics of the
            Middle Classic Period at Tikal. In Maya Archaeology and Ethnohistory,
            edited by Norman Hammond and G. R. Willey, 38-50. Austin: University of
            Texas Press.
    1980    The Shape of Time: Some Political Implications of a Four-Part Figure.
            American Antiquity 45:727-39.
Comas, Juan
    1966    Caracteristicas fisicas de la familia linguistica maya. Instituto de Investi-
            gaciones Historicas, Serie Antropologica, no. 20. Mexico: Universidad
            Nacional Autonoma de Mexico.
    1969    Algunos craneos de la region maya. Anales de Antropologia 6:233-48.
            Instituto de Investigaciones Historicas. Mexico: Universidad Nacional
            Autonoma de Mexico.
Danien, Elin C. and Robert J. Sharer, eds.
    1992    New Theories on the Ancient Maya. Philadelphia: The University Museum,
            University of Pennsylvania.
Diebold, A. Richard, Jr.
    1960    Determining the Centers of Dispersal of Language Groups. International
            Journal of American Linguistics 27:1-10.
Dumond, Don E.
    1987    A Reexamination of Eskimo-Aleut Prehistory. American Anthropologist
            89:32-56.
Dyen, Isidore
    1956    Language Distribution and Migration Theory. Language 32:611-26.
Edmonson, Munro S.
    1971    The Book of Counsel: The Popol Vuh of the Quiche Maya of Guatemala.
            Middle American Research Institute, Publication no. 35. Tulane University.
    1978    Some Post Classic Questions about the Classic Maya. In Third Palenque
            Round Table, vol. 4, edited by Merle Greene Robertson and Donnan Call
            Jeffers, 9-18. Monterey: Pre-Columbian Art Research, Herald Printers.
Eggan, Fred
    1934    The Maya Kinship System and Cross-Cousin Marriage. American Anthro-
            pologist 36:188-202.
    1950    Social Organization of the Western Pueblos. Chicago: University of Chicago
            Press.
    1952    The Ethnological Cultures and Their Archaeological Backgrounds. In
            Archaeology of the Eastern United States, edited by James B. Griffin, 34-45.
            Chicago: University of Chicago Press.

1954        Social Anthropology and the Method of Controlled Comparison. American Anthropologist 56:745–63.

1966        The American Indian. Chicago: Aldine Publishing.

1980        Shoshone Kinship Structures and Their Significance for Anthropological Theory. Journal of the Steward Anthropological Society 11:165–93.

Eggan, Fred, ed.
1937        Social Anthropology of North American Tribes. Chicago: University of Chicago Press.

Fash, William L.
1991        Scribes, Warriors, and Kings. New York: Thames and Hudson.

Farriss, Nancy M.
1984        Maya Society under Colonial Rule: The Collective Enterprise of Survival. Princeton: Princeton University Press.

Flannery, Kent V., and Joyce Marcus, eds.
1983        The Cloud People: Divergent Evolution of the Zapotec and Mixtec Civilizations. New York: Academic Press.

Ford, Anabel
1980        Late Classic Maya Settlement Patterns: An Interpretation of Economic Determinants of Settlement. Paper presented at the 79th Annual Meetings of the American Anthropological Association, Washington, D.C.

Fox, James A., and John S. Justeson
1986        Classic Maya Dynastic Alliance and Succession. In Supplement to the Handbook of Middle American Indians, edited by Victoria Reifler Bricker. Vol. 4, edited by Ronald Spores, 7–34. Austin: University of Texas Press.

Fox, John W.
1978        Quiche Conquest: Centralism and Regionalism in Highland Guatemalan State Development. Albuquerque: University of New Mexico Press.

1987        Maya Post-Classic State Formation. Cambridge: Cambridge University Press.

1990        On the Rise and Fall of Tulans and Maya Segmentary States. American Anthropologist 91:65–81.

Freidel, David A.
1981        The Political Economics of Residential Dispersion among the Lowland Maya. In Lowland Maya Settlement Patterns, edited by Wendy Ashmore, 371–82. Albuquerque: University of New Mexico Press.

Freidel, David A., and Linda Schele
1988        Kinship in the Late Preclassic Maya Lowlands: The Instruments and Places of Ritual Power. American Anthropologist 90:547–67.

1990        Dead Kings and Living Temples: Dedication and Termination Rituals among the Ancient Maya. In Word and Image in Mayan Culture, edited by William F. Hanks and Don Rice, 233–43. Salt Lake City: University of Utah Press.

Freidel, David, Linda Schele, and Joy Parker.
1993        Maya Cosmos: Three Thousand Years of Shamanism. New York: William Morrow.

Gossen, Gary H.
1974        Chamulas in the World of the Sun: Time and Space in a Maya Oral Tradition. Cambridge, Mass.: Harvard University Press.

Green, Roger C.
1981        Location of the Polynesian Homeland: A Continuing Problem. In Studies in

Pacific Languages and Cultures in Honour of Bruce Briggs, edited by Jim Hollyman and Andrew Pawley, 133-58. Aukland: Linguistic Society of New Zealand.

1986 Some Basic Components of the Ancestral Polynesian Settlement System: Building Blocks for More Complex Polynesian Societies. *In* Island Societies: Archaeological Approaches to Evolution and Transformation, edited by Patrick V. Kirch, 51-54. Cambridge: Cambridge University Press.

Greenberg, Joseph H.
1987 Language in the Americas. Stanford: Stanford University Press.

Greenberg Joseph H., Christy G. Turner II, and Stephen L. Zegura
1986 The Settlement of the Americas: A Comparison of Linguistic, Dental, and Genetic Evidence. Current Anthropology 27:477-98.

Guiteras-Holmes, Calixta
1966 Cambio de un sistema Omaha a un sistema bilateral entre los Tzotziles de Chiapas. Etnologia y Folklore 1:46-63. Havana.

Hammond, Norman
1978 The Myth of the Milpa: Expansion in the Maya Lowlands. *In* Pre-Hispanic Maya Agriculture, edited by Peter D. Harrison and B. L. Turner II, 5. Albuquerque: University of New Mexico Press.

Hanks, William F.
1990 Referential Practice: Language and Lived Space among the Maya. Chicago: University of Chicago Press.

Harrison, Peter D.
1977 The Rise of the Bajos and the Fall of the Maya. *In* Social Process in Maya Prehistory: Studies in Memory of Sir Eric Thompson, edited by Norman Hammond, 469-508. New York: Academic Press.

1978 Bajos Revisited: Visual Evidence for One System of Agriculture. *In* Pre-Hispanic Maya Agriculture, edited by Peter D. Harrison and B. L. Turner II, 249-53. Albuquerque: University of New Mexico Press.

Harrison, Peter D., and B. L. Turner II
1978 Pre-Hispanic Maya Agriculture. Albuquerque: University of New Mexico Press.

Haviland, William A.
1966a Maya Settlement Patterns: A Critical Review. Middle American Research Institute, Publication no. 26, pp. 21-47. New Orleans: Tulane University.

1966b Social Integration and the Classic Maya. American Antiquity 31:625-31.

1972 A New Look at Classic Maya Social Organization at Tikal. *In* Ceramica de cultura Maya, no. 8, edited by James C. Gifford, 1-16. Philadelphia: Department of Anthropology, Temple University.

1975 The Ancient Maya and the Evolution of Urban Society. Museum of Anthropology Miscellaneous Series, no. 37. University of Northern Colorado.

1977 Dynastic Genealogies from Tikal, Guatemala: Implications for Descent and Political Organization. American Antiquity 42:61-67.

1981 Dover Houses and Minor Centers at Tikal, Guatemala: An Investigation into the Identification of Valid Units in Settlement Hierarchies. *In* Lowland Maya Settlement Patterns, edited by Wendy Ashmore, 89-117. Albuquerque: University of New Mexico Press.

1985 Population and Social Dynamics: The Dynasties and Social Structure of Tikal.

Expedition 27(3):34-41.

Hill, Robert M. II, and John Monaghan
 1987 Continuities in Highland Maya Social Organization: Ethnohistory in Sacapula, Guatemala. Philadelphia: University of Pennsylvania Press.

Jones, Christopher
 1977 Inauguration Dates of Three Late Classic Rulers of Tikal. American Antiquity 42:28-60.

Jones, Christopher, William R. Coe, and William A. Haviland
 1981 Tikal: An Outline of Its Field Study (1957-1970) and a Project Bibliography. *In* Supplement to the Handbook of Middle American Indians, edited by Victoria Reifler Bricker. Vol. 1, edited by Jeremy A. Sabloff, 296-312. Austin: University of Texas Press.

Jones, Christopher, and Linton Satterthwaite
 1982 The Monuments and Inscriptions of Tikal: The Carved Monuments. Philadelphia: University Museum, University of Pennsylvania.

Josserand, J. K.
 1975 Archaeological and Linguistic Correlations for Maya Prehistory. Actas del 41 Congreso Internacional de Americanistas 1:501-10. Mexico City.

Justeson, John S., William Norman, Lyle Campbell, and Terrence S. Kaufman
 1985 The Foreign Impact on Lowland Mayan Language and Script. Middle American Research Institute, Publication no. 53. Tulane University.

Kaufman, Terrence S.
 1964 Materiales linguisticos para el estudio de las relaciones internas y externas de la familia de idiomas mayanos. *In* Desarrollo cultural de los Mayas, edited by Evon Z. Vogt and Alberto Ruz L., 81-136. Mexico: Universidad Nacional Autonoma de Mexico.
 1976 Archaeological and Linguistic Correlations in Mayaland and Associated Areas of Meso-America. World Archaeology 8:101-18.

Kelley, David H.
 1962 Glyphic Evidence for a Dynastic Sequence at Quirigua, Guatemala. American Antiquity 27:323-35.
 1976 Deciphering the Maya Script. Austin: University of Texas Press.

Kintz, Ellen R.
 1990 Life under the Tropical Canopy: Tradition and Change among the Yucatec Maya. Ft. Worth: Holt, Rinehart and Winston.

Kirch, Patrick V.
 1984 The Evolution of the Polynesian Chiefdoms. Cambridge: Cambridge University Press.
 1985 On the Genetic and Cultural Relationships of Certain Polynesian Outlier Populations. American Journal of Physical Anthropology 66:381-82.
 1986 Rethinking East Polynesian Prehistory. Journal of the Polynesian Society 95:9-40.

Kirch, Patrick V., and Roger C. Green
 1987 History, Phylogeny, and Evolution in Polynesia. Current Anthropology 28:431-51.

Koenig, Seymour H., and George O. Williams
 1985 Modeling Lowland Maya Settlement Patterns. *In* Fifth Palenque Round Table, 1983, edited by Merle Greene Robertson and Virginia M. Fields. Pebble

Beach, Calif.: Robert Louis Stevenson School.

Kroeber, A. L.
1948      Anthropology. New York: Harcourt Brace.

Laughlin, Robert M.
1977      Of Cabbages and Kings: Tales from Zinacantan. Smithsonian Contributions to Anthropology, no. 23. Washington: Smithsonian Institution Press.

Lee, Thomas A., Jr.
1979      Coapa, Chiapas: A Sixteenth-Century Coxoh Maya Village on the Camino Real. Maya Archaeology and Ethnohistory, edited by Norman Hammond and Gordon R. Willey, 208–22. Austin: University of Texas Press.
1989      La arquelogia de los altos de Chiapas: Un estudio contextual. Mesoamerica 18:257–93.

Lee, Thomas A., Jr., and Sidney D. Markham
1976      Colonial Coxoh Acculturation: A Necrotic Archaeological and Ethnohistoric Model. 42d Congres International des Americanistes, Paris.

Lees, H. W.
1956      Shiro Hattori on Glottochronology and Proto-Japanese. American Anthropologist 58:176–77.

Lounsbury, Floyd G.
1976      A Rationale for the Initial Date of the Temple of the Cross at Palenque. In Second Palenque Round Table, edited by Merle Green Robertson, 211–24. Palenque Round Table Series 3. Pebble Beach, Calif.: Robert Louis Stevenson School.

Luckenbach, Alvin H., and Richard S. Levy
1980      The Implications of Nahua (Aztec) Lexical Diversity for Mesoamerican Culture-History. American Antiquity 45:455–61.

McGee, Jon R.
1990      Life, Ritual and Religion among the Lacandon Maya. Belmont, Calif.: Wadsworth

MacKinnon, J. Jefferson
1981      The Nature of Residential Tikal: A Spatial Analysis. Estudios de Cultura Maya 13:223–50.

MacLeod, Murdo J.
1973      Spanish Central America: A Socio-Economic History, 1520–1720. Berkeley and Los Angeles: University of California Press.

MacNeish, Richard S.
1981      Second Annual Report of the Belize Archaic Archaeological Reconnaissance. Robert S. Peabody Foundation for Archaeology, Phillips Academy, Andover, Mass.

MacNeish, Richard S., S. Jeffrey K. Wilkerson, and Antoinette Nelken-Terner
1980      First Annual Report of the Belize Archaic Archaeological Reconnaissance. Robert S. Peabody Foundation for Archaeology, Phillips Academy, Andover, Mass.

Marcus, Joyce
1976      Emblem and State in the Classic Maya Lowlands: An Epigraphic Approach to Territorial Organization. Washington, D.C.: Dumbarton Oaks.
1978      Archaeology and Religion: A Comparison of the Zapotec and Maya. World Archaeology 10:172–91.

1982a    The Plant World of the Sixteenth- and Seventeenth-Century Lowland Maya. *In* Maya Subsistence: Studies in Memory of Dennis E. Puleston, edited by Kent V. Flannery, 239–73. New York: Academic Press.

1982b    Review of *Lowland Maya Settlement Patterns* edited by Wendy Ashmore, University of New Mexico Press, 1982. American Antiquity 47:899–902.

1983a    Lowland Maya Archaeology at the Crossroads. American Antiquity 48:454–88.

1983b    On the Nature of the Mesoamerican City. *In* Prehistoric Settlement Patterns: Essays in Honor of Gordon R. Willey, edited by Evon Z. Vogt and Richard M. Leventhal, 195–242. Albuquerque: University of New Mexico Press.

1992     Mesoamerican Writing Systems: Propaganda, Myth, and History in Four Ancient Civilizations. Princeton: Princeton University Press.

Mathews, Peter, and Linda Schele
1974     Lords of Palenque—The Glyphic Evidence. *In* First Palenque Round Table, part 1, edited by Merle Greene Robertson, 63–75. Pebble Beach, Calif.: Robert Louis Stevenson School.

Miller, Mary Ellen
1988     The Meaning and Function of the Main Acropolis, Copan. *In* The Southeast Classic Maya Zone, edited by Gordon R. Willey and Elizabeth Hill Boone, 149–94. Washington: Dumbarton Oaks.

Millet Camara, Luis
1984     Logwood and Archaeology in Campeche. Journal of Anthropological Research 40:324–28.

Morley, Sylvanus G., George W. Brainerd, and Robert J. Sharer
1983     The Ancient Maya. 4th ed. Stanford: Stanford University Press.

Newman, M. T.
1960     Population Analysis of Finger and Palm Prints in Highland and Lowland Maya Indians. American Journal of Physical Anthropology 18:45–58.

Pawley, A., and K. Green
1971     Lexical Evidence for the Proto-Polynesian Homeland. Te Reo 14:1–36.

Proskouriakoff, Tatiana
1963–64  Historical Data in the Inscriptions of Yaxchilan, parts 1 and 2. Estudios de Cultura Maya 3:149–67; 4:177–203. Mexico: Universidad Nacional Autonoma de Mexico.

Puleston, Dennis E.
1977     The Art and Archaeology of Hydraulic Agriculture in the Maya Lowlands. *In* Social Process in Maya Prehistory: Studies in Memory of Sir Eric Thompson, edited by Norman Hammond, 449–67. London: Academic Press.

Rands, Robert L., Ronald L. Bishop, and Garman Harbottle
1978     Thematic and Compositional Variation in Palenque Region Incensarios. *In* Third Palenque Round Table, vol. 4, edited by Merle Greene Robertson and Donnan Call Jeffers, 19–30. Monterey: Pre-Columbian Art Research, Herald Printers.

Renfrew, Colin
1992     Archaeology, Genetics, and Linguistic Diversity. Man 27:445–78.

Robertson, Merle Greene
1985     The Sculpture of Palenque. Vol. 3, The Late Buildings of the Palace. Princeton: Princeton University Press.

Romney, A. Kimball
  1957    The Genetic Model and Uto-Aztecan Time Perspective. Davidson Journal of
          Anthropology 3(2):35-41.
  1967    Kinship and Family. *In* Handbook of Middle American Indians, vol. 6, edited
          by Manning, Nash, 207-37. Austin: University of Texas Press.
Ruz Lhuiller, Alberto
  1964    Aristocracia o democracia entre los antiguos mayas? Anales de Antropologia
          1:63-76.
  1977    Gerontocracy at Palenque? *In* Social Process in Maya Prehistory: Studies in
          Honour of Sir Eric Thompson, edited by Norman Hammond, 287-96. New
          York: Academic Press.
Sabloff, Jeremy A.
  1975    Excavations at Seibal, Department of Peten, Guatemala: Ceramics. Memoirs
          of the Peabody Museum of American Archaeology and Ethnology, vol. 13,
          no. 2. Harvard University.
Sabloff, Jeremy A., and Gair Tourtellot
  1991    The Ancient Maya City of Sayil: The Mapping of a Puuc Region Center. New
          Orleans: Middle American Research Institute, Tulane University.
Santley, Robert S., Thomas Killion, and Mark Lycett
  1986    On the Maya Collapse. Journal of Anthropological Research 42:123-60.
Sapir, Edward
  1916    Time Perspective in Aboriginal American Culture: A Study in Method.
          Geological Survey of Canada, Memoir no. 90 (Anthropological Series no. 13),
          Ottawa.
Saul, Frank P.
  1968    Review of *Caracteristicas fisicas de la familia linguistica maya* by Juan
          Comas. American Anthropologist 70:1032.
Schele, Linda
  1977    Palenque: The House of the Dying Sun. *In* Native American Astronomy,
          edited by Anthony F. Aveni, 42-56. Austin: University of Texas Press.
  1978    Genealogical Documentation on the Tri-Figure Panels at Palenque. *In* Third
          Palenque Round Table, vol. 4, edited by Merle Green Robertson and Donnan
          Call Jeffers, 41-70. Monterey, Calif.: Robert Louis Stevenson School.
  1982    Maya Glyphs: The Verbs. Austin: University of Texas Press.
Schele, Linda, and David Freidel
  1990    The Forest of Kings: The Untold Story of the Ancient Maya. New York:
          William Morrow.
Schele, Linda, and Mary Ellen Miller
  1986    The Blood of Kings: Dynasty and Ritual in Maya Art. New York: George
          Braziller.
Serrano Sanchez, Carlos
  1973    Nota preliminar sobre los dermatoglifos digitales en dos poblaciones Mayas
          de Yucatan. Estudios de Cultura Maya 9:17-28.
  1975    Les dermatoglyphes des populations Mayas du Mexique et d'autres groupes
          Mesoamericains. Doctoral Thesis of 3d Cycle, Université de Paris.
  1976-77 Estudio comparativo de los dermatoglifos digitales de los Zoques y otros
          grupos indigenas del sureste de Mexico. Estudios de Cultura Maya 10:17-29.

Serrano, Carlos, and Julieta Arechiga
 1978 El proceso de cambio biologico en poblaciones indigenas: El caso de los Mayas. Estudios de Cultura Maya 11:15–29.
 1979 Estudio bioantropologico de surco palmar transverso en los Mayas Yucatecos. Estudios de Cultura Maya 12:15–32.

Sharer, Robert J.
 1974 The Prehistory of the Southeastern Maya Periphery. Current Anthropology 15:165–87.

Sharer, Robert J., ed.
 1978a The Archaeology and History at Quirigua, Guatemala. Journal of Field Archaeology 5:51–70.
 1978b The Prehistory of Chalchuapa, El Salvador. 3 vols. University Museum Monograph no. 36. Philadelphia: University of Pennsylvania Press.

Sharer, Robert J., and James C. Gifford
 1970 Preclassic Ceramics from Chalchuapa, El Salvador, and Their Relationships with the Maya Lowlands. American Antiquity 35:441–62.

Sharer, Robert J. and David W. Sedat
 1987 Archaeological Investigations in the Northern Maya Highlands, Guatemala. Philadelphia: University Museum, University of Pennsylvania.

Siemens, Alfred H.
 1978 Karst and the Pre-Hispanic Maya in the Southern Lowlands. In Pre-Hispanic Maya Agriculture, edited by Peter D. Harrison and B. L. Turner II, 117–43. Albuquerque: University of New Mexico Press.
 1982 Pre-Hispanic Use of Wetlands in the Tropical Lowlands of Mesoamerica. In Maya Subsistence: Studies in Memory of Dennis E. Puleston, edited by Kent V. Flannery, 205–25. New York: Academic Press.

Stuart, David
 1987 Ten Phonetic Syllables. Research Reports on Ancient Maya Writing, no. 14. Washington, D.C.: Center for Maya Research.

Swadesh, Morris
 1952 Lexicostatistic Dating of Prehistoric Ethnic Contacts. Proceedings of the American Philosophical Society 96:452–63.

Tedlock, Barbara
 1982 Time and the Highland Maya. Albuquerque: University of New Mexico Press.

Thompson, Richard A.
 1974 The Winds of Tomorrow: Social Change in a Maya Town. Chicago: University of Chicago Press.

Turner, B. L. II
 1974 Prehistoric Intensive Agriculture in the Maya Lowlands. Science 185:118–24.
 1978 Ancient Agricultural Land Use in the Central Maya Lowlands. In Pre-Hispanic Maya Agriculture, edited by Peter D. Harrison and B. L. Turner II. Albuquerque: University of New Mexico Press.
 1983 Comparison of Agrotechnologies in the Basin of Mexico and Central Maya Lowlands. In Highland-Lowland Interaction in Mesoamerica: Interdisciplinary Approaches, edited by Arthur G. Miller, 13–47. Washington, D.C.: Dumbarton Oaks.

Turner, B. L. II and Peter D. Harrison, eds.
 1983 Pulltrouser Swamp: Ancient Maya Habitat, Agriculture, and Settlement in

Northern Belize. Austin: University of Texas Press.

Villa Rojas, Alfonso
1947    Kinship and Nagualism in a Tzeltal Community, Southeastern Mexico. American Anthropologist 49:578-87.

Vogt, Evon Z.
1955    American Subcultural Continua as Exemplified by the Mormons and Texans. American Anthropologist 57:1163-72.
1960    On the Concepts of Structure and Process in Cultural Anthropology. American Anthropologist 62:18-33.
1961    The Navaho. *In* Perspectives in American Indian Culture Change, edited by Edward H. Spicer, 278-336. Chicago: University of Chicago Press.
1963    Courses of Regional Scope. *In* The Teaching of Anthropology, edited by David G. Mandelbaum, Gabriel W. Lasker, and Ethel M. Albert, 183-90. American Anthropological Association Memoir no. 94.
1964a   Ancient Maya Concepts in Contemporary Zinacantan Religion. VIe Congres International des Sciences Anthropologigues, vol. 2, 497-502. Musée de l'Homme, Paris.
1964b   The Genetic Model and Maya Cultural Development. *In* Desarrollo cultural de los mayas, edited by Evon Z. Vogt and Alberto Ruz L., 9-48. Mexico: Universidad Nacional Autonoma de Mexico.
1969a   Zinacantan: A Maya Community in the Highlands of Chiapas. Cambridge: Belknap Press of Harvard University Press.
1971    Addendum to Summary and Appraisal. *In* Desarrollo Cultural de los Mayas, edited by Evon Z. Vogt and Alberto Ruz L., 428-47. 2d ed. Mexico: Universidad Nacional Autonoma de Mexico.
1973    Gods and Politics in Zinacantan and Chamula. Ethnology 12:99-114.
1976    Tortillas for the Gods: A Symbolic Analysis of Zinacanteco Rituals. Cambridge: Harvard University Press.
1978    Bibliography of the Harvard Chiapas Project: The First Twenty Years 1957-1977. Peabody Museum, Harvard University.
1983    Ancient and Contemporary Maya Settlement Patterns: A New Look from the Chiapas Highlands. *In* Prehistoric Settlement Patterns: Essays in Honor of Gordon R. Willey, edited by Evon Z. Vogt and Richard Leventhal, 89-114. Albuquerque: University of New Mexico Press.
1985    Cardinal Directions and Ceremonial Circuits in Mayan and Southwestern Cosmology. National Geographic Research Reports, no. 21, 487-96.
1992    Cruces Indias y Bastones de Mando en Mesoamerica. *In* De palabra y obra en el nuevo mundo. Vol. 2, Encuentros interetnicos, edited by Manuel Gutierrez Estevez, Miguel Leon-Portilla, Gary H. Gossen, and J. Jorge Klor de Alva, 249-94. Madrid and Mexico: Siglo XXI.
1994    Fieldwork Among the Maya: Reflections on the Harvard Chiapas Project. Albuquerque: University of New Mexico Press.

Vogt, Evon Z., ed.
1969b   Handbook of Middle American Indians, vol 7. Austin: University of Texas Press.

Vogt, Evon Z., and Ethel M. Albert, eds.
1966    People of Rimrock: A Study of Values in Five Cultures. Cambridge: Harvard University Press.

Vogt, Evon Z., and Thomas F. O'Dea
    1953      A Comparative Study of the Role of Values in Social Action in Two South-
              western Communities. American Sociological Review 18:645-54.
Vogt, Evon Z., and Alberto Ruz, eds.
    1971      Addendum to Summary and Appraisal. *In* Desarrollo cultural de los Mayas,
              edited by Evon Z. Vogt and Alberto Ruz L., 428-47. 2d ed. Mexico: Universi-
              dad Nacional Autonoma de Mexico.
Vogt, Evon Z., and Catherine C. Vogt
    1980      Pre-Columbian Mayan and Mexican Symbols in Zinacanteco Ritual. *In* La
              antropologia Americanista en la actualidad: Homenaje a Raphael Girard. Vol.
              1, 499-523. Mexico: Editores Mexicanos Unidos.
Wallace, Douglas C., and Antonio Torroni
    1992      American Prehistory as Written in the Mitochondrial DNA: A Review. Human
              Biology 64:403-16.
Warren, Kay B.
    1992      Transforming Memories and Histories: The Meanings of Ethnic Resurgence
              for Mayan Indians. *In* Americas: New Interpretive Essays, edited by Alfred
              Stepan, 189-219. New York: Oxford University Press.
Wasserstrom, Robert
    1983      Class and Society in Central Chiapas. Berkeley and Los Angeles: University
              of California Press.
Watanabe, John M.
    1983      In the World of the Sun: A Cognitive Model of Mayan Cosmology. Man
              18:710-28.
    1992      Maya Saints and Souls in a Changing World. Austin: University of Texas
              Press.
Wauchope, Robert, ed.
    1964-76   Handbook of Middle American Indians. 16 vols. Austin: University of Texas
              Press.
Willey, Gordon R.
    1978      Prehispanic Maya Agriculture: A Contemporary Summation. *In* Prehispanic
              Maya Agriculture, edited by Peter D. Harrison and B. L. Turner II, 235-336.
              Albuquerque: University of New Mexico Press.
    1980      Toward a Holistic View of Ancient Maya Civilization. Huxley Memorial
              Lecture, 1979. Man 15:249-66.
    1981a     Maya Lowland Settlement Patterns: A Summary Review. *In* Lowland Maya
              Settlement Patterns, edited by Wendy Ashmore, 385-415. Albuquerque:
              University of New Mexico Press.
    1981b     Recent Researches and Perspectives in Mesoamerican Archaeology: An
              Introductory Commentary. *In* Supplement to the Handbook of Middle
              American Indians, edited by Victoria Reifler Bricker. Vol. 1, edited by Jeremy
              A. Sabloff, 3-30. Austin: University of Texas Press.
    1989      Vogt at Harvard. *In* Ethnographic Encounters in Southern Mesoamerica:
              Essays in Honor of Evon Zartman Vogt, Jr., edited by Victoria R. Bricker and
              Gary H. Gossen, 21-32. Austin: University of Texas Press.
Willey, Gordon R., Richard M. Leventhal, and William L. Fash, Jr.
    1978      Maya Settlement in the Copan Valley. Archaeology 31(4):32-44.

# The Contributors

KAREN I. BLU is Associate Professor of Anthropology at New York University.

JENNIFER S. H. BROWN is Professor of History at the University of Winnipeg.

The late CHARLES CALLENDER was Associate Professor of Anthropology at Case Western Reserve University.

JUNE M. COLLINS is Professor Emeritus of Anthropology, State University College at Buffalo.

RAYMOND J. DEMALLIE is Professor of Anthropology and Director of the American Indian Studies Research Institute at Indiana University.

LORETTA FOWLER is Professor of Anthropology at Indiana University.

JERROLD E. LEVY is Professor of Anthropology at the University of Arizona.

BRUCE B. MACLACHLAN was Associate Professor of Anthropology at Southern Illinois University, Carbondale, when he conducted his study on American Indian law.

JOSEPH MAXWELL is Assistant Professor of Education in the Graduate School of Education, Harvard University.

ALFONSO ORTIZ is Professor of Anthropology at the University of New Mexico.

TRILOKI NATH PANDEY is Professor of Anthropology at the University of California, Santa Cruz.

ERNEST L. SCHUSKY is Professor Emeritus of Anthropology at Southern Illinois University, Edwardsville.

415

The late JAMES G. E. SMITH was Curator of North American Ethnology, Museum of the American Indian, Heye Foundation, New York.

ANNE S. STRAUS is Professorial Lecturer, Master of Arts Program in the Social Sciences, at the University of Chicago, and Senior Research Consultant, American Indian Economic Development Association.

GREG URBAN is Professor of Anthropology at the University of Pennsylvania.

EVON Z. VOGT is Professor Emeritus of Anthropology at Harvard University.

GARY WITHERSPOON is Professor of Anthropology at the University of Washington.

# Index